ABINGDON PREACHER'S ANNUAL 1993

ABINGDON PREACHER'S ANNUAL 1993

COMPILED AND EDITED BY

John K. Bergland

ABINGDON PRESS
Nashville

ABINGDON PREACHER'S ANNUAL 1993

ISBN 0-687-00569-8
ISSN 1047-5486

Library of Congress ISSN 1047-5486

MANUFACTURED IN THE UNITED STATES OF AMERICA

This book is dedicated to our five grandsons:
Trey, Tyler, Eric, Tucker, and Drew

It's been my joy to baptize each of them. I have high hopes for their lives and for their growing devotion to Christ and the Word of God.

And when the days are evil, they teach me to pray.

Contents

□

CONTENTS

CONTENTS

CONTENTS

SECTION II

SERMON RESOURCES

CONTENTS

PREFACE

□

This book is intended to help pastors who preach to the same hearers week in and week out. It provides a starting place, a subject or subjects, a calendar, and some suggested purposes for that demanding progression of Sunday services that is the preacher's weekly deadline. *When* is easy. *Where* to begin is relatively uncomplicated. *Why* is almost impossible. In describing a traffic accident, when it happened can be documented. Where it happened is a matter of record. The why is always a matter of interpretation.

The when of preaching is simply a matter of calendar. This book follows the Sundays and the calendar of the Christian year. The when of Easter determines the when of Pentecost.

Where does the preacher begin? Where does he or she get an idea? Will you begin in the contemporary moment with a recognized personal or social need, or will you begin in the tradition, following the movements of the Christian year and the suggested lectionary lessons? In the *Abingdon Preacher's Annual* the lectionary is where we begin. The assigned Sunday lessons suggest the controlling themes, issues, and answers.

Why certain preachers are featured here; why they write what they write, and preach what they preach; why their message sparks an inspiration or recognition of faith; why it seems to miss the mark completely is a mystery. *Why* is always difficult.

This book follows the calendar of the year and the lectionary lessons for those Sundays. The Common Lectionary has been revised, effective Advent 1992. Because many readers may still be using the 1983 lectionary during this transition period, I have based my brief commentaries on the earlier lectionary. However, all but four of the sermons are based on texts that appear on the same Sunday in *both* the 1983 and 1992 editions of the Common Lectionary (Cycle A).

I have written a brief synopsis of each lesson and some illustrations and ideas that hopefully will help prompt the move from text to sermon. This section is called "Interpretation and Imagination."

PREFACE

The sermons are from a broad representation of ministers, both geographically and denominational. Several of them are preachers of The Protestant Hour, others are homiletics professors, and some you will recognize as distinguished pastors. Some of the preachers are not widely known, but are faithful to their calling as servants of the Word.

The appendix (Section II) also includes a helpful overview of the Common Lectionary (1983) lessons for Cycle A and the Cycle A lections for the Revised Common Lectionary (1992).

Louise Stowe Jones, a preacher of the Protestant Hour, has written children's sermons, one for each month, except July, which you will find in Section II.

I am indebted to all who have helped in this project. The pastors who have written sermons and prayers for the book are named in the table of contents. My son, Bob Bergland, a United Methodist pastor and chairperson of the Conference on Worship, has helped with numerous resources, suggestions, and material to fill in the gaps. My secretaries Marcia Moritz and Lisa Bryant have been of great help. Without them I would have given up the task long ago. Debra Sepp has typed long sections of the manuscript.

There was a scrawny old mule with blinkers and harness hooked up to a heavy wagon. The farmer took the reins and said, "Well, get up Jacob, get up Esau, get up Ezekiel, get up Daniel, get up Peter, get up Paul, get up Mr. John." When he said, "get up Mr. John," the old mule began to pull the wagon. A man standing by said, "Your mule sure has a lot of names." "No," the farmer said. "Just one. It's Mr. John. When I spoke his name you saw him start pulling." "But why did you say all those other names first?" the man asked. "Mr. John is a very smart mule," the farmer answered, "If he thought he was pulling this wagon all by himself, he wouldn't even try."

John K. Bergland
Pentecost 1991

Section I

□

FIFTY-TWO WEEKS OF SUNDAY SERMONS

JANUARY 3, 1993

□

Second Sunday After Christmas

The Christ Child, born in a stable in an obscure Judean village, ultimately will manifest God's glory and reveal his truth to the far corners of the earth. Magi from the East were the first to seek him.

The Sunday Lessons

Isaiah 60:1-6: Hymns and poems of triumph and joy that celebrate the return of captives and the restoration of Israel are gathered in chapters 55–66 of Isaiah. This passage bids defeated and fallen people to "Arise, shine," and reflect the glory of the Lord, which once more rests upon the nation. Enslaved children return home. Poverty is replaced by wealth. "You shall . . . be radiant" (v. 5).
Ephesians 3:1-12: Paul was in prison because he advocated equality for the Gentiles. Insights into the mystery of Christ and the hidden purposes of God have been revealed by the Spirit. Paul was made an apostle to the Gentiles to preach the unsearchable riches of Christ.
Matthew 2:1-12: Wise men, a learned group well acquainted with the stars and watchful of the heavens, saw a new star and followed it. These magi of ancient Persia came to Jerusalem and asked Herod the king, "Where is the newborn king?" A worried king inquired of his scholars concerning the expected birthplace of the Messiah. "In Bethlehem of Judea." The wise men found the child there and worshiped him with gifts.

Interpretation and Imagination

Aesop's Fables came from the land of the wise men. One of them is about star gazing. "An astronomer used to wander outside each night to observe the heavens. One evening, as he wandered through town with his eyes fixed on the sky, he fell into a deep well. He cried for help until a neighbor arrived and called down to him. Learning what had happened, the neighbor said, ‘Why pry into the heavens when you cannot see what is here on the earth?’” (quoted in *Parabola, The Magazine of Myth and Tradition,* Vol. XV, No. 2, 69).

There are several “earthy” but important aspects to the account of the wise men’s journey following the star: Jesus was born to Jewish parents who lived as Jews among Jews. He was born in Bethlehem of Judea in the land of Judah. It was the birthplace of King David and the fitting place for the birth of a prince, the son of David. Born near shepherds’ fields, he was expected to shepherd Israel. Religious leaders, well versed in holy Scripture, were so passive that they missed the privilege of visiting the newborn King.

Political powers, represented by the puppet king Herod, were so insecure that they could not tolerate the challenge of change found in this child. Leaders, though well placed for leadership, are always and forever cursed by their unworthy judgments. Herod ordered his soldiers to kill all male children two years old and younger.

A representative group of foreigners, the first to bring him gifts, reminds all Gentile seekers that the gospel is for everyone everywhere. No one knows how they ascertained that Christ had been born; how they read the stars. No one knows why they wanted to worship the newborn king of the Jews; no one knows how many wise men there were (tradition says three). But we do know that their gifts were costly and appropriate for any king—gold, frankincense, and myrrh. (JKB)

THE WISDOM OF DOUBTING

Matthew 2:1-12

A SERMON BY H. MICHAEL BREWER

There are some bits of common knowledge that everyone knows. Everybody knows, for instance, that every fourth year is a leap year. But it’s not. Look it up.

Everybody knows that a brick falls faster than a penny. But Galileo disproved that theory several centuries ago.

Everybody knows that in the movie *Casablanca*, Humphrey Bogart said, "Play it again, Sam." Except that Bogie never said those words in that movie.

And everybody knows that three kings arrived in Bethlehem, fast on the heels of the shepherds, to pay homage to a baby in a manger. Except Matthew doesn't confirm any of that. First of all they weren't kings; they were professional scholars, perhaps members of a priestly class in Persia. Neither does Matthew tell us how many there were. For all we know there could have been two or there could have been ten. (Although, I have to admit that "We two kings of Orient are" would never catch on, and I don't see how you could squeeze ten wise men on the front of a Christmas card.)

And as far as these guys kneeling in the straw among the livestock, Matthew never says a word about a stable or a manger. He says that Mary and Jesus were in a house—and no wonder. Joseph's family had plenty of time to settle in. The wise men tell Herod that they first saw the star two years earlier. And the Greek word used to describe Jesus in this story is not the word for baby, but a word which means "child" or "toddler." Jesus is a couple of years old by the time the magi arrive.

I'm sorry if I've shattered any illusions today. I only bring it up to point out that just because everybody believes something, that doesn't necessarily make it true. Sometimes the smartest thing, the wisest thing you can do is to doubt what everybody knows is true. Christianity requires that kind of healthy doubting, and the wise men are good models for us in that respect. They were wise enough to doubt what everyone else believed was true.

Everybody has always known, for instance, that it is better to be in charge, better to call the shots, better to be a leader. But the wise men were wise enough to become followers. Through the configuration of the stars God whispered to these magi, "Hey, come on. Follow my light. I've got someplace I want you to go, and somebody I want you to meet." The magi set out in the best tradition of Abraham and Sarah. Into the desert, into the night, going God-only-knows-where. But that's all right. The magi didn't have to know where they were going. God was in the lead, and they only had to follow. And they got there, too, didn't they?

I remember sometime back I set out to visit a new family for the first time. First I called and got directions, very clear directions. I came to an intersection. The directions said turn left. I looked around, got my bearings, and said to myself, "That just has to be wrong." So I turned right. Pretty soon I didn't even know what state I was in. Forty minutes later I managed to backtrack to the same intersection. This time I followed the directions. Five minutes later I arrived at my destination.

We Christians are *followers* of Jesus Christ. We believe that God knows more than we do about where we ought to be and how we ought to get there. We believe that Jesus Christ lived a human life, and knows far more than we do about living humanly. We also believe that the surest way to get lost is to chart our own course and ignore God's lead. So we do our best to be followers. In following we find there is freedom, opportunity for creativity, and even occasions for leadership. One of the things I have learned as a pastor is that I lead best by following well.

What else does everybody know? Everybody knows that it's better to get than to give. The wise men doubted that, too, and came with gifts in hand. It's not that the wise men didn't receive a great deal from God. They did, of course. But they were so eager to give something back. They were so determined to offer their worship, to give homage, to unwrap the gold and myrrh and frankincense. Those are expensive gifts, and since these travelers were not kings, we may assume that the presents must have cost them dearly. But still they brought them, still they rejoiced in giving them.

We Christians are a giving folk, too, at least that's what we believe. We believe that God has given us so much that we just can't help but spend our lives giving something back: giving to God, giving to each other, giving to people we don't even know. Show me a Christian who isn't a giver, and I'll show you a Christian who isn't wise yet in the ways of joy and gratitude.

Near the end of the story Matthew tells us that God warns the magi not to return to Herod, so they depart for home by a different way. Everybody knows that you shouldn't rock the boat. Keep things the way they are. Maintain the status quo. Come on now, how many of those New Year's resolutions are you really going to keep? We don't like to change. But the wise men were wise enough to let God turn them around, change their plans, and point them in a different direction.

In our branch of the Christian family we are fond of saying that the church must be reformed and always reforming. The motto means that no matter how much you tinker with the church, there is still room for improvement. The same thing goes for members of the church. There is still room for you and me to grow. There are some plans we have made that ought to be changed. There are areas in our lives that call for repentance. And there are some directions we have chosen that will not lead us home. Change and repentance and growth can be hard, but the alternative is to hide forever in the cocoon and never gain our wings.

Silly old magi. Left the easy life to follow a star. Spent their life savings. Risked their lives with sandstorms, bandits, and murderous kings. And all so that they could visit some runny-nosed kid. Everybody knows they should have drawn the shades on that star. Everybody knows they should have stayed home and played it safe. Everybody knows that they should have hung on to their money. Everybody knows that's how life should be lived.

May God give us the wisdom to doubt what everybody knows and to chart our course according to what God knows.

Suggestions for Worship

Call to Worship: (Ps. 72:3-5):

PASTOR: May the mountains yield prosperity for the people, and the hills, in righteousness.

PEOPLE: May he defend the cause of the poor of the people, give deliverance to the needy. . . .

PASTOR: May he live while the sun endures.

PEOPLE: And as long as the moon, throughout all generations.

Act of Praise: Psalm 72:1-14.

Suggested Hymns: "Who Is He in Yonder Stall"; "We Three Kings"; "The Boy-Child of Mary."

Opening Prayer: God All-Wise, free us from the folly of pride and self-sufficiency, so that we may find the true wisdom from above, which is the mind of Christ Jesus. Amen.

Pastoral Prayer: God of New Beginnings, on the threshold of this new year we turn to you who are our hope and joy. Your love is always new and fresh. Free us from the heavy burdens of past guilt and failure. Cast our sins into the depths of the sea, and tread our transgressions underfoot.

In this new year open our hearts to the grace that is sufficient for all our needs. Teach us to depend on Christ our Lord in every trial and temptation. The Spirit you have put within us is greater than the spirit of the world, and in you we are more than conquerors.

Open our hands to share freely the gifts of your bounty with those in need. Show us ways to help the homeless and hungry. Guide us into ministries for broken families. Let us give comfort to the sick, the dying, and the bereaved. Where there is conflict and turmoil, help us to be peacemakers.

Open our mouths to speak the good news of the risen Lord. Let us bear witness to those who have not heard. Let us be examples to those who have not believed. Let us encourage those who have not lived up to their own faith.

Open our eyes, Lord, to every shining sign of your presence, every token of your will, and every opportunity of thankful service. This we ask in Jesus' name. Amen.

JANUARY 10, 1993

□

First Sunday After Epiphany

God's chosen servant was endowed with the Holy Spirit. The church, Body of Christ and an extension of the Incarnation, now represents God throughout the nations.

The Sunday Lessons

Isaiah 42:1-9: This lesson from the servant songs of Isaiah tells of the one chosen by God and given as a covenant to the people, "a light to the nations" (v. 6). He brings true justice and peace. God's spirit is given to him.
Acts 10:34-38: All the Gospels agree that Jesus' ministry began after his baptism. Peter's missionary sermon recalls Jesus' baptism as the time of his anointing. The endowment of the Holy Spirit was his source of power.
Matthew 3:13-17: John the Baptist felt he was the one who needed to be baptized, but instead he was the baptizer. Jesus came to him to be baptized. A voice from heaven declared, "This is my Son, the beloved with whom I am well pleased" (v. 17). Matthew uses the story to liken Jesus to Moses, who passed through the waters of the Red Sea.

Interpretation and Imagination

In a democracy, our style does not set one apart as especially chosen. The special anointing of kings is foreign to the experience of modern Americans. *Megatrends*, a book of the eighties that discusses ten directions transforming our lives, makes the point that hierarchies are being replaced by networks. The pyramid structure, with its great high priest or general or chief executive officer, is no longer trusted as good management. The only time we tolerate strong leadership is in times of crisis. Group dynamics have taught us to focus on members of the group rather than solely on the leader.

Are the biblical teachings concerning Christ no longer acceptable? Scriptures such as "Behold my chosen servant," "This is my Son," and "There is salvation in none other" hold up Jesus' unique and singular Lordship.

This story of Jesus' baptism begins with John saying, "I need to be baptized by you" (v. 14). Most of us agree with Matthew's point that Jesus' baptism did not imply that he was inferior to John in any way. Joined with the servant song from Isaiah, this lesson reminds us that Christ came not to be served but to serve, not to be saved but to save, not to be glorified but to glorify God.

Trusted leaders seldom display their power and popularity. Force or the threat of harm never enters into their dealings with subordinates.

Isaiah's servant song describes the way of such great leadership. "Here is my servant. . . . He will not cry or lift up his voice, . . . a bruised reed he will not break, and a dimly burning wick he will not quench" (vv. 1-3). Christ's quiet strength is even now "a light to the nations." (JKB)

JESUS IN THE JORDAN

Matthew 3:13-17

A SERMON BY H. MICHAEL BREWER

The Jordan River begins as a trickle, high in the snowy mountains of northern Israel. Eventually it broadens into a lazy river that meanders like a green ribbon through the length of Palestine. Even in the Judean desert the banks of the Jordan are alive with trees and bushes that draw moisture from the river. The river was a natural place for John to begin his ministry when he came out of the wilderness, preaching repentance and baptism for the forgiveness of sins.

From Jerusalem and the surrounding environs great crowds gathered to hear John and to be baptized. Some thought that John was the messiah, but he denied that. "I baptize you with water for repentance, but one who is more powerful than I is coming after me," he said. "He will baptize you with the Holy Spirit and fire" (v. 11).

Then one day Jesus the Messiah came down to the Jordan River to see John. He wanted to be baptized, but John was troubled by the request. Surely the Holy One of Israel could have nothing to confess, no sins for which to repent. "Do you come to me?" asked John. "I need to be baptized by you" (v. 14). But Jesus insisted, and assured John that it was right and proper for the Messiah to be baptized in the same river with the sinners.

Why should that be so? Why should Jesus take on a baptism of repentance. Perhaps another story will help to illuminate the biblical story. In the 1800s a Christian missionary named Damian went to minister among the people of the Hawaiian islands. The islands were a tropical paradise, but the coming of the Europeans had introduced new diseases to the isolated islanders. Among the new sicknesses was leprosy. For a while lepers were sent to a special hospital in Honolulu, but when the hospital filled up, the king of the islands decreed that henceforth all lepers would be banished to an uninhabited island called Molokai. Exiled from friends and family, the lepers were abandoned to live on Molokai without housing, medical care, or an adequate supply of water. There they stayed until death claimed them.

Damian was tormented every time he saw some member of his congregation carried off to Molokai, until finally the missionary felt the call to go there himself. Although Damian went to serve, the lepers of Molokai greeted him with suspicion. He was the only European on the island and the only healthy person on Molokai. What were his motives, they wondered. How could they accept one so different from themselves?

In order to win the trust of the natives, Damian identified himself with them by living as they lived. Until decent huts could be built, he slept in the open as they did. He helped lay the pipe to bring clean water into the village. He shared their food and their water. Damian participated in their lives in every respect. It is possible to minister to lepers and remain reasonably safe from the disease by taking some precautions. But Damian would allow nothing to distance him from the people he had come to help. He brought hope, dignity, and love to Molokai. Eventually he died there, himself a victim of leprosy.

Damian felt he could only help those poor people by becoming one of them. He gave up all privileges and lived their life. I think that is what Jesus had in mind at the Jordan River. By his very birth, the Son of God emptied himself and took the form of a servant. He was heaved helpless and squalling into the cold world the same as you and I. He endured the stubbed toes and disappointments of growing up. He knew the joys and sorrows of life in a family. He studied a trade and learned to support himself by the work of his own hands. He knew the delight of a cool breeze and the misery of a sweaty, relentless summer day. In nearly every way, Jesus Christ became like us. Although without sin himself, Jesus did not remain aloof from sinners.

At the Jordan River Jesus cast his lot with us once and for all. He trudged across the same muddy bank and waded into the same chilly water. He let himself be lowered beneath the water along with all the sinners. Jesus could have stood apart from the multitudes, but these were the very people he had come to save. On Molokai a healthy man identified himself with the sick; in the Jordan River Jesus, the sinless one, identified himself with sinful humanity. Christ committed himself to face the same hurts, problems, and worries that you and I endure, so that we could learn to trust him. In this way he came to help us.

Let me say it once more. In his baptism Jesus identified himself with us and entered into the fullness of our lives. When you and I are baptized it means that we have identified ourselves with Christ and entered into the fullness of his life. What John the baptizer predicted about the Messiah came to pass on Pentecost. The risen Lord baptized his people with tongues of flame and the power of the Holy Spirit. From that time on the believers identified themselves with their Lord. They bore Christ's brand. They carried his name. They lived the kind of life that Jesus had lived. Jesus was baptized so that he might be like us. We are baptized so that we can be like Jesus.

Of course, it is not fire or water that makes us into the likeness of Christ. It is the Holy Spirit who does this. The Spirit moves in and through the sacrament of baptism and continues to shape us through all the span of our years. It is the Spirit who teaches us to love and forgive. It is the Spirit who convicts us of sin and assures us of forgiveness. The Spirit whispers to our hearts that in Christ you and I are beloved sons and daughters of God, beloved children with whom our Father is well pleased. Thanks to the

Spirit we are growing daily into the fullness of the stature of Jesus Christ.

The Spirit came to Jesus as he stood in the Jordan and allowed Jesus to enter into our lives. The Spirit comes to us in baptism, allowing us to enter into the life of Jesus Christ. The Jordan River brings life wherever it flows, even in the desert. Wherever the Spirit flows, it too brings life. The Spirit moved at the Jordan; the Spirit baptized in fire at Jerusalem; and that same Spirit is still moving, still baptizing, still bringing life to all whose hearts are open to his coming!

Suggestions for Worship

Call to Worship (Ps. 29:1-2, 11):

PASTOR: Ascribe to the LORD, O heavenly beings, ascribe to the LORD glory and strength.

PEOPLE: Ascribe to the LORD the glory of his name; worship the LORD in holy splendor.

PASTOR: May the LORD give strength to his people!

PEOPLE: May the LORD bless his people with peace!

Act of Praise: Psalm 29.

Suggested Hymns: "The Church's One Foundation"; "Open My Eyes, That I May See"; "When Jesus Came to Jordan."

Opening Prayer: Loving God, immerse us in your love so that we can be washed clean of sin. Open the fountain of your grace within us and fill us to overflowing with the water of life in Jesus our Lord. Amen.

Pastoral Prayer: Holy and Redeeming Lord, although you made us in your image, our rebellious ways have distorted that image and our lives bear little likeness to the example of Christ

Jesus your Son. Use the presence of Christ as a mold into which our lives may be poured. Shape the clay of our potential according to your will for us. Conform us to the image of Christ, in whom human life was perfectly fulfilled.

Where we are selfish, make us kind. Where we are envious, make us generous. Where we are indifferent, make us compassionate. Where we are cowardly, make us courageous for justice. Where we are contentious, make us peaceable. Where we are grudging, make us forgiving. Where we are spiteful, make us loving.

Make us quick to pardon and slow to blame. Make us eager to serve and reluctant to demand. Commit us to humility and turn us away from pride. Dispose us to gentleness and free us from harshness. Make us zealous for the needs of neighbors and forgetful of our desires.

In all things teach us to live like Christ until that day when his glory will be fully revealed in us! Amen.

JANUARY 17, 1993

□

Second Sunday After Epiphany

The rites of temple sacrifice are not a part of our religion, but the mission of a saving Christ is central. Being claimed by that saving power is also central.

The Sunday Lessons

Isaiah 49:1-7: This second servant song of Isaiah recounts God's calling of Isaiah, who from his conception was named the prophet to bring Israel back to God. His witness is no small thing. It will reach to the ends of the earth.

I Corinthians 1:1-9: Paul's greeting to the church at Corinth speaks of the call of God. Paul, called by the will of God, wrote to Corinthians who were called to be saints. Grace and peace, God's richest blessing, are the wishes in Paul's salutation. Although there are divisions at Corinth, Paul begins, "I give thanks to my God always for you" (v. 4).

John 1:29-41: John the Baptist's testimony concerning Christ recalls the Spirit descending as a dove from heaven and notes that while he baptizes with water, Jesus baptizes with the Holy Spirit. Two of John's disciples followed Jesus. One of them, Andrew, found his brother Simon and said, "We have found the Messiah" (v. 41). Jesus' mission to take away sin and his call of disciples are central.

Interpretation and Imagination

"You never really know a man until you live with him," she said. It's true about so many things in life. You never really know a place until you've been there, even though you've read about it or seen pictures of it. There is no substitute for firsthand experience.

"Where are you from?" they asked. Their blunt question revealed their deeper questions. Who are you really? What are your purposes? What's your game? If we can be with another, share a conversation or a meal or the hospitality of their home, we learn some things that cannot be gained any other way. So John's disciples, curious about who Jesus was and about the nature of his ministry, asked the question, "Where are you staying?" "Come and see," he said (vv. 38-39).

Many of us who find little power that changes anything (takes away sin) in our Christian experience need to recover a sense of being in the presence of Christ: Being with him when he heals; with him when he stills the storm; with him when he calls little children or feeds the multitudes; with him when he forgives sins; with him in the garden and at the cross; with him on Easter morning. Meditation is the way.

Henry Sloane Coffin, preaching on this text, ridiculed the dictionary definition of the word *kiss*: "To smack with pursed lips (a compression of the closed cavity of the mouth by the cheeks giving a slight sound when the rounded contact of the lips with one another is broken)." He noted that the description is accurate, but it is of little use to a mother who kisses her child or to lovers who thrill to each other's acceptance.

Doctrinal statements and ancient creeds will not, by themselves, lead to the discovery of mercy and knowledge of the life-giving power of Christ. That comes to those who make their home with Christ. They don't depend on hearsay or on words read. They are intent upon being with him and, in so doing, are not disappointed. (JKB)

A MATTER OF IDENTITY AND DESTINY

I Corinthians 12:27

A SERMON BY JOHN WESLEY COLEMAN

Today we remember Martin Luther King, Jr. We remember his parsonage birth on that winter day in 1929. We remember his brutally inflicted death in the early spring of 1968.

Throughout these past few days in church and school auditoriums; across the airwaves by radio and television; in communities, rural and urban, throughout the length and breadth of the land could be heard recordings of King's resonant voice proclaiming "I have a dream!" The rhythmic chant and eloquent words, from what is probably King's most famous speech, have been memorized and his delivery imitated by more people in more places on more programs than possibly any other speech by any other person throughout the pulsating panorama of recorded history.

However, I do have a concern. And that concern is related to the element of truth contained in that old and familiar adage that declares, "familiarity breeds contempt." Could it be that the constant bombardment of King's dynamic message, delivered on the steps of the Lincoln Memorial in our nation's capital on that blistering but intoxicating, exciting, history-making August afternoon in 1963, could cause it to become so trivialized, so burdened with triteness from overuse, that those glowing and glorious ideas have become meaningless cliches? It has the capacity to cause momentarily nostalgia-inducing reminiscences, perhaps, but hardly the force or power to effect any transformation in human conduct.

The passage of time is so swift, relentless and clothed in irrevocable inevitability. Two and a half decades have passed since those days of glorious but costly defiance. In moments of recollection and reflection one can still hear the cadence of determined marching feet and the syncopated chant of young brothers behind us calling for "Freedom! Freedom! Now! Now!"

In memory the sounds are hardly as clear and pronounced as they once were. They have dissipated with the passage of time, as has the intensity of and commitment to the struggle. These have faded with the years and are now but dim, almost inaudible sounds from a long ago time and a distant place.

But one still remembers. One still remembers the pain, the ridicule, the suffering that so many endured with the burning, heartfelt conviction that the earth was in labor and a new world was being born. The "now" for which they cried has escaped us. The hope once invested in "the dream" has eluded us. The "here" is past; the "now" is history.

The dead shadows of dreams that once inspired visions of a glorious tomorrow have been embalmed with the voices of heroes of that dim yesterday that is but the haunting ghost of unfulfilled promises. Post-mortems are in vogue. But eulogies are empty words that fall meaninglessly upon the coffins of the damned. One grows tired of dreaming and there's a weariness upon our world. Skeletons now dance upon the graves of our martyrs. The blood of yesterday's battles has seeped into the ground.

But even in the face of all of the diluted optimism, occasional disillusionment, and the periodic pangs of hope-smothering disappointment, I can still feel the electricity that we all felt—caught up in an almost mystical sense of invincibility, unity, and purpose—as Martin caused the very gates of heaven to vibrate with his witness to his unshakeable faith and persistent hope, proclaiming over and over again, *"I still have a dream!"*

In response to my earlier query, No. Neither King's memory, nor his dream can ever be trivialized as long as there are those of every race, religion, clime, and culture who, through honest, sincere, and committed action, hunger and thirst for "liberty and justice for all." King fervently believed that a church truly committed to Jesus Christ was predicated upon the firm conviction that liberty and justice, freedom of opportunity, and a sense of possessing infinite value as a human being were basic rights of every individual born of God.

He further believed that the church's mandate from Christ was received as the anointing of power through the Spirit in relation to obedience. How did Christ himself speak of the power of the Spirit's anointing? "The Spirit of the Lord is upon me, because he has anointed me to bring good news to the poor. He has sent me to proclaim release to the captives and recovery of sight to the blind, to let the oppressed go free, to proclaim the year of the Lord's favor" (Luke 4:18-19).

Thus, King intensely, earnestly, and devoutly believed Paul's glowing and glorious exhortation that is our text for today: "Now you are the body of Christ and individually members of it" (I Cor. 12:27). I personally subscribe to the opinion of those exegetes who are much more knowledgeable than I (and without hesitation aver the same for Martin, based upon my understanding of positions taken by him on issues regarding such matters) that Paul, in regarding the church as "the body of Christ," was not dealing in metaphor or simile, but conveying what he believed to be an ontological reality.

Operating under this conviction, King brought with him to the struggle expectations of the church's obedience to the mandate of Christ to oppose all forces of oppression in human society; forces that would foster policies, practices, and programs predicated upon racism, sexism, classism, or any other "ism" that demeans, degrades, or is destructive to the ennobling aspects of the human personality.

Operating under this conviction, I, as do others who profess belief in Jesus of Nazareth as the very Christ of God, contend that the church, as the Body of Christ, is the continuing incarnation by which the will, way, ministry, and mission of Christ is a continual presence in human society; that the Incarnation recently celebrated at Christmas, was not, and is not, a once-for-all-time event, but is, in fact, a day-by-day, hour-by-hour occurrence. It happens over and over and over again and again and again through the church and through Christians reaching out to help where there is pain; to care where there is nakedness and deprivation; to care where homelessness finds people bedding down on freezing sidewalks and in frigid alleys separating inhospitable buildings on busy city streets. Christ is there through the church and through caring Christians committed to him in love. To be the Body of Christ, as the church, is our identity and also our glorious destiny.

In our text Paul affirms the concept of the continuing incarnation finding expression as the church, committed to doing the will of Christ in the world: "Now you are the body of Christ and individually members of it" (v. 27). "For," as Paul said earlier, "just as the body is one and has many members, and all the members of the body, though many, are one body, so it is with Christ. For in the one Spirit we were all baptized into one body—Jews or Greeks, slaves or free, male or female, Methodists or Presbyterians—and we were all made to drink of one Spirit" (see vv. 12-13).

For King, it would appear that Paul's words presaged what King often referred to as "The Beloved Community." As the scholar Walter Rast so effectively states,

> When Jesus thought of community he conceived of something entirely new as coming about through his ministry. The church would manifest a new form of humanity the world had little

> known before. It would be a new kind of assembly left here on earth as a continuing witness to the Messiah's mission, a witness not simply in words but in every visible expression of its life.

For King, this new form of humanity to be found in a new kind of organizational mode, under the Lordship of Jesus Christ, was naught but the church, "The Beloved Community," the continuing incarnation, empowered by the impetus of sacrificial love and willful obedience to the anointing, indwelling Spirit of the eternal God. And the church, by the actualization and authentication of its professed faith in and commitment to Jesus Christ, would be instrumental in the ultimate dawning of the reign of a more humane social order upon the earth.

In his allegiance to Jesus Christ, and as a result of his love for him, King lived out Paul's admonition found in chapter eleven of his first letter to the church at Corinth: "Be imitators of me, as I am of Christ" (v. 1). King tried, as much as was humanly possible, to live according to his understanding of God's will for his life, as it was revealed to him through the life and work of Jesus Christ. We remember him today because of what he was able to achieve through the complete subordination of his will to the will of God.

In reflecting upon the life of Martin Luther King, Jr., some days ago, I was struck with amazement at the number of similarities between the experiences of Jesus and those of King. At so many points in his life King acted as one who was conscientiously trying to follow in the footsteps of Christ.

Take the way in which each, by the sheer cohering force of personality, was able to bring together the diverse and conflicting personalities of those who followed them into a harmonious unified group, where disagreements and misunderstandings were laid aside because of each group member's shared allegiance to and affection for the one whom they followed.

For example, just look at those who followed Christ. There was Matthew, with the deviousness and calculating tendencies of one who had been a tax collector; there was Peter, who was often given to outbursts of emotional upheaval; James and John, with political ambitions which led them to covet positions of power; there was Simon the Zealot, a fire-breathing revolutionary; and so on. Around King there were personalities no less diverse, with no less potential for conflict and incompatibility. There was Jim Beval, Jesse Jackson, Wyatt Walker, Andy Young, C. T. Vivian, Hosea Williams, and so on—truly a varied and potentially volatile mixture of personalities if ever there was one.

As it was with Jesus, so it was with King. Both were able to bind such diversity into a oneness that would change history, by no other means except the cohering force of personality.

Consider also the similarity in the experiences of both Christ and King on the night before their deaths. Each faced their moment of resignation.

Jesus, in the Garden of Gethsemane: "Father, if it be thy will, let this cup pass from me. Nevertheless, not my will but thy will be done."

King, in that last speech in Memphis: "I'd like to live a long life, longevity has its place. But that really doesn't matter to me now; I just want to do God's will."

"Thy will be done," said Jesus. "I just want to do God's will," said King.

Consider, also, the way in which each responded to the cry of human need. I used to think of how different history might be if King had followed the original plan and not gone to Memphis when he did.

I can recall so vividly the last time many of us saw King alive. Black preachers from across the nation assembled in Miami, Florida, at the Ministers Leadership Training Program. Three times we were compelled to vacate the Sheraton Hotel due to bomb scares. We were there to finalize plans for what was to be the Poor People's Campaign, a movement representing the poor of every race in the land.

Though possessed with a severe throat infection King took us to the mountaintop on that morning. Into that meeting Ben Hooks (who had been recently appointed a judge) and Jim Lawson brought the story of the need and the appeal from the struggling, oppressed trash collectors in Memphis. They called to King to help them in their struggle, and King had to go to Memphis.

For me this was reminiscent of Jesus who had to respond when those in need cried to him for help. Even in the moment of his dying he had to delay death to respond to a repentant thief on the cross beside him, who in his final moment cried out, "Jesus, remember me when you come into your kingdom" (Luke 23:42). Jesus stopped dying long enough to assure that forgiveness-seeking reprobate of a place with him in eternity, "Today you will be with me in Paradise" (v. 43).

Lastly, consider the final commitment of self to God by both Jesus and King. Tradition has it that Jesus' final word from the cross, his final words in his earthly life were, "Father, into your hands I commend my spirit" (Luke 23:46).

King's final words were very similar. He had stepped out on the balcony of the motel and was chatting with Jesse Jackson who introduced him to Ben Branch, the music director of Operation Breadbasket. King asked Branch if at the meeting that night he would play "Precious Lord, Take My Hand." As the words left his lips a shot rang out, and moments later Martin Luther King, Jr.—the apostle of nonviolence—was dead.

"Father, into thy hands, I commend my spirit," said Jesus. "Precious Lord, take my hand," said King.

We remember him today because of our conviction that this world is a better place because King passed this way.

King closed his last speech in this life by reciting Julia Ward Howe's "Battle Hymn of the Republic."

> Mine eyes have seen the glory of the coming of the Lord;

ending with that resounding refrain,

> Glory, glory, hallelujah!
> His truth is marching on.

History reveals that King's truth—that the oppressed of the world would overcome—is marching on. In Romania that truth is marching on. In East Germany that truth marched on. In South Africa that truth is marching on. One day soon in the struggling countries of Latin America and the Middle East that truth will march on. The downtrodden will throw off the shackles of oppression and overcome.

We remember Martin Luther King, Jr., and know this world is a better place because of him.

On this occasion for celebrating the memory of God's prophet, Martin Luther King, Jr., let us remember him with thanks to

God for his life as we remember the words of the gospel song, the title of which contains King's last words in this life: "Precious Lord, take my hand."

Suggestions for Worship

Call to Worship (Ps. 40:1-3):

PASTOR: I waited patiently for the LORD; he inclined to me and heard my cry.

PEOPLE: He drew me up from the pit, out of the miry bog,

PASTOR: [He] set my feet upon a rock, making my steps secure.

PEOPLE: He put a new song in my mouth, a song of praise to our God.

Act of Praise: Psalm 40:1-11.

Suggested Hymns: "Let All Mortal Flesh Keep Silence"; "There Is a Fountain Filled with Blood"; "Just as I Am, Without One Plea."

Opening Prayer: Gracious God, Giver of all speech and all knowledge, teach us, beyond all words, that even though we speak in the tongues of angels but have not love, we are only noisy gongs and clanging symbols. And teach us, beyond all ideas, that even though we understand all mysteries and all knowledge but have not love, we are nothing. Called to be disciples of Christ Jesus, we await your word with all those who call upon your Name. Amen.

Pastoral Prayer: O God of Jesus, on whom the Spirit descended and in whom the Spirit lived, we draw near to you in his name. Gathered here in the knowledge that you walked among us in him, we take comfort from your nearness. You are still our judge, but now we are assured that your judgment will be tempered with justice and your justice, with mercy.

We thank you, gracious God, for the Spirit that dwelled in Jesus. Let that same Spirit descend upon us that we might exclaim with John, "Behold, the Lamb of God!"

Open our eyes, O Lord, and let the light that shone in Jesus shine in us and through us. And let the light fall also upon our neighbors, that we might become one in our witness to that which dwells in every person ever born on earth. Amen. (From Everett Tilson and Phyllis Cole, *Litanies and Other Prayers from the Common Lectionary: Year A* [Nashville, TN: Abingdon Press, 1989], 31-33.)

JANUARY 24, 1993

□

Third Sunday After Epiphany

Jesus' ministry, which set no limits and was not turned back at any boundary, began in "Galilee of the Gentiles."

The Sunday Lessons

Isaiah 9:1-4: When Jerusalem was destroyed and the exile begun, Galilee was swallowed up by pagan influences. Isaiah's consolation is addressed to this land. Matthew's Gospel quotes the prophet's words: "The land of Zebulun, land of Naphthali . . . Galilee of the Gentiles" (Matt. 4:15).
I Corinthians 1:10-17. Chloe's people reported there were divisions in the church at Corinth. Some claimed Paul as leader; others, Apollos; others, Cephas. "Has Christ been divided?" Paul asks. "Were you baptized in the name of Paul?" (v. 13). The apostle was thankful he had baptized only two of them.
Matthew 4:12-23: Galilee was populated by Gentile pagans. Some pious Jews hardly thought it worthy to be part of the holy land. Jesus' ministry began there, reaching out to all nations. By the Sea of Galilee he called Peter and Andrew. They left their nets and followed. He called James and John, who left their boat and their father.

Interpretation and Imagination

Solidarity is a word introduced to our consciousness during the last decade. It has been an important word for socialists for a long time, and is now the key word of the international labor movement. When workers joined in rebellion against a party dictatorship in Poland, "Solidarity" was their cry. The letterhead of American labor organizations AFL and CIO announced in bold print, "Solidarity Day 1983."

Solidarity means being united, standing side by side, working together. The Christian concepts of unity, neighbor, community, and fellowship are akin to its meanings.

Jürgen Moltmann published a sermon entitled "Solidarity" (*The Power of the Powerless*, Harper & Row, 1983). He says, "It is not merely political aggression and economic exploitation that ruin people. Suffering, guilt, fear, and grief destroy us too, because they isolate us. Nothing is more important than to find people who stand by us in trouble, and stay beside us, and bear our burdens."

The marks of a segregated and broken society are just as evident in any state and county of America as they were in Zebulun and Napthali, that holy land filled with pagans. We've called our nation "the melting pot" and our church "pluralistic," yet our communities reflect how we only love folks like ourselves and fear those who are different. Feminists, evangelicals, and homosexuals caucus separately. Togetherness and community that only reflect "birds of a feather" are not a fulfillment of the messianic hope for all nations.

Moltmann calls for "solidarity of creative love," saying, "It is a hopeful and creative community only if I sit beside someone I do not agree with, and stay there." (JKB)

FROM DARKNESS INTO LIGHT

Isaiah 9:1-4
Matthew 4:12-23

A SERMON BY M. CLAIRE CLYBURN

As a child, I had a very particular way of positioning myself for sleeping: I would lie on my stomach in a very straight line, with my stuffed toy nestled close to my head. This strategy was to ensure that none of my extremities would hang over the edge of the bed. I didn't want the monsters who lived under the bed to be able to reach up and grab me during the night. To this day, when I am falling asleep, I make sure that all of me is securely positioned underneath the covers.

Monsters. Darkness. Closets. Things that go bump in the night. A child's fear of the dark is one of the most universal and consistent fears, for darkness is the place where the wild things are; where ugly, terrible, and scary creatures lie in anticipation, waiting for us to become vulnerable by lying down and falling asleep.

Now I lay me down to sleep;
I pray the Lord my soul to keep.
If I should die before I wake,
I pray the Lord my soul to take.

That childhood prayer struck fear in my heart every time I muttered the words. What might happen that would keep me from waking the next morning?

Isn't it odd that the places and situations that look innocent enough by day should become avenues of terror and fright by night? By day, a closet is a place to hang clothes and stuff toys. By night, it's a doorway to a secret tunnel of unknown lands. By day, under the bed is a place to kick your toys or your shoes so your room looks cleaner than it really is. By night, it's a hideout for monsters, whose job is to reach up and grab you, unawares, when you are defenseless.

For most of us, becoming adults has not necessarily cured us of our fears of the dark. Oh, the closets may be a little bigger and filled with business suits instead of building blocks, but at night, when the lights are out and our children are tucked in bed to wrestle with their fears, our own monsters come to life and taunt us once more.

Am I a loving wife? Am I a caring husband? Am I raising my children right? What about my own parents? Will I get that promotion? Can I keep my kids off drugs? When will I slow down? Why do I never seem to be satisfied? Where is God in the midst of my chaotic life?

By day, we function pretty well through this maze of life—paying bills, getting family schedules coordinated, even managing to eat high-fiber/low-fat diets once in a while—and the fears of our unknowns are held at bay, pushed safely behind our aerobics classes and microwave dinners. But when our world slows down a bit, the fears creep—no, *rush*—into our lives, our hearts, our minds, our souls, and torment us once again.

"The people who sat in darkness have seen a great light" (Matt. 4:16). Something in us tells us this is true, that this is the only hope worth holding on to, that there is a way out of this fearful trap. And somewhere we have seen a light—if only we could find it again! If only it would find *us*.

It's the light we need, isn't it? By daylight our lives are

manageable. It's only when the darkness closes in around us that we become afraid, just as when we were children. Only now, our darknesses take many different forms, and the light seems so hidden from our view.

The darkness of betrayal: having spent your life in partnership with one who let you down in your time of need. The darkness of uncertainty: believing in an ideal or a dream that is unable to sustain you any longer and will not come to pass. The darkness of suffering: when you or one you love bears a pain you cannot remove. The darkness of death: the sinking realization that all your best efforts to attain immortality will not, finally, save you from that universal human drama.

"The people who sat in darkness have seen a great light." We begin our search for this light—a light that burned once with such intensity!—hoping against hope that it will turn out to be more than a flickering candle that dances with every breath until a strong wind snuffs it out completely.

Do you recall what it's like to wake up in the middle of the night in an unfamiliar place? Sometimes a nightlight glows down the hall, providing a small amount of light, or security, against the darkness of the night. How reassuring it can be to see a faint glow, providing orientation against the hazy murkiness. Sometimes a lamp has been left on in the den down the hall and its steady glow almost beckons you into the room, into safety. One Christmas at my parents' home I found myself sleeping in my old bed. I awoke in the middle of the night and lay there for a long time, listening for any sounds of life. The door to my room was shut, so the only light was from the moon outside. I tossed and turned for what seemed like hours, waiting only for the sky to brighten enough for me to legitimate getting up. Later at breakfast, I related my tale of a sleepless night. My father asked me why I didn't just get up and sit with him in the living room, since he had been up most of the night as well!

Sometimes there are sources of light in our lives—nightlights that orient us, lamps that beckon us, even moonlight that calms us—reminding us that the spell of darkness can be broken. But sometimes these lights can confuse us and even blind us with a false sense of security. We get so comfortable with reading by the light of a 60-watt bulb that we forget what power a ray of sunshine can have. We settle for the predictability of artificial light and are startled, even scared, when the radiance of pure sunlight penetrates our bodies and warms our souls.

What has happened to us that we have contented ourselves with that which is false? We run to artificial sources of light, or joy, or pleasure, and hide ourselves from the light of truth. We have even tried to be our own light, our own truth, to be the answers to all our questions, to content ourselves with nightlights instead of moonlight, with lightbulbs when only the clear brilliance of sunlight can illumine us.

"I am the light of the world," Jesus said. We would so dearly love to believe him, but other lights have captured our attention. They cannot hold it, however, any more than they can shine on their own.

Here is the good news: "The people who sat in darkness have seen a great light, and for those who sat in the region and shadow of death, light has dawned" (Matt. 4:16). The light *has* dawned in Jesus Christ! We did no more to create it than we did to create ourselves. Imagine—a light not of our own making! We have only one task: to bask in its glow. And like the new green plants, which grow instinctively toward the sun, our exposure to the light of Christ beckons us to grow toward him, to live in the warmth of his glow, and to reflect the light of his love to others. No longer do we have to question our attempts to create the light we need. No longer do we have to remain in the darkness of our fears, our faults, or our failures. The light of Christ floods our being.

It is as if you were seated on the ocean's shore, early one morning. The only colors you see are the dark blues and blacks of the water and sky, and the faint, silvery glow of the wavecrests as they break on the beach. Then slowly, without your moving, the colors begin to lighten on the water. They draw your eye to the horizon, where the sky is changing hues before you. First crimson, then pink, then finally pale yellow appear above the horizon. Then, almost without warning, the sun bursts into the sky. Color and light flood you and, incredibly, begin to warm your soul. The hazy shapes of darkness give way to clear impressions of the new day. The light of Christ, which is his love, is this real.

I mentioned the unintentional all-nighter at my parents' home one Christmas. The next night was Christmas Eve. After church we came home and crawled into our beds, exhausted but elated after a midnight service. I slept hard that night and awoke the next morning to see the rising sun streaming through the east window in my room. It was Christmas Day, and with joy I awoke to greet the glorious day. This Christmas sun is our bright morning star, our Christ who dispels even the longest darkness.

"What has come into being in him was life, and the life was the light of all people. The light shines in the darkness, and the darkness did not overcome it." (John 1:3-5) He is waiting to enter your darkness. He is waiting to make you fit you to walk in the light.

Suggestions for Worship

Call to Worship (Ps. 27:1, 4):

PASTOR: The LORD is my light and my salvation; whom shall I fear?

PEOPLE: The LORD is the stronghold of my life; of whom shall I be afraid?

PASTOR: One thing I asked of the LORD, that I will seek after:

PEOPLE: To live in the house of the LORD all the days of my life.

Act of Praise: Psalm 27:1-6.

Suggested Hymns: "Joyful, Joyful, We Adore Thee"; "Lord of the Dance"; "O Zion, Haste."

Opening Prayer: O God, Father of all light, you sent your only Son, Jesus, to be the light for all the world. Grant that we might be illumined by the truth of Jesus Christ, and so live in love with him, who reigns with you and the Holy Spirit, now and forever. Amen.

Pastoral Prayer: God of grace and love, in the beginning you created light and called it good. You have given us the one true light in Jesus Christ, who illumines our paths and calls us to enter your presence. In this season of Epiphany we offer you praise for the gift of your Son.

Lord, hear our prayers for a hurting and broken world. We ask for the courage and grace to share the light of Christ's love with our families, our friends, our neighbors, our co-workers. Grant that the light of Christ might dwell in us and strengthen us to reach out in peace to our sisters and brothers in need.

Lord, fit us for the ministries into which you have called us, and give to us the grace to serve you with joy, trusting in your love and goodness.

We ask our prayers in the name of Jesus, the light of the world. Amen.

JANUARY 31, 1993

□

Fourth Sunday After Epiphany

A new portrait of citizens of the kingdom of God is painted in the Beatitudes.

The Sunday Lessons

Micah 6:1-8: Legal terminology suggests that God will bring suit against Israel. The mountains will hear his case. The sixth verse asks the question, "With what shall I come before the LORD?" Sacrifices of flock and field and even a first-born child are set aside. Justice, kindness, and humility are the way.
I Corinthians 1:18-31: Paul reminds the Corinthians that God did not choose the rich, the wise, or the powerful to be his representatives in the world. Human wisdom and resources must yield to the power of God, whom Christ manifests on the cross. For the Jews it is a stumbling block; for pagans, foolishness. For those being saved, it's the power of God.
Matthew 5:1-12: The Beatitudes are introduced at the beginning of the Sermon on the Mount as an inaugural. Eight blessings accompany values that still contradict existing standards. The ninth addresses those who are persecuted as dissenters.

Interpretation and Imagination

In a preaching class at Duke Divinity School, the assigned texts were stories found in the first eleven chapters of Genesis. Through random choice Captain Robert Von Buskirk, a Vietnam veteran, was assigned to preach the story of Cain and Abel. Student preachers were to focus on the intersection of "the story" and "our story."

About midnight the Green Beret captain called my home saying, "Do you know where the burden of the text is for me? It's when God says to Cain, 'Your brother's blood is crying out to me from the ground'" (Gen. 4:10).

That's true of all of us. The blood of our brothers and sisters is crying from the ground. Wanting progress, we have pushed others aside. Wanting to live better, we have caused others to die. Wanting our time in the world to last longer, we threaten the times. Anti-nuclear witnesses remind us that time is running out.

Name any continent, and you will name a battlefield. Name any nation, and you will name a place of conflict. Name any city, and you will name a site of violence. Name the name of Jesus, and you will name that light which manifests true blessedness and teaches the way of it. The Beatitudes are his manifesto. "Blessed are the peacemakers" (Matt. 5:9).

Disarmament is no easy issue. One may refuse to defend against any oppressor and willingly accept the certain suffering and possible death that follow. One may intend to live and, if necessary, die without armament but in that personal choice require others—neighbors, family, nation—to face the reality of evil's oppression without means of resistance and defense.

Is it not plain that only in a kingdom of meekness, purity, and hunger for the righteousness of God can we have peace? The Beatitudes must be a call to confession and penance, or they will never be a benediction. (JKB)

KINGDOM LIVING FOR KINGDOM PEOPLE

Matthew 5:1-12

A SERMON BY M. CLAIRE CLYBURN

Doesn't it seem that our whole culture is devoted to reminding us that our chief goal in life is to be happy? Advertising sells products based on how much happier or more satisfied we will be if we purchase that particular product. Part of a job performance evaluation asks you to consider your own level of happiness in your work. When a couple is ending a relationship, it is usually precipitated by one person admitting that he or she is no longer happy. Many of us have bought into the idea that life's main purpose is to make us happy, and we believe we have an inherent right to complain when we are not. (How else do you explain the popularity of talk shows?)

Many people have looked at the scripture lesson for today as a prescription for happiness. Several years ago I participated in a musical drama with this idea. It featured a seeker, played in mime, who wandered around looking for happiness. She encountered a sign-carrier who told her about peace, a sad clown who told her about mourning, and so on. At the conclusion of her search, she tried to achieve happiness by simultaneously doing all the things she had learned. My job as a chorus member was to laugh at her pitiable attempt to carry a sign, cry, and jump up and down, an effort which left her frustrated and hopeless. We sang to her, "You've got to get it together if you want to be happy" (Buryl Red, *Lightshine!*). And just a few years ago Robert Schuller published his comments on the Sermon on the Mount, *The Be-Happy Attitudes*.

Perhaps we have looked at what the world offers us—high mortgages, a break-neck pace to keep up with our peers, and nagging doubt about our worth in a company full of people who dress, look, and act like we do—and found ourselves wallowing in our own emptiness. Or maybe we have believed that we alone could solve any problem that confronted us and have reluctantly realized that we do not have all the answers, that we did not make ourselves, and that we surely cannot save ourselves. Somewhere along the road we have become convinced that the appropriate goal for our lives is to content ourselves with comfortability, with security, and with pride.

So why in the world would we look to Jesus to confirm this notion, and particularly this passage? Even a quick perusal of the teachings tells you that if we are going to take Jesus seriously, we will have to give up trusting in what society tells us to value.

"I don't want to depend on God, for that keeps me vulnerable. I want to be self-actualized." Jesus answers, "Blessed are the poor in spirit."

"I'm not going to cry any more; it's time for me to get over this situation and move on with life. I just don't care any more." Jesus says, "Blessed are those who mourn."

"I want the American dream like anyone else. I want real estate, I want to invest my money, I need a bigger home. I want, I want, I need, I need . . ." Jesus counters with "Blessed are the meek."

"I'm tired of being a bleeding heart. I worked for what I have; let other people do it, too." And Jesus simply says, "Blessed are the merciful."

"Of course we need strong defense. That's what makes this country great." "Blessed are the peacemakers."

Matthew tells us that, seeing the crowds, Jesus withdrew to a mountain and began to teach his disciples. He didn't go up there to get a better view of the people or even to be better heard. Jesus withdrew from them and called his followers around him. He is not giving out instructions to all of society, nor is he teaching the secret of self-actualization. He is, quite simply, telling them what God is like. This is kingdom talk for kingdom people. To the uninitiated it sounds quite bizarre, hopelessly out of step with the times, and just plain upside down.

But to those who wish to follow Jesus it is music to our ears, for it describes what life in God's kingdom can be like. It describes who God's people are. God's people are poor in spirit because they have learned to trust in God alone. God's people mourn when they consider the state of the world and its refusal to hear the good news. God's people hunger and thirst for righteousness because they long for the day when God's justice will prevail. God's people are merciful because they know they have received mercy. God's people are pure in heart because they have learned that God is not mocked. God's people are peacemakers because Jesus Christ is their peace. God's people tolerate persecution because they know they are not called to be happy but to be faithful.

Can you imagine what would happen if the church believed it is called to be a kingdom community? Maybe then we would spend less time ordering and protecting our hierarchies and more time building up the Body of Christ. Perhaps then we would spend less energy trying to decide who fits our definitions of normalcy and instead concentrate on becoming a people of forgiveness. Perhaps then we would spend less time organizing ourselves into caucuses of power blocs and more time seeking God's will for the entire community.

Philip and Barbara joined a church when they moved to a new town because it seemed like the thing to do. They went most Sundays if they were in town. Philip enjoyed ushering, and Barbara loved to sing in the choir. When their children were born, they brought them to the church to be baptized, and the pastor was glad to come to their home and talk with them about raising their children in the Christian faith. It was a very happy time in their lives.

One evening Philip was late arriving home from a business trip. Barbara was anxious but knew he would call if anything were amiss. When the phone rang at 11:30 P.M., she expected it to be Philip explaining his delay. She was not prepared for the voice on the other end of the phone, distant and clinical, that informed her of Philip's tragic death in a traffic accident. Numb and in shock, Barbara called her pastor. Within hours people were in and out of her home, bringing food, taking care of the children, answering the phone. In the weeks to come, she only vaguely remembered the funeral. She was on automatic pilot as she tried to feed and dress her toddlers. After some months, Barbara found herself with an exhausting but seemingly manageable schedule.

One day, Barbara found herself standing up and telling her story. She was appreciative of all the church members had done for her, but she continued to need help. "When I brought my children to be baptized, you promised to help me raise them in the faith. I need your help. I cannot do it alone." A full minute passed in silence. A couple stood and offered to keep her children once a week. One man, an accountant, offered to help her organize her finances. Another person offered a monthly meal. The congregation rallied around Barbara and her children.

Sound impossible? What's even more impossible is continuing to believe that we must face the challenges of life alone. Kingdom people have experienced the life of community, which brings peace and forgiveness, and where mercy is practiced and justice is longed for. Jesus never intended that we try to follow his teachings in a vacuum; the church is his gift to us, which makes possible the living out of his word.

Kingdom life is hard because it is the way of the cross. It may not lead to happiness, at least the way the world defines it, and it will require perseverance precisely because the world doesn't value this life-style. Kingdom life is also risky. If we are to take Jesus seriously, we will no longer be able to hate other people but will instead have to ask for the grace to practice forgiveness. We will want to seek righteousness instead of perpetuating injustice. We may even be asked to give up a comfortable way of life if we take Jesus seriously. These risks might not even be worth it if we aren't convinced that God is like this with us.

It is our joyous task as a congregation of followers of Jesus to create a community where forgiveness is real, where peace is genuine and healing, where dependence on God is trusted and valued, where people are not afraid to mourn because they know your comforting arms will surround them.

Jesus has not promised happiness. Instead, he has promised the kingdom of heaven, a life with God, and a community of faithful disciples really loving one another. I invite you to imagine this community. I encourage you to pray for the grace to create this kind of congregation and for the courage to live the upside-down life-style of a child of God's kingdom.

Perhaps no prayer better sums up Jesus' teaching about life in the kingdom than the prayer of Saint Francis.

> Lord, make me an instrument of thy peace;
> where there is hatred, let me sow love;
> where there is injury, pardon;
> where there is doubt, faith;
> where there is despair, hope;
> where there is darkness, light;
> and where there is sadness, joy.
>
> O Divine Master,
> grant that I may not so much seek
> to be consoled as to console;
> to be understood, as to understand;
> to be loved, as to love;
> for it is in giving that we receive,
> it is in pardoning that we are pardoned,
> and it is in dying that we are born to eternal life.
> ("The Prayer of St. Francis," *The United Methodist Hymnal)*

Suggestions for Worship

Call to Worship (Ps. 37:3-7):

PASTOR: Trust in the LORD, and do good; so you will live in the land, and enjoy security.

PEOPLE: Take delight in the LORD, and he will give you the desires of your heart.

PASTOR: Commit your way to the LORD, trust in him, and he will act.

PEOPLE: He will make your vindication shine like the light, and the justice of your cause like the noonday.

PASTOR: Be still before the LORD, and wait patiently for him.

Act of Praise: Psalm 37:1-11.

Suggested Hymns: "Come Thou Almighty King"; "Lord Speak to Me"; "What a Friend We Have in Jesus."

Opening Prayer: O God of peace, in the ministry of Jesus you gave us the means to envision life in your kingdom. Grant us the courage to live new lives of faithfulness, trusting in your grace, which is sufficient to meet all our needs. We pray in the name of Christ, who lives and reigns with you and the Holy Spirit, now and forever. Amen.

Pastoral Prayer: Lord of life, by your grace you have called us to be your children, and in your love you have showered us with the blessings of life: families to nurture us, friends to encourage us, work to challenge us, rest to restore us. We are thankful, Lord, for the gift of your son, Jesus Christ, who by his life, death, and resurrection created a new community of disciples. We count it a privilege to share in this community of faith. Lord, give us a vision of life in your kingdom. Give us the grace to seek to live according to your will, not counting the cost but looking to the day when your kingdom will reign supreme. Give us the courage to live as a community of faithful followers. Shower us with mercy so that we might extend that mercy to others. Remind us of your forgiving love that we might forgive others. Enable us to be peacemakers so that others may see in us the gospel of Christ. And keep us in love with you so that in all things we might give you praise. We pray in Jesus' name. Amen.

FEBRUARY 7, 1993

□

Fifth Sunday After Epiphany

A central message of Epiphany is that the light shines in the darkness. The glory of God is manifest in Jesus Christ. The community of faith bears witness.

The Sunday Lessons

Isaiah 58:5-10: The fast, which is pleasing to your God, shares bread with the hungry, breaks the yoke of oppression, and cares for the homeless. When you pour yourself out to them "then your light shall rise in the darkness" (v. 10).
I Corinthians 2:1-11: Paul did not come to the Corinthian church with lofty words of wisdom. He offered a crucified God so that faith might not rest in the wisdom of humans, but in the power of God. Blind rulers of this age "crucified the Lord of glory" (v. 8).
Matthew 5:13-16: The true followers of Christ will influence everything around them like the salt of the earth, the light of the world, a city on a hill. We do not light a lamp and put it under a bushel (v. 15).

Interpretation and Imagination

Nietzsche once said, "They must sing better songs, ere I learn belief in their saviour. His disciples must look like the saved." Many of us have not been very earnest about good works that give glory to God. All of us are caught up in moral confusion about what is right and what is wrong. Professor Paul Mickey, commenting on the tensions evident in The United Methodist Church, noted, "We all agree on justification by faith. It's the question of sanctification . . . that divides us."

The text is an audacity. Who dares to say "I am the light. I am the salt. I will be seen and be cause for thanking God." Most of us would confess that our ethical confusion and half-hearted obedience deny us the right to claim to be the example of Christ.

A pastor, painfully aware of his failure and broken promise, asked, "Do I have any right to call myself a Christian?" The answer is given by Paul and echoed in the church across the years. "No, not if you trust in your own rightness." But if you know you have no right to be called Christian, and that you now stand in grace and in the spotlight of divine judgment, then, "Yes, you are the light."

Remember those who have been so named. Peter, the bold and impetuous disciple who claimed too much and denied his Lord. A tax gatherer, a woman of the street, a doubter, the timid who fled, the nearsighted who could never see, the dull who seldom understood, the calloused who cared too little.

As a church, we falter and fail when we make our tasks great and our failures too significant. In so doing, we ignore the exceeding greatness of our Lord and belittle his power to those who believe. We take the gift lightly when we fail to strive for the highest good that we know. (JKB)

SALT AND LIGHT

Matthew 5:13-16

A SERMON BY ALTON H. McEACHERN

Salt is common and inexpensive today. In earlier times, however, salt was rare and expensive. Roman soldiers were paid in part with salt—thus our English word *salary*. Ancient governments taxed salt. In the Tower of London you will find salt cellars among the crown jewels, dating from 1640. On the American frontier, pioneers often settled near salt licks, and during the Civil War salt was a scarce commodity in the South, due to the naval blockade.

Jesus paid his disciples, and us, a compliment when he said, "You are the salt of the earth" (v. 13). We still call a person of integrity and character "the salt of the earth." It is no mean title.

Salt flavors, makes its presence known. Just a pinch of salt can affect the taste of food. As salt makes a sore spot sting, Christian ethics can sting the conscience of secular society. Salt also preserves fish and fresh meat. Good men and women preserve society. Sodom would have been spared had Abraham been able to find ten good men there. And it was one of the ancient prophets who was called Israel's defense, not its army or alliances.

France underwent a bloody revolution two hundred years ago. England was spared a similar fate, at least in part, because of the spiritual renewal sparked by John Wesley's preaching. Christians are called to influence every area of life for good and for God—business, government, education, and home life. Christian values can penetrate society and affect the attitudes and policies of individuals and governments.

Jesus also gave a warning, lest we become proud. He said that salt that loses its flavor is worthless. In Jesus' time, salt from the Dead Sea was liberally mixed with other chemicals. When exposed to the weather, the pure salt would filter out, separating from the worthless chemical residue. It's only use was to be thrown on a path like gravel or ashes.

Likewise, when Christians become guilty of moral compromise they lose their flavor. The secular environment in which we live can dilute our moral influence. This makes us powerless to permeate and change the world with Christian values. In America today the church is seldom persecuted; most often we are ignored. Has the church lost its savor and moral influence in society?

The salt of the earth is no hermit theology. Salt gives itself, just as Jesus gave himself to others. It does not hide in obscurity but penetrates and changes its environment. Christians dare not try to selfishly smuggle their own soul into heaven. We are to share the Savior's savor in our common life. Faith is personal, but it is not private. Our sphere of influence is the world.

Jesus did not call us "the honey of the earth," but "the salt of the earth." Notice, also, that he did not say we have the *potential* to become the salt of the earth; we already *are*. Our faith, like salt, is to penetrate society, sharing the Christian ethic and ideals. We are meant to flavor and preserve our culture.

Dare we attempt to live up to the Master's high compliment and heed his warning? Faith is meant to be shared, that persons and the world itself can be changed, and the kingdom of God come on earth. After all, this is what we pray for each time we recite the Lord's Prayer. This is the Master's challenge!

"You all are the world's light; you are a city on a hill that cannot be hid. Have you ever heard of anybody turning on a light and then covering it up? Don't you fix it so that it will light up the whole room? Well, then, since you are God's light which he has turned on, go ahead and shine so clearly that when your conduct is observed it will plainly be the work of your spiritual Father" (Clarence Jordan, *The Cotton Patch Version* [New York: Association Press, 1970], 22-23).

We live in a sin-darkened world, despite all the bright lights. God is light. The prophet Isaiah said, "The people who walked in darkness have seen a great light" (9:2). And the psalmist sang, "The Lord is my light and my salvation" (27:1). His burning presence is our glory.

Jesus came into our dark world of sin, evil, and death to show us the Father and make our salvation possible. "In him was life, and the life was the light of men. The light shines in the darkness, and the darkness has not overcome it" (John 1:4-5 RSV). The Master said, "I am the light of the world" (John 8:12). He is the source of light; our light is derived from him. "Apart from me you can do nothing" (John 15:5).

The first century was also a time of spiritual darkness and longing. People worshiped many gods but were ignorant of the true and living God (see Acts 17). Religion had degenerated into a cold legalism for many, bringing little joy and peace. Wickedness and corruption were rampant—child exposure, prostitution, and homosexuality were practiced among the Greeks and Romans, for example. People had no real hope for life after death; there was no place to turn for the assurance of divine forgiveness and eternal life.

Jesus came into this world of spiritual darkness, preaching the gospel of God. He showed us the Father as one who cares for us, and one with whom we can live in a loving relationship. He is our dear Abba Father—approachable. On the cross Jesus provided for our forgiveness, at the cost of his life's blood. On that first Easter morning he conquered death itself, giving us the assurance of immortality. Jesus said, "I am the light of the world" (v. 14) and so he is!

Jesus also said, "You are the light of the world" (v. 14), as impossible to hide as a city built on a hilltop. For Christians to keep their faith secret is a contradiction—hiding their light under a bushel. The nature of faith calls for it to be shared. We are to tell the good news and extend the gospel's influence. A sincere witness to our faith will attract others to Christ and the church.

Believers let their lights shine as beacons or lighthouses. They warn the world about the dangers of life and death without Christ. Planes have crashed because fog obscured the airport beacon lights. Ships would wreck on reefs were it not for the warning lighthouses on shore. Christians witnessing to their faith can provide crucial direction in a confused and spiritually darkened world.

How do we shine for Christ? By our good attitudes and actions. While we are not saved *by* good works, we are certainly saved *for* good works. Jesus said, "Let your light shine before others, so that they may see your good works and give glory to your Father in heaven" (Matt. 5:16). Note that our good works are not to draw attention to ourselves but to the heavenly Father. I once heard a woman say of her pastor, "You could warm your hands by his love!" The love of God in him led her to faith in Christ.

Jesus did not say we have the potential to become the light of the world; he said we *are*. Letting our faith shine, sharing the knowledge of Christ is not an elective. It is a given. It is not a matter of whether we will let it shine, but how brightly. Piety that is cold, austere, and phony repels people. Positive goodness attracts. It is warm, loving, and sincere.

There is also an urgency to letting our faith shine. People who die without Christ are lost. We must share our faith "while it is day," while we have the opportunity. Now is the time for us to bear witness to Christ, just as now is the time to believe in him. Putting it off is unsafe.

Note the common characteristic of salt and light—they penetrate. Salt permeates meat and preserves it. Light penetrates darkness and dispels it. The kingdom of God penetrates society and transforms it. Salt and light depict Christian conduct. These strong metaphors call us to believe and to share our faith, and teach us what we are to be and what we are to do.

Suggestions for Worship

Call to Worship (I Cor. 2:9-10):

PASTOR: As it is written; "What no eye has seen, nor ear heard.

PEOPLE: Nor the human heart conceived, what God has prepared for those who love him"—

PASTOR: These things God has revealed to us through the Spirit;

PEOPLE: For the Spirit searches everything, even the depths of God.

Act of Praise: Psalm 112:4-9.

Suggested Hymns: "Go, Tell It on the Mountain"; "We've a Story to Tell to the Nations"; "Ask Ye What Great Thing I Know."

Opening Prayer: Lord Christ who came into our sin-darkened world as light, shine in our hearts and through our daily witness to your transforming power. As salt penetrates and preserves, let us bear a telling influence in our society, to your glory. Amen.

Pastoral Prayer: Father, in midwinter we lift our hearts heavenward in praise and adoration. "Great is the Lord and greatly to be praised." May we catch a glimpse of the mystery to stir our hearts in worship and praise. Slow our pace, that we may look beyond the daily routine to trace your guiding hand as love in our lives. Make us salt and light in our world.

We confess our sins before you: deliberate and unkind acts, as well as the good we've neglected. Purge our thoughts and cleanse our spirits. Now be pleased to give us the assurance of divine pardon, and having experienced your forgiveness, enable us to forgive ourselves and others.

Your grace leaves us in amazement. You do not give what we

ask but better than we ask. Accept our tribute of praise and thanksgiving from thankful hearts, for all your bountiful blessings.

Lord we pray in intercession for others. Grant healing for those who are ill and bereaved, especially your servants ________. Grant wisdom and direction for all who feel confused and uncertain. Uphold our president and governor and all persons in positions of responsibility. Bless all who join us in divine worship today. Through Jesus Christ our Lord. Amen.

February 14, 1993

□

Sixth Sunday After Epiphany

A new ethic is set before citizens of the kingdom of God: "You have heard that it was said to those of old. . . . But I say. . . ."

The Sunday Lessons

Deuteronomy 30:15-20: The lesson emphasizes the freedom to choose rather than the inclination to sin. Loving God, obeying God's voice, and cleaving to God represent choosing life.
I Corinthians 3:1-9: The Corinthian church was divided and marked by jealousy and strife. Paul challenged this party spirit saying, "I planted, Apollos watered, but God gave the growth" (v. 6). Attitudes of superiority and envy are evidence of spiritual immaturity.
Matthew 5:17-26: The law of Moses was not set aside by Christ. He called instead for a higher righteousness that exceeded that of the scribes and Pharisees. "But I say to you that if you are angry with a brother or sister, you will be liable to judgment" (v. 22). The rabbis prescribed 613 laws. Jesus called for a perfect holiness that goes beyond law.

Interpretation and Imagination

"It's impossible for anyone to obey those commandments." The young man who spoke these words was serious in his intent to be a good follower of Jesus Christ. He was also honest with himself and did not look for easy excuses. He wanted to know what ethical response was called for by these teachings.

Three interpretations have been employed to soften their demand: (1) Jesus only wants his disciples to strive for perfect righteousness—the goal is always out of reach; (2) The law is an impossible ideal, causing us to realize our dependency upon grace; and (3) It's only a short-term ethic, called for in a heroic moral effort in the last days. These views evidence some truth, but should not set aside this primary message: the kingdom of

God is here now. Jesus Christ sets God's highest demands before the citizens of that kingdom and bids us to obey.

In the corporate structure some believe that they cannot be concerned with ethics. Profit is the name of the game. Individual needs in conflict with corporate needs produce a moral dilemma that cannot be resolved. Military strategy sets aside moral restraint when winning is the name of the game. The choices between good and evil are never easy. We are less than helpful when we offer generalities and gloss.

George Bernard Shaw, in his drama *Major Barbara*, depicts a munitions manufacturer asking his twenty-four-year-old son about his career plans—literature, philosophy, law, the church, the army. When the father asks bluntly, "Is there anything you know or care for," the young man replies, "I know the difference between right and wrong." The father's cynical response points to the dilemma. "What, no capacity for business, no knowledge of law, no sympathy with art, no pretension to philosophy, only a simple knowledge of the secret that has puzzled all the philosophers, baffled all the lawyers, muddied all the men of business, and ruined most of the artists. The secret of right and wrong—at twenty-four, too." (JKB)

HOW TO BE GOOD AND MAD

Matthew 5:17-26

A SERMON BY ALTON H. McEACHERN

"You have heard . . . but I say . . ." In the Beatitudes Jesus described the kingdom person. He encouraged his disciples to live as salt and light in the world. Then Jesus redefined the life of grace and God's intention, by comparing and contrasting life under the law and life under grace.

The law said "no murder"; Jesus said "no anger" (vv. 21-22).

The law said "no adultery"; Jesus said "no lustful look" (vv. 27-28).

The law said "no divorce without a decree"; Jesus said God's intention is "no divorce" (vv. 31-32).

The law said "no false swearing"; Jesus said "don't swear at all" (vv. 33-34).

The law taught "limited retaliation"; Jesus said "don't retaliate" (vv. 38-39).

The law said, "love your neighbor"; Jesus said "love your enemy" (vv. 43-44).

Obviously, Jesus held up an absolute ideal, an impossible ethic, pointing us to a way higher than legalism. These attitudes and actions describe the kingdom person and character. We may try to soften Jesus' teachings, but they are hard. While we will fall short of this ideal, nevertheless, we must strive to achieve it, always relying on divine grace.

In Scripture, we see murder first in Genesis 4. Murder is prohibited in the Ten Commandments. Human life is sacred because it is a gift of God; therefore murder is wrong.

Unintentional murder is also wrong. Killing can occur, for example, when people mix drinking and driving. That is the most lethal mixed drink. Such irresponsibility can lead to murder.

The commandment also prohibits self-murder. Our bodies are not our own; they are the dwelling place of the Holy Spirit. Therefore, to neglect good health care, or to abuse one's body with food and drink or lack of proper rest is a violation of this commandment.

Jesus went further than the commandment. He went beyond the act of murder to the attitude that leads to it. Behind the action, he cited the motive that produces it. Sin is rooted in our intention.

Anger without a cause was probably not the original saying of Jesus. It sounds like a scribal gloss intended to soften Jesus' absolute ethic. Paul wrote, "Be angry but do not sin" (Eph. 4:26). We are not to let sunset find us nursing our anger and resentment.

The anger Jesus prohibited is not the "short-fuse" variety, which flares up quickly and is gone, though that is harmful enough. The type of anger Jesus condemned in this passage is the smoldering, festering, coddled variety, which becomes an obsession and blots out the sun for us.

The law is an external code—Jesus is calling for inner control. The courts can act only after a crime has been committed. Jesus would have us go beyond our actions to our motives, and root out anger before it leads to sinful action.

Anger can lead us to treat others with contempt. To call another "fool" is more than an insult. The Greek word *moras* literally means "an empty-headed moron." Pride and snobbery can lead to such contempt. And murder may begin with contempt for another. When we lose respect for human beings, we can easily begin to see them as despicable objects rather than persons. This sort of thing occurs in war. The enemy is given an insulting name and we feel free to destroy him. He is no longer regarded as a person. Contempt is a moral disease that affects both people and nations.

Jesus had a harsh word for those who are angry, who hate, and feel contemptuous of others. He said those persons are in danger of hell's fire (v. 22). Such thoughts and attitudes make people fit for the trash heap. Jesus showed us a higher way. Faith and works, worship and ethics go together.

Is anger good or bad? That depends on how it is expressed and used. Anger is like fire: good in a fireplace, bad in a closet. It can warm or destroy. In much the same way, anger can oppose evil and aid communication, or it can destroy a relationship. Anger can be useful as an alarm system but devastating as a way of life.

Consider the things that made Jesus angry. It was not the gospel writers who called him, "Gentle Jesus, meek and mild." Jesus did not tolerate hypocrites—people who say one thing but do another. He became angry at those who exploited the poor and turned his Father's house of prayer into a den of thieves. We dare not exploit others in the name of religion!

Jesus had no patience with those who loved systems (orthodoxy) more than persons. Recall the reaction of such persons to his healing on the Sabbath. Jesus made fun of those who judge others when they are worse sinners themselves. He told about a man with a beam in his eye trying to get a speck of sawdust out of someone else's eye!

The apostle Paul got angry when he confronted Simon Peter over the admission of Gentiles into the early church. Fortunately, Paul's point of view prevailed, and Christianity became a universal faith.

What makes you angry? Is it usually some moral issue—or minutiae? Are you most often upset over injustice or over your own injured pride? There is a difference in being angry with others and being angry on behalf of others. Anger and righteous indignation ended human slavery, sweat shops, and child labor. The anger of the Allies ended Fascist terror and death camps in Europe. But we are more apt to get angry over a missed elevator than over social injustice.

How are we to be good and mad? Ask yourself, "*Why* am I angry?" Jesus' anger was rooted in compassion for others. It was never due to what was done to him. He prayed for his enemies and taught us to do the same.

Next ask, "*How* am I expressing my anger?" Did I repress it—smile outside but burn inside. Do I pretend that everything is okay while resentment gnaws at me? Or do I give healthy expression to my anger?

Jesus taught us to take the initiative to go to persons who are offended with us, or with whom we feel offended. We are to express our feelings openly and not behind their backs. That is "clean anger," which can clear the air and restore broken relationships.

Ask, "*What* is my anger doing?" Does it help by confronting hurt feelings and making things right? Or does my anger destroy relationships with others? Is my anger constructive or destructive? We must learn to love the sinner while hating the sin—God does.

"Be angry but do not sin" is a tall order! The wise person learns how to be good and mad. There is a real contrast between the world's values and those of the kingdom person. Jesus challenges us to follow the higher way. By dealing with our attitudes and motives we can exercise greater control over our actions. Preventing sin is better than seeking pardon.

Suggestions for Worship

Call to Worship (Ps. 119:2-3, 7-8):

PASTOR: Happy are those who keep his decrees, who seek him with their whole heart.

PEOPLE: [Who] walk in his ways.

PASTOR: I will praise you with an upright heart, when I learn your righteous ordinances.

PEOPLE: I will observe your statutes; do not utterly forsake me.

Act of Praise: Psalm 119:1-8 (Response 3).

Suggested Hymns: "Come, Thou Fount of Every Blessing"; "I Love to Tell the Story"; "I Am Thine, O Lord."

Opening Prayer: O Thou whose holy anger cleansed the Temple, teach us how to be good and mad about the right issues. Let us never grow comfortable with the oppression of others, in the name of divine justice. Amen.

Pastoral Prayer: Dear Father, along with angels and the church triumphant we unite our hearts in adoration and praise. We join with millions of believers around the world in divine worship on the Lord's Day.

"God of grace and God of glory, on thy people pour thy power; crown thine ancient church's story; bring her bud to glorious flower."

Father, we confess our sins before you. We have given first significance to secondary causes. We become angry at slights real or imagined and fail to get mad when others are unmercifully oppressed. Teach us how to be good and mad. Forgive our sinful attitudes and actions, great and small.

Our hearts overflow with thanksgiving when we pause to consider your provision of our every need, and many extra as well. Truly your grace is amazing. Accept the worship of our grateful hearts.

We remember before you all who need your grace and favor, especially your servants ________. Comfort all who are troubled. Calm and assure those who are afraid. Make us all equal to our tasks. Through Jesus Christ our Lord. Amen.

FEBRUARY 21, 1993

□

Last Sunday After Epiphany (Transfiguration)

The Transfiguration ends Christ's ministry in Galilee. Now, he journeys to the cross. Christ's teaching and healing clearly manifest his messianic power. The Mount of Transfiguration is the final assurance of that power.

The Sunday Lessons

Exodus 24:12-18: Moses went up on Mount Sinai. The glory of the Lord settled on the mountain. For six days it was covered by a cloud. On the seventh day God spoke from the cloud. Below the people saw, "Glory . . . like a devouring fire" (v. 17).
II Peter 1:16-21: The author of this late New Testament book (about A.D. 125) appeals to the authority of Simon Peter's firsthand experience. The first-century church, constantly challenged because of their belief in Jesus as Son of God, loved the Transfiguration story.
Matthew 17:1-9: Matthew is conscious of the Old Testament parallels found in the mountaintop experiences of Moses and Elijah. This mountaintop theophany manifests Christ above the Law and the Prophets as the final revelation of God.

Interpretation and Imagination

It is not hard to believe in the power of God when all things go well. In Galilee, crowds thrilled to the insight and truth Christ's parables revealed. In Galilee, crowds were amazed by the power evidenced in the miracles.

But the power of Christ seemed thwarted and contradicted by the cross. A king crowned with thorns, spit upon, mocked, and nailed to a cross was no king at all. One finally dead and buried could hardly be seen as the manifestation of God. Indeed, it would seem to put an end to the dream that this Galilean Jesus was the Messiah.

In first-century Israel the most believable authorities regarding the might and right of God were Moses, the great law giver, and Elijah, the greatest prophet. Holy mountains were associated with their moments of vision and call. The early church loved this story of Transfiguration, when the glory of God shone upon the carpenter from Nazareth on his way to Jerusalem and the cross.

The realities of anguish and agony and all the terrifying perils of life could not cower those New Testament Christians. With the assurance that comes to one who has been to the mountain, they did not fear even death itself. Now, they could state the sinister facts bluntly, denying nothing, minimizing nothing, explaining nothing away. Their hearts were bold and their eyes undimmed. They had been to the mountain.

Many confronted by the harshness of life and all that threatens it are left with a fear that cries out to God in despair. Life's tragedies prompt angry demands that God explain the contradictions of life. The New Testament Christians, however, saw deeper mysteries and were convinced of realities more lasting that lead us toward the cross.

"There is God's beloved," they say. "That's what happened to him in God's world. That's what happened to him even with God in charge. Now listen to him, follow him to the other side of darkness."

It's hard to believe in a crucified God. Morality, right teaching, health, and wholeness are the religious authority we have come to trust. The mystery of a mountain meeting, the ambiguity of the language of the boundary, the awesome experience of the voice of God may have little credibility in twentieth-century scientific thought. Yet thanks be to God for the transfiguring light that still shines. (JKB)

THE MYSTERY ON THE MOUNTAIN

Matthew 17:1-9

A SERMON BY WILLIAM KELLON QUICK

As we think about the life of Jesus, his Galilean ministry comes to a climax in Matthew's Gospel, in an event that is called "the Transfiguration."

It is an incident that Jesus specifically asked the three disciples who were present—Peter, James, and John—not to mention to anyone. The way Matthew tells it, Jesus and these three withdrew from the crowds and the other disciples. Jesus led them up a mountain and began to pray. From timc to time, Jesus sensed the need to retreat, to go into seclusion, and Mt. Tabor provided a greater sense of isolation.

In this "twilight zone" they experienced some strange happenings. They heard Jesus speak as if with some unseen persons. They saw his face overcome with awe. We are told they fell on their faces and were afraid.

There was a radiance about Jesus that they had not seen before. One minister described it as a luminous presence, not caused by something shining *on* him like a spotlight, but of something that was shining *within* him. There was something incandescent about his face; somewhat like a dull sky with dark clouds, suddenly set ablaze by a setting sun. How changed the clouds now appear! All that was commonplace and unattractive about them is gone. Now they glow and sparkle—gold, purple, and all the colors of the rainbow blend beautifully. Are these the same dull clouds we looked upon moments ago? Yes, but they have been wonderfully transfigured.

And here we see Jesus wonderfully changed! But his outward splendor was the reflection of an inner glow.

Suddenly Moses and Elijah appeared and talked with Jesus. It was widely believed by Jews in Jesus' day that prominent figures of Old Testament history would appear at the end time of this world and play a part in the events leading up to it. In the last days, false prophets were expected to appear. So by their presence with him, Moses and Elijah—two great representatives of the Law and the Prophets—testify to Jesus as the true Christ. Peter, James, and John realized that Jesus was in the same class as the spiritual giants of their heritage. Was this not natural for them—and us? When we admire someone, we instinctively begin to compare that person with someone we highly respect or has profoundly influenced us. When I think of the assassination of John F. Kennedy, a cartoon comes vividly to my mind, showing Abraham Lincoln with his head buried in his hands, weeping. Lincoln, a century earlier, had also been killed by an assassin's bullet. The cartoonist, who obviously had admired Lincoln, linked the past to the present in that tragic moment and put Lincoln and Kennedy in the same class. We not only compare those whom we admire with our heroes from the past, but we also sense a kind of historical continuity between them.

Is it any wonder, then, that following this impression, when Jesus was conversing with Moses and Elijah, Peter made a ludicrous suggestion: "This is such a momentous hour let us build a memorial here and now. It is good for us to be here so let's construct three tabernacles for Jesus and the two prophets" (v. 4, paraphrase). Peter was so taken with the experience he wanted to abide there forever. How natural an impulse! We like to savor such high moments, but we can't prolong them. Ecstasy cannot be continued. Emotional mountaintops are transient. Life's highest moments may be foretastes of glory, yet, as much as we'd like to retain that special sense of God presence, time marches on, and we descend once again from the mountaintop to the valley where we are called to live out our lives. I have never known a single soul who could live and work day by day with emotions at a high peak of pressure. Peter wanted to build a memorial, and memorials are all right. But no shrine can truly capture one's mountaintop experience.

We are told, at this point, that a bright cloud overshadowed them all and they heard a voice saying, "This is my Son, the Beloved; listen to him!" (v. 5). The voice reveals to Peter, James, and John what had been revealed at Jesus' baptism: to listen and to follow what Jesus had to say. It is still so. Hear Christ's words. Catch Christ's spirit. Obey Christ's law, "listen to him."

There are some significant lessons for us in the Transfiguration. The first is this: Our great mountaintop religious experiences never last. They are powerful moments, and may indeed be for many a conversion in which life is transformed. But they are fleeting, transient, momentary.

John Wesley, founder of Methodism, went reluctantly to a prayer meeting on Aldersgate Street in London, on the night of May 24, 1738. Wesley, son and grandson of Anglican clergy, and ordained himself, had returned to Britain six months prior from a stint as a missionary to the Indians in the colony of Georgia. Heartsick, depressed, and filled with doubt about his own faith and relationship with God, he wrote, "I came to America to convert the Indians, but who, O Lord, will convert John Wesley?"

On that fateful night of May 24, at about a quarter to nine, while someone was reading Martin Luther's Preface to the Book of Romans, Wesley records an extraordinary moment in his *Journal*. "I felt my heart strangely warmed. I felt that I did trust Christ, Christ alone for salvation, and an assurance was given me that he had taken away my sins, even mine." Something came alive in the soul of Wesley at that moment. However, we tend to forget that Wesley would soon record serious doubts of what happened that night.

Another moment when a giant of the faith was seen to doubt his own experience of assurance, was at the time of Jesus' baptism, when John the Baptizer was privy to a happening hidden from the understanding of others present. He saw the Holy Spirit descend upon Jesus in the form of a dove and heard the voice from heaven saying, "This is my beloved Son in whom I am well pleased." Yet later, when John was imprisoned and facing death, he revealed the doubts that accompany one whose faith is being tested. He told his disciples to go to Jesus and ask him whether he was the "one who is to come" or whether they were to wait for another (Luke 7:19)—a clear indication that even his mountaintop experience and its attendant depth of faith were not to last forever. Why?

The great moments of experiential joy and liberation never last. The radiance will fade; the vision will pass. Such moments are significant emotional experiences, and we should praise God for them. They come all too rarely for too many people. And they can be a stepping stone to something more powerful or significant, just as romantic love can be, and as Jesus' experience was. But one thing for certain, they cannot remain just as they are. We cannot remain the same. We have to come back to earth.

The second significant lesson is in the exhortation, "Listen to him." This is the divine imperative, the essential requirement—to hear and to heed what Jesus has to say.

During Holy Week, 1990, our country mourned the death of an eighteen-year-old youth who waged a five-year battle against both AIDS and the unreasoning fear many people have of its victims. Ryan White, the Indiana lad, contracted the killer infection from a tainted blood-clotting agent during treatment for hemophilia, at the age of thirteen. He became a national voice for children with AIDS. He was on the cover of *People* magazine and made friends with national and international celebrities. His story of fighting both AIDS and discrimination became a part of our national consciousness.

One of Ryan White's gifts to us, apart from his indomitable fighting spirit and refusal to become maudlin, was his staunch, undaunted faith. In a national television interview, Ryan said, "I believe in God and I believe when we die we go to a better place. I am not afraid." Ryan had an immovable faith in God and from that faith he drew strength. There was no doubt in his mind about immortality. He was so firm in his religious convictions, not even a television anchorman dared question it.

Ryan White lived out his faith to the end. His ethical behavior and positive faith touched the soul of America.

Our first response to the gospel call, whatever turn life may take, is to listen to Jesus. Listen! Seek first the kingdom of God and his righteousness. If you hold a grudge, be reconciled to your brother or sister. The inside of the person, like the cup, is more important than the outside. If you wish to save yourself, lose yourself in service to God and others. Depend on God as a child depends on a parent.

The greatest crisis in the church today is the failure to live out the faith we profess. The world waits and watches the Christian.

There is an old story about a young missionary assigned to India. He sought and received an audience with Mahatma Gandhi, the father of modern India. He inquired of Gandhi, "Do you have any advice for a young missionary?" It is reported that Gandhi looked at him and said, *"Be like Jesus!"*

At the Transfiguration, the glory was upon Jesus, but Peter, James, and John shared in that mystical experience. How precious are such moments! How we long for their recurrence. How mysteriously they come and go. They saw. They heard. They shared this incomparable moment. Though the ecstasy was real, it was brief, and they had to return to their ordinary preoccupations. And Jesus, too, no longer appeared the same.

Matthew says Jesus told them to "Tell no one about the vision" (v. 9). This speaks not merely of the absence of words, but of the presence of a meaningful mystery too deep for words. Perhaps their silence tells us more about the mystery on the mount than any spoken word could ever tell.

Suggestions for Worship

Call to Worship (II Pet. 1:16-19):

PASTOR: "Our Lord Jesus Christ . . . received honor and glory from God the Father.

PEOPLE: "[The] voice was conveyed to him by the Majestic Glory, saying, 'his is my Son, my Beloved, with whom I am well pleased.'

PASTOR: "So we have the prophetic message more fully confirmed.

PEOPLE: "[We] will do well to be attentive to this, as to a lamp shining in a dark place."

Act of Praise: Psalm 2:6-11.

Suggested Hymns: "Immortal, Invisible, God Only Wise"; "To God Be the Glory"; "God of Grace and God of Glory."

Opening Prayer: O God, whose Son sought you in daily prayer and communion, we come this day seeking your grace and forgiveness. Stir us, O Lord, in this hour of worship, that we may rise up and go forth filled with your spirit to do your will and bring to our world the gift of loving service for the sake of Jesus Christ, in whose name we pray. Amen.

Pastoral Prayer: We give you thanks, O God, that our Lord has walked life's road before us. We remember that he knew hard work and hunger, thirst and pain; that he experienced joy and sorrow; that he met the crises of life and like us, was tempted across the years of his life.

As he drew apart from the crowds to think and pray, seeking your direction, we come to this place of worship seeking guidance and strength for our daily lives. Through our worship, may the Christian life become more meaningful, simpler for those who find life confusing, and happier for those who face disappointment.

Grant, O Lord, that we may look ever to you for our guidance and direction. From you alone can we learn the true meaning of life. Help us to commit our ways unto Him who is the way, the truth, and the life.

As we seek to live out our faith in the world, touching the lives of men and women, help us to be friends to all. Help us to cheer the suffering by our sympathy. Enable us to offer some word of hope to those who find daily life hopeless. If anyone needs us, make us ready to offer some kindness without any feeling of self-righteousness, for no reason except Christian love. Enable us never to be ashamed to show whose we are and whom we serve, through Jesus Christ our Lord. Amen.

FEBRUARY 28, 1993

□

First Sunday in Lent

The temptation and fall in the garden tell of our estrangement from God. The temptation of Christ in the wilderness and his obedience tell of Christ's victory over evil. Beginning with the temptation story, salvation history is recounted in the days of Lent.

The Sunday Lessons

Genesis 2:4*b*-9, 15-17, 25; 3:1-7: Knowingly and willingly, the creature disobeyed the Creator. This story of temptation and fall is filled with theological issues. The central issue is estrangement from God. Man and woman caused themselves to be ashamed and alone.

Romans 5:12-19: The apostle Paul contrasts the sin of Adam with the salvation of Christ. The disobedience of Adam and the obedience of Christ are emphasized.

Matthew 4:1-11: After a forty-day wilderness fast, Jesus was tempted by the devil but remained faithful. Matthew remembers that Israel's faithfulness was tested in forty years of wilderness wandering. Israel failed. Quoting from Moses' teachings, he lifts up Christ's obedience.

Interpretation and Imagination

"There's no way to get this crowd innocent," the preacher said. He was right about that. Though most of us would like to restore simplicity and freedom to our lives, we cannot. We have compromised ourselves with self-centered relationships and obligations. The right that we have known to do we have not done. The wrong that we should have hated we have too often embraced.

At first, the forty days of Lent were a time for men and women to prepare for their baptisms. They recounted the salvation story of disobedience and broken promises, of wilderness journeys and of God's faithfulness in providing a way. The goal was a new and right relationship with God.

How may one get right with God? By cutting off every imperfect relationship? Certainly not. By renouncing every obligation that seems unworthy? Surely not! As heroic as such disciplines may be, they will never restore the simplicity and freedom of innocence to our lives. Giving up pie and cookies for Lent won't make it right. Nor will reading the Bible, attending church, and praying more faithfully for forty days settle the matter of sin in the world.

The realities of sin, the evidence of our depravity, and the constant temptation to serve other gods have left us as embarrassed and alone as Adam was in the presence of God.

Christ is the way. He brought every relationship within the influence of one great relationship and subordinated every claim to the final authority of God. Isn't that our primary quest?

We would like to be free from sin and compromise. We long to return to childlike simplicity in life. We dream of being held firmly in the love of a divine parent. Thus, we are called to bring everything about ourselves under the gracious influence of God, revealed by Jesus Christ. (JKB)

THE AGGRAVATION OF TEMPTATION

Matthew 4:1-11

A SERMON BY MARTHA H. FORREST

Today is the first Sunday of the season of Lent—the forty-day period of the church year when we are especially mindful of our human frailties, our sins. We have always been sinners, since the time of Adam and Eve. And God has certainly tried in every way imaginable to bring us back to obedience. Finally, out of desperation, God sent his only Son, Jesus Christ, to lead us back by glorious examples of obedience, leading to his death on the cross. Now, Jesus is the Son of God, he's divine; but he's also the Son of a human mother. The hymn that we sing at Christmas time, "That Boy-Child of Mary," tells us:

> Gift of the Father, to human mother,
> Makes him our brother of Bethlehem.

Born of our heavenly Father and his human mother Mary truly makes Jesus our brother—he is human like us. Divine and human! And in his humanity, he was tempted to sin, just like us.

It was dusk, and the day had been balmy and pleasant. Jesus gathered his disciples around him to teach them, and I imagine he said something like this:

I was baptized by my cousin John. He had been preaching a baptism of repentance in the Judean desert. But when I presented myself to him at the Jordan River, he seemed uncomfortable. He tried to get me to change my mind, saying that we had things in reverse, that I should be baptizing him instead of the other way around. But I finally convinced him, and when he drew me up out of the water, an awesome thing happened. Heaven opened up, and a dove flew down and landed on my shoulder. It was God's Spirit, and I clearly heard God's voice say that I was his own dear Son and that he was pleased with me.

Imagine how I must have felt. Of course I felt chosen, I felt special; but I also felt confused and anxious, and yes, maybe a little afraid. I felt a need to get away by myself to think things out and to pray, and God's Spirit helped me by leading me off into the desert to be alone. I spent forty days and nights there—praying, fasting, trying to sort out my thoughts. Sometimes, being away from other people helps me in my perception of what is happening, and I certainly did feel a tangible oneness with God. I emptied myself those forty days by not eating, by cutting out the nonessentials, by aloneness; and I felt at peace with a clarity of thought not often achieved.

But then, aloneness changed into unwelcomed company, because the devil came and taunted me with sarcasm: "*If* you are God's Son, order these stones to turn into bread" (v. 3 GNB). Not only did he want me to misuse God's power to selfishly feed myself, he tried to make me doubt that I was even God's own Son. "If," he had said! But I had heard God call me by this name with my own ears at my baptism. I realized that I didn't need to justify myself to the devil, I didn't need to prove myself to the ruler of evil. I'm also glad that I have had a good education in the Scriptures because God's truth came to me in a passage I've known since I was twelve years old. Do you remember when

God's children were wandering in the desert for forty years, and they started to complain because they were hungry? They accused God of starving them to death. He heard their complaints, and each morning after that, manna was sent down from heaven for them to eat. God had made them hungry to test them, to see if they would obey his commands. And then, he gave them this strange new food from heaven to teach them that humankind must not depend on bread alone to sustain them; they also need every word that God says to nourish them (Deut. 8:3).

We know that God was testing the Israelites, as I was tested in the desert, because Moses reminded them of it when they got to Moab just before they were to go into the Promised Land. There Moses was asking the people, yet another time, to be obedient to God. I, myself, choose obedience to my heavenly Father, and I told the devil this when I quoted the Scripture to him; but he wouldn't go away. In fact, he took me away to Jerusalem, to the very highest part of the Temple, and began to mock me again. "If," he said, "If you are God's Son, let me see you jump off and then save yourself." And then he began using Scripture to state his case. He quoted from the book of Psalms, the very hymnbook and prayer book we use in worship now. I can still almost hear the devil telling me to go ahead and jump, that God would keep me from being killed or maimed. Then the Evil One dared to quote one of the prayers for protection.

> God will put his angels in charge of you
> to protect you wherever you go.
> They will hold you up with their hands
> to keep you from hurting your feet on the stones.
> (Ps. 91:11-12 GNB).

I confess. I was sorely tempted to jump. It certainly crossed my mind to go ahead and do it; to let God save me, and be rid of the devil once and for all. But then I remembered another scripture—when Moses reminded the Israelites that they were not to test the Lord our God as they did at Massah (Deut. 6:16). You men know it. The Israelites had begun to complain, because they were thirsty. Their thirst made them so hostile that Moses was afraid they would kill him. So he began praying to God for direction. God answered him, saying that he was to take some of the leaders with him to the place we now call Massah and Meribah, "testing" and "complaining." He was to hit the rock there with his walking stick, and call the people to drink the water that poured out of it (Exod. 17:1-7). I, like Moses told the Israelites, told the devil that we are not to put the Lord our God to test. I so wanted to be obedient to God, and I thought this would surely be the end of all this tempting business. But, it wasn't.

The devil took me again, this time to a high, high mountain where we could see all around us the great kingdoms of the world. I stood there with the Evil One in the cold, biting wind that so often lashes about on a mountain top, and I felt an inner chill as he pointed out and described to me the riches and the power of each of these leading nations. I waited for the words I knew were coming, and I clearly noticed that he didn't mock me this time. I had waited to hear the words: "*If* you are God's Son . . ." but they didn't come. Instead, he said quietly and convincingly, "I will give you all these kingdoms and all of their resources and wealth, *if* you kneel down and worship me" (v. 9, paraphrase).

I thought of all the people I could feed, all the people I could shelter, all the people I could heal, if I were the great ruler of all the kingdoms we saw below. It was a tempting offer. I wondered how it would feel to be a powerful king with such vast riches! But, then, I remembered yet another scripture from Moses' great speech to the Israelites when he gave them the Ten Commandments, which God had given him on Mount Sinai. Moses told our wayward ancestors that they should:

> Have reverence for the LORD your God, worship only him, and make your promises in his name alone. Do not worship other gods, any of the gods of the peoples around you. If you do worship other gods, the LORD's anger will come against you like fire and will destroy you completely, because the LORD your God, who is present with you, tolerates no rivals. (Deut. 6:13-15 GNB).

And who has set himself up to be in competition with my Father since the world was created? Who is a false god every bit as much as Baal? Who has constantly slandered God to people, and people to God? The Tempter, the Prince of Demons, Beelzebub, the devil, Satan!

I gathered my resolve and told him distinctly, "Go away, Satan! The Scripture says 'Worship the Lord your God and serve only him!'" (v. 10 GNB).

Something in my determination to resist caused him to believe me and go away, for the time being; and God sent his angels down to accompany and to help me.

Then, I went on to Galilee and began the work my Father had for me. I went to Galilee and preached to all who would hear—they were to repent. I began choosing you who are my helpers, and you follow me as I preach the good news about God's kingdom, as I teach and heal the people.

Jesus paused to reflect. He stared off into the distance. He had finished talking, and the disciples were astounded and silent. Their leader, a man who claimed to be the Messiah, had been tempted as they often were. He was like them, yet different because he resisted the devil to obey God in the fullest: to be the Savior of us all! Amazing!

Suggestions for Worship

Call to Worship:

PASTOR: Out of the depths I cry to you, O LORD;

PEOPLE: Let your ears be attentive to my cry for mercy.

PASTOR: If you kept a record of sins, O LORD, who could stand?

PEOPLE: But with you there is forgiveness; therefore you are feared.

PASTOR: I wait for the LORD,

PEOPLE: And in his word I put my hope.

Act of Praise: Psalm 130.

Suggested Hymns: "I Love to Tell the Story"; "Yield Not to Temptation"; "Beneath the Cross of Jesus."

Opening Prayer: Loving Father, who forgives your sinful children through your Son, Jesus Christ, give us the strength to resist temptation so that we may follow the example of our Brother who was obedient. In his name we pray. Amen.

Pastoral Prayer: Dear God, we come together today to praise and to worship you. You are the God of love and of judgment, and we are eager to kneel down and give you honor.

Thank you for your compassionate love—you always love us even when we are unlovable. And thank you for your saving gift of forgiveness—you forgive us when we are unworthy of your favor.

And, gracious Father, please continue to forgive us. We confess that we are sinners, so often frail and weak in the face of temptation. We do wrong when we want to do right; we do harm when we want to give help; we do evil when we want to do good.

Help us to be more like your Son, Jesus, who was tempted but remained strong in his faith. In Jesus' name we pray. Amen.

March 7, 1993

□

Second Sunday in Lent

Life need not be inclined to death. The promise of God, the grace of God, and the mercy of Christ combine to say "whoever believes need not perish . . . will be saved."

The Sunday Lessons

Genesis 12:1-8: For twelve chapters, Genesis tells the story of humanity's disobedience and rebellion. Now, the promise of God takes control. God is the chief actor in this story.
Romans 4:1-17: Some believed that God's salvation and blessings could be merited and should be earned. Not so, says Paul. They are a gift. The promise rests on grace and is for all who "share the faith of Abraham" (v. 16).
John 3:1-17: Nicodemus, a ruler of the Jews, had questions. How can a man be reborn? How can human nature be changed? How can life be eternal? In John's Gospel eternal life is understood not only as life after death, but also as life that is abundant and true. Such life is possible now to one who believes.

Interpretation and Imagination

A video interpreting a prison ministry, for persons who had "wasted it," been found guilty, and put away, was entitled *Believe a Man Can Change*. Most persons working with our prison systems have given up rehabilitating criminals. Punishment for crime is the reason one is sent to jail. That makes the claim of this Christian prison ministry all the more staggering. Do you believe that men and women can change?

Some will be quick to say, "No! Humanity is just as bad or even worse than it has been. Life is not dear. We squander freedoms, sacrifice soldiers, slaughter unborn babies, drug our senses, indulge our appetites, rob the poor, oppress the weak, and hasten the deaths of many and even ourselves. Days of Lent have come and gone. Sermons have been preached, churches built, and converts baptized, but the world is not one bit better for any of it."

The lessons of this day fly in the face of such evidence. There *is* new life to be had. One may be born again and born to life that is good enough to last forever. This is the message that is anchored in the purposes of a God of promise, grace, and mercy.

We have seen many wonderful improvements in the quality of life in this generation. Travel, communications, nutrition, housing, health—all reflect the progress of humanity. Government will manage resources and populations in the interest of positive change. Yet none of this is as basic to life itself or as eternal with promise as the kind of change wrought through being "born of the Spirit" (v. 8).

"How can these things be?" asked Nicodemus (v. 9). It's like the wind; like the breath of life; like a desert storm that changes everything when it has passed; like a steady breeze that fills a well-trimmed sail; like clean new air when the shutters are open wide. Listen. (JKB)

NICODEMUS, A BORN-AGAIN CHRISTIAN

John 3:1-17

A SERMON BY MARTHA H. FORREST

I've noticed that teenagers today seem to be a lot bigger, taller than we were at that age. When I was in the sixth grade in 1952, I was five feet, four inches tall, and I still am. I weigh what I did then, too.

Look around the sanctuary now and notice how much bigger the kids are today. Next time you go to the mall, look at the kids—they're taller. I guess it's all that good food and vitamins we gave them.

I used to collect Early American primitive antiques. I don't now because we live in the parsonage, and I'm glad of it, because it encourages us to travel light. My grandmother also collected Early American primitives, and she gave us a walnut three-quarter bed for a wedding present. It was lovely. It made up beautifully with a colorful quilt, but it sure wasn't practical. It was too short and too narrow. We obviously were bigger, taller people than people were in the eighteenth century. I figured this to be true when my parents and I went to England and visited John Wesley's home. His bed was tiny, his preaching robe was tiny, and his shoes looked like a preschooler's.

Our youngest child, Steve, weighed ten pounds when he was born. I wasn't too surprised, since about all I could wear the month before he was born was a huge gray dress from K-Mart and a big pair of floppy red tennis shoes. Ten pounds he weighed, and he was always bigger and taller than the other children he played with. Steve's twenty-one years old now—a heavy weight wrestler and weight lifter—six feet, four inches tall and around two hundred and fifty pounds. So, can you possibly imagine him being born again? I can't.

This was Nicodemus's problem. He couldn't imagine it. He was too literal in his thinking, too specific, too precise. How can I, he probably thought, a grown man, possibly be born again?

I have never much cared for the term "born again," as in "Are you a born-again Christian?" because it reminds me too much of the often-asked-on-the-street-corner question, "Are you saved?" which usually makes me want to ask, "Saved from what?" But then, my mind is often too literal; too logical. I suppose yours is too.

Nicodemus was a Pharisee, a teacher of the Law that God gave to the Jews through Moses; an interpreter of the Law, one who studied the Law and who thought logically. He even acted in a logical, controlled manner by coming to see Jesus at night. After all, he would have lost credibility if he'd been seen in the broad daylight talking to the man named Jesus who said he was the Messiah. And he used clear, concise thinking when he acknowledged that Jesus was a teacher sent by God, because who could possibly perform miracles if God wasn't with him. But his well-trained mind balked at Jesus' abrupt comment that no one can see the kingdom of God unless he is born again. How could a woman give birth to a full-grown man? It just doesn't follow the natural laws of life, not to mention the Law.

And aren't we just as law abiding? Never play cards on Sunday. Never go to the movies on Sunday. Never read the funny papers on Sunday. Never sew on Sunday. These were some absolutes from my childhood. And we have them even now—don't clap in church, don't put flowers in front of the cross on the altar table, don't wear dangling earrings to church—obey these rules, and you'll be sure to go to heaven.

As Nicodemus stood there, perplexed, Jesus went on to say that no one would ever enter the kingdom of God unless he was born of water and of the Spirit. Nicodemus had probably already heard of Jesus' baptism in the Jordan River by John the Baptist, and this incident must have spoken to him of "born of water" (v. 5). We Pharisees (and we mothers who like to be in control) have a fine understanding of the baptism of water. Water cleans up the dirty. Water flushes out the system. Soap and water wash the bad words out of your mouth. These are some of our basic rules, along with drinking eight glasses of water every day; don't touch a dead body or you will be ritually unclean; or never wear clean, white shoes after August or before Easter.

But born of the Spirit? Nicodemus wanted to know what this meant, and Jesus seemed astounded that he still wasn't catching on. "You are a great teacher in Israel, and you don't know this?" (v. 10 GNB). Jesus asked, "You do not believe me when I tell you about the things of this world; how will you ever believe me, then, when I tell you about the things of heaven?" (v. 12 GNB).

I guess Nicodemus must have felt a little slow, but then he caught the glimmer of when John the Baptist told the messengers (who had been sent by the Pharisees, incidentally) that he baptized with water, but the man who came after him baptizes with the Holy Spirit. Nicodemus remembered that John had relayed to them that the one who came after was much greater, because he existed before John was ever born, and that God had told him that he would see the Spirit come down and stay on the man. John had actually said that this man is the Son of God. John had seen with his own eyes the Spirit come down from heaven in the form of a dove and light on Jesus.

And then, Nicodemus really got it. It was like a fresh new wind, and it blew away the dusty, old thinking of the Pharisees. It became clear to him, almost like a cartoon light bulb over his head, that Jesus was talking about a baptism of real change, an inner change of the heart, not just a cleaning up on the outside. It was a baptism of repentance—turning away from our wants and wishes and turning toward God's. It was a transfer of our controlling every aspect of our lives to accepting God's control. It was a brand new understanding that God is in charge of this world, not us.

Because of our sinful nature, we like to be in charge. Just before we were born, we were not in control in our mothers' wombs. Our mothers' bodies were in control. If your mother took drugs, so did you, because her body controlled yours. If she smoked and drank, so did you, because her body controlled yours. But, after you were born, you started taking control by crying when you were cold, crying when you were wet, crying when you were hungry—every baby knows that crying gets to them every time.

Sinners we all are, from birth on up. But we can change! God wants us to change. God wants us to change so much that he sent his only Son. God loves us so much that he sent his only Son, not as a Pharisaic judge, but as a Savior, our Savior. This is what being born of the Spirit is—welcoming Jesus Christ as our Lord and Savior.

God has always loved his children, even during the forty years in the wilderness when Moses was leading the Israelites to the Promised Land. But God got so tired of them whining and complaining that he sent poisonous snakes to bite and kill many of them. God still loved them, though, and told Moses to make a bronze snake and mount it on a pole, and lift it up high so that those who looked at it would be healed of their bites (Numbers 21:4-9). Moses lifted up the bronze snake to heal the people, and God lifted up his only Son to heal the people again.

I've often wished that I could have our oldest child, Rob, over again. The oldest child always gets practiced on; the oldest child always catches the parental mistakes. I know, because I am the oldest child. I wanted so much to be a good mother, I followed all the Dr. Spock rules, and I made Rob follow all the rules that now seem so unimportant. He was probably the cleanest little boy in North Carolina, with all the baths and washings of clothes. But sometimes I didn't see or hear the spirit of what he did or said, because I was busy obeying the rules.

Well, what happened to Nicodemus? Did he turn away from his sins and follow Jesus? I think he did. And I think this, because John goes on to tell us in chapter 7 that as Jesus gained popularity with the people, the Pharisees and the Chief Priests felt more and more threatened. So they sent guards to arrest Jesus, but the guards came back empty handed and in awe of Jesus' words. The Pharisees were annoyed and accused the guards of being fooled by the one who some were calling the Messiah. But Nicodemus stood up for Jesus, saying that the Law prohibited them from condemning a man without hearing him. Nicodemus had certainly stuck his neck out, because the Pharisces mockingly asked, "Well, are you also from Galilee? Study the Scriptures and you will learn that no prophet ever comes from Galilee" (v. 52 GNB).

Later, we read that Jesus died on the cross, and that Joseph of Arimathea, a secret follower of Jesus, asked Pilate for the body. Pilate agreed, and a man helped Joseph lay Jesus to rest. The helper brought a hundred pounds of spices. They lovingly wrapped the body with linen cloths and the spices, according to Jewish custom. Then they buried Jesus in a new tomb in the garden where he had died. Joseph's helper was Nicodemus. (John 19:38-42).

Suggestions for Worship

Call to Worship (Ps. 33:18, 20-21):

PASTOR: Truly the eye of the LORD is on those who fear him.

PEOPLE: On those who hope in his steadfast love,

PASTOR: Our soul waits for the LORD; he is our help and our shield.

PEOPLE: Our heart is glad in him, because we trust in his holy name.

Act of Praise: Psalm 33:18-22.

Suggested Hymns: "Love Divine, All Loves Excelling"; "Spirit Song"; "Alas! and Did My Savior Bleed."

Opening Prayer: Loving God, the giver of life, who patiently waits for us to turn away from our sins, help us to be born again so that we may mature in faith. May our commitment be fresh and alive, rather than stale and stillborn.

All this we pray, through Jesus Christ our Lord. Amen.

Pastoral Prayer: Almighty God of all creation, the one to whom we look for nurturing, we come to your church to show you love and adoration.

Thank you that we were born into this world. Thank you for caring for us and providing for our needs. Thank you for the opportunity of rebirth, which you offer to us through your Son, Jesus Christ. Thank you for the marvelous gift of life eternal, available to us all.

Forgive us when we are prideful, when we are controlling, when we are self-centered. We confess that we are all sinners in need of your merciful grace.

Help us to put our confidence in you, Holy Creator, and in you alone. Through your Son we pray. Amen.

MARCH 14, 1993

□

Third Sunday in Lent

Water from a desert rock and living water for the woman at the well are the subjects of these lessons. Here, the life-giving qualities of water are used to symbolize renewal.

The Sunday Lessons

Exodus 17:3-17: The people complained, "Why did you bring us out of Egypt, to kill us . . . with thirst?" (v. 3). Moses' rod, which had parted the waters at the sea, now brought forth water from the rock. The place was named Meribah (complaining) and Massah (proof).
Romans 5:1-11: At a time when we were helpless, "while we were still weak, at the right time Christ died for the ungodly" (v. 6). Making the case for justification by faith, Paul speaks of God's love "poured into our hearts through the Holy Spirit" (v. 5). That Christ died for us while we were yet sinners is God's proof of his love for us.
John 4:5-42: Water, the symbol of Christian initiation, is also used to symbolize constant renewal. A Samaritan woman was surprised by Jesus' request for water. To share a cup would be considered unclean. Jesus' offer of "living water" (v. 10) and promise of "a spring of water gushing up to eternal life" (v. 14) prompt her response.

Interpretation and Imagination

Professor John Marsh, commenting on this Gospel lesson, notes, "It is not what God's people can do for him that is determinative, but rather what he can do for them." The story of the woman at the well contrasts the drink that is asked for with the living water to be given.

In first century Israel a Jewish male was certain that he was superior in the eyes of God to a woman of Samaria. Samaritan women, according to Jewish law, were "menstruants from their cradle" and, therefore, always unclean. The assumption was that God is better pleased with the ways of Jews than Samaritans.

We, too, make rival claims about being God's favorites. Most of our confidence in superior status rests on our belief that our religious practice is more pleasing to God and our obedience more faithful. The true Israel is not formed and renewed by what we do or by any religious practice. The Christ who offers himself as "living water" is the source of life.

"Like the woman at the well, I was thirsting for things that could not satisfy," are the first words of a gospel song that concludes with the plea, "Fill my cup, Lord." What are those things that fail to satisfy? Money, power, popularity, knowledge, works righteousness? It will be easier to point to such emptiness than it will be to speak convincingly about living water.

Proof of life-giving water is what we want. It is not theological argument that convinces, but rather, action and presence. (JKB)

HOW JESUS DEALS WITH SIN

Romans 5:6-10

A SERMON BY SUSAN GLADIN

Sometimes a preacher, faced with a certain text, feels that things can't be said any better than they already have. Paul's words in this letter to the Romans are already a sermon; a sermon communicated in words so eloquent and beautiful that trying to say anything more seems pointless and trite. When I read the first eleven verses of this fifth chapter, I am left with that feeling.

But Paul's words were written in the first century to some of the very first Christians. And though some things never change, others change beyond recognition. We are Christians, too, and humans, and while we have much in common with those early Christians, we have even more differences. These differences cause us to hear these words differently, to interpret them into our own lives differently, even to live them quite differently than the first-century Christians Paul addressed.

I try to imagine hearing these words for the first time, like the early Christians did. I try to imagine being raised in a tradition wherein salvation must be earned through daily attention to right living and good works. I try to imagine living in the fear that my wrong deeds and evil thoughts—even my evil dreams—might somehow incur the wrath of God. Imagine living like that and then meeting Paul. He tells you that you are already saved; that Christ died for you, even while you were still a sinner. He tells you that your own efforts can't earn God's love, because it has already been given to you. Imagine hearing that for the first time! What a relief it would be to believe that! What a gift has been given in those words!

While we were still sinners, Christ died for us. We have been given the gift of life—a gift we didn't earn, and certainly didn't deserve.

I wonder if those early Christians found it hard to accept those words and that gift. I know that we twentieth-century Christians find it hard. We tend to proclaim God's unconditional love, then say, "But . . ." and follow with the conditions. We are seldom able to separate God's grace from the conditions that we feel we must follow to claim it. We simply find it hard to accept a gift, especially one that we feel we don't deserve. We can't seem to give up the struggle to earn God's love and approval.

In the same manner, when someone we don't know, or don't know well, gives us something of value, we feel uncomfortable. We don't know what we've done to deserve such a gift, and deep down inside we believe that gifts should, at least on some level, be earned and deserved.

A young preacher had moved to the mountains for a summer internship, and was puzzled because the mountain parishioners were showering his family with gifts. He hadn't been there long enough to earn their respect or adoration, and he accepted the gifts reluctantly, with protestations such as "You shouldn't have" or "I don't deserve this!" Some gifts he even tried to refuse. Finally, a wise mountain woman pulled him aside. "We're not giving to you because of who you are or what you have done. We give because of who we are. When you accept our gifts, you accept us for who we are. Please accept them graciously."

Those mountain people were giving themselves and demonstrating their love in their giving. In many traditions, including that of the Native Americans, giving a gift is a way of giving a part of yourself. And, conversely, accepting a gift is a way of accepting another person into your heart. Either way, the focus is on the *giver,* not on the recipient.

But in our society, we tend to focus on the recipient, whether it be ourselves or someone else, and we tend to question the degree to which the gift was deserved. In my human service work we see this played out almost daily. We're in the business of giving to the poor, and we give as the direct result of our faith in God. But far too often we question the deservedness of the recipient, and fail to recognize the spirit of the giver. "We give because of who we are."

It is a common mistake. When a gift is given, we tend to focus on the recipient—what did I do to deserve this gift? But what about the very act of giving and the spirit of the giver? Have we missed an important message here?

What did we do to deserve this gift Paul conveys through his words in Romans 5? How did we earn this gift of life and salvation? This question is the crux of the Christian faith, and the question I see people struggle with more than any other. What did I do? What must I do? How much do I have to do? When do I have to do it?

Sometimes the questions are asked in genuine fear and concern for our own salvation. We want to be sure we understand the rules so that we can follow them faithfully and achieve our place in heaven. We want to do what is right and pleasing to God.

Sometimes the questions are asked out of arrogant self-righteousness. We want to set up the rules in such a way that we can play the game successfully but others can't. Thus we can feel more secure among an elite who have earned their place in heaven. Either way, we are motivated by fear.

And of course, there are those who claim to know all the rules and will happily let you in on the secret if you'll just send $25 today (and more tomorrow).

Rules, rules, everywhere are rules. What must I do?

Time and time again the biblical writers give us the answer. "You don't have to do *anything,* it has already been done." But, despite having the answer, we keep asking the question.

You see, our perspective is all wrong. We can't seem to stop looking at ourselves. We stare at ourselves and wonder why we can't see God. We listen to our own fears stirring in our hearts and thundering in our brains and wonder why we can't hear God. If we could just shift our gaze upward, and tune our ears outward, we could learn what Jesus came to teach us: Focus on the giver, accept the gift. The gift is given because of the giver. God gives because of who God is, not because of who we are.

"God proves his love for us in that while we still were sinners Christ died for us" (v. 8). What did we do to deserve this? *Nothing.* We didn't earn this distinction. It has nothing to do with who we are. It has everything to do with who God is and how fully and freely God loves us.

We were still weak, we were ungodly, we were enemies, but we were reconciled to God through the death of his son. We will be saved by his life. We are even able to boast of God! Paul is big on freedom. Elsewhere he wrote "for freedom Christ has set us free" (Gal. 5:1). Paul has little tolerance for rules and regulations. The value of the gift lies with the giver.

Paul's message was radical to his time, just as it is radical to ours. He had to deal with the fears of the crowds who predicted that chaos would ensue if people were told that salvation was freely given, and not to be earned.

But Paul was right, and the fearful crowds were wrong. Paul understood God's love in the context of a parent's love. The child who is secure in a parent's love is mature and wise, able to be loving and giving. It is the insecure child who scraps and fights for his rightful place. It is the insecure child who quits trying to earn his place, and takes on a self-destructive life-style. It is the insecure child who is outwardly submissive and obedient, but inwardly cold and unfeeling. Paul knew that the world's problems are created by insecure children. Paul knew the power of this message—that God's love is proven to us, even while we were still sinners. We are secure in God's love.

Paul knew that the message of God's unconditional love would free us to be loving and giving. Paul knew that confidence in God's love would empower us to be the Body of Christ. Paul knew that, as secure children, we could be agents in bringing about the kingdom of God.

But I don't think Paul knew we'd still be rejecting his message some 2,000 years later. He didn't realize the power of the human ego to remain self-focused. He didn't realize just how insecure we all are.

Sally and Susan were ages five and three, respectively. They shared the same parents, and the same home, and even looked like sisters, but that was as far as the resemblance went.

Sally, the elder, was a little adult: prim and proper, always on the best behavior, always seeking to please. She said "yes ma'am" and "no ma'am," picked up her own clothes, and never, never talked back.

Susan, the younger, was a little hellion. Her energy was boundless, and it was always focused on some negative behavior. She yelled back, she never cleaned up after herself, and, with just a moment to herself, she would empty cabinets and canisters, torture the cat, or injure her sister. She was always angry, always fighting for her rights; for her place in the family. Sometimes it seemed she had just given up on ever doing anything right, and so set out to do as many things wrong as possible.

Sally and Susan were insecure children. Sally, the compliant one, was always trying to earn her place and everyone's approval. She never did anything wrong, but she had no spirit, no self-esteem. What little she gave to others was given only to gain acceptance for herself. Sarah was a slave to the rules that she thought would bring her love and acceptance. But she lived in fear of rejection.

Susan was the defiant one. Her insecurity translated into rebellion. She fought for her place, and challenged anyone, including the cat and her sister, that she perceived as getting in her way. She realized early on that she couldn't outdo Sarah in goodness, so she gained attention through badness. It was Susan's name that resounded through the house. And she didn't care about the tone in the voice. Someone was calling her name. That was what mattered.

Here is a prayer for Sally and Susan. It is for you and me, along with Sally and Susan. It is a prayer for insecure children everywhere—for all of us, Sallys and Susans, everywhere. This is a prayer for those of us who still argue with Paul, for those of us who haven't lifted our eyes or opened our ears. This is a prayer for the children of God.

Sally, I love you. I love you as a daughter, though you are not my own. I love you when I wake in the morning, and I love you when I fall to sleep at night. Susan, I love you in spite of your goodness, but not because of it. I love you for trying to win my love, but I love you most when your eyes flicker with the recognition that love is not something that will disappear with a cross word or a wrong deed. When your little body sleeps at night, weary from the work of being good, my love does not diminish. You are a child of God, and God's love does not disappear, not even when sleep brings dreams that you can't control. I love you, Sally, but not because of your goodness.

Susan, I love you. I love you as a daughter, though you are not my own. I love you when I wake in the morning, and I love you when I fall to sleep at night. Susan, I love you in spite of your disobedience, but not because of it. You challenge my love, and when you realize that you can't conquer it, you will sigh and relax and accept what you now fight for. You will know a freedom you have never known. Susan, you are a child of God. With God's love you will someday recognize that God has made a place for you and for Sally, and even for the cat. I love you Susan, and nothing you can do will change that.

Sally and Susan, lift up your eyes and see God's love. Tune your ears outward and hear God's voice. There is a message being spoken for you. There is a hand reaching out to you. Look into the eyes of the Giver. You are a child of God. God proves his love for us even while we are sinners—weak and ungodly. We have been reconciled and justified, though we didn't earn it and we don't deserve it. God gave and God gives. Accept that gift. Love the Giver. Amen.

Suggestions for Worship

Call to Worship (Ps. 95:1-2, 6-7):

PASTOR: O come, let us sing to the LORD;

PEOPLE: Let us make a joyful noise to the rock of our salvation!

PASTOR: Let us come into his presence with thanksgiving;

PEOPLE: O come, let us worship and bow down,

PASTOR: Let us kneel before the LORD, our Maker!

PEOPLE: For he is our God, and we are the people of his pasture.

Act of Praise: Psalm 95.

Suggested Hymns: "O For a Thousand Tongues to Sing"; "Blessed Assurance"; "Pass Me Not, O Gentle Savior."

Opening Prayer: Lord, we come thirsty before you this morning. Our throats are dry, and ache for those waters that only you can provide. Through Moses you gave water and your presence to the Israelites who wandered in the desert. At a deep well you once gave the Samaritan woman water to nourish her spiritual thirst. Lord, open our spirits to accept your healing water. Quench the thirst that we carry in our souls. Open our hearts to be vessels that will contain the gift you have given us through your son, Jesus Christ. Amen.

Pastoral Prayer: Blessed are you, O Lord our God, creator of the universe, who has given your people the gift of your boundless love. Blessed are you, O Lord our God, creator of the universe, who loves the sinner, the ungodly, and the enemy—who loves me. We thank you for your gifts that bring us life, salvation, and reconciliation. We thank you for the ways that you allow us to know you and love you, not as distant worshipers, but as adoring children who can feel your gentle arms around us. Through your grace we have the gifts of justification and peace. Blessed are you, O Lord our God. Blessed are you. Amen.

MARCH 21, 1993

□

Fourth Sunday in Lent

A clear-sighted prophet, a king with vision, a new-sighted man, and Christ, who is light, are the personalities of these lessons.

The Sunday Lessons

I Samuel 16:1-13: Jesse's youngest son, David, the shepherd boy, was brought before the prophet Samuel. "Rise and anoint him" (v. 12). The sacrifice and the oil indicate this king was appointed by God. The name David (beloved) has never been forgotten in Israel, where people long for another like him.
Ephesians 5:8-14: "For once you were darkness, but now in the Lord you are light" (v. 8). Images of darkness and light dominate this passage. "The fruit of the light is found in all that is good and right and true" (v. 9). The deeds of secrecy are called barren.
John 9:1-41: The sight of a man blind from birth was restored. Controversy with the Pharisees followed, and finally, the man was expelled from the synagogue. "One thing I do know, that though I was blind, now I see" (v. 25). The authority of Jesus, who had come from God, is lifted up as John's Gospel skillfully points to spiritual blindness through the healing of physical blindness.

Interpretation and Imagination

We frequently pray for divine guidance. Deliverance from blindness and nearsighted errors, and a clear perception of truth are primary goals in our religious quest. The emphasis on spiritual guidance is a common characteristic of all religions. The Old Testament lesson teaches, "The LORD does not see as mortals see" (I Sam. 16:7) and tells of the clear vision of prophet and king. The Epistle lesson lauds the goodness of light and proclaims, Christ shall give you light. Pharisees asked, "Surely we are not blind, are we?" (John 9:40). John's Gospel claims for Christ and for Christian believers light that shines in darkness.

In the clear light of a twentieth-century day, a March day in 1993, can divine guidance be known? Should it be trusted? How can it be gained?

Elbert Russell, a Quaker who was dean of Duke Divinity School, quoted Isaac Pennington, who claimed that the divine "Light is an infallible Light, and the eye that sees is an infallible eye." The dean agreed with the first part of the statement, but made the point that humans have no infallible guidance. He doubted that any given human eye sees the divine light infallibly. The idea of guidance should not be confused with any claim to infallibility.

In times past, mystics seeking divine guidance have tried to dull their physical senses. A hair shirt and a cave were the trademarks of those who wanted to see as God sees. Sacrifice appropriate to clear vision in this moment of history means paying the price of diligent research; it means not loving traditional beliefs too much; it always means surrender to the revealed truth in Jesus Christ. (JKB)

AN EYE-OPENING EXPERIENCE

John 9:25

A SERMON BY MICHAEL BROWN

John Killinger tells of a man who visited one day in a classroom for visually impaired children. Troubled by what he saw, the man remarked (rather insensitively), "It must be terrible to go through life without your eyes." A young girl quickly responded, "It's not half so bad as having two good eyes but still not being able to see." Her point was well made. There are varieties of blindness. And perhaps none is more tragic than that which affects "the eyes of [the] heart" (Eph. 1:18).

This morning's lesson identifies several forms of blindness, only one of which is *physical*. That was the malady affecting the beggar who was brought to the Temple. John says he was "a man blind from birth" (v. 1). Obviously the victim of a genetic disorder, he had never seen the faces of friends, nor the soft beauty of grass bending to the wind, nor the radiant smiles of children. If you saw the movie *Mask,* you'll recall a scene where the young boy who was the central character of the film tries to explain to a girl who was blind from birth what blue looked like. She reminds him that blue is a meaningful concept only to people who have seen it. The beggar in this morning's story was like that, "a man blind from birth," John called him, whose concepts of the world around were all fashioned from sound, smell, taste, and touch. From the day of his delivery he had never been able to see.

A second type of blindness identified in this story is *theological.* Popular opinion in that day and age decreed that suffering was the result of sin. You remember how Job's associates accused him of being a sinner. They were sure no one would be so terribly afflicted unless God were punishing that person for some unspeakable transgression. Theirs was a God of justice, not mercy. In fact, the Old Testament at one point suggests that God remembers "the iniquity of parents" against "the third and fourth generation" of their children (Exod. 20:5).

In some ways that point of view seems almost credible even still. I was reading recently of numerous illnesses that can be transmitted to a child prenatally, many of them resulting from conscious decisions that parents make. Will I smoke during pregnancy? Will I use drugs while carrying this baby? The article related heartbreaking stories of newborn infants already addicted to heroin or cocaine and of babies born carrying the AIDS virus because either mom or dad used IV drugs or was sexually promiscuous. The disciples obviously believed that children can inherit sin (even guilt) from their parents. So when confronted with the beggar at the Temple door, they asked Jesus, "Who sinned, this man or his parents, that he was born blind?" (v. 2). What they missed, obviously, was the compassionate nature of God that Jesus had been diligently trying to get across through his repeated references to God as "Father" (Parent). Jesus had labored to teach them about mercy and grace and how theirs was a God who wished only good for his children, whether they deserved it or not. The disciples, at least at this point, were theologically blind.

Another type of blindness the story underscores is *prejudicial.*

This is demonstrated in the neighbors and worshipers who had seen the beggar at his post every day over the years. They had come to believe that "he was what he was." They were unwilling to concede that he could ever change or become different. And even after he was touched by Christ, after his eyes were opened and he became a new man, those neighbors remarked, "[It is not him,] but it is someone like him" (v. 9). They were, to the very end, unwilling to alter their opinion once it had been formed.

Still another blindness illustrated in the lesson is *emotional.* That was the case for the parents of the man born blind. You recall, of course, how they responded to his healing. The young man himself gave credit where credit was due. Jesus had opened his eyes and had given him a new lease on life, and he proclaimed to all who would listen: "He [Jesus] is a prophet!" (v. 17). But the Pharisees, who were seeking to discredit Christ, challenged the man's parents to offer an explanation for what had transpired. Most moms and dads would have been laughing or weeping for joy. But this mom and dad were, instead, nervously counting what Dietrich Bonhoeffer called "the cost of discipleship." How much did they stand to lose by being honest? They knew the Sabbath laws, and that Jesus had apparently broken them. They knew their son's standing in the religious community was seriously compromised by his praise of Christ. They knew that they, too, would be ostracized and cut off from their friends, family, and community of faith if they assumed too bold a defense of Jesus. So, they offered the coward's way out: "We do not know how it is that now he sees, nor do we know who opened his eyes. Ask him; he is of age. He will speak for himself" (v. 21). They were myopic in their self-centeredness. They could only see as far as their own interests, their own security. As the child observed in Dr. Killinger's story, how tragic it is "having two good eyes but still not being able to see."

The final blindness presented in this account is *spiritual.* That is evident in the actions of the Pharisees. Jesus had become a threat to them and to their standing in the community. He was saying things they had not said and doing things they could not do, and in many quarters people were paying more attention to his words than to theirs. He was even causing dissension within their own ranks. The lesson puts it this way: "And they were divided" (v. 16). Increasingly the Pharisees were becoming convinced that Jesus had to be silenced. Indeed, in the story immediately preceding this one, John tells us that they had "picked up stones to throw at him," and Jesus had been forced to hide from his attackers (8:59). It was the sabbath when Jesus healed the man born blind. That provided ammunition to those legalists who were more concerned with religious rules and orders than with love, and who were already searching diligently for some public stone to cast at the Rabbi from Nazareth. "[Jesus] is not from God," they said, "for he does not observe the sabbath" (v. 16).

At a large inner-city church a few years ago, a teenage boy ran up the steps and pounded on the locked office door. A voice inside answered, "The office closes at 5:00. Come back tomorrow." "I'm being chased," the boy yelled. "They're going to kill me. Please! Let me in!" The voice behind the door replied, "Our trustees set the rules. I'd like to help, but it's past 5:00. Come back tomorrow." Within seconds there was gun fire, and a teenage boy bled to death on the steps of a church that was so bound by the rules that it was paralyzed to offer help to someone in need. The Pharisees were so bound by their adherence to the Law that the pain and disability of a beggar at the Temple door was ignored. Ritual took precedence over compassion. They were spiritually blind.

Blindness, it seems, comes in many forms. Sherlock Holmes put it to Watson this way: "You see, but you do not observe." I suspect we are all familiar with stories of people those words would describe. I recall something that occurred in my hometown when I was a teenager back in the mid-1960s. One Saturday an elderly farmer parked his rusty pickup truck on the edge of an automobile dealership's parking lot. He crawled out, adorned in overalls and wearing a straw hat, and began looking at the new cars on the lot. It was lunch time on a Saturday, and the dealership was shorthanded. Only three salesmen were there, and one secretary was working inside. Two of the salesmen were devoting their attention to the same prospective buyer, a well-dressed gentleman in his early thirties. The third salesman was devoting his attention to the new secretary. Wishing to divert him, she twice pointed out the fact that the man in the overalls was browsing around among the new cars, and no one had offered to assist him. The salesman replied: "Old McDonald out there can look all he wants, but I'm not wasting my time on someone who can't afford to buy." After growing weary of being ignored, "Old McDonald" climbed back into his truck, drove one block south to a rival dealership, picked out one of their new top-of-the-line models and, reaching into his overalls, pulled out a fistful of cash and paid for the car. The salesmen at the first dealership could adequately be described in biblical fashion: Having eyes, they did not see (Mark 8:18).

How easy it is to look at other persons and not see them in their true light. How easy it is to misjudge others because of external issues like age, race, economic status, sex, political affiliation, or even things as superficial as fashion. The Pharisees looked at the Messiah and saw him as a threat instead of a blessing. The neighbors at the Temple looked at the man whose blindness had been healed and said, "[It is not him,] but it is someone like him." Having eyes, they would not see.

Similarly, for better or worse, we sometimes do not see ourselves in proper perspective. I recall an occasion when I was losing the battle against some unwanted weight. My wife and I were at dinner with a delightful young couple, each of whom was quite trim. I remarked that at their age I, too, was slim and athletic. I continued how difficult it was to look in a mirror and realize that my formerly slim self had become fat. The young lady across the table, attempting to be gracious, answered, "Oh, Michael, you're not fat. You're just portly." Immediately the thought crossed my mind that the Pillsbury Doughboy is "portly." "Svelte" would have been a nice choice of words, or even "slender." But I had never before seen myself as "portly." It was, however, that eye-opening description which led to a renewed commitment on my part to diet and exercise.

Am I a sinner? Am I guilty of prejudice, greed, insensitivity, arrogance? Whatever I am, I tend to become comfortable being that way. In fact, it is easy to become virtually oblivious to truth about self unless someone comes along to open our eyes that we may see. Only then can true transformation become a possibility.

Jesus does that for us, even as he did for the beggar by the Temple door. He opens our eyes that we may see others as they truly are and that we may see ourselves, not only as we are, but as we yet may become.

And so our story closes with that beautiful testimony of faith: "One thing I do know, that though I was blind, now I see." The blind beggar was blind no more. Christ had opened to him a new world, limitless in scope and potential. He had become a new person with a new fortune because of the touch of the Master's hand. Whatever my blindness may be, theological, prejudicial, emotional, or spiritual, new vision comes to me in the same way, with the touch of the Master's hand.

A dear friend not long ago discussed with me her decision to leave a financially lucrative career to enter full-time service to troubled and abused youth. Her income has literally been reduced by 75 percent. She has been forced to sell her lovely home and move into a small rented apartment. Her nine-to-five schedule has increased due to the addition of "on-call" hours to her regular office/field service routine. Often she works weeks without a day off, carrying with her the pains and problems of disadvantaged kids, and working diligently toward some sort of resolution. Her entire life-style has been turned upside down. I asked what prompted the decision, and she replied, "Christ did. For the first time in my life, this past year I have begun to see myself as someone who is loved, unconditionally, no matter what. And that liberated me to be able to love others the same way." Then with a broad smile she added, "After forty years of stumbling around this world, at last I am able to see why I'm here."

Jesus encountered a man born blind, touched him with divine power and infinite love, and the man proclaimed,

> I once was lost but now am found,
> Was blind but now I see!
> (John Newton, "Amazing Grace")

What Jesus did for that beggar he can do for us if we give him the chance. He can open the eyes of our hearts that we may no longer stumble in the world's darkness, but at last might truly see why we are here.

Suggestions for Worship

Call to Worship (John 4:23-24):

PASTOR: The hour is coming, and is now here, when the true worshipers will worship the Father in spirit and truth.

PEOPLE: **For the Father seeks such as these to worship him.**

PASTOR: God is spirit,

PEOPLE: **And those who worship him must worship in spirit and truth.**

Act of Praise: Psalm 23.

Suggested Hymns: "When Morning Gilds the Skies"; "Freely, Freely"; "What Wondrous Love Is This."

Opening Prayer: Everlasting Father, Prince of Peace, you have revealed your kingdom to every nation. Your light shines in every corner of this world. There is no night that is night to you. Bless your church today and fill us with the light of Christ, that we too may reflect your glory, through Jesus our Lord. Amen.

Pastoral Prayer: O Holy God, we long for a closer walk and a deeper friendship with you. Your word teaches that if we continue to walk in darkness we cannot have fellowship with you. And so your word has called us to confession.

Let the prompting of your Spirit convict us of our sin. Speak, Holy Spirit, of the wrong that we have done. Speak, Holy Spirit, of the good we have not done. Help us to amend those things that we can still make right. Heal the hurts that we have caused but cannot cure. Help us to forgive each other as Christ forgives us.

Merciful God, you know our weakness. Our sin is always in full view of your all-seeing eyes. We cannot escape your judgment, neither can we flee from your far-reaching love. So, just now, we reach out with sorrow, but also with joy to grasp your hand. By the grace of Christ and the strength of the Spirit, help us to walk more readily in your ways. Amen.

March 28, 1993

□

Fifth Sunday in Lent

The theme of these lessons is life. Not dry bones, not a body rotting in a grave, but the life-giving power of God is the message of the church.

The Sunday Lessons

Ezekiel 37:1-14: Two images of death appear in the text, the valley of dry bones and graves. The question, "Can these bones live?" (v. 3) was addressed to a people who had lost hope. So was the prophecy, "Come from the four winds, O breath, and breathe upon these slain, that they may live" (v. 10). God's power and initiative are revealed.
Romans 8:1-11: Paul does not suggest that human nature has infinite qualities that deny death. Rather, he states the opposite: "The body is dead" (v. 10). His primary message is one of life, not death, and his confidence is in "the Spirit of him who raised Jesus from the dead."
John 11:17-45: "I am the resurrection and the life" (v. 25). The raising of Lazarus is the context for this great Christian claim. Both Martha and Mary made the speech that suggests death ends all hope: "Lord, if you had been here, my brother would not have died" (v. 32). Jesus answered, "Did I not tell you that if you believed, you would see the glory of God?" (v. 40).

Interpretation and Imagination

The accident was followed by the kind of urgent activity that one expects in life-threatening emergencies. The young woman, critically injured, was given first aid at the scene. In the rush of ambulance, emergency room, and intensive care, every life-support system was used. Family, friends, and pastor came immediately. People prayed. Then, it was over, and the hopeless resignation and brokenhearted grief quieted the frenzied effort with an awful finality.

We know some things can forestall death; but once it has claimed its victim, nothing can undo it. Indeed, the finality of death has often been employed by the church to prompt people to get right with God while there is still time, or at least to get one's estate in order. A man reflecting on a sermon that emphasized death and brooded on human mortality said, "That was as morbid as the six o'clock news."

Spinoza wisely observed, "There is nothing on which a free man lets his thoughts dwell less than on death, for true wisdom is a meditation, not on death, but on life." John 11 concludes with a focus on the death of Christ, but only to bear witness to the resurrection and the life.

Abundant life is more than not dying. The lover of Tithonus in Greek mythology was able to gain immortal life for her friend, but she neglected to request perpetual youth. He lived on and on, only to shrivel with age and grow weak with infirmity. At last the gods pitied him and turned him into a grasshopper. Life worthy of immortality is akin to the new life of Lazarus and the new faith of Mary. It adores Christ and rejoices in freedom. (JKB)

TWO FUNERALS

John 11:17-45

A SERMON BY WILLIAM R. WHITE

The last two weeks had not gone well for Pastor David Zwanziger. On Tuesday the week before, Howard Iverson, David's friend, neighbor, and parishioner, died. Howard and his wife, Elsie, retired from farming about the time the Zwanzigers moved to Blackhawk. They quickly adopted the Zwanziger's children, who called them Gramps and Grandma. David and Howard, along with the Iverson's only son, Donald, often went ice fishing together. Donald teaches accounting at the University of Wisconsin, in La Crosse, forty miles away.

The service, held last Thursday, was simple. It began with three of Howard's favorite Bible passages, which he had picked years ago. Next there was a sermon, a prayer written by Donald's wife, Iris, and two hymns sung by a barbershop quartet from La Crosse.

Elsie sat passively through the entire service, displaying no emotion.

After the benediction, the pall bearers began to wheel the draped casket down the aisle. Donald, with his mother on his arm, followed. Suddenly Elsie collapsed. Someone screamed. A nurse in attendance pushed her way through the frightened congregation. David sprinted to his office to call the rescue squad. The people stood by in stunned silence. The EMS team rushed into the church, carefully lifted Elsie onto a cart, and wheeled her to a waiting vehicle. Many followed the rescue squad to the curb and watched as the ambulance, siren crying, sped to its destination four blocks away.

It seemed a few minutes when the phone call from Blackhawk Community Hospital confirmed everyone's worst fears: Elsie had died instantly.

David, who followed the ambulance to the hospital, came back to the church where there were a few women eating potato salad and meat sandwiches in the church basement. Unable to talk, he went to his office and stared at the walls. Later in the day he found himself at the Iverson home with Donald and Iris. He tried in vain to think of something to say—a word of comfort, a word of hope. Everything he thought of seemed trivial. He didn't even invite the family to pray, fearing he wouldn't know what to say. Finally he broke the silence. "When do you plan to have your mother's funeral?" David asked.

"As soon as possible," Donald replied. "Probably Saturday. Everyone who is coming is already in town," he reasoned.

The Saturday service was by far the most difficult funeral David had ever conducted. When he stepped to the pulpit to speak he sensed everyone in the room was recording his every word. People were hoping the pastor would help make sense of the situation. But David felt hollow, and he was certain his words sounded empty.

On Monday, his normal day off, David made visits he had neglected the previous week. First he stopped at the retirement center, Ebenezer Home. Normally David enjoyed joking with the aids, playing euchre with a couple of men, and praying with others. On this day he found Ebenezer depressing.

It was worse when he visited the hospital. He nearly choked when he walked down the corridor at the hospital. What was that smell? One of the patients was a small boy who had leukemia. David greeted the mother, spoke briefly with the boy, said a prayer and left. He felt like Robo-pastor. It was not a very engaging visit.

That night after the children left the supper table, David's wife Doris asked, "What's wrong?"

"I'm sick of this season," David said. "I've had enough of Lent. It is time for a bit of Easter."

Fifteen minutes later, the phone rang. It was Knute Lee, a retired pastor who reminded David of a marine sergeant. Knute usually omitted greetings or salutations. "David, you normally study next Sunday's text on Tuesday mornings. Do you plan to do so tomorrow?"

David hadn't even thought about it. "I guess so," he muttered.

"Then I will be at your office at 9 A.M. We'll read and study together." Before he could respond, Knute hung up. David wasn't sure he wanted anyone in his office in the morning, but there was no denying Knute. Knute was one of the most persistent men David had ever met.

When David arrived at church the next morning about 8:55, Knute was in the kitchen brewing a pot of coffee. He was clearing the coffee table in David's office for Bibles and note pads when Donald Iverson walked in unexpected. David was about to tell Knute that they would postpone their study when the old pastor spoke to Donald. "We are about to study the gospel for the Fifth Sunday in Lent. Would you like to join us?"

David was surprised when Donald eagerly accepted the invitation and sat down. Knute offered a prayer and asked Donald to read the story of Jesus and Lazarus.

Donald had read but a few verses when David began to feel ill. The longer Donald read, the worse David felt. By the time the reading was completed, he told his companions he was unable to continue.

"Do you think you have the flu?" Donald asked kindly.

"I don't know what it is," David confessed. "I've had something for several days."

"What strikes you about this story?" Knute asked ignoring the state of David's health.

A flash of irritation swept through David. He felt like saying, "Knute, will you listen. I'm not feeling well." Instead, he answered the question. "It isn't the most significant thing in the story, but I am struck by the first words of both sisters. Jesus walks miles to get to the place and immediately they try to lay a guilt trip on him. 'If you had been here, my brother would not have died.' I hear things like that a lot."

"It is not a very cheery story, is it?" Donald said.

David agreed. "A man gets ill; Jesus, for some strange reason, takes his time leaving; the man dies; his disciples are afraid they are going to get killed; Martha rags on him once he arrives; and it ends with the high priest plotting his death. It's enough to make you sick."

Knute nodded. "And you did."

"I don't think the way I feel has anything to do with the story," David protested.

Knute leaned forward, put a hand on David's arm and spoke gently, "How do you evaluate your part in the two Iverson funerals?"

Tears immediately filled David's eyes. "I'm afraid I wasn't a very good pastor. I was too shocked to be of much help to Don and Iris on Thursday, and I was almost disoriented at Elsie's funeral. I'd say it was pretty pitiful." He turned to Donald, "I'm sorry I was of so little help."

Donald looked surprised. "I didn't see it that way at all. Iris and I weren't looking for any great words of wisdom the night Mom died. We were both grateful for your presence. You reacted like Jesus did when he saw the grief of the family. He wept. I am very grateful that you were with us during that difficult time." Donald wiped his eyes with tissue. "The reason I came by this morning was to thank you. You helped me understand that I was not the only one who had experienced grief. I lost my parents, but you lost dear friends. Everything you did told me that you loved them dearly. That was very important to me."

"I couldn't even pray with you," David said choking back the tears.

"I found the entire visit a prayer. It was enough just to have you with us. I told Iris this morning that I have felt the presence of God more powerfully in the last week than ever before in my life. She said something that baffled me at first, but makes more sense as I think about it. She said, 'Faith sees best in the dark.'

The more I think about it, the more I like it. What does that say to you?"

Knute broke in. "The first thing it says is that your wife is a perceptive person and a fine theologian. More people lose faith over affluence than poverty. Bright lights and good times make us think we can walk alone. Tough times and darkness make us long for God's light."

Donald picked up the Bible. "Mind if I respond to Knute's question? I am struck by the presence of death everywhere in this story. Perhaps it is because I've been thinking about death a lot lately, but I can even smell it. Martha says, 'Lord, already there is a stench because he has been dead four days.' It just seems to me that the odor is everywhere. People die before their time, often in tragic ways. Some are killed in accidents, while others inject death into their bodies through drugs, steroids, or alcohol. The money we so desperately need for life—for the care of the very young, the very old, and the very poor—is invested in weapons of death. The smell of death is everywhere."

Knute asked, "And do you see any hope?"

Donald nodded. " 'I am the resurrection and the life.' That is the hope. The hope isn't in humans, it is in God. God can bring life in the midst of death. God weeps over the death of his creation, just as Jesus wept, and just as David wept. But, of course, with this one important distinction; God is not willing to let death be the last word. Howard and Elsie are in the hands of God. That is a very great comfort."

It was Knute's turn. "The world uses death as a tool. Like the high priest says, it is a matter of expediency. He figures that it is no big deal that one person die so that the rest of the nation might not suffer. That is not so different from what our high priest, we call him president, said about the loss of life in Panama. Governments are willing to lose a few for the sake of the program. Governments also use death as a threat, like the Soviet tanks rolling through the streets of Lithuania. God uses death, too. He uses his own death in order that 'the scattered children of God might be made one.' "

David had listened intently to the exchange of the two men. "Donald is right. Death is everywhere. I started to feel nauseated when Elsie died. Since that time I have smelled death everywhere I went. When he read the story, it became overpowering. By the way, I'm feeling better."

Donald leaned over and hugged his friend. Tears filled David's eyes. "I'm afraid I have had a few things backwards. I have tried to be the resurrection and the life. It was not enough to point to the one who is resurrection. I had to have answers and I had to be strong. When I had no answers and no strength, I felt like people were blaming me, just as Martha blamed Jesus. But Donald and Iris don't need me to be their comfort. The one who is the resurrection and the life is comfort enough."

Knute nodded. "Even pastors need to hear the good news. Let me offer one more image from this story. I am struck by Lazarus coming forth from the grave, with the burial clothes wrapped around him. He has just been resurrected, but the signs of death were still evident. I see this as a parable of our time. We live by the grace and power of God, but death is still very much present. Jesus is the resurrection and the life, but we still live in a world of pain. Sickness, disease, anger, hatred, war—these are but a few of the burial clothes wrapped around us."

Knute let his words sink in before he concluded. "Jesus issues a command, 'Unbind him, and let him go.' We all need to be unwrapped. David needed to be unwrapped from his need to play God, because that is certainly death. Others need to be unwrapped from hatred or envy or greed, other bandages of death. The more deeply we enter into Jesus' life, the more deeply we need to experience resurrection."

The men finished their study about 10:30. At 12:45 David came home for lunch. Doris asked, "What did you do this morning?"

David laughed. "I got sick. And I got better. Seriously, after our study I went to the hospital to visit the little boy with leukemia. Then I made a visit at Ebenezer."

"I thought you just made those visits yesterday." she said.

"No, that was Robo-pastor. But today he got undressed. He took off a few bandages. It is amazing what you see when you take the wrapping off. It was wonderful. And you know what? It even smelled different today."

That is the good news from back home where this morning they are marveling over the great promise, "I am the resurrection and the life. Those who believe in me, even though they die, will live."

Suggestions for Worship

Call to Worship (Ps. 116:5-7):

PASTOR: Gracious is the LORD, and righteous;

PEOPLE: Our God is merciful.

PASTOR: When I was brought low, he saved me.

PEOPLE: Return, O my soul, to your rest, for the LORD has dealt bountifully with you.

Act of Praise: Psalm 116:1-9.

Suggested Hymns: "Stand Up, Stand Up for Jesus"; "There Is a Fountain Filled with Blood"; "Hymn of Promise."

Opening Prayer: Gracious God, we confess that we often choose death over life. We choose war over peace, anger over love, selfishness over sharing. Help us to so learn Christ's way of life that we will reject the way of death and show the power of the resurrection in all that we say and do, through your Son, Jesus Christ our Lord. Amen.

Pastoral Prayer: Creator God, we pray for this congregation and its leaders. Grant them a vision of your mission. Through their guidance let us feed the hungry, cloth the naked, and announce good news to the poor.

We commend into your hands, dear God, all those who need your gift of healing. Bless those who suffer bodily pain and restore them to wholeness. We pray for those who suffer the pain of separation from friends, family, or children. Assist us in being agents of your mercy and grace in their lives.

We pray for those who have wandered into the far country. Keep them safe and hasten the day when they will desire to return home. Upon their return, let this be a welcoming place, a place where we celebrate their return with rings, robes, sandals, and a party.

Remind us once again, good Lord, of the virtue of simplicity. Let us not pretend to be more than who we are, desire more than we need, spend more than we can afford, or consume more than is just. Let us find our completeness in you, as did our Savior, Jesus Christ, who for our sakes, became poor that he might make many rich.

Holy Father, kindle in the hearts of all your children the love of peace, guide the leaders of the nations, so that your kingdom will go forward in peace, and the earth will be filled with the knowledge of your love. Amen.

April 4, 1993

□

Passion/Palm Sunday

The entry into Jerusalem hails the beginning of Christ's reign. It is also the beginning of the final conflict, his passion and death.

The Sunday Lessons

Isaiah 50:4-9*a*: The prophet is not intimidated by insults and beatings. His devotion to God's message brings the might of God to this prophet. "It is the Lord God who helps me" (v. 9).
Philippians 2:5-11: This ancient hymn proclaims that Christ, though in the form of God, accepted our human condition and suffered and died. His humility resulted in his exaltation. "At the name of Jesus every knee should bend . . . and every tongue should confess that Jesus Christ is Lord" (vv. 10-11).
Matthew 21:1-11: Riding a donkey on a road carpeted by coats, Jesus entered Jerusalem amidst palms and praise. "Hosanna to the Son of David!" (v. 9). Matthew carefully notes Zechariah's prophecy, "Your king is coming to you" (v. 5).
Matthew 26:14–27:66: The passion and suffering of Christ through betrayal (Judas), denial (Peter), rejection (the crowd cried, "Crucify,"), beatings, taunting, and, finally desolation ("Why have you forsaken me?" [27:46].) ended in death. Then, the temple curtain was torn in two. The earth shook, and, no longer mocking, a soldier confessed, "Truly this man was God's Son" (27:54).

Interpretation and Imagination

Reversal and contradiction are rampant in the passion of Christ. The crowd that shouted, "Hosanna," soon shouted "Crucify." The steward became the betrayer. The bold Peter became a timid liar. Hope turned to despair. Joy became sorrow. Life became death.

There is in the midst of it all, however, another reversal that will deny contradiction. The victim becomes victor. The foolish king is King indeed. The mockery of soldiers is replaced by awe.

Ave crux—unica spes are ancient Latin words, long honored by the church. Hail Cross, our only hope! This, too, is a contradiction. In his book *The Power of the Powerless*, Jürgen Moltmann recalls the phrase and notes that hope means life and love, and that the cross is a disappointed hope, a betrayed love, a godforsaken death. Then he asks, "What has hope to do with the cross? How can a death become the foundation for a unique hope for living?"

Moltmann answers by reminding his readers that at "the centre of the Christian faith is a history: The history of the living and dying, death and resurrection of Christ. A history of Christ's passion."

Every great passion is marked by suffering. If we will not know sadness, we cannot know joy. If we could not feel pain, we could not know comfort. Without conflict there is no growth. True passion for a new order accepts the cost of it—obedience, suffering, disappointment, a cross.

Often, we want to turn back, deny it, wash our hands of it, but then, again, we're confronted by his cross. It always seems to be standing amid broken promises and broken dreams and above the ruins—the ruins of hate, injustice, selfishness, war, poverty, and death. Standing there, it makes the horizon. Hail cross, our only hope. (JKB)

THE TRAGIC TRIUMPH OF CHRIST

Matthew 21:1-11

A SERMON BY WILLIAM R. CANNON

The classical definition of tragedy is the depiction of a strong, dominant person struggling against forces that are sure to overcome and defeat that person. The climax of tragedy is not the defeat but rather the point at which the person almost succeeds. The climax in the human tragedy of the life of Jesus, which ended in the crucifixion, is Palm Sunday, when Jesus made his triumphal entry into Jerusalem and received the homage of its citizens as their king. At that point it appeared as if he had succeeded in establishing the kingdom of God on earth. At no other time in his career was his messiahship so generally and completely recognized as it was on Palm Sunday.

That day began in an act of amazing generosity. Jesus sent two disciples into a nearby village and told them that they would find a donkey and its colt tied outside a house there, which they were to unloose and bring to him. If the owner should object, all they had to say was, "The Lord needs them" (v. 3), and without further ado he would send them. And this is precisely what happened. Without asking the purpose or debating its merits, the owner of those animals sent them just because Jesus requested that he do so. He did not know the disciples, and they did not know him. But he knew Jesus, and that was enough. He realized that the needs of Jesus and his kingdom were more worthwhile and important than any needs of his own.

I was present with a pastor when he received an urgent call from his conference for financial help to meet an emergency. Immediately he picked up the phone and called certain of his members. All he said was: "This is your pastor. A dire need has arisen. Please write a check to help meet it and put it in the mail to me today." I was astounded at his action. His explanation was that they knew he would not call them unless he believed the cause he represented was worthy of their Christian charity. He said that they never failed to respond.

What a person gives in time, energy, and resources to the cause of Christ is more indicative of his or her commitment than anything else. We use the tithe as the minimum of our income to be given to God through the church, but this is applicable only to persons of very limited means and with heavy family obligations. People of ample means should give much more, giving to Christian charity as much, where possible, as they spend on themselves. "From everyone to whom much has been given," said our Lord, "much will be required" (Luke 12:48). John Wesley made this entry in his private diary less than eight months before his death: "As my sight fails me much, I do not purpose to keep any more Accounts. It suffices that I gain all I can, I save all I can, and I give all I can, that is, all I have" (John Wesley, *Journal*, ed. Nehemiah Curnock, Bicentenary Issue, Vol. VIII [London: Epworth Press, 1938], 83).

The glamor and glory of Palm Sunday lay in the enthusiastic welcome the people gave Jesus and the hospitality they showed him as he entered Jerusalem. The crowd that came down from Galilee with him swelled into a multitude when it was joined by the throngs that came out of the city to greet Jesus. Both those who came to meet him and those that followed him cut branches from the palm trees and strewed them in the road before him. This was the custom that the Jews practiced in those days to welcome a hero. They had done this a century earlier to honor Judas Maccabaeus after he had thrown off the oppressive yoke of the Seleucids and extricated the Temple from profanation by Antiochus Epiphanes, who had erected his own statue there. Our equivalent today would be the tape and confetti the citizens of New York City shower on our heroes as they parade down Broadway. General Eisenhower, for example, was given the biggest welcome anyone had ever received from New Yorkers, when he returned victorious over the Nazis in the Second World War. Likewise, presenting the keys of the city to a celebrity on a visit to our town is similar though far less significant, than the adoration shown to Jesus on Palm Sunday.

Some of the people actually took off their cloaks, the finest garments they owned, and spread them in the way before Jesus, allowing them to be trampled on by his donkey. Sir Walter Raleigh did the same thing when he threw his cape at the feet of Queen Elizabeth I to keep her from soiling her shoes in the mud. He would not have done this for just anybody. He did it because she was his queen. The people of Jerusalem did what they did because they recognized Jesus as the Messiah. They acknowledged him as their king. Consequently, they shouted their hosannas, which meant, "Save now, we beseech thee." They called him the Son of David, the one who comes in the name of the Lord, thereby recognizing him as their sovereign and welcoming the establishment of his kingdom in their midst. They pledged their allegiance and obedience to him.

Absolute obedience to Jesus Christ and allegiance to him and his kingdom before and above all other allegiances is the hallmark of being a Christian. Jesus is totalitarian in his rule over his followers. We either give him everything, including ourselves, or he will accept nothing from us. Our attestation of allegiance to him is null and void unless it is complete. Jesus said, "So likewise, whosoever of you does not forsake all that he has, cannot be My disciple" (Luke 14:33 NKJV).

Jesus' triumph on Palm Sunday would have been complete if this outward show of generosity, welcome, hospitality, submission, and obedience on the part of the people had been a genuine display of their inner feelings and the commitment of their total being to him and his kingdom. No doubt, the people thought it was and at the time acted sincerely in their response to him. But unfortunately, it was not. Their loyalty was short-lived. Before the end of the week they had changed their minds about him. On Friday, he, whom they had heralded as Messiah and king on Sunday, was denounced by them as imposter, rebel, and blasphemer, and deserving of death as a criminal. Jesus' triumph on Palm Sunday was tragic, all the more so, because it had been so glamorous and glorious, and because the very people who staged it were to betray him to his enemies in the end. He had no kingdom after all—that is an earthly one—for all his subjects either rebelled against him or deserted him. Like the last Roman emperor in battle with the Turks at the walls of Constantinople, he might well have opined, "What good is an emperor without an empire!"

The reason for this sudden reversal of the people in their attitude toward Jesus was that they had misunderstood the personality of their king and the nature of his kingdom. They expected him to be an all-powerful, temporal ruler, proud and mighty, triumphant over all their enemies, who would release them from Roman servitude. They expected his kingdom to displace the Roman Empire, making Jerusalem the capital and the center of world commerce, so that they would become rich and influential. They overlooked the fact that Jesus had ridden into the city on a donkey, the beast of burden, not on a white steed of conquest. And they forgot their own history. The judges had ridden white asses when they had gone about the country adjudicating the wrongs of the people and assuring justice by meting out judgment. Jesus portrayed kingship as servanthood: "The greatest among you will be your servant" (Matthew 23:11). And he demanded justice and righteousness just as the judges had done, for he drove the greedy merchants and money changers out of the Temple and overturned their tables of trade. His goal in life was holiness, not fame and fortune and victory over one's enemies. Because of all this, the people deserted him. They had followed him for what they had expected to get out of him; when he did not give them what they wanted, they left him. Jesus wanted them to give him their lives and with him, to serve God by serving God's people.

That is what Jesus wants of us as well. Jesus did not come to enrich his devotees with material goods, the comforts and conveniences that money can buy. Nor was his mission to empower his followers to rule over others and to attain eminence in the secular world. His religion is not a means of self-aggrandizement and worldly success. The greed and corruption that characterize contemporary society are the antithesis of his kingdom and the denial of his gospel. He taught that only the meek shall inherit the earth and that the pure in heart alone will be able to see God. Too many today confess his name while, by their behavior and business activity, they deny his precepts and make a caricature of his way of life. With our lips we declare Jesus' triumph over sin and death, but by our deeds we debase the triumph of Palm Sunday, turning it into the tragedy of Good Friday.

This Palm Sunday, may Christ enable us to see the attractiveness of holiness and sense the abiding joy of service to others and also give us the power of their fulfillment in our own lives, that his triumph may be ours both now and throughout eternity.

Suggestions for Worship

Call to Worship (Ps. 118:26-27):

PASTOR: Blessed is the one who comes in the name of the LORD.

PEOPLE: We bless you from the house of the LORD.

PASTOR: The LORD is God, and he has given us light.

PEOPLE: Bind the festal procession with branches, up to the horns of the altar.

Act of Praise: Psalm 118:19-29.

Suggested Hymns: "All Glory, Laud, and Honor"; "Were You There"; "Go to Dark Gethsemane."

Opening Prayer: O gracious God, who gave your Son recognition by the people of Jerusalem as their Savior and King on Palm Sunday, give us now the discernment to appreciate his mission to the world and to us today, and the grace to receive his blessings and use the benefits of his mission to your glory and the salvation of humankind. Amen.

Pastoral Prayer: O God, whose everlasting abode is heaven and yet whose reign is over all the earth, we thank you for your providence and your constant watch over us day and night, so that nothing we think or do escapes your notice and our every need is before your eyes. Satisfy our needs, we pray you, not according to what we desire, but according to what is best for us and is in keeping with your purpose for our lives. We realize our waywardness, the stubborn pursuit of our own ends, the greed and callousness toward the welfare of others we display in our daily activity, our selfishness, and our inward and outward sin. We degrade the name of Christ by pretending to follow him when in reality we chart our own course and seek success and fame as the secular world defines them. Forgive us, we pray, and transform us into new persons after the pattern of Christ. We pray for the church, that she may live as his faithful bride and be his true agency in the redemption of the world. Help us to be a help to others, seeking like our Saviour to heal the sick, strengthen the weak, be company to the lonely, enrich the poor and provide them with work and the means of accomplishment, and bring to all the solace of your gospel. We pray, O Lord, for peace with justice and respect for human rights in all parts of the world. Help us to treat our enemies as if they were our friends. All this we pray in the strong name of Jesus. Amen.

April 11, 1993

□

Easter Day

We have watched earthbound saviors from beginning to end, and we know how little they finally leave us. The risen Christ leaves empty tombs, resurrection, life.

The Sunday Lessons

Acts 10:34-43: Peter preached at Caesarea, where Cornelius and the first Gentiles believed and were baptized. His compelling argument was that he and others "were chosen by God as witnesses, and who ate and drank with him after he rose from the dead" (v. 41).
Colossians 3:1-4: Because of the victory that Christ has won for us, we need not be bound by such earthly things as immortality, evil desire, and covetousness. Dead to this world, our devotion centers on heaven's very best. "Set your minds on things that are above" (v. 2).
John 20:1-18: John's Gospel records eyewitness accounts of the empty tomb and the risen Christ. Mary saw the stone "had been removed from the tomb" (v. 1). Peter and John went inside and noted the empty gravecloths, "and he saw and believed" (v. 8). The weeping Mary Magdalene looked in to see two angels. Meeting one she thought to be a gardener, she heard Jesus speak her name. "Go to my brothers and say to them, 'I am ascending to my Father and your Father' " (v. 17).

Interpretation and Imagination

Two great questions come with the gift of life. We will face them whether we want to or not. The first is this: How to do the right thing and avoid doing what is wrong. The second is, Will death and dying be the end for me? Easter is the Christian answer to these questions when it asks, "Grave, where is your victory," and reminds us that "the sting of death is sin . . . sin defeated by the victory of Christ."

In first-century Jerusalem, a real man, Jesus, lived out these questions in the middle of the human story that is still our story. God was being thwarted by evil; love was challenged by hate; life was mocked by death. For a broken-hearted woman and two frightened men, the first Easter morning was heavy with defeat. Then Mary saw the risen Lord. We also sing, "The strife is over. The victory is won."

What evidence is there that death is defeated, that the powers of wrong are set aside? Even today, people will weep beside graves.

The evidence offered in the first century is still the compelling evidence of the twentieth. Men and women who saw and believed shared the good news. If it were a vague hope, their story would have been silenced in a month. "People won't believe it. I know what I saw, but I just don't speak of it anymore," was the plaintive despair of one uncertain dreamer. Not so for those who witnessed the power of Easter. They went to their deaths certain about life. Today, the evidence of resurrection is in the goodness and vitality of Christian men and women in whose lives Christ reigns forever. (JKB)

GLORIOUS EASTER!

John 20:1-18

A SERMON BY WILLIAM R. CANNON

Easter is the most glorious day in the Christian year. Though Christmas is almost equally venerated as the anniversary of our Savior's birth and signal of the Son of God coming into the world to save us from our sins, Easter testifies to the success of his mission. For on that day he conquered our worst enemy, death, and rose in victory from the grave, conferring on us the benefits of his triumph. "But in fact Christ has been raised from the dead," Paul proclaims, "the first fruits of those who have died. For since death came through a human being the resurrection of the dead has also come through a human being; for as all die in Adam, so all will be made alive in Christ" (I Cor. 15:20-22).

Unlike other major religions, Christianity bases its claims not on ideas and their attractiveness, but on historical events, on hard facts, on incidents that actually took place and made their impact on those who witnessed them. "We declare to you what was from the beginning, what we have heard, what we have seen with our eyes, what we have looked at and touched with our hands, concerning the word of life" (I John 1:1).

The greatest of such events—indeed, the greatest event in all history, secular as well as sacred—is the resurrection of Jesus Christ from the dead. His resurrection relegates death to only an incident in life, merely a point in its continuity and development, not its fatal end. It demonstrates our transition through death from the temporal to the eternal and out of the carnal into the spiritual, and introduces us to a new realm of existence in the everlasting kingdom of God. "When this perishable body puts on imperishability, and this mortal body puts on immortality, then the saying that is written will be fulfilled: 'Death has been swallowed up in victory' " (I Cor. 15:54).

Therefore, on this Easter Sunday we shall consider the gospel account of the resurrection as narrated by John. Mary Magdalene was the person who made its discovery—that is, the one who found Jesus' tomb empty, which had to be accounted for. She was a woman, and in the patriarchal society of that day, women were subservient to men. A report from a woman would have been questionable, especially a report about an event so extraordinary that it defied common sense. That is, no doubt, why she ran to find some of the disciples to corroborate her discovery and verify her findings. Nonetheless, it was she, not they, who made the discovery, which goes to show what an important part a woman played in the beginning of the Christian faith and in the origin of our religion. Just as the Virgin Mary gave birth to our Savior and nourished him in his infancy, so Mary Magdalene, when everyone thought that Jesus' life had ended on the cross, was the first to discover that his tomb was empty. It was her devotion to the person who had rescued her from sin that caused her to stand by him during his crucifixion, even when all but one of his disciples had deserted him, and, when he had died, to help Nicodemus and Joseph of Arimathea wrap his body in spices and place it in the sepulcher. Now, on the day after the Sabbath, it was her love for Jesus that brought her back again to his grave while it was still dark, so that she might pay her respects to her departed friend.

Peter and John came themselves to the sepulcher to see with

their own eyes what Mary Magdalene had described to them. When they had seen for themselves, they had no option but to believe her report. And so they went back to tell the others what had happened. But the truth is they did not really know what had happened. They, like Mary Magdalene, assumed that Jesus' body had been removed from Joseph of Arimathea's sepulcher and placed in some less pretentious grave. They did not remain in the garden. They did not make any effort whatever to ascertain the facts in the situation, to find out how the removal had taken place and where Jesus' body had been buried. They forgot he had told them that he would rise again from the dead. They thought their career with him had ended with his crucifixion.

Mary, in contrast to the disciples, remained in the garden, more concerned than ever over what had happened to the body of her Lord. She had discovered the empty tomb; but like Peter and John, she had not discerned the reason why it was empty. She had gone to the sepulcher that morning, looking for the corpse of Jesus and had made a remarkable discovery. But she did not know what it was she had discovered.

This was also true of Columbus. He discovered a new world, but he did not realize it. He had sailed from Spain expecting to find a new route to the Indies. What he found was not the Indies, but the previously undiscovered Western Hemisphere. Two more continents, as a result of his voyage, were added to the western geographers' map of the world. Teresa of Avila thought she had found solitude in the silence of her cell in the convent. But what she really found in that silence was not solitude, but the vision of God, which in middle age threw her, body and soul, into the hurly-burly of the world. She worked determinedly till the day she died, against fierce opposition, to achieve what she took to be the will of God for Spanish monasticism, confessing in old age, "My body is old and weak, but my desires are still young and vigorous."

Mary stood at the sepulcher, weeping and lamenting the loss of Jesus. Even the sight of two angels and their salutation did not console her. When Jesus came up behind her, she did not recognize him, but thought he was the gardener and asked him what he had done with the body of her master. Jesus had to disclose himself to Mary before she recognized him and realized he was alive.

The resurrection of Jesus from the grave is a historical fact for Christians. The evidence for it was the empty tomb and a missing body, which no one had removed and was nowhere to be found. The most convincing evidence, of course, was that the person whose corpse had been buried was alive and visiting once again with his friends.

But the heart of this Gospel lesson is that all Mary Magdalene could discover on her own was the empty tomb. Jesus had to take the initiative and disclose himself to her before she could grasp the fact that he had risen from the dead. Discovery in itself is inadequate in matters that pertain to our understanding of God and his relationship to us, and the purpose he has for our lives. Our resolve to find God is important and will carry us a long way on our religious quest. But then God must meet us on the way, come up to us and call us by name, as Jesus did Mary Magdalene in the garden. He must enable us to know that it is he, so that we cannot help crying out in submission and joy as she did, Rabboni, Master. "Faith" in the living Christ, though dependent upon the fact of Jesus' resurrection, is, nonetheless, a personal gift from God to us.

It is important to observe that the announcement of Jesus' birth was made publicly. It was good news for all the world. The angel proclaimed, "I am bringing you good news of great joy for all the people" (Luke 2:10). The resurrection, or at least the verification of it, was a private event. The risen Christ appeared only to his devoted followers, not to the general public. Paul indicates that the most who ever saw him in his post-resurrection state on earth was just above five hundred people, all of whom were his followers (I Cor. 15:6). Others might have ascertained from the examination of eternal evidence that the resurrection had taken place, but they could not see and hear the risen Christ unless he chose to disclose himself to them. The guards at the sepulcher felt the earthquake and witnessed the angel roll back the stone from the entrance and knew the resurrection was taking place, but they never saw the risen Christ.

The good news that Christ was alive and that his power and grace were still available to those who believe had to come through witnesses—those who had actually seen him and been in his presence. The first of these was Mary Magdalene. After she had discovered the empty tomb and had her discovery verified by Peter and John, then had seen and talked with her risen Master, she went immediately to the disciples and told them all that had happened. Their risen Lord then came to them and dealt with them as he had with Mary Magdalene in the garden. And it was their declaration of the Easter events that convinced the minds and won the hearts of others, and thereby produced the Christian faith. The reliability of their testimony was confirmed by their adherence to it. Their declaration that Jesus rose from the grave and came back to them caused them to be ridiculed, mocked, despised, persecuted, and even put to death, until the world began to realize that people will not endure what they endured to disseminate a falsehood, nor will they suffer martyrdom to promote a lie. Because of its results, the resurrection of Jesus from death and the grave is reckoned to be one of the most reliable events in all history.

But if it is just a historical event to us, like the Battle of Hastings or even the American Revolution, something to be known and discussed, we have missed entirely the glory of Easter and denied ourselves its power and its life. As Augustine observed, in his conversation with Alypius before their conversion, the unlearned, by accepting Christ as their Saviour, start up and take heaven by force, while they with all their learning continue only to debate and discuss and delay. Easter becomes glorious for us, not in our recalling what happened at Jesus' tomb on that first Easter, but in what we allow to happen to us this Easter day by inviting anew the risen Christ into our lives, and loving and serving and proclaiming him as Mary Magdalene did so long ago. "Blessed are those who have not seen and yet have come to believe" (John 20:29).

Suggestions for Worship

Call to Worship (Ps. 118:14-17, 24):

PASTOR: The LORD is my strength and my might; he has become my salvation.

PEOPLE: There are glad songs of victory in the tents of the righteous:

PASTOR: "The right hand of the LORD does valiantly."

PEOPLE: I shall not die, but I shall live, and recount the deeds of the LORD.

PASTOR: This is the day that the LORD has made;

PEOPLE: Let us rejoice and be glad in it.

Act of Praise: Psalm 118:14-24.

Suggested Hymns: "Christ the Lord Is Risen Today"; "Up from the Grave He Arose"; "The Day of Resurrection."

Opening Prayer: O God, who brought from death to life your Son, Jesus Christ, and made him to be our Savior and our Lord, enable us this Easter to experience anew his presence in our lives and to follow him all our days on earth that we may live with him forever in heaven. Amen.

Pastoral Prayer: O God, whose power and glory and whose majesty and dominion were manifested in the fullness of creation so that all might believe, through the resurrection of your Son, our Lord and Savior Jesus Christ, we gather in your presence this Easter Sunday to thank you for that inestimable gift. We join our voices with the heavenly hosts in magnifying and praising your holy name both now and forever more. In doing this, we realize our unworthiness and we confess our many sins and manifold wickedness. We know that we do not deserve your attention, and we feel uncomfortable in your presence. Yet we take confidence in the knowledge that it is your disposition always to have mercy. Forgive us our sins, we pray, have mercy on us for Jesus Christ's sake, and give us the will and power always to please you. We pray, not only for ourselves, but also for others, remembering that if we concern ourselves with the welfare of our friends only, our devotion to you is incomplete, for you taught us to love our enemies. Bring about through us, we pray, the realization of the ideals of your heavenly kingdom here on earth, so that peace, justice, and love will prevail among us. Hear our prayer, O God, for we pray it in the name of Jesus Christ, our risen Savior. Amen.

April 18, 1993

□

Second Sunday of Easter

We are like Thomas. We weren't there when it happened. We are like the first readers of I Peter. We despair because the eschaton is delayed, and we doubt that it's coming. Converts from doubt to faith are given words to profess—"My Lord and my God."

The Sunday Lessons

Acts 2:14a, 22-32: This lesson is a part of Peter's sermon at Pentecost. "This man . . . you crucified. . . . But God raised him up" (vv. 23-24). Psalms 16 is quoted, "My flesh will live in hope" (v. 26), even though the psalmist David died and was buried.

I Peter 1:3-9: Peter's letter, written to encourage those who would face persecution, begins with the theme of a "living hope through the resurrection." The words of verse 8, "though you do not see him now, you believe in him," remind us of the Gospel reading for this day.

John 20:19-31: Jesus appeared to the disciples in the evening and greeted them, saying, "Peace be with you" (v. 19). Thomas, who was not there, was told of the appearance and said, "Unless I see the mark of the nails in his hands . . . I will not believe" (v. 25). After his confession of faith, the Lord says, "Blessed are those who have not seen and yet have come to believe."

Interpretation and Imagination

"Please! Won't someone just say what really happened! What's the truth of the matter. Can anyone tell me?" The reports were vague, and this man who hated ambiguity wanted certainty.

Thomas wasn't content with hearsay. He wanted to see for himself. Most of us are like Thomas; we want assurance.

Such fear and suspicion about the unknown prompt a narrow and rigid mentality, not only in religion, but also in economics, foreign policy, politics. Variance cannot be tolerated, and categories too confining for reality block out truth.

When one is in a lively debate, one is likely not in the presence of timid uncertainties, but rather among those who believe. Honest doubts are not evidence of weakness but of strength. How blessed are those who have not seen but believe. Yet it is the experience of many followers of Christ that as a believer stands in the position of assurance, he or she is simultaneously engaged in a continuing struggle with doubt.

Then comes the day when we know in whom we believe. The matter is settled. Jesus Christ is Lord. He is Victor. For the person of faith, the quarreling ends. Singular truth is known in spite of diversity. Doubt itself expresses faith. (JKB)

THE HOLY WEEK VISITOR

John 20:19-29

A SERMON BY WILLIAM R. WHITE

Just one year ago, March 31, Maundy Thursday evening, at about ten o'clock, Pam Nesheim breathed a sigh of relief and sat down at the piano. It had been a long day and she had finally managed to get the children to bed. Her husband Rick, a nervous wreck for most of Holy Week, was upstairs working on his Good Friday sermon. Rick, who never looked forward to preaching, found Holy Week with its four sermons in eight days pure torture. Playing the piano was a release for Pam who worried whenever Rick worried. Did he really have the stuff to be a pastor?

As she began to play "Moonlight Sonata," she heard pounding near the back of the house, and the door open noisily. Pam leaped from the piano, dashed to the kitchen, and discovered a small man with a very large beard weaving into the room. He knocked over a chair and leaned on the kitchen sink. Melanchton, the Nesheim's large dog, wagged his tail and began to lick the stranger's hand. Pam edged her way to the stairs and tried not to sound as frightened as she felt. "Rick" she shouted, "could you come down here? Immediately! We have a guest."

By the time Rick got downstairs, he found the guest sitting at the kitchen table, quite confused and quite intoxicated.

Melanchton had his shaggy head buried in the man's lap. "Rick," Pam said, "do you know Delbert Matson?"

"People call me Fuzzy," the man mumbled. "Your wife tells me this is the Lutheran parsonage. You ain't lived here too long."

"Just over four years," Rick replied.

"I'm an atheist," Fuzzy said emphatically.

At that moment Rick was more concerned about the man's sobriety and the occasion of the visit than he was his faith. "What brings you out our way?" he asked.

"Best I can remember, I'm headed home."

"Where's home?" Rick inquired.

" 'Bout half a mile south of the Hanson farm on Country Trunk B."

"You must be a neighbor of Marie Bolstad."

"Neighbor! I'm her brother. Moved in with her five years ago when Milt died. Horrible thing it was too. That's another reason I ain't a believer. Why'd God do a thing like that to Milt? Left Marie with a big farm and no kids to help. You call that fair?" Fuzzy shook his finger at the pastor to accent his sentences.

Marie Bolstad, a small woman who sat two rows from the back in church each Sunday, always looked tired. Rick knew she was a widow who farmed alone, but had no idea that she lived with a brother.

Pam reentered after leaving to check on the children. "Delbert, I don't see a car outside. How did you get here?" The parsonage was located on a small hill about a quarter of a mile from their rural church and over a half mile from the nearest family.

Fuzzy looked puzzled, "I was driving when I left The Boondocks. I've really got myself in hot water this time. Marie will be ashamed of me again."

Pam looked at Rick with alarm. The Boondocks, a seedy bar, was more than six miles from their home. Rather than find out more about transportation, she asked, "Who would like coffee?"

"We both would," Rick answered. Pam was surprised. Rick had never drunk a cup of coffee in the ten years she had known him. Later, when the story was finally told, she discovered Fuzzy didn't drink coffee either. That night both drank for the sake of the other.

As they sat around the kitchen table Fuzzy told his story. His father died when he was 11. All through high school and for two years after graduation, he worked with Doc Benson, a veterinarian. In order to avoid the army, he enlisted in the Navy and a year later was assigned to duty in Vietnam.

One day in Vietnam, he and a buddy, Goose, were riding watch on a small boat traveling up a river looking for snipers, when a sniper found Goose. "The day they sent Goose home in a bag I got drunk and stayed that way until they sent me home," he cried.

"You must have been frightened to death," Rick said, absorbed in the story.

"Frightened, powerfully lonely, and mad," Fuzzy insisted. "Nobody understood that I had lost my best friend. Nobody cared that I had only one good buddy and he was dead. Right then and there I decided not to believe in God anymore. And I haven't."

"You think God is dead?" Pam asked.

"If he ain't, he doesn't want to get involved."

For nearly an hour Fuzzy poured out one bitter story after another. He told of employers, neighbors, and friends who turned against him once he came home. He was critical of everyone but Marie.

When Fuzzy seemed to be more alert, Rick took his guest home. Marie came to the door, saw her brother standing with her pastor and cried, "Fuzzy, every day you find a new way to embarrass me."

Before Rick left that night he offered to help Fuzzy search for his pickup the next morning. At Fuzzy's request, Rick arrived at the Bolstad place about 7:30 A.M., before too many people were on the road. They found the pickup three miles from the parsonage, keys in the ignition and the gas tank empty. It was nearly ten o'clock by the time they gassed up the old truck and waved good-bye.

That night as he stood greeting people at the door for Good Friday services, Rick saw Marie accompanied by a small man in a suit. It was Fuzzy. As he entered the church he whispered to Rick, "Don't get your hopes up. I'm doing this for Marie."

The sermon for Good Friday was based on the words of Jesus, "My God, my God, why have you forsaken me?" Rick told the people that the cross was a place of loneliness for God, who lost his only son. "The cross is a sign of God's solidarity with all the abandoned of the world," the pastor continued. "Sin separates us from others and God. The cross unites us."

Sugar Valley Lutheran Church, where Rick serves, is on the edge of the unincorporated village of Prairie, five miles west of Blackhawk. The village consists of a grocery store, cafe, hardware store, a tavern, and about 190 people.

By Saturday morning, when Rick stopped by Disrud's Grocery, all 190 people knew the story of the pastor's Thursday night visitor. "Heard you worked late Thursday night," Milt Disrud said cheerfully as Rick entered the store. Before he left town a half dozen people stopped him to tell a Fuzzy story. A kind and gentle man before he went into the service, Fuzzy was radically different when he returned from Vietnam. "He can't keep a job, pastor," one man confided. "When something goes wrong, and it always does, it is always someone else's fault. Each time people fire him he gets more bitter."

"I always thought he ought to be a veterinarian," a lady whispered. "There isn't an animal in the county that won't lay at his feet." Rick smiled as he thought of Melanchton's quiet greeting.

On Easter, Fuzzy was in church again. And again he went out of his way to speak to Rick. "An hour listening to your nonsense is a small price to pay for peace at home," Fuzzy explained.

As Rick told the story of Easter from Mark's Gospel, he focused on the angel's message to the women, "Go, tell his disciples and Peter that he is going ahead of you to Galilee; there you will see him, just as he told them."

"Even though Peter and the disciples had betrayed and denied Jesus; he still kept his promise to them. Easter hope is even for those who deny God," he said.

During communion Fuzzy sat alone, perhaps the only person in the white frame church who did not come to the altar.

On Monday morning, Pam's mom arrived to take care of the children, allowing Rick and Pam to spend a couple of days in Madison. On Thursday morning, his first day back in the office, Rick saw an old pickup turn into the church's parking lot. It was Fuzzy.

Rick met him at the door and invited him in. Instead he pushed his yellow "Renk's Seeds" cap back on his head and leaned against the wall. "You preachers ain't used to a normal work week, eh?" he said with a smile on his face. "Work three and take off three."

Rick thought about explaining that he always took a couple days off after Easter, but just smiled.

"I know you took aim at me last week," Fuzzy said becoming more serious. "But it didn't work. I still don't believe. God is cruel. He lets too many good people die." He stared at the pastor, letting his words sink in.

Rick didn't wait long to break the silence. "Don't you beat all, Fuzzy. You claim you don't believe in God and then you get mad at him. You sure burn up a lot of energy being angry at someone who doesn't exist."

Fuzzy squinted his eyes and stared at the pastor with a puzzled expression.

Rick spoke softly. "Fuzzy, I don't know what happened in Vietnam, but I know you've been mad at the wrong person for a lot of years. I wasn't taking aim at you on Good Friday, but this much I'll tell you, your heart wasn't the only one that broke when Goose was killed. The cross is God's way of participating in all of the pain in this world."

Neither man spoke for a long time. Then Rick said quietly, "I expect that someday you'll face God when you face yourself, including your drinking."

Fuzzy didn't reply. He just stared impassively at the pastor. Then he turned, walked to the pickup, and drove away.

When he got home that night Rick told Pam, "I'm afraid we've seen the last of Fuzzy for a while."

Rick was wrong. The next Sunday Fuzzy was in church again. The next Monday he was at the pastor's office again. This time when he was invited into the study, he entered wordlessly and sat down.

"I didn't have a very good day yesterday," he began. "In fact I didn't have a good night either. Part way through church, I figured out what was happening. It wasn't you aiming at me, it was God. He looked me straight in the eye and said, 'Put your finger here, and put your hand in my side. Don't be faithless, believe.' Not only did he say it once, he said it over and over again to me and Thomas."

Rick interrupted. "Who is Thomas?"

Fuzzy looked surprised. "You know, the disciple. Finally, about midnight both of us, me and Thomas, took him up on his offer and stuck our hand into his wound. When I pulled mine out it was dripping blood. Before you could blink me and Thomas cried out together, 'My Lord and my God.' "

The little man began to cry. Then he sobbed. Finally he looked up and said. "I'm ready to get help. Please."

That was a year ago. It has been a rocky but fruitful twelve months for Fuzzy. Two days after he left Pastor's Nesheim's office he entered a detoxification program. As he said, he was ready. He was ready to stop blaming others, including God, for what had happened. He was willing to listen to others, particularly at AA meetings, which he attended faithfully. He was willing to listen to God. And he was willing to stop trying to do everything himself. He was also ready to be a part of a community, which he found at Sugar Valley.

April, May, and June were rocky, but in July Fuzzy was hired as an assistant to a young vet in Blackhawk. The young doctor has been patient, and Fuzzy has improved his work habits every month.

Last Tuesday Rick approached his new friend with a request. "The story of Thomas is the gospel again for the Sunday after Easter. I wondered if you would be willing to read it in church."

Fuzzy responded immediately. "It sure has become my favorite story. Yah, I'll read it." Then he smiled and concluded, "And while I'm up there I might say something else. I might say something about amazing grace and the Lord's offer for us to turn from doubt to faith. Maybe this year someone else will put his hand in the Lord's side."

Suggestions for Worship

Call to Worship (I Pet. 1:3-4, 8):

PASTOR: Blessed be the God and Father of our Lord Jesus Christ!

PEOPLE: By his great mercy he has given us a new birth into a living hope through the resurrection of Jesus Christ from the dead,

PASTOR: And into an inheritance that is imperishable, undefiled, and unfading, kept in heaven for you.

PEOPLE: Although you have not seen him, you love him; and even though you do not see him now, you believe in him and rejoice with an indescribable and glorious joy.

Act of Praise: Psalm 16:5-11.

Suggested Hymns: "Christ Is Risen"; "He Lives"; "Christ Is Alive."

Opening Prayer: We confess, dear God, that we are in bondage to sin and cannot free ourselves. Our attempts to take control of our lives and the lives of others has ended in failure. Our only hope is that through your grace we may be restored to wholeness, through your Son, Jesus Christ our Lord.

Pastoral Prayer: Risen and everliving Lord, we praise you for the hope you have brought us by your resurrection. You have conquered death and given us the assurance that we shall one day stand before your throne with the faithful of all time, and praise you with an undying and perfect love.

As spring brings new signs of life to the earth around us, let this Easter season bring new vitality to your universal church. We pray that we, your holy church, will be strengthened to assist the nations in beating swords into plowshares, feeding the hungry and giving hope to the oppressed. Let us love justice more than we love comfort, and peace more than personal position.

O God, the giver of all life, look with love upon the fathers and mothers of this congregation. Let them look at their children with wonder and joy. Make them teachers and examples of faith for their children, so they may share with their children the salvation you have prepared for them through Jesus Christ.

We give you thanks, great God, for the gift of music and those who bring it to us. We thank you for those who accompany, those who play instruments, and those who sing. Through their gifts here on earth, help us to glimpse your beauty in the life to come.

All these things, and whatever else you see that we need, grant us, dear God, for the sake of him who died and rose again, Jesus Christ our Lord. Amen.

April 25, 1993

□

Third Sunday of Easter

More times than we would like to admit, our congregations gather feeling, "There's nobody here but us folks." Hearts may be strangely warmed—indeed they may burn within us as we recognize the risen Christ in our midst.

The Sunday Lessons

Acts 2:14*a*, 36-47: This is a record of the response to Peter's sermon preached on the first Pentecost. Many were baptized and then "devoted themselves to the apostles' teaching and fellowship, to the breaking of bread and the prayers" (v. 42). A sense of awe was everywhere (v. 43).

I Peter 1:17-23: "If you say 'Our Father,' you must stand in awe of him," who judges each. Through the living Word of God, you have been born anew of immortal parentage. We aren't ransomed with perishable stuff like silver and gold.

Luke 24:13-35: Two disciples on the road to Emmaus were joined by the risen Lord. At first they failed to recognize him, but then knew him in the breaking of bread. "Were not our hearts burning within us . . . while he was opening the scriptures to us?" (v. 32).

Interpretation and Imagination

The essential elements of Christian worship are Word and Sacrament. Protestants have tended to emphasize the Word as the primary manifestation of Christ's presence. Roman Catholics have emphasized the Mass as the truest presence of the risen Christ. In recent times Protestants and Catholics alike have recognized the importance of both Word and Sacrament. The story recorded by Luke lifts up the bread blessed and broken and Scriptures taught and explained as a meeting place with the risen Christ.

From time to time, I attend meetings where nobody's there.

Oh, to be sure, many seats are occupied, and there are numerous replies of "present" when the roll is called; but there is no authentic presence. Conversations, reports, and speeches are mostly empty phrases that fail to command either attention or action.

At other times I've been in a real meeting where word is an event and language is a happening. An eventful word is "You're fired." That gets your attention and something happens. A language happening is "I love you." Suddenly ears really hear and eyeballs become windows right into the soul.

Some of the best meetings—those where we know we are indeed together—have at their center the sharing of bread. Sometimes it happens in church, and there's the strange warmth from the mysterious presence of the risen Lord. Sometimes it happens when I no longer hear the voice of the preacher, but the other voice saying, "You're eternally mine. You weren't bought with silver or gold, but with blood." (JKB)

THE WALK TO EMMAUS

Luke 24:13-35

A SERMON BY WILLIAM KELLON QUICK

Over a period of forty days, the Gospels chronicle a series of resurrection appearances of the living Christ. Yet until we discover what they mean, our lives—yours and mine—will not be deepened by the spiritual impact of these events.

The followers of Jesus were perplexed, baffled, sad and fearful. Jesus was dead. His voice was silenced. Hope had given way to despair. Let's try to relive the story.

The women on that Easter morn, according to Luke, had gone to anoint the body of Jesus but found only an empty tomb. They hastened to tell "the eleven disciples and all the rest" what they had found, but "the apostles thought that what the women said was nonsense, and they did not believe them" (v. 9, GNB).

The scene now shifts from the women to two followers of Jesus on their way to the village of Emmaus. They walked, hearts heavy with grief.

I have walked that same road. When I made my first pilgrimage to Israel, I asked an Arab Christian, whose family's

Palestinian roots go back over a thousand years in the Holy Land, "Is there any place one can be reasonably assured of walking where Jesus walked?" I have been skeptical, you see, about people who go to the Holy Land and come back with slides to tell of "walking where Jesus walked." Two thousand years of shifting sands, the destruction of the old city of Jerusalem, and the radical changes brought by twenty centuries had convinced me that this was an impossibility.

He quickly responded, "There are two historic sites where I am convinced you can do just that. One is the steps to what we know today as the Church of the Cockcrow. The other is the Old Roman road in the ancient village of Emmaus. The ancient stone road was built by Rome long before Jesus was born."

"I'll take you," he said, typical of Christian Palestinian hospitality.

On the way I learned there are two Emmaus villages. One is spoken of by the Jewish historian Josephus, some four miles from Jerusalem, chosen by Vespasian as the site for a colony of Roman soldiers. The other is off the Jaffa Road.

He took me to the old village of Emmaus and I walked that historic Roman-built road with the remains of the massive wine vats and oil presses on either side. "The wine of Emmaus was so famous" my Palestinian host said, "that folks as far away as Spain bought wine from this village."

Of course, we cannot authenticate this stretch of road to Emmaus. But the Gospel tells us that, following the Crucifixion, two dispirited disciples walked this road on the journey back home from Jerusalem.

Cleopas and his companion, later given the name Simon, are reliving the tragedy of Passover week, climaxed by the scene on Golgotha. Conversing about those tragic events then is just as normal as when a loved one dies today, and we want to know all we can learn about the circumstances leading to their death. Rather curiously we want to recount the final earthly events before the death of one we loved.

The Emmaus travelers are suddenly joined by a stranger who walks beside them. When questioned about their discussion, they are shocked by his apparent ignorance and express surprise that anyone living in Jerusalem could be unaware of recent happenings.

They share the reasons they are downcast. Jesus of Nazareth, whom they had expected to deliver Israel from its present occupation by Roman troops and bring in the kingdom of God, is dead! Rumors had reached them that the tomb was empty. Jesus, however, had not been seen. Disappointment is echoed in their words, "We had hoped that he was the one. . . ."

Then the stranger rebuked them for their slowness in believing the prophets. They invite him to their home, and in taking the loaf at table, blessing and breaking the bread, he discloses himself to their astonished eyes. In joyous disbelief they recognize him, and then he vanishes out of sight.

What lessons can we learn as late-twentieth-century modern Christians from this immortal story?

First, many of us rejoice in good news but are often reluctant to share it. I have been turned off by the popular religious slogan, "Keep the Faith." Now, if one is speaking of remaining steadfast and true to the Christ of the gospel, then by all means, do so! As far as I am concerned, however, Christians should be encouraged, and sent forth to "*Share* the Faith."

The faith is meant to be shared. Obviously, we cannot share something that is foreign to us. Harry Denman, perhaps the greatest twentieth-century lay-evangelist in Methodism, was fond of saying, "There are two things a person cannot do. You cannot tell someone something you don't know. You cannot lead someone where you are not going."

To share the faith means a Christian is available to other people:

- like Andrew, who brought his brother, Peter, to Christ;
- like the woman at the well who ran to her village with the good news, "Come and see a man who told me everything I have ever done!" (John 4:29);
- like Peter and John encountering the man who was a cripple from birth, "I have no silver or gold, but what I have I give you" (Acts 3:6);
- like Zacchaeus who climbed a tree to see Jesus but whom Jesus saw first and then invited himself to Zacchaeus's house;
- like a zealot named Saul who, when blinded, gave himself in endless journeyings to take the gospel to Jew and Gentile, male and female, bond and free.

To share the faith means we translate belief in Jesus into concern and action. We are available to others.

To read the accounts of the post-resurrection appearances is one thing. To sense the overwhelming presence of a living Christ is quite another. One can treasure what one reads, but one is compelled to share intense experiences. I've experienced no greater joy in thirty-seven years as a pastor than to see men and women discover the loving presence of Jesus and translate that presence into compassionate ministry, which finds expression in significant, loving service.

A second lesson we can learn from the Emmaus story is the way Jesus reveals himself to us in simple and ordinary acts. It is a staggering revelation to learn that these two—Cleopas and Simon—were not in the Upper Room. They were not among the twelve apostles. But obviously, they had been present in some setting with Jesus during his ministry, and now he is present in their home in Emmaus.

Jesus had come into their home at their invitation. They share an ordinary meal in an ordinary Jewish house, with an ordinary loaf of bread. In this act, as Jesus breaks the bread, these men recognize him.

What a lesson! We believe Christ is present at the Communion table. He is also present at the table in our own homes. To emphasize the reality of his presence, I frequently pray as a part of the grace before meals, "O Christ, who oft revealed yourself in the breaking of bread, remind us that you are with us in this moment at this table." He is not only host in his church, he is the guest—the unseen guest—in every home.

This story speaks to us about the gift of hospitality. Hospitality *is* a gift. These men might never have recognized Jesus had they not invited him into their home! Do we hesitate to invite him? He waits for that invitation. Christ will never force his way into any heart. There are dispirited people all about us. Why not invite Jesus into your home, into your heart?

Albert Schweitzer is considered by many to be the greatest missionary of the twentieth century. Schweitzer reminds us:

> He comes to us as One unknown, without a name, as of old, by the lakeside, He came to those men who knew Him not. He speaks to us the same word: "Follow thou me!" and sets us to the tasks

which He has to fulfil for our time. He commands. And to those who obey Him, whether they be wise or simple, He will reveal Himself in the toils, the conflicts, the sufferings which they shall pass through in His fellowship, and, as an ineffable mystery, they shall learn in their own experience Who He is.
(Albert Schweitzer, *The Quest of the Historical Jesus* [London: A. & C. Black, 1922] 401).

Suggestions for Worship

Call to Worship (Ps. 116:12-14, 16; I Pet. 1:23):

PASTOR: What shall I return to the LORD for all his bounty to me?

PEOPLE: I will lift up the cup of salvation and call on the name of the LORD;

PASTOR: I will pay my vows to the LORD in the presence of all his people.

PEOPLE: O LORD, I am your servant; I am your servant, . . . You have loosed my bonds.

PASTOR: You have been born anew, not of perishable but of imperishable seed, through the living and enduring word of God.

Act of Praise: Psalm 116:12-19.

Suggested Hymns: "Come, Christians, Join to Sing"; "Come, Ye Faithful, Raise the Strain"; "Thine Be the Glory."

Opening Prayer: O risen and blessed Lord, who would walk with your sad and grieving followers on the Emmaus Road, draw near to us and walk with us in these troubled times, so that our faith may be strengthened, and we may rejoice to bear witness to our resurrected Lord. In his name we pray. Amen.

Pastoral Prayer: O triumphant and victorious Lord, we praise you for bringing new life into our world. In this glorious season, we rejoice that from the grave you brought us a new promise, "Because I live you shall live also."

We give you thanks that the darkness of night has passed, gloom has been chased away, and morning has broken. In the midst of our fears, our disappointments, our grief, we lift voices of unending praise for the good news from Joseph's tomb.

Be especially near to those who are slow to believe, whose eyes are blinded, whose hearts have grown cold, and, because of doubt or denial, find no joy in Christ's resurrection. Open our eyes, unstop our ears, warm our hearts, and, by your Spirit, come into our midst that the mystery of the resurrection may become real to us and to your whole church today. In Jesus' name. Amen.

MAY 2, 1993

□

Fourth Sunday of Easter

Throughout Scripture, the shepherd image portrays the one who feeds, protects, and saves the flock—sheep that are often killed and destroyed.

The Sunday Lessons

Acts 2:42-47: This description of the early church is summed up in the words, "They devoted themselves to the apostles' teaching and fellowship, to the breaking of bread and the prayers" (v. 42). For a time, Christians in Jerusalem held everything in common.
I Peter 2:19-25: Peter writes to those suffering persecution. After urging slaves (all are in some serving relationship) to respect even their oppressors, Peter lifts up Christ as the example of a suffering servant and concludes, "You were going astray like sheep, but now you have returned to the shepherd and guardian of your souls" (v. 25).
John 10:1-10: False leaders who kill and destroy are contrasted with the true shepherd. Two symbols reveal the ministry of Jesus—the good shepherd and the gate to the sheepfold. Sheep stealers kill the sheep. The good shepherd "lays down his life for the sheep" (v. 11). There is one door to the fold, one source of life, one way to find pasture, one gate of heaven. "I am the gate. Whoever enters by me will be saved" (v. 9).

Interpretation and Imagination

For long months stretching to years, laborers patiently worked to build a cathedral; it was blasted into ruins in one bombing raid. A minister, through years of study, prayer, and discipline, became the kind of pastor who was loved and trusted; then in a lustful and deceitful moment, his good character was wasted so that only God in Christ could redeem.

Almost anyone can quickly kill and easily destroy. Every pig can root up pastures and tramp down the flowers in a moment—flowers that only God can create and destroy. It is far better to protect life than it is to exploit and waste it.

Still in politics, the military, and some pulpits, false leaders trust aggression more than patience. Survival is the name of the game in which the strong and the swift kill and destroy. But it's an impatient and cowardly way.

The Christ and every child of eternity who bears his name are committed to something more noble and eternal. It may seem frail and foolish to the aggressive ones, but it sends us out to unnoticed places—feeding the hungry, caring for children, helping the poor, nursing the sick, calling for justice, and always steadfast in suffering because we're centered in eternity. It's the style of the Good Shepherd.

Don't simply moralize the text. Christ is the chief actor in it. (JKB)

THE SHEPHERD AND THE SHEEP

John 10:1-10

A SERMON BY WILLIAM KELLON QUICK

One of the most beautiful analogies in Scripture between God and humankind is that of a shepherd and his sheep. One of the most familiar and best loved passages in our Judeo-Christian heritage is the opening verse of Psalm 23, "The Lord is my shepherd, I shall not want." Jehovah, the Lord God of Israel, is shepherd to the Israelites.

The prophet Isaiah pictured the Messiah as the shepherd of the sheep: "He will feed his flock like a shepherd, he will gather the lambs in his arms, and he will carry them in his bosom, and gently lead those that are with young" (Isaiah 40:11 RSV).

Is there any picture of Jesus more loved than that of him as the Good Shepherd? It is deeply woven into the language and the imagery of the Bible.

The rough and stony ground of the dry, brown, sun-burned Judean plateau was home to the shepherd, staff in hand, watching over his scattered flock. His was a difficult life. No flock could graze those semi-arid Judean hills without a shepherd. His task was to be vigilant from early dawn until night.

The selfless shepherd is constantly alert for the welfare of his flock. There was always the need to guard against the wild animals, not to mention the robbers and sheep stealers. Sheep do not take care of themselves, as many of us suppose. More than any other livestock, they require endless attention and meticulous care.

Is it accidental that Jesus has chosen to call us sheep?

Sheep and human beings share similar behavior in many ways: fears and timidity, stubbornness and stupidity, a mass mind and perverse habits are all parallels of profound importance.

Is it strange that Jesus declared, "I am the good shepherd" (v. 11)?

He is the understanding shepherd, the concerned shepherd who cares enough to seek out and save even one lost man or woman. Here is a majestic linkage between God and his children, the immortal and the mortal. It implies a profound, yet practical, working relationship between human beings and their Maker.

This memorable and searching parable of the shepherd and his sheep presented a challenge to Israel's religious authorities. If we fail to consider the occasion and the audience, a true understanding of the story is concealed from us. Therefore, let's look at the setting.

In the previous chapter, John tells the story of Jesus giving sight to a man born blind. The blind beggar's confession that Jesus had opened his eyes aroused the jealousy of the Pharisees, and they cast him out of the synagogue. To an Israelite the dread of excommunication was second only to the fear of death. As a matter of fact, such ostracism cut him off from his circle of friends, the community of faith, and made him an object of scorn and derision.

Having heard what had happened, Jesus sought him out. Once again the blind man stands before the Son of God and a second miracle of faith is performed. He confesses, " 'Lord, I believe.' And he worshiped him" (John 9:38).

Once again we witness a strange reversal of life. Those who call themselves believers are blind, and a blind man becomes the one whose eyes are opened! Jesus here contrasts himself with the Pharisees as the true shepherd. In this setting, Jesus gives the parable of the shepherd and his sheep.

It is helpful for us to understand the purpose of the sheepfold if we are to understand this teaching of our Lord.

The pastoral sections of ancient Palestine were infested with wild beasts. Shepherds in each village shared a large sheepfold as common property. The sheepfold was enclosed by a wall ten to twelve feet high.

At nightfall the shepherds converged on the village and led their flocks to the gate of the fold. Then they would go home or to some place of lodging for the night. The sheep were guarded through the night by the porter who protected them against robbers, thieves, and wild animals, until the shepherds returned the following morning. One by one, each shepherd was allowed to enter through the gate of the sheepfold, calling by name the sheep that belonged in his flock. Palestinian sheep were largely kept for their wool and were often with the shepherd for years. Each one had a descriptive name such as "black leg" or "brown ear" or "white nose." The sheep would respond to their shepherd's voice and were led to the new day's pasture.

Jesus marks the true shepherd as the one who enters the fold by the gate and does not climb over the wall as a thief or robber. The porter opens the gate because the shepherd proves himself when the sheep respond to his voice.

In this lesson of John, our Lord leaves no doubt that entry into the fold is through the door, and Jesus himself is that door. Jesus has pointed out generally what constitutes a true shepherd. Now he speaks more plainly. "I am the gate" he says. "All who came before me are thieves and bandits" (vv. 7-8). Jesus refers here not to the Old Testament prophets—but to the false pretenders and messiahs who arose and led many astray. Implicit is the claim that Jesus is the true Messiah and the gate to the sheepfold. He also suggests that since he is the gate, "Whoever enters by me will be saved, and will come in and go out and find pasture" (v. 9).

What is Jesus' message for the church today in this teaching?

First, pastors in the late-twentieth-century church are called, once again, to become shepherds. In fact, the very word *pastor* (Eph. 4:11) is Latin for shepherd.

When Christ completed his earthly ministry, he appointed others to shepherd his flock. His first call to Simon Peter was "Follow me, and I will make you fish for people" (Matt. 4:19). His final encounter with Simon Peter finds him talking not of fishing but of shepherding. The first call suggests the evangelist; the final call suggests the pastor.

Remember that encounter? The boasting Peter is asked three times if he loves Jesus. Peter responds each time, "Lord, you know I love you." Initially comes the charge, "Feed my lambs"—the weak and feeble of the flock. These are the ones who have the first claim on the pastor. Twice more Jesus probes Peter's heart and affection, "Do you love me?" (John 21:15-17).

Peter had been called as an apostle and boasted at the Last Supper in the Upper Room that his love was superior to that of the others. Then following the seizure in the Garden he fled in the night and later cursed and denied knowing the Galilean. Now his love for Jesus is challenged by the Master. Affirming his love he is instructed, "Feed my sheep." In other words if you truly love me, here is the way to demonstrate it: shepherd the flock!

That charge, that call, is ours today. We are to be fishers, or evangelists, winning persons to Christ. To make disciples is the church's first responsibility. However, those who have been won need shepherding—to be cared for, fed, and defended.

An ecumenical case study of church dropouts in upstate New York revealed the tragic news that many who dropped out of the church felt they had no shepherd. Their stories told of bringing personal, family, or spiritual crises to the attention of their pastors. Either out of busyness, carelessness, or neglect, the pastor—the chief shepherd—did nothing to minister to the need of the flock.

Once again the call comes to every pastor: "If you love me . . . feed the flock." Despite the laborious work, the discouraging response, the harsh criticism, and often little appreciation, it is the love of Christ—his for us and ours for him—that compels us to be his hands, his feet, and his voice. When all is said and done, the welfare of the flock is dependent upon the shepherding care. It is the Master in people's lives who makes the difference in their destiny!

Secondly, the church community is called to share the shepherd's ministry. Leadership in the church brings with it a responsibility "to tend the flock of God that is in your charge, exercising the oversight, not under compulsion but willingly, as God would have you do it—not for sordid gain but eagerly. Do not lord it over those in your charge, but be examples to the flock" (I Pet. 5:2-3). Paul urges the elders of Ephesus to take heed to all the flock over which the Holy Spirit had made them overseers (Acts 20:28).

The community of faith is not a spectator-oriented, passive form of Christianity. A vital, tangible faith is one where followers of the Good Shepherd are doers of the Word and not hearers only.

A pastor in the South was in his office on a Saturday morning. The phone rang and a woman said, "I'd like to order five pounds of barbecue, a pound of slaw, and two dozen hush puppies. I'd like to pick them up in an hour." The somewhat surprised minister who had failed to identify himself replied that she must have the wrong number. The woman insisted, "You're the crowd that's advertised the barbecue special, aren't you?" "No," replied the pastor, "you have a wrong number." Then, seemingly annoyed, she asked, "What's your business?" Before the pastor could answer, she hung up.

That's a good question for the church today: "What's our business?" Is it barbecue suppers, covered-dish dinners, rummage sales, art auctions? Is the church making a difference? Is the church true to its mission?

All around us are dramatic examples of people hurting and estranged; people desperately searching for a place to feel wanted and accepted. At the heart of the good news is the concept of grace. Grace is the unearned, unmerited love of God, given freely. The real task of the church is to communicate this grace and help other people experience it. Through the sacraments, the Scriptures, and the spoken word, grace is offered. Grace is also effectively shared person to person as we care for and encourage one another. Pastors are called to train the laity as under-shepherds, to share in tending the flock.

Finally, the Shepherd "calls his own sheep by name . . . and the sheep follow him because they know his voice" (vv. 3-4). Throughout the Gospels, we find illustrations of this time and again.

One day Jesus passed through Jericho. Zacchaeus, the rich tax collector, climbed a tree in order to see Jesus. But Jesus saw him first and said, "Zacchaeus, hurry and come down; for I must stay at your house today" (Luke 19:5). Jesus called one of the sheep by name and the sheep promptly responded.

A striking example of the Shepherd calling the sheep by name is found in John 11. Lazarus had died. Jesus went to Bethany, to the cave where Lazarus is buried. The gravestone is rolled away and Christ calls the sheep by name, "Lazarus, come out" (John 11:43). The sheep at once responds.

Perhaps the most touching example of the sheep knowing the Shepherd's voice is found in John 20. Very early on that first Easter morning, Mary Magdalene visits the Savior's tomb. She finds the stone rolled away and the tomb empty. Suddenly she sees a man she supposes is the gardener.

He speaks, and a moment later calls her by name, "Mary." In an instant she identifies him. What enabled her to identify Jesus? The moment he called his sheep by her name she "knew his voice."

Down through the ages it has been so. There is a call that goes forth to us all. The hymn writer, Cecil Alexander, has put it:

> Jesus calls us o'er the tumult
> Of our life's wild, restless sea;
> Day by day his sweet voice soundeth,
> Saying, "Christian, follow me!"

This outward call is for an inner commitment. Amid the chaos of a confused, sick society, Christ comes quickly as of old and invites us to follow him—to put our confidence in him. It is an invitation from the Shepherd himself, Jesus Christ, and if the sheep look to him, he will keep them together. Otherwise they are sure to stray in a torn and distracted world.

I pray no congregation may be as sheep without a shepherd. Born out of his love for us, may our love for him, the Great Shepherd, enable us to love his sheep, love his work, and love our role as a shepherd. Amen.

Suggestions for Worship

Call to Worship (I Pet. 2:24-25):

PASTOR: [Christ] himself bore our sins in his body on the cross,

PEOPLE: **So that, free from sins, we might live for righteousness;**

PASTOR: By his wounds you have been healed.

PEOPLE: **[We] were going astray like sheep, but now [we] have returned to the shepherd.**

Act of Praise: Psalm 23.

Suggested Hymns: "He Leadeth Me: O Blessed Thought"; "Savior, Like a Shepherd Lead Us"; "Where He Leads Me."

Opening Prayer: O God, the Great Shepherd of the sheep, grant us sight and insight to follow your leading and walk in your way, so that whether over some treacherous road or in green pastures, we will know the one who walks before us, who will never lead us astray. In the name of Jesus Christ our Lord. Amen.

Pastoral Prayer: O God, whom to know is to love and to love is to serve, forgive us for wandering away in paths that lead nowhere and for listening to voices that would beckon us to become straying sheep.

We come to this moment in worship and prayer in the knowledge that all we like sheep have gone astray.

We have prayed for your kingdom to come and your will to be done. Yet so often, God, we mean by others rather than ourselves.

We seek your pardon for our wandering ways and for the sorrow we have inflicted upon you and upon those who love us.

Help us to walk in your way, to find rest in the shelter of your fold, ever mindful that you are grieved when even one of your sheep is outside the fold. Protect us from the dangers of this mortal life and grant us both the desire and the will to walk always in obedience to the Great Shepherd, Jesus Christ our Lord. Amen.

MAY 9, 1993

□

Fifth Sunday of Easter

The questions regarding destiny are answered when Jesus says, "I go to prepare a place for you" (John 14:2).

The Sunday Lessons

Acts 7:55-60: Stephen began his challenge by saying God did not dwell in a house made with hands, not even Solomon's temple. Then he incited his hearers wrath when he accused them of rejecting and killing God's messengers (vv. 48-53). They cast him out of the city and stoned him to death. Dying, Stephen prayed, "Do not hold this sin against them" (v. 60).

I Peter 2:1-10: This passage, employed by reformers to teach the priesthood of all believers, has at its center the image of a stone. The rejected stone (Christ) has become the chief cornerstone for the spiritual temple of a special community. "You are a chosen race, a royal priesthood, a holy nation, God's own people, in order that you may proclaim the mighty acts of him who called you" (v. 9).

John 14:1-14: Thomas asks, "How can we know the way?" (v. 5). Philip says, "Show us the Father, and we will be satisfied" (v. 8). Jesus, who is "the way, and the truth, and the life" (v. 6), replies, "Whoever has seen me has seen the Father" (v. 9), and promises, "The one who believes in me will do greater works than these, because I go to the Father" (v. 12).

Interpretation and Imagination

"It's a good contact and one that we will want to cultivate." These words, spoken by the president of a private university, referred to a man who could influence the decisions of a corporation capable of making sizable gifts to private education. Such contacts are important to universities. Indeed, a point of contact is always important.

A mother whose son was in jail wrongly accused lamented, "I

can't help him. I'm poor. I'm uneducated. I'm a nobody who doesn't know anybody." Her next question indicated the reason for the call, "Do you know anyone who can help us?"

Only a moment's reflection will bring to mind the importance of someone to contact. When seeking a job, applying for admission to college, making an insurance claim, or getting help with clogged plumbing, an address or phone number is always needed, but we'd prefer someone to contact.

Both priest and missionary are important contacts with the sovereignty of God. Yet none is as important as the one who has come from the Father and returns to the Father. The sobering question for all who would know God is that asked by the Son: "Have I been with you all this time . . . and still you do not know me?" (v. 9).

The good news for all who long for safe lodging and peace at last is, "In my Father's house there are many dwelling places. . . . that where I am, there you may be also" (John 14:2-3). (JKB)

LEGACIES OF THE LIVING LORD I

John 14:1-14

A SERMON BY JAMES F. JACKSON II

Have you ever been remembered in a will? Have you ever inherited anything? According to the experts, most people with means received their wealth either directly or indirectly through inheritance. Someone said that there are two ways to accumulate great riches: You can work hard, save your money, and invest it wisely; or you can be born into a wealthy family and inherit what they have. Most people of means have come by it through the latter path. It is more an accident of birth than a result of cleverness.

Susan and I had an experience with inheritance several years ago. We were in the process of building a lake house for family retreats. We had exhausted all of our financial resources, when I received a letter from a lawyer in Florida saying that a relative I had only seen once had left me a legacy of $5,000. I could not believe it! I felt overwhelmed and undeserving. If I had mowed her lawn every Saturday and she had never paid me, I would have felt differently. But I knew she had only remembered me in her will because she had found my name in her family tree.

I know what some of you are thinking: "Nothing like that will ever happen to me. If everyone in my family dies and leaves me everything they have, I'll have to file bankruptcy. I can't pay their debts and mine too!" But I have good news for you. You have already received a great inheritance. It is a legacy from our living Lord.

In John 14–16, Jesus tells his disciples that he is going away. He comforts them by giving them a series of promises that are to be delivered to them by the Holy Spirit. Jesus told them that when the Holy Spirit comes, "he will take what is mine and declare (deliver) it to you" (John 16:14). Like the inheritance I received, the legacies that he promised are totally undeserved. They are gifts of grace.

For the next two weeks I would like to read and to interpret portions of the last will and testament of our Lord Jesus Christ. What he promises is not to all people in general, but only to those who believe in him (John 1:10-11; 8:43-44; 14:17). If you believe in Jesus and are a follower of his, then you are in his family and your name is in the will.

First of all, he has made us the promise of a supernatural place (John 14:1-6). Jesus describes it as a permanent "dwelling place." It is not like the "earthly tent" in which we now live. It is a "house not made with hands, eternal in the heavens" (II Cor. 5:1). A tent is a temporary, fragile dwelling for a sojourner. What Jesus has promised us is a permanent dwelling for those who have completed the journey of life. Perhaps that is the reason I prefer the old King James word "mansions" to "dwelling places" or "rooms."

Jesus further described our "dwelling place" as something he is preparing for us now, that he might share with us for eternity. "I go [to] prepare a place for you . . . that where I am, there you may be also," he said (John 14:2-3). Wow! These verses tell us what Jesus is doing right now—preparing a permanent dwelling place for us. They also tell us that Jesus will be with us there.

The New Testament is filled with promises of our eternal inheritance. Paul told us that we will be "joint heirs with Christ" (Rom. 8:17). Peter spoke of "an inheritance that is imperishable, undefiled, and unfading, kept in heaven for you" (I Pet. 1:4).

Jesus even tells us how to get to our dwelling place. He says, "I am the way, and the truth, and the life. No one comes to the Father except through me" (John 14:6). What did Jesus mean by these narrow words? Is he claiming to be the exclusive path to God? I think that he is.

Did you know that Christianity is the only religion in the world that does not teach that we must be perfect to be saved? Judaism has a sacrificial system for forgiveness, but Jewish Law provides no forgiveness for those who sin intentionally (see Lev. 4:2, 13; Num. 15:30; Heb. 5:2). Have you ever known something was wrong but did it anyway? So have I. In Buddhism you must avoid every form of pleasure and pain to be saved. According to Hindu tradition, you keep coming back in a higher or lower life form until you perfect your life. In Islam you must perfectly keep the Law of the Koran to be saved. Only in Christianity are sinners saved as they are. No wonder Simon Peter said to Jesus, "Lord, to whom can we go? You have the words of eternal life" (John 6:68).

How would you like to know for sure that when you die you are going to heaven? Well, you can know. You have the promise of Jesus. Listen to him: "If it were not so, would I have told you that I go to prepare a place for you?" (John 14:2).

You also have the presence of his Spirit now as a downpayment, guarantee, a seal that his promise is true (see John 6:27; II Cor. 1:22; 5:5; Eph. 1:13; 4:30; II Tim. 2:19). Paul says that we are not slaves, but children of God by adoption, and the Holy Spirit bears witness with our spirit that it is true. And if we are his children, then our name is in the will. We are heirs (Rom. 8:15-17). Remember, the Holy Spirit is the one who takes the inheritance we have been promised and delivers it to us (John 16:14).

Can you imagine the excitement the disciples felt on the day of Pentecost when they realized that they were one day going to heaven? No wonder they became fearless!

Perhaps you remember the story of the great Norwegian explorer, Roald Amundsen. He was the first to discover the magnetic meridian of the North Pole and the first to discover the South Pole. On one of his trips to the North Pole he took a homing pigeon with him. When he finally reached the top of the world, he opened the cage and set it free. Imagine the joy his family felt thousands of miles away when they looked up and saw the pigeon returning. They thought, "He's alive. He made it. He will return."

That is exactly what the disciples felt at Pentecost! Jesus had made them some powerful promises. He had said, "Because I live, you also will live" (John 14:19). When the dove-like Spirit descended on the disciples at Pentecost, they knew he was alive, that he would return, and that all his promises were true.

You can know the same joy his disciples knew today. Your name is in the will! You are his child. His Spirit is available to you today.

Suggestions for Worship

Call to Worship (John 14:6, 8-10):

PASTOR: Jesus said, "I am the way, and the truth, and the life. No one comes to the Father except through me."

PEOPLE: "Lord, show us the Father, and we will be satisfied."

PASTOR: Jesus said, "Whoever has seen me has seen the Father. How can you say, 'Show us the Father'?"

PEOPLE: "Do you not believe that I am in the Father and the Father is in me? . . . The Father who dwells in me does his works."

Act of Praise: Psalm 31:1-8.

Suggested Hymns: "For the Beauty of the Earth"; "The Battle Hymn of the Republic"; "Happy the Home When God Is There."

Opening Prayer: To you, O God, we bring our failures, our disappointments, our unfulfilled longings, and our famine-stricken spirits. You alone can supply our deepest needs: grace, strength, eternal life. Come, Lord Jesus, and grant to us those things that only you can give. In Jesus' name. Amen.

Pastoral Prayer: Eternal Father, we thank you for this blessed day of rest and worship. With the angels and archangels and with all the company of heaven, we rejoice that death is finished, that love prevails, and that nothing can separate us from your love. Let no hesitancy in believing, no heaviness of circumstances, no dullness of heart, no familiarity of past worship services deprive us of the joy and peace you intend for us today.

Loving God, we are a company of people who love you. We pray that you will give us whatever it takes to enable us to run the race of life for your glory. Help us to be the kind of followers who invite rather than hinder faith. Give us a vision of the invisible world that you have promised so that we may continue to be faithful when times are hard. Keep in front of us the example of our Savior to always stand beside those who are in need.

Gracious Lord, in whose sight all people are precious, hear us as we pray for those whose lot in life makes doubt easier than faith: for the prisoner who is separated from his or her loved ones; for the addict whose whole world turns on the next fix; for the unemployed and the underpaid for whom survival is an all-consuming fear; for those who despise themselves and are unable to believe anyone could care; for the recently bereaved who vacillate between anger and self-pity; for the highly successful who have clawed their way to the top only to discover that they were happier when they owned less and trusted more; for those who are so numbed by the stress of life that they are unable to hear the gospel which we believe. God you are able to do more for us than we have faith to ask. Give us faith to see the light that streams from Joseph's garden tomb touching and changing the lives of the people for whom we pray.

These things we ask in the name of Jesus of Nazareth who taught us to pray. Amen.

May 16, 1993

□

Sixth Sunday of Easter

We are not left alone. Even as Christ speaks of his departure, he promises the continued presence of the Holy Spirit. "I will not leave you orphaned" (John 14:18).

The Sunday Lessons

Acts 17:22-31: Paul, preaching at the Areopagus, spoke of an altar inscribed, "To an unknown god" (v. 23). The true God, "not far from each one of us" (v. 27), has appointed one to "judge the world in righteousness" (v. 31 RSV). You can be sure of his authority because God raised him from the dead.
I Peter 3:8-22: Peter's letter, addressed to Christians under persecution, encourages them to do what is right in spite of their suffering. "Do not repay evil for evil" (v. 9). Christ is the example, "the righteous for the unrighteous, in order to bring you to God" (v. 18). The passage contains an early Christian hymn about Christ's death and resurrection.
John 14:15-21: Jesus desires love and obedience. "If you love me, you will keep my commandments" (v. 15). He promises a continued presence and counselor, the Spirit Paraclete. The Greek word means "legal assistant, advocate," and suggests counsel, both prosecuting and defending, a Spirit of truth that will make the requirements plain. The result is that you know and obey the commandments of the risen, victorious Christ, and "You also will live" (v. 19). This does not mean that God's love is conditional upon our obedience, but that love prompts obedience.

Interpretation and Imagination

Every war leaves countless orphans who grow up in the street. No one cares where they are. No one tells them what to do. Without comfort or counsel, they go it alone.

You cannot live in the Gospel lesson for today unless you

realize the possibility of being left alone, orphaned and desolate. It can happen that one becomes so accustomed to being all alone that he or she fails to notice how devilish, how inhuman, how tragic, and how contrary to meaning and fulfillment all living becomes when every permanent relationship is radically struck from one's heart and life.

Indeed, some may want to be alone. When reading the words, "He will give you another Advocate, to be with you forever" (John 14:16), one may think, "That's confining. Who wants to contend with the permanent presence of a chaperone?"

Still, in our best moments, we are grateful when someone cares. We're strengthened by accountability. A nation is given character by the constant influence of constitutional law. And we are blessed by the knowledge that we cannot live without God. That's when we hear gladly, "I will not leave you orphaned" (John 14:18).

Often we associate the gift of the Spirit with ecstasy and wonderful happenings. The Gospel lesson points to the work of the Spirit that is counsel and comfort. Responses of love and obedience follow.

It was once said of a man, "He had another passion, a jealous absorbing passion, that made him live in a world different from ours."

You've seen that dynamic at work. A controlling love that makes one eager, enthusiastic, and even compulsive in obedience. You've witnessed it in the church. "If you love me, you will keep my commandments" (John 14:15). (JKB)

LEGACIES OF THE LIVING LORD II

John 14:15-21

A SERMON BY JAMES F. JACKSON II

There is a wonderful story that dates back to the time when the Romanian church was under the control of the state. At that time all unauthorized church groups were forced to meet underground. A woman who was on her way to an evening Bible study class was stopped at a roadblock. The police asked her where she was going and what she would be doing there. She could not lie, but neither did she want to cause herself or her friends to be arrested. After a moment of hesitation, she said, "My older brother has died, and I am going to a reading of the will."

As we saw last week, John 14–16 is Jesus' last will and testament. He talked to them about the things they would receive as an inheritance after his death. He told them that the Holy Spirit would deliver to them the legacies he had promised (John 16:14).

Last week we also read and commented on the first part of the will: the promise of a supernatural *place*. This week we will look at a second legacy of our living Lord, also contained in last week's Gospel lesson: the promise of supernatural *power* (John 14:7-14).

Jesus promised his disciples that when he left they would experience no loss of power. Conversely, he said that they would have even greater power—power to do his works and even greater things than he had done. Jesus added that the disciples would access this promised power through prayer. It was as though he was saying to them, "I am only a prayer away. If you need anything, just ask the Father for it in my name."

Much has been made about Pentecost being a reversal of the Tower of Babel story in Genesis 11:1-9. At the Tower of Babel the languages of the human family were confused. At Pentecost people from different linguistic backgrounds were able to understand one another (Acts 2:1-11). The thing that is the most interesting about these two stories to me is not that Pentecost represents a miracle of language, but that it represents a miracle of power. In Genesis 11:6 we are told that God confused their language because he knew that if they became unified, they would be able to do anything they proposed to do. Nothing would be withheld from them. At Pentecost they became unified and empowered, and nothing would be impossible for them.

If most of us believed that we had this kind of power through prayer, we would pray differently. But what does it mean to pray "in Jesus' name?" Is he saying, "Name it and claim it?" No, it means two things: asking for things that are consistent with the mind of Christ as best you know it, and asking for whatever will glorify him most. Listen again to the critically important verse: "I will do whatever you ask in my name, so that the Father may be glorified in the Son" (v. 13). In other words, the spirit of all our prayers should be, "Lord, I want your highest and best will in this situation. I want whatever will glorify you most." When we pray in this spirit, nothing is impossible. I like the way Saint Paul said it: "Now to him who by the power at work within us is able to accomplish abundantly far more than all we can ask or imagine . . ." (Eph. 3:20).

What does the promise of supernatural prayer life have to do with the Holy Spirit? According to Paul, "we do not know how to pray as we ought," and when we do not have the words to express our prayers to God, he searches our hearts and "intercedes for the saints according to the will of God" (Rom. 8:26-27).

The third legacy we have from our living Lord is the promise of a supernatural *helper* (John 14:15-21). The disciples were troubled (John 14:1) because they had no idea where their help would come from in the future. Jesus had been their helper, their counselor, their comforter, their advocate for three years. Now what was going to happen to them?

Notice that Jesus did not try to comfort them with the kind of cliches we use: "Cheer up, things could be worse"; "When the going gets tough, the tough get going"; "When you get to the end of your rope, just tie a knot and hold on"; "Grin and bear it." We tell people to be more macho, to handle things by themselves.

Jesus offered "another Advocate" (v. 16). He promised them that the Holy Spirit would come and take his place. The second paraclete would be of the same substance as the first paraclete—an exact duplicate, without any variation. The other helper would bring them resources outside themselves that would equip them to be the disciples Jesus had called them to be.

Can you see what this promise would have meant to an apostle like Peter? Peter did pretty well when Jesus was around. He walked on water (Matt. 14:25-29) and spoke divine revelation (Matt. 16:16-17). But when Jesus was not around he failed miserably (Matt. 26:69-75). Jesus was promising Peter another helper, who would not only stand beside him as Jesus did, but one who would also live within him (John 14:17; Gal. 2:20; Col. 1:27). He assured his disciples that the one being sent in his place would reveal himself to them (John 14:21).

When I was in the ninth grade our family lived in Waycross, Georgia. My hero at Waycross High was an All-State, All-American halfback named Marvin Hurst. I worshiped him. I did whatever I could to be near him. One day one of Marvin's friends declared war on me because I had spoken to his girlfriend. He sent me word that he planned to murder me behind the cafeteria during the lunch period. I sat quiet at lunch hoping the 225-pound, All-State tackle would forget about his death threat. But finally the time came for me to die. Someone told me that he was waiting for me outside. I started the death march not knowing that Marvin, who had been sitting at my table, was walking behind me. When I went out the back door of the cafeteria I could see my murderer. He stood there with his arms crossed, rocking from toe to heel, glaring at me. I was terrified! Then I noticed that Marvin was standing beside me. He said to his friend, "I know that Jackson spoke to your girlfriend and you are angry about it. Well, you go ahead and do what you think you have to do. But I want you to know that if you fight him, you fight us." I crossed my arms, rocked from toe to heel, glared, and the bully walked away.

Do you get the message? We have a supernatural helper.

Don't live below your privileges. You are his child. Your name is in the will. He has promised you a supernatural place, a supernatural power, and a supernatural helper. These legacies are available to you today and need only to be claimed.

Suggestions for Worship

Call to Worship (Ps. 66:8-10, 13):

PASTOR: Bless our God, O peoples, let the sound of his praise be heard,

PEOPLE: Who has kept us among the living, and has not let our feet slip.

PASTOR: For you, O God, have tested us; you have tried us as silver is tried.

PEOPLE: I will come into your house with burnt offerings; I will pay you my vows.

Act of Praise: Psalm 66:8-20.

Suggested Hymns: "Come, Thou Almighty King"; "Be Thou My Vision"; "Spirit of God, Descend upon My Heart."

Opening Prayer: Heavenly Father, we confess the sins that no one knows and the sins that everyone knows. We confess the sins that burden us and the sins that we enjoy. We confess our individual sins and our corporate sins. We confess our intentional sins and our unintentional sins. Father, forgive us. Grant to us the grace that your Son purchased for us. Send your Holy Spirit to us that we may live differently in the future. Through Jesus Christ our Lord. Amen.

Pastoral Prayer: Eternal God, we pause to offer you the only thing that is truly ours to give—our praise and our thanksgiving.

We praise you for who you are. You fill all things, and yet you are inexhaustible. You speak and bring things into existence, and yet reveal yourself most clearly through silence. You are holy, and yet you love people who are under the bondage of sin.

We also come to thank you for what you have done for us. We thank you for our families, the people who share our aloneness and drive away the demons of despair, for our friends, the people who are like family for us, those to whom we are bound in covenant relationship; for our church, the mother of our faith, the people of yours who have so often been the instrument of your grace to us.

O God, who created and sustains us, hear our prayer for those things for which you have taught us to pray.

We pray for your kingdom to come and your will to be done. Show us what you would have us to do as individuals and as your church. Reveal your will to us and give us the courage to be obedient.

We pray for daily bread. Like children, we come asking you to meet our deepest needs and longings. We ask you to meet the needs of our sisters and brothers which tug at our hearts today.

We pray for forgiveness for those things we have said and done which are disobedient to your Law. We ask that you will give us grace to forgive those who have spoken unkindly of us and done evil to us.

We pray for guidance and restraint that we will not fall into temptation. We ask that you will deliver us from those areas in which we are enslaved to patterns of self-destruction and evil.

We pray that you will keep us from being confused by the illusions of this world. Remind us that the things of this world which look like the Kingdom, the power, and the glory are not. Yours is the Kingdom, the power, and the glory—forever.

We offer these petitions in the name of Jesus Christ. Amen.

MAY 23, 1993

□

Seventh Sunday of Easter

The lessons lift up an essential part of our life together in the community of faith—confident prayer that is open to the presence of God.

The Sunday Lessons

Acts 1:6-14: Before His ascension Jesus promised, "You will receive power when the Holy Spirit has come upon you; and you will be my witnesses . . . to the ends of the earth" (v. 8). Back in the Upper Room in Jerusalem, the disciples "were constantly devoting themselves to prayer" (v. 14). Two things are emphasized—the gathered community and the prayerful expectation of the Spirit.
I Peter 4:12-14; 5:6-11: Laws had been passed that made it a crime to be a Christian. Peter writes, "Do not be surprised at the fiery ordeal" (4:12). Those who bear Christ's name should expect to suffer. He adds encouragement. "After you have suffered for a little while, the God of all grace . . . will himself restore, support, strengthen, and establish you" (5:10).
John 17:1-11: The priestly prayer of Christ consecrates his death and then consecrates his disciples and the church. Desiring glory for God, Christ prays to be glorified: "Glorify your Son so that the Son may glorify you" (v. 1). He prays for believers, that they may continue to glorify God in this world. "I am no longer in the world, but they are in the world (v. 11). I have been glorified in them" (v. 10).

Interpretation and Imagination

When a mission has ended and the last meal together is over, when all the anxious questions have been asked and the final farewells spoken, some are going to be left behind. That was the experience of the disciples.

They had come to that upper room from the streets of

Jerusalem. It was a place under a sloping roof, poor, and almost bare. There was a table. A water jar stood near the door. A towel hung from a peg. Christ washed the disciples' feet there. They ate bread from the same loaf and drank from a shared cup. That night it became a holy place as Christ consecrated his death and their life alone in the world, all to the glory of God.

Christ prayed for us in that upper room. He prayed for our witness in his behalf and for unity and love among his disciples. He prayed that we might know the same oneness with God that he knew. It is no wonder that the disciples, left alone in the world, returned to that upper room. There they gathered, waiting for the Spirit.

What prompts one to pray? The realization that you're on your own will cause you to pray. So will your sense of weakness and your fear of the unknown. But prayer that is only the plaintive cry of a lonely sheep will have little power in the world. Prayers that speak only of sick bodies, empty pockets, and a violent world are so nearsighted that they can never know the glory of God.

True prayer begins with God. Its first prompting is in the promise of the Spirit. Its true model is Jesus praying. Its glory is in one's unity with God.

Such prayer is not dependent on an act of my will. Nor is it sustained by my disciplines and piety. God is both the beginning and the end of prayer. Separation and suffering may demonstrate our need for help, but prayer starts with God. (JKB)

TURMOIL AROUND THE TABLE

John 17:1-11

A SERMON BY JOHN WESLEY COLEMAN

As the world around us becomes more and more enveloped by the majesty and magic of springtime, one is, possibly more than usual, given to periods of reverie and remembering. In witnessing the miraculous transformation in nature produced by the warming of spring and the promise of summer, one becomes caught up in a sense of expectancy. This sense of anticipation is inspired by recalling the joys of times past. Even as we look forward to the future, the past is very much a part of us.

One of the cherished memories of my own childhood is that of the family gathered together at the table at dinner time. Only moments before, the sounds of childish squabbles and differences filled the air and accompanied us as we took our places around the table—mild turmoil reigned all about. Dad's voice would intervene with a gentle firmness as he would say, "Let us offer thanks to God." Suddenly silence prevailed, and all differences were put aside for the moment as we were lifted to God in prayer. It was not just a prayer of thanks for the evening meal, but one of concern for our family, the church, our nation, and the world. All these and more were lifted to God in those evening prayers at table.

The words of our text were the words Jesus offered in prayer to God. As Jesus the Christ realized the end of his earthly sojourn was drawing near, he was confronted by the reality that the world is a place inundated by faithlessness, violence, and evil. Our Lord also realized that it was into this environment that his little group of disciples was called to go, without him, to proclaim the gospel of faith by word and deed. Thus Jesus offers to God his final prayer for the original band of disciples.

But let us place Jesus' prayer in its context. The time is eventide. The shimmering shadows of dusk are slowly, almost reluctantly, settling on the little city of ancient Jerusalem. The city has grown quiet now; the shopkeepers have closed their shops for the day, and the sellers in the marketplace have collected their wares and left for home. The first trilling sounds of the night birds can be heard from tree limbs on the Mount of Olives and in the Garden of Gethsemane, only a short distance away. Children are no longer playing in the streets. The world has grown silent as everyone has gone home to partake of their evening meal.

In the gentle hush of that twilight in early spring, in a little room on the upper floor of a little house on a little street in this ancient little city, sits Jesus of Nazareth at dinner with his twelve closest friends. He knows that his time on earth is almost done, that the end of his earthly sojourn is at hand, and he is sharing a last meal with those who have been his constant companions during his brief ministry—a ministry that spanned only three years.

In the quietness of that upper room Jesus is speaking. He is breaking the painful, sorrowing news that he must leave them, and he is making them an unbelievable promise. Thus he speaks:

> "Do you remember when the crowds gathered around us to hear the message from the Father, the message of his will and his way for those who are his children?
>
> "And do you remember when the thousands who gathered around us became hungry for food, and though there was no apparent way to do so, still we fed them?
>
> "You thought that was miraculous, and so it was.
>
> "Do you remember when desperate loved ones brought those who had suffered illness for so long a time, and those sick ones were healed of their diseases?
>
> "You thought *that* was miraculous, and so it was.
>
> "Do you remember those who were blind, who came and had their sight restored; those who were lame, who walked away cured of their crippling infirmities; and those whose minds had broken under the daily pressures of life, who were brought back to quiet, peaceful sanity and serenity?
>
> "You thought that all these were miraculous, and so they were.
>
> "Well truly I say to you—all that you have seen me do *you* will do also, and even *greater* works than I have done *you* will do when I have gone.
>
> "You will feed those who are hungry, you will clothe those who are naked, you will bring sight to those who are blind, and the hope of a new day and new opportunity to those imprisoned in dungeons of despair and need. All these and *more* you will do after I have gone."

As the supper and the evening wore on, there was something in the scene and the setting that deeply concerned our Lord. It was not fear over what awaited him beyond the horizon of tomorrow; he was totally accepting of the Father's will, he would not shun the cross. No, what caused him so grave a concern was his awareness that there was turmoil around the table. Jesus looked at his disciples, deep within their hearts, and saw there the potential for conflict, disagreement, and misunderstanding that could *literally* tear them apart.

Jesus looked around the table at those with whom he had intimately shared the last three years of his life, and was now sharing this last supper before his death. Out of their individual differences, personalities, ambitions, and varying understandings of his true purpose for them as his disciples, he saw a potential for such antagonism, hostility, enmity, and tension, that without their overriding commitment to and love for him, they would have been at each other's throats.

It was their love for him that had bound them together as one, and now he would no longer be with them, sharing their history. Jesus had good cause to be concerned, for there *was* "turmoil around the table." See them; sense the attitudes and the atmosphere present in that upper room.

There was Matthew, with the calculating tendencies of one who had been a tax collector; the impetuous Peter, often given to outbursts of emotional upheaval; there were James and John, whose political ambitions led them to hunger for positions of power and influence in the new order that they *thought* was about to dawn; Simon the Zealot, with the fierce, fire-breathing tendencies of a revolutionary; and more. Jesus saw in that little group, men possessed with such differences that *without* him there was little, if any, reason or possibility for them to be joined together or bound as one in common hope or purpose.

Realizing the presence of such tension and turmoil, Jesus, the Christ of God, lifted them to the Father in a great and passionate prayer: "Holy Father, protect them in your name that you have given me, so that they may be one, as we are one" (v. 11).

Some moments before, our Lord had prayed his farewell prayer for his disciples. While at table he asked them to remember him and the measure of his love for them. Paul has written of this:

> Jesus . . . took a loaf of bread, and when he had given thanks, he broke it and said, "This is my body that is for you. Do this in remembrance of me." In the same way he took the cup also, after supper, saying, "This cup is the new covenant in my blood. Do this, as often as you drink it, in remembrance of me." (I Cor. 11:23-25)

From that day to this, and down through the endless ages until he comes again, this sacrament of memorial to our Lord's love, life, death, and resurrection is to be for us, and for all who would be his disciples. It is a lesson to inspire our emulation and a bond that unites us in cohering unity. The inspired words of Charles Wesley say it so well:

> Jesus, united by thy grace
> And each to each endeared,
> With confidence we seek thy face
> And know our prayer is heard.
>
> Touched by the lodestone of thy love,
> Let all our hearts agree,
> And ever toward each other move,
> And ever move toward thee.
> ("Jesus, United by Thy Grace")

Christ Jesus knew that without unity and oneness his disciples could not fulfill the glorious destiny promised them—that, after he had gone, even greater things than had been witnessed during his earthly ministry would be accomplished in his name for the good of the world and humankind, and to the glory of God (John 14:12).

And the oneness was achieved, for not long after Christ Jesus' death, resurrection, and ascension, the followers of the risen Lord came together and committed themselves to live not for themselves, but for Christ.

When they made that commitment, as we shall recall in just a few days when we celebrate Pentecost, the Holy Spirit came upon them with such power and might that others caught the vision and inspiration and made the same commitment. Then others and again others and on and on, until within a few years, that small group had grown to such strength in the Spirit that they became known, even to their enemies, as "those who have turned the world upside down."

And they did, too. A small group of first-century men and women had committed themselves so totally, so completely to Jesus Christ, that the impact of their faith and faithfulness transformed much of the known world. As a result of that radical transformation, millions upon millions of people around the world this morning call themselves Christians. These Christians are gathered together in thousands upon thousands of churches all over the world today, even as we are, singing praises to the God who made himself known in Jesus Christ, and proclaiming the truth and hope for the world found in the Gospels about this same Jesus Christ.

There is still turmoil around the table this morning, as there has always been. The presence of almost three hundred denominations that make up the Christian church is surely sufficient evidence of that fact. The mission of proclaiming the risen Christ to the whole world by word *and* deed is still before us. And though we are fractured and splintered, there is yet a oneness that unites us: our common love for and allegiance to our Lord and Christ, who prays for us even now: "Holy Father, protect them in your name that you have given me, so that they may be one, as we are one."

Again, Charles Wesley provides us with words that should be our response, and our commitment to strive to imitate the Christ whose love, mercy, grace, and sacrifice save us.

Help us to help each other, Lord,
Each other's cross to bear;
Let all their friendly aid afford,
And feel each other's care.

This is the bond of perfectness,
Thy spotless charity;
O let us, still we pray, possess
The mind that was in thee.
("Jesus, United by Thy Grace")

Amen and amen.

Suggestions for Worship

Call to Worship (Ps. 68:3-4):

PASTOR: Let the righteous be joyful; let them exult before God;

PEOPLE: Let them be jubilant with joy.

PASTOR: Sing to God, sing praises to his name;

PEOPLE: His name is the LORD—be exultant before him.

Act of Praise: Psalm 68:1-10.

Suggested Hymns: "Crown Him with Many Crowns"; "Precious Lord, Take My Hand"; "Breathe on Me, Breath of God."

Opening Prayer: Eternal God, our Savior, who sent Jesus into the world to reveal your divinity and to glorify our humanity, we approach you in the mood of his expectant disciples. Come to us, as you came to them, and bring to us, as you brought to them, the assurance that Christ lives and is alive forevermore. Let that assurance move us, as it moved them, to celebrate our oneness with you in word and deed. Amen.

Pastoral Prayer: Gracious God, we come before you in prayer, not because we know how or what to ask, but because we know there is no one else to whom we can turn. We know, too, that you will meet us where we are and as we are, even though we betray the goodness for which we praise you and are quicker to demand justice than to grant it. When we ponder our faithful moments, we bless you for having created us in your image; but when we consider our unfaithful moments, we bless you for not having remade yourself in our image.

Waiting together after Jesus' departure, the disciples were assured the Holy Spirit would empower them to become witnesses for Christ and to continue his works. Sometimes, more conscious of the absence than the presence of the Holy Spirit, we feel no great surge of power charging through us. Not only do we acknowledge our weakness, O God, but we are ready to assume responsibility for it. Many of our tasks hardly require our strength; they certainly do not demand yours. Others, instead of advancing your purpose, frustrate it. Forgive us, dear God, for not using the powers you have given us or, worse, for not enlisting them in the service of your will. Forgive us, too, for complaining about the cost of discipleship or, worse, for confusing inconvenience with sacrifice. Deliver us from the temptation to compound the sin of loose talk with the search for cheap grace. . . .

Hear our prayer, O Lord, and incline us to seek its answer in obedience to your will. Amen. (From *Litanies and Other Prayers for the Common Lectionary: Year A*, by Everett Tilson and Phyllis Cole [Nashville: Abingdon Press, 1989] 78-81.)

MAY 30, 1993

□

Pentecost Sunday

Our source of peace and power is Christ's resurrection victory over sin and death, and in the outpouring of God's Spirit. Pentecost is the birthday of the church.

The Sunday Lessons

Isaiah 44:1-8: Water poured out on dry and thirsty land brings new life. The Spirit of God poured out upon Israel will transform God's people. All people will identify themselves as belonging to God and his chosen nation. There is no other God; no other "rock" to build upon (v. 8).

Acts 2:1-21: Luke begins his account of the Acts of the Apostles by telling of the outpouring of God's power. Wind and fire are his images. "There came a sound like the rush of a violent wind. . . . Tongues, as of fire, . . . rested on each of them" (vv. 2-3). Filled with the Holy Spirit, they began to speak in other languages. Instead of babble and confusion, there was understanding and unity.

John 20:19-23: John's Gospel records the gift of the Spirit as a resurrection day happening rather than a Pentecost event. The disciples were hiding behind locked doors, and suddenly Jesus appeared in their midst. His greeting was one of consolation, "Peace be with you" (v. 19). His gift was the Holy Spirit. "As the Father has sent me, so I send you. . . . Receive the Holy Spirit" (vv. 21-22). They were changed and empowered to become the church.

I Corinthians 12:3-13: Every believer is gifted. The gifts of the Spirit are many and varied, but each gift given is for the benefit of all. One and the same Spirit works all these things.

Interpretation and Imagination

Fire transforms. A raging wind changes most things when it passes. Every fresh new breeze cleanses the atmosphere. Each new breath bears life as its gift. Wind and fire are the symbols that describe both the power and the gift of the Holy Spirit. It brings change and new life.

The disciples were hiding behind locked doors. They were timid, confused, and seemingly without a leader. The risen Christ then stood in their midst, bearing gifts. "Receive the Holy Spirit," he said, and their timidity became courage, their lostness set aside by purpose and direction.

The Word of God, which we view as the very presence of the risen Christ in the church, speaks to each of us today. His words to you are, "Receive the Holy Spirit." You will hear in your own language and experience. You must speak with the tongue given you. Believe that the words of our Lord are for us today. They are meant for us. They are meant to give us peace and power.

The outpouring of the Spirit is not private and individual. It is given for the mission of the church, and it is shared in the communion of believers. It calls and equips us to join together in service for Christ and the world. It melts and molds us into a unity that reflects his love. Confusion and dissension about the work of the Spirit result when we try to box this powerful reality into our small experiences and wooden doctrines.

We neglect the Spirit when we cling too much to our old ways and our old understandings. We limit our possibilities to be the church when we look for manifestations of the Spirit only in the miraculous and express its power only in ecstasies. The tongues become a confusing babble when we claim too much for ourselves. (JKB)

THE COMPANY OF THE GIFTED

I Corinthians 12:3-13

A SERMON BY RALPH K. BATES

Do you have charisma? A young woman in the perfume department of a large department store asked the customers, "Would you like to have charisma?" If they responded, "Yes," she would spray a perfume called "Charisma" on them and say, "Now you have charisma." *Charisma,* according to Paul, is not something you put on or spray on, but, as in the Greek, is a "gift from God."

It was so important for the early Christians to understand the nature of spiritual gifts that they are recorded in the twelfth chapter of I Corinthians and Romans, and in the fourth chapters of Ephesians and I Peter.

Paul begins by naming the gifts. Through the Spirit, one is given the gift of prophecy. Prophecy is more *forth*telling than *fore*telling. A prophet is one who speaks the word of God with authority.

To another is given the gift of wisdom. The gift of wisdom comes from spending hours and hours in prayer listening to God. The Pharisees often marveled at Jesus' wisdom and authority and wanted to know where he went to school. It was on the quiet hills of Galilee as he listened to the Father.

There is the gift of knowledge. Knowledge is more than understanding, it is being able to say the right thing at the right time. I have known a few people with this gift. I have watched and listened as they spoke words that calmed the uncertainty and smoothed the troubled waters. The writer of Proverbs says it precisely: "A word fitly spoken is like apples of gold in a setting of silver" (Prov. 25:11).

There is the gift of faith. A person with this gift speaks boldly and confidently for God. They believe that faith can move mountains.

There are gifts of healing and miracles. Healing miracles are mysterious to the modern mind, but I have personally known those who had this gift to bring healing to seemingly impossible situations.

There is the gift of exhortation. An exhorter might be defined as one who encourages or enables another. Recently, a person described this experience in these words: "When I am with John, I feel like I'm at a party and I'm the guest of honor." It raises a disquieting question. What happens to people when they are around us? Are we a delight or a drag? Are we liberating or limiting? Are we a boost or a burden? Do people in our companionship blossom or bloom, or fade and fall?

Notice that there is the gift of gifts. There are people who know how to give gifts. It has been a challenge for me to know a good friend who owns a productive business and has committed 50 percent of his profits to God. I love to be with people who have the gift of gifts. They are exciting and adventuresome.

There is the gift of mercy, of compassion, loving and caring for other people. Recently, while teaching a course on spiritual gifts, I asked the group to list their gifts. A young woman doctor who works in a trauma unit responded spontaneously, "I have the gift of mercy."

There is the gift of evangelism, telling others about Jesus Christ. Persons with this gift are excited, enthusiastic, and effective in sharing their faith. No one, in my opinion, does it better than Dr. Billy Graham. However, I have known lay persons and ministers who were equally effective.

There are twenty-seven gifts, and according to Paul, God is the giver of these gifts. All God's children have charisma.

Next, look at some of the characteristics of gifts. Paul suggests that gifts are given for the purpose of building up the church as the Body of Christ. They are personal gifts, but not given for personal use. They are given for the purpose of God. Every Christian has at least one gift, and many of us have more than one. Some of us have one talent, another two talents, still another five talents.

Gifts are also given to do a particular task. When God calls us to the task of ministry, he gives us the gifts and the energy to do the job. When those gifts are fully energized, they are beautiful to behold. One of the most obvious examples is the field of athletics. I enjoy watching a gifted athlete who is fully energized. In the 1988 Olympics there was a Japanese skater, eighteen years of age, who captivated the audience. No one expected her to excel, but she was grace-gifted. As she skated through her routine, the announcer commented, "She looks as if she is enjoying every moment." She was so vivacious that the minute she finished her routine, she broke into tears, and the audience broke out in a spontaneous standing ovation. She had performed so well under pressure that all of us who watched were caught up in the magic of the moment.

The same thing happens when the gift, the situation, and the person are caught up in the will of God. Something beautiful happens. One is enabled to do things that seem beyond one's ability. I remember being surprised by a comment made to me after a worship service. A woman walked to the altar, took my hand, looked me in the eye and said, "You are a very ordinary-looking person, but when you preach, you preach with the power of a giant." To say the least, I was speechless—but I knew what she was saying. The sermon that night, as well as the preacher, was grace-gifted.

Another thing I've discovered about gifts is that one cannot achieve giftedness. I don't care how hard one works, gifts cannot be earned. They do not depend on intelligence, personal appearance, or personal magnetism. Gifts are God-given.

I have observed that those who possess gifts are eager to use them. The teacher is eager to teach, the preacher is eager to preach. If you have the gift of hospitality, you love to entertain. If you have the gift of helping, you are eager to serve.

I have also learned that one can discount and disqualify gifts. There is a sense in which we use our gifts or we lose them. Through attitudes, behaviors, and actions we can limit or destroy the effectiveness of our gifts.

When we use God's gifts for his purpose, the ego never gets in the way. You don't go around begging for compliments, you don't go away hurt if somebody doesn't say that you are the greatest person in the world. You know that it is something God has done through you, enabling you to go far beyond anything you could ordinarily do. The focus is on God, not you.

Have you discovered your gifts? You do have charisma. Gifts, like talents, have to be discovered, developed, and used. In the 1960s, one of the exciting events in group experience was the strength bombardment. One was given a marker and asked to stand before a black board. The members of the group called out the strengths of that person who wrote them down without comment. Many of us found ourselves writing down strengths that we didn't know we had. It was exhilarating. This same procedure would help us identify our spiritual gifts.

We also find our gifts through prayer. In communion and relationship with God we discover his will for our lives. We listen as he calls us into service and servanthood. God opens the doors, but it is our opportunity and choice to walk through those doors. God would not give us a gift unless there was an opportunity to appropriate that gift.

We find our gifts by being in the right place at the right time with our gifts. I have found that the right person in the right place at the right time enables a church to go forward. If the wrong person with the wrong gift is in the wrong place at the wrong time, the church will neither grow nor prosper.

So many of us hide our gifts under a bushel or in the ground. When one person withholds a gift, the Body of Christ is crippled. Paul tells us that the Body of Christ is one body with many members. "The eye cannot say to the hand, 'I have no need of you,' nor again the head to the foot, 'I have no need of you' " (I Cor. 12:21). When all the gifts in the body are functioning, we have a powerful body.

Lloyd Ogilvie helps us to see what happens in a dysfunctional family in his book, *You Have Charisma* ([Nashville: Abingdon Press, 1975], 19-20). He tells of sitting down in his office with a church member, a woman forty-five years of age, to share with her that her husband no longer loved her. He wrote, "I had to tell her that her husband didn't love her anymore and wanted a divorce." Her response was, "Well, I'm not surprised that he doesn't love me, because I don't even love myself." He continued, "She negated her gift with a cranky negatism." She made her home a hell by her control, jealousy, and possessiveness. Dr. Ogilvie asked her, "How long have you been in the church?" "Forty-five years," she responded. "How long have you been hearing about God's love?" "Forty-five years." She had heard about God's love for forty-five years but had never been a recipient of that love. She began to affirm God's gift, and slowly and surely let God's love into her life, and she was filled with new tenderness and warmth. Later, her husband, to whom she was estranged, began to notice the difference. He asked for her hand in marriage and lovingly remarked, "I want to live the rest of my life with you. I really need you." Her charisma had become an undeniable, irresistible, magnetizing power for new love.

If God encountered you on your daily routine and asked, "Do you have charisma?" what would you say?

Suggestions for Worship

Call to Worship (Ps. 104:31, 33-34):

PASTOR: May the glory of the LORD endure forever;

PEOPLE: May the LORD rejoice in his works—

PASTOR: I will sing to the LORD as long as I live;

PEOPLE: I will sing praise to my God while I have being.

PASTOR: May my meditation be pleasing to him, for I rejoice in the LORD.

Act of Praise: Psalm 104:24-34.

Suggested Hymns: "Morning Has Broken"; "I'm Goin'a Sing When the Spirit Says Sing"; "Spirit of Faith, Come Down."

Opening Prayer: Eternal Wisdom, incarnate Word, when you first spoke, the world was made. When you taught, truth was revealed. When you died on the cross, hate was conquered by love. When you arose from the grave, death was defeated by life eternal. Surely you rule all creation with your strong and tender care. Come and show us the things that belong to our peace. Amen.

Pastoral Prayer: Gracious and loving God, you are able to do exceeding, abundantly above all that we ask or think. You are the author and giver of gifts. Our problem is that we do not know how to receive gifts. We want to work for gifts, be worthy of gifts, to merit gifts. We want to earn gifts. Getting something for nothing, when we don't deserve anything, creates an attitude of suspicion and a feeling of uneasiness. Even when we receive a gift, we feel that we are obliged to repay. In our way of thinking, it is more blessed to give than to receive.

It is also frightening to believe that you could give us a gift that we would never use. We are alarmed to think of the possibility of unused potential. We would never forgive ourselves for misusing your gifts, so we hide our gift under a bushel or bury it in the ground. We cannot risk that which could be developed a hundredfold ending in bankruptcy.

It alarms us to know that when we fail to use our gifts, we lose them. When we withhold one gift from the body, it cripples the body; when one of us is hurt, we are all hurt. We do not want to be responsible for anyone but self; unity is too risky.

MAY 30

O God, if we dared listen to you today, what would you say? If we gave you a chance to work in our lives, what would you do? If we placed our lives in your hands, where would you take us? Give us courage to claim our gifts, daring to use our gifts, and power to expend our gifts for the unity of the Christian congregation and for the challenge of the world community. In the name of the Father, Son, and Holy Spirit. Amen.

June 6, 1993

□

First Sunday After Pentecost (Trinity Sunday)

Our hope as Christians rests in the belief that God loves us. That sovereign love, first seen in the goodness of creation, is proven by the grace of Christ and brought near by the fellowship of the Spirit.

The Sunday Lessons

Deuteronomy 4:32-40: The Lord, through many great and wondrous happenings, chose and made Israel to be his people. This election and revelation of God's power and presence was based on love. "Keep his statutes and his commandments" (v. 40).

II Corinthians 13:5-14: The second Corinthian letter, addressed to rebellious converts, is more gentle than the first. Paul writes, "Examine yourselves to see whether you are living in the faith" (v. 5). His final blessing offers grace, love, and fellowship.

Matthew 28:16-20: Evangelism and catechism are the commission given to the church. It is by all the power of heaven and earth that we are commissioned. It follows that all nations must know this Ruler. Conversion and nurturing will always be the ultimate goals of the church's life and work. Our baptisms and our baptizing are "in the name of the Father and of the Son and of the Holy Spirit" (v. 19).

Interpretation and Imagination

The doctrine of the Trinity, one God in three persons, is not clearly set forth in Scripture. It was gleaned from the experience and understanding of early Christians. They were monotheists who believed in one sovereignty that set the world on its foundations and continues to rule forever. Challenged by the charge that they worshiped three gods, and confused by the separateness and unity of Father, Son, and Spirit, they tried to explain that mystery through the doctrine of the Trinity. We have learned the formula, but "three in one" has provided as much confusion as clarity. Still, we hold fast to these convictions. God is the creator. Jesus of Nazareth is God in flesh and God victorious over sin and death. The Holy Spirit is the pervading comfort and power of God among us now.

From time to time the church, though claiming to be trinitarian, has become unitarian—giving allegiance to only one person of the Trinity. Trinity Sunday is a time to see it as a whole.

A Christian theologian, commenting on the sermon of a Christian preacher, was appalled by his reference to three natures of God. I looked up the definition of the word "nature" and understood his concern. The first definition is "the intrinsic characteristics and qualities of a person or thing." The second refers to "disposition and essence." Sometimes, the word is used to refer to a type, but in trinitarian thought we jealously protect the nature of God as the same for each person of the Trinity. Does it seem picky to worry over the distinction between "nature" and "person"? Trinity Sunday also sees the distinctive work of each person in the Trinity. We dare to claim it all. "God in three persons, blessed Trinity." (JKB)

GOD'S POWER IN TODAY'S WORLD

Deuteronomy 4:32-40

A SERMON BY RALPH K. BATES

Most of us would agree that God is all powerful. We call him "the Almighty" and sing, "How Great Thou Art." If the Bible consistently agrees on any one point, it is that God is a God of power. But the question haunts us, If God is omnipotent, why does he allow this world to be so destructive? If all the claims of God are true, why do bad things happen to good people, especially Christian people?

As we observe God's power, it is obvious that his power permits destruction. We live in a destructive world. We destroy our environment, one another, and ourselves. Nations destroy nations. God allows the Soviet Union to war against the Baltic States. He allowed the allied coalition to destroy the Iraqi forces in Kuwait. He allows apartheid in South Africa. He allows the government in China to suppress freedom demonstrations. He allows hunger, homelessness, AIDS, drug addiction, rape, murder, and adultery. These conditions cause many people to question God's power.

Not everyone is as confident of God's power as Moses was when he spoke to the children of Israel in the wilderness. He asked the children of Israel, "Has anything as great as this ever happened before? . . . Have any people ever lived after hearing a god speak to them from a fire, as you have? . . . Before your very eyes he used his great power and strength" (v. 32-34 GNB). Moses was confident that his God was a God of power.

How confident are we in the power and strength of God? We may not have seen God's power, but we have seen the power of modern man. Look, for example, at modern technology. Before the *Columbia* went into space for the first time, my wife and I spent a day at Cape Canaveral with Dr. Richard Smith, the Deputy Marshall of the Kennedy Space Center. He gave us a guided tour of the *Columbia* space craft. It was awesome! I told my wife that I could not believe that anything that big could ever get off the ground. As we climbed the scaffolding around the space craft, Richard pointed to the two booster rockets and said, "Each one of those rockets can deliver 2.65 million pounds of thrust." Now that's power.

Many of us have seen the results of the technological power of the A-bombs dropped on Hiroshima and Nagasaki. We have seen the destructive effects of napalm in the jungles of Vietnam and in the Persian Gulf. In the war with Iraq, we have seen the power of the Scud and the Patriot missiles.

We have seen the political power of a John Kennedy and the financial power of a Donald Trump. We have seen the literary power of a T. S. Eliot, the analytical power of a Sigmund Freud, and the moral power of a Mother Theresa or Alexander Solzhenitsyn. We live in a world of power. However, in the minds of many, God's power does not measure up to technological power.

The secular mind questions God's power. In time of war we would rather have the Tomahawk missile or the nuclear bomb; in sickness, a trained medical doctor, and in financial difficulty, a good banker. Who needs God in a world where man is so proficient? Rabbi Harold S. Kushner reflects on this problem in his book *Who Needs God?*

People are asking whether God is more powerful than a nuclear bomb. Is he more powerful than a 747? Is he more powerful than the laser? Where do we go to find the answer? Is there a Moses around? Is there a prophet? Who has the answer?

Jesus helps us more than anyone to understand God's power when he said, "The kingdom of heaven is like a mustard seed" (Matt. 13:31). Is that power? Look at the tiny seed and tell me what you think. It's one of the smallest of all seeds, yet when fully developed, it becomes a bush so large that the birds come and fill its branches while eating the delicious seeds. Jesus went on, "It's like leaven which a woman places in a lump of dough" (Matt. 13:33, paraphrase). Leaven does its work as it fills the entire lump of dough. God's power works from small and simple beginnings, expanding slowly, steadily, and surely. What kind of power is that?

Recently I was speaking to a group of ministers at Camp Sumatanga. After one of the sessions, I told a friend of mine what I would be preaching the following Sunday and that I was wrestling with the theological issue of God's power. He gave me an outline that he credited to Dr. Wallace Hamilton. I would like to share it with you.

God's power must be consistent with his person and with his character. Paul touches on this idea when he says, "For we cannot do anything against the truth, but only for the truth" (II Cor. 13:8). Matthew expresses a similar idea when he says, "A good tree cannot bear bad fruit, nor can a bad tree bear good fruit" (Matt. 7:18).

If God is all powerful, and I think he is, then he must use great discretion in implementing his power. If God is love, and I think he is, then his power must be consistent with love. Frederick Buechner, in his book *The Magnificent Defeat* (New York: The Seabury Press, 1966, p. 34), puts this into perspective:

> So the power of God stands in violent contrast with the power of man. It is not external like man's power, but internal. By applying external pressure, I can make a person do what I want him to do. This is man's power. But as for making him be what I want him to be, without at the same time destroying his freedom, only love

> can make this happen. And love makes it happen not coercively, but by creating a situation in which, of our own free will, we want to be what love wants us to be.

If God is to use his power consistently to interfere with one dispute, he must interfere with all disputes. If God stopped the Persian Gulf Crisis, he would have to interfere with the personal disputes in my private life. That would take away God's gift of free choice, and what would life be without options?

If God refused to use his power to save his Son from the cross, it was because he refused to use his power inconsistently with his character. If God had ruthlessly destroyed those who taunted and insulted Jesus on the cross with the power of "more than twelve legions of angels," we would have observed a God of law and not a God of grace. If God had chosen to force his way into the historical event of the crucifixion, then he would also choose to force his way into our private lives and interfere with our freedom of choice. Love works by freedom, not by force.

God's power is not only consistent with his person, it is consistent with his patience. God is infinite, we are finite. God is timeless, we are bound by time. The Bible tells us that if we live beyond three score and ten, we are living on borrowed time. God can afford to not be in a hurry. God can wait. He has time to let his patience work.

Notice how the mustard seed grows, how the leaven works. Jesus started with twelve disciples. At Pentecost, 120 persons went into an upper room to wait, to tarry, and to pray. When the day of Pentecost had fully come, they were filled with the Spirit. They left the upper room, walked out into the world and turned it upside down. They started a revolution that will not end until the leaven leavens the meal and the mustard seed brings forth a hundredfold.

The seed and the leaven do their work in God's own time. God can wait for an Augustine to be born. He waits until Augustine writes a book, *The City of God*, which lays down principles that create revolution in the world. He waits for a Luther to create a Protestant Reformation. He waits for a John and Charles Wesley to bring spiritual springtime to the eighteenth century. He waits for a Patrick Henry, a John Adams, and a John Weatherspoon to create a new nation under God. He waits for a Bonhoeffer, a

Barth, and a Tillich. He waits for mothers to fight against drunk driving. He waits until spouse abuse, child abuse, sexual harassment, abortion, and drug addiction fill the consciousness of modern society. He waits until war, injustice, hunger, and homelessness become major issues. I believe this is the power of God patiently guiding the events of the world toward his Kingdom. We would be wise to listen to the council of the poet, Francis Quarles:

> My soul, sit thou a patient looker-on;
> Judge not the play before the play is done:
> Her plot hath many changes; every day
> Speaks a new scene; the last act crowns the play.

God's power is not ostentatious. He never leaps from temple pinnacles. He doesn't take the shortcut of political expediency, neither does he manipulate a person through bread or riches. His power is consistent with his character and his patience.

God's power is also consistent with his purpose. I believe Dr. Leslie Weatherhead was right when he wrote that God's ultimate power could not be frustrated. Today there are Christian communities all over the world. That seems to be God's plan. I read recently that when the Africans want to carry the gospel to a new tribe, they do not send a book, they send a family. There are families all over the world that are living, working, praying for the kingdom of God. That's how God's power works. People working for peace, a better environment, women's rights, children's rights, the rights of the aging, and those who have handicaps.

It would be nice if God would break into our lives, solve all our problems, settle all our disputes. But remember this: If God is to be consistent, then he would then interfere with the affair of lust, the addiction to alcohol, the high from a drug, the lie, the cheating, the stealing; and he would turn our personal lives into shambles. No there is only one way for God to use his power: by permission and invitation. Then things really begin to happen.

Recently I saw the idea of God's power vitally at work in the life of an individual; as Moses said, "Before [my] very eyes, [God] used his great power and strength" (v. 34 GNB). As a minister, I attend many meetings and invoke the blessings of God. Recently

I went to a banquet sponsored by an outreach arm of United Methodism called "Urban Ministries." It was a time of personal sharing concerning the power of God. A dignified man walked to the microphone. He told us that he had been hooked on drugs, alcohol, and womanizing. He had lost his dignity and was isolated from his wife and three daughters. One day a minister showed up at his house to take his three daughters to church. He was angry and walked toward the preacher with the intention of beating him up. The minister won the day by simply listening to the cry for help which came disguised from the man's lips. He invited him to church. He refused to go because he had no suitable clothing. They went to Urban Ministries and found clothing. The man's life was slowly changed from death to life. Today, he is an active member of the Community Church, and an active worker in the Urban Ministries Program reaching out to others. When the man left the platform, his oldest daughter, whom he had introduced earlier, stood and applauded him. She, also, had seen the power and strength of God with her own eyes.

"Do not be deceived; God is not mocked, for you reap whatever you sow" (Gal. 6:7). How is that for power?

Suggestions for Worship

Call to Worship (Ps. 33:8-9, 11-12):

PASTOR: Let all the earth fear the LORD;

PEOPLE: Let all the inhabitants of the world stand in awe of him.

PASTOR: For he spoke, and it came to be; he commanded, and it stood firm.

PEOPLE: The counsel of the LORD stands forever, the thoughts of his hearts to all generations.

PASTOR: Happy is the nation whose God is the LORD.

PEOPLE: The people whom he has chosen as his heritage.

Act of Praise: Psalm 33:1-12.

Suggested Hymns: "Holy, Holy, Holy! Lord God Almighty"; "O God in Heaven"; "O Love, How Deep."

Opening Prayer: O Lord, your ways are beyond understanding, yet your truth is always before us. Listen to the prayers of your people that we may find your help and guidance in every time of need. Amen.

Pastoral Prayer: Gracious and loving God, to no one else can we draw so near; with no one else can we share our secrets; with no one else can we so be ourselves. You knock at our heart's door to offer love and friendship. You walk with us through the deep places of life with a guiding light and a helping hand. You work in our midst in strong and silent ways. You invite us to follow you while you walk before us to lead the way and beside us to steady our steps. When we move toward you, we experience your coming toward us.

But there is also within us that which we call "rebel" something that pulls us away from your love into our lust, from your likeness into our humanness. We reject your friendship, resist your leadership, and reserve our love for self. The good that we would do, we do not do. With blind eyes we stumble along the path of self-centeredness.

Thank you, God, for not giving up on us, for not leaving us in isolation. Forgive us when you come to us and find no fruit on the barren fig tree—nothing but leaves. Speak comfortably to us in our warfare, and reassuringly to us in our indecision. Help us, like the Prodigal, to come to ourselves and go home to the Father's house.

Enable us to open our eyes, unstop our ears, and move from our illusions of pride to the reality of your purpose. Enable us to wake up to your will, to walk in your way, and to work in your world. In Jesus Christ our Lord. Amen.

JUNE 13, 1993

□

Second Sunday After Pentecost

Self-centered privilege, often referred to as "rights," will let you take more than you give. Those commissioned by Christ for his mission give more than they take.

The Sunday Lessons

Genesis 25:19-34: There was a wrestling match within Rebekah's womb as the twins struggled together. Esau, the red and hairy one, was born first, but his brother was not far behind. He had taken hold of his twin's heel. "So he was named Jacob" (v. 26). Years later, when Esau came from the fields hungry, he sold his birthright to Jacob for a bowl of red stew (v. 30).
Romans 5:6-11: We are "justified" (v. 9) and "reconciled" (v. 10) to God through Christ's death. While we were yet sinners Christ died for us. It is the proof of God's love for us. We are those who have sinned and are estranged. Paul never speaks of God being reconciled to humankind; we must be reconciled to God.
Matthew 9:35–10:8: Seeing the crowds, "harassed and helpless, like sheep without a shepherd" (9:36), Jesus commissioned twelve disciples and sent them out to preach and heal. He gave them the authority to resist evil. The mission was not for profit; its message: "The kingdom of heaven has come near" (10:7).

Interpretation and Imagination

"Birthright" suggests favor and favorites. A mother of ten children was asked, "Do you have a favorite?" "Yes," she answered. "The one who is sick, until he is well. The one who is away, until she comes home."

The first-born son of a patriarch's favorite wife was the favored child in ancient Israel. Ishmael and his slave mother, Hagar, were sent away into the wilderness by Abraham (Gen. 21:14). He also sent away the sons born to him by Keturah (25:6). It was to Sarah's son Isaac that Abraham gave all he had (25:5).

Isaac was the father of twin boys. His favorite was Esau, but Rebekah loved Jacob (Gen. 25:28). The birthright—the twins wrestled for it in their mother's womb—was bartered and exploited, sold cheaply, then taken by a deceitful trick. But it was *the* birthright, and with it came blessing and promise. Jacob, the younger son, received the commissioning blessing and so we say, "The God of Abraham, Isaac, and Jacob."

The men Jesus chose and set aside for a special ministry were given extra resources and authority. Christ himself had a special relationship with the Father. Yet none of it was for their own power, prosperity, or glory. The blessing was for the sake of others.

For more than three decades the church has been burdened with the lobbying and demands of special interest groups. Each seeks representation, empowerment, and a goodly portion of everything. The church is not stronger because of it, nor has it become more inclusive. Crowds of outcasts and outsiders, like sheep without a shepherd, never gain the blessing of belonging to a good king and a heavenly kingdom. Christ's command has not changed: "You received without payment; give without payment" (Matt. 10:8). (JKB)

IF WINTER COMES

Romans 5:1-9

A SERMON BY DAVID W. RICHARDSON

Despite the rightful insistence we hear calling us to live in the present, the fact remains that we must often look to the future to find hope. When cold weather and snow begin to weary us, we can hardly be faulted for looking to a warmer and better time. Let us think of the wintry cold and also of the wintry soul.

No one could argue against the reality of winter, but we need more than present reality. We need to have hope for and in the future. The English poet Shelley penned these words to express the present reality and future hope: "If winter comes, can spring be far behind?"

Shelley knew what we know: there is no "if" winter comes! This fact was made even more unpleasant by the dampness of the England Shelley knew more than a century and a half ago.

Another Englishman, Rudyard Kipling—living about a century after Shelley, but still in a time when homes lacked central heating—wrote, "Never again will I spend another winter in this accursed bucketshop of a refrigerator called England."

Likewise, the winter that comes to the soul is hardly to be desired. Yet it comes. If it can be said, "Into every life a little rain must fall," it can also be said, "Into every life winter comes." This is not a condition unique to us and our contemporaries. Job complained, "I am allotted months of emptiness, and nights of misery are apportioned to me. . . . The night is long, and I am full of tossing until dawn" (7:3-4). What Job calls "nights," I call "winter."

Every person faces unhappiness, disappointment, and grief if he lives for at least several decades. Perhaps you find it hard to believe, but Jesus shared the wintry feelings. The Gospels do not always portray Jesus as the pleasant man with little children, nor the peaceful man so often pictured. If we think of winter as unhappiness and disappointment, then Jesus had his share and more. To think that Jesus was untouched by such events as the death of John the Baptist and the betrayal by Judas is to miss what the Gospels want us to know. When confronted by the death of Lazarus, Jesus wept. The Gospel writers did not intend for us to think that Jesus was somehow above such emotions. In fact, just the opposite is true. How little his family and friends, his disciples, and his enemies understood what he was doing. To say that this did not affect Jesus would be nonsense.

Having accepted the fact of the coming of the wintry cold and the wintry soul, let us think of what brings winter. William Cowper, who wrote, "God moves in mysterious ways his wonders to perform," called "Winter [the] ruler of the inverted year."

Winter cold comes because we are not long enough nor close enough in the warmth of the sun's rays. Our souls need warmth and closeness in fellowship with God and other humans. Do you recall the story of the Chinese student at the University of Michigan who, having failed his courses at the university, climbed into the attic of a church and stayed there several years? He did not want his parents to know of what he considered his disgrace.

When I say he experienced the wintry cold and the wintry soul, I mean it. Ann Arbor is very cold in the winter, and surely the church attic was cold. At night he came down into the church to get more clothing from the church rummage sale and food from church dinner leftovers. His worst suffering, however, was the loneliness. Sundays were especially lonely because he was near many people, and yet he was not really a part of them. Of course, he was finally discovered. How heartwarming it is to know that the church took him into their fellowship. If there is someone here now or in the future who needs our fellowship, I hope we will not let a difference of color make us want to prevent someone's entering our fellowship. And if someone now or in the future feels that he or she has disgraced himself or herself, let that be unimportant also. Let's not cause winter to come to anyone because we do not open our fellowship.

What we do or don't do to someone might cause winter to come. One way we might bring winter is to give someone the "cold shoulder." Another way is by dampening a person's enthusiasm unjustly. Many years ago Colonel Low, a professor at St. Joseph's College in Bardstown, Kentucky, was fired by the trustees of the college. Why? Because he wrote a pamphlet advocating a railroad to the west coast. You will know that he wrote a long time ago and that the trustees were shortsighted men when I tell you that Low was fired on the ground of insanity. The trustees knew that anyone who wrote about the possibility of a train going to the west coast had to be insane.

Let's not overlook what we do to ourselves. One of the church's prayers includes these words, "Deliver us, when we draw nigh to thee, from coldness of heart and wanderings of mind." It may be that we consciously turn our minds from God. A cartoon showed a man and his wife looking into the next yard where neighbors were on their knees and bowing before a huge, cold-looking black figure. The man, surprised at the actions of his neighbors, says to his wife, "I thought the Saunders were agnostics." The fact is that the only time some people get on their knees is to work in the garden or lawn. The fact is that many so-called agnostics really worship. They worship status or money or popularity or their lawns. Worshiping something other than God can bring winter to us and to others.

Let us also realize that not every wintry condition is our fault. To say that disappointment and grief come to a man because he has done wrong is to echo the so-called friends of Job, whose views have long been repudiated by Jews and Christians alike. Let there be no such people here. It may be that a person's troubles are brought on by his or her actions, but not necessarily. Certainly, we should not let winter or the threat of winter freeze us into inaction.

Job was told by his "friends" that he suffered bad health and the loss of his goods because he had sinned. We can thank God that he does not treat us so severely. Though not God's fault, sometimes the innocent suffer, and sometimes life treats us harshly, and bad things happen unexpectedly. This does not mean that we are overcome. Even in the bad times, we can generally do something. William and Mary College was damaged and closed during the Civil War. After the Civil War it opened, but shortly closed again for seven years. Yet the president of William and Mary daily acted in hopes of a better future. Despite the fact that there were no students or faculty and that the buildings had fallen into disrepair, the president went out every morning to ring the bell.

We can be thankful for the examples of persons who remain unvanquished. In 1943 a British soldier, with others who had been captured, was forced to build the railroad from Bangkok to Burma. He told of being in a place where men were forced to work in cold water that came above their knees. They had to carry a part of the track to the spot and get down on their hands and knees to fit the joints together. When they were down on their knees, the cold water came up to their necks. The soldier writes of the noise made by the chattering of teeth.

Then he heard the noise of men singing. As each man joined in singing, he was helped, then he helped buoy another man's spirits. Even though no effort was made to harm the Japanese, the Japanese officer and his guards were frightened by this. He could hardly believe his eyes and ears as he muttered, "These men have been working thirty hours. For twelve hours they have had no food. They are wet and cold. I am wet and cold, and yet they sing." A British officer told his captor that he had witnessed a display of the spirit which he could never hope to conquer.

Even when the situation seems to prevent us from doing anything, there is something we can do, if only to sing or to pray.

Christians are called to be harbingers of hope. Though the chill of winter is a present reality, we do not forget that spring will come. We affirm that by being faithful and obedient to God, we can bring in the hope and the warmth of spring. Paul, who knew this truth from personal experience, wrote, "Let us rejoice in our troubles, for we know that trouble produces endurance, endurance brings God's approval, and his approval creates hope" (Rom. 5:3 GNB).

Let us think of the sequence of winter to spring and find hope through some of the Beatitudes. For example, the winter of feeling poor in spirit is followed by the spring of the kingdom of heaven; the winter of mourning is followed by the spring of being comforted by God; and the winter of hungering and thirsting for righteousness is followed by the spring of being satisfied (Matt. 5:3-4, 6).

A popular song of some time ago contained the words, "Love turns winter to spring." If you feel cold in your heart, hear again the words, "God has shown us how much he loves us—it was while we were still sinners that Christ died for us!" (Rom. 5:8 GNB). I would not want to be impervious to anyone's suffering or troubles, but I do want to affirm what the assurance of God's love can do and has done for many people.

In the winter, a man has an unusual occupation; one that can be helpful to our thinking. During the winter this man goes into various areas of the northwest and measures the amount of snow in order to tell how much water will be in the rivers in the springtime. It is in the winter that he tells of what will happen in the spring.

Our mission is to go to those people who are locked in wintry conditions to tell them that spring will come, of the sufficient water of eternal life. What we do, even though little, makes a difference. Those who have shoveled snow know the cumulative effect of one little flake falling after another. By themselves these small flakes are insignificant. When they are joined by others, they have quite an effect.

You can have a good effect. So don't give up hope. Bring hope to others. Shelley knew what we know: "If winter comes, can spring be far behind?"

Suggestions for Worship

Call to Worship (Ps. 46:1-2, 10-11):

PASTOR: God is our refuge and strength, a very present help in trouble.

PEOPLE: Therefore we will not fear, though the earth should change, though the mountains shake in the heart of the sea.

PASTOR: "Be still, and know that I am God! I am exalted among the nations. I am exalted in the earth."

PEOPLE: The LORD of Hosts is with us; the God of Jacob is our refuge.

Act of Praise: Psalm 46.

Suggested Hymns: "Holy Spirit, Truth Divine"; "God of Love and God of Power"; "Lead On, O King Eternal."

Opening Prayer: God of power, God of love, you are forever caring. You are always strong. In our loneliness, help us to trust your love. In our weakness, help us to know your power. In our worship, help us to truly praise you that we may live with faith and hope and love. Amen.

Pastoral Prayer: We thank you, our Father, for the life and knowledge you have revealed to us through your Son, our Savior. We praise you, O God, for the joyful hope and the fullness of peace that are your gifts to us through him. We pray, O God, for an increase of love and a flowering of justice that are worthy of his name.

By the power of your Holy Spirit, remake us, mold us, fill us, and use us as faithful witnesses for Christ our Lord. Cast out every evil spirit that has found a place among us—cast out pride, envy, and greed; cast out fear, suspicion, and distrust. Help us to know the unity of the spirit and the bonds of peace in our own community of faith.

Then, through the powerful grace of our Lord Jesus Christ, make us hungry and thirsty for a right relationship with you, O God, and with all of your children. Make us hungry for human kindness, for Christlike forgiveness, and for heart-felt compassion. Make us thirsty for peace and unity, for solidarity with all your children everywhere.

May our worship and discipleship, our prayer and praise, our gifts and service, our thoughts and deeds, be done in the spirit of Christ. Make us new creatures in Christ, who by his grace are worthy of the name Christian. Amen.

JUNE 20, 1993

□

Third Sunday After Pentecost

Followers of Christ who share his mission should also expect to share his rejection, humiliation, and suffering.

The Sunday Lessons

Genesis 28:10-17: In an unsettled, wilderness place, Jacob slept on a pillow of stone. He dreamed of a ladder that reached heaven. God gave to him the promise he had given to Abraham and Isaac. Jacob named the place Bethel or "the gate (meeting place) of God." "This is none other than the house of God, and this is the gate of heaven" (v. 17).
Romans 5:12-19: Paul contrasts the sin of Adam with the obedience of Christ. Estrangement and condemnation resulted from Adam's disobedience. Abundant grace and a new and right relationship with God came, as a free gift, through Christ's perfect obedience.
Matthew 10:24-33: As disciples, subordinate to the teacher, they could not expect better treatment. Christ was opposed and rejected. They would be also. Yet that should not prompt timidity or fear. Share Christ's teachings openly. Proclaim the message from the housetops. "Whoever denies me before others, I also will deny before my Father in heaven" (v. 33).

Interpretation and Imagination

We have been told, through many piquant sayings, that it is better to be silent than to speak. A taciturn farmer taught our adult Sunday school class on occasion. He was full of quips concerning the worth and wisdom of silence. Some I remember are: "An ounce of 'keep your mouth shut' is better than a ton of explanation"; "I've never been hurt by anything I didn't say"; "Smart people speak from experience. Smarter people, from experience, don't speak."

But this man, who so honored silence, was highly regarded as a strong witness to Christian faith. Never was he described in terms of weakness, timidity, or fear. There is another proverb that bears repeating. "Silence gives two signs of weakness—to be silent when one should speak, and to speak when one should be silent."

Christ taught his disciples that the teachings they had received in comparative privacy, that were whispered, should be proclaimed openly for maximum attention. Don't fear those who are hostile to the Christian witness. Don't accommodate them with privacy and silence. They may be able to reject, ridicule, and even kill the body, but they cannot kill the soul.

Neutrality is not allowed in the critical matters of life. A woman had just been shot to death in the house on Carver Street. Another woman, who would later be called as a witness to the murder, walked back to her car saying: "I don't know nothing. I haven't heard nothing. I haven't seen nothing." She was terrified. What would the killer do to her if he knew she had heard the gunshot? (Fayetteville *Observer-Times*, 31 May 1991). But her real fear could not keep her neutral.

"Do not fear!" Christ says to his witnesses. Then he reminds us that God marks the fall of every sparrow. "You are of more value than many sparrows" (v. 31). Both bold witness and timid silence will have lasting consequences, and will be known in the courts of the Almighty. Let our confession of Christ be fearless and faithful. (JKB)

WHO DO YOU FEAR?

Matthew 10:24-33

A SERMON BY T. M. FAGGART

The year was 1969. Three men were sitting in the board room of the local bank, discussing the run-down condition of the local elementary school. In fact, no repairs had been made since it had been integrated two years before. The plaster was falling from the ceilings. Windows were broken out and had not been replaced. The heating in the boys' toilets was broken. The school was badly in need of repair. The three men were a banker, a local automobile dealer, and a United Methodist preacher.

"I can't confront the county school board. They invest their cash flow monies with me," said the banker.

"They buy their trucks and automobiles from me," said the auto dealer.

Then together they said, "Preacher, that leaves you." But the United Methodist preacher responded, "The chairman of my Pastor-Parish Relations Committee is an important member of that school board."

All of life is marked by a conflict of relationships and mixed loyalties. To witness for truth and justice often risks one's business, friendships, economic well-being, and peaceful relationships.

"I need a sanity check," Jeff said. The whole church staff snapped to attention. The statement was new, his sincerity startling. "I'm getting ready to take twenty-five youths on a weekend retreat with only three counselors."

All of us laughed. We were a happy group. All our programs were going full steam ahead. Confidence abounded. "It'll be all right," assured the program director. "Those youths have been together for years. We can trust them. But don't forget—risk goes with the job."

It's true now; it has always been true. There is no witness without risk. But there is no gospel without witness. When Jesus sent his disciples out into the world he knew that; therefore, he spoke those words of sober warning and confident encouragement that are recorded in the morning lessons.

He made two major points: (1) If Christ was ridiculed and rejected (they called him a representative of the devil), his servants should not be surprised if they too meet ridicule and rejection. (2) If you take counsel with your fears of rejection, be sure that you know the ultimate rejection. Don't fear the shadow and ignore the reality. Don't fear one who can only kill the body. Fear God, who deals with souls.

Are we willing to stand for Christ? To acknowledge him before others no matter the risk?

Church history is filled with the names and stories of those who stood for Christ against a host of enemies—ill-conceived doctrine, evil structures, and ruthless values in both the church and the world. Luther, Calvin, Zwingli, Knox, Bunyan, Wesley, Martin Luther King, Jr., and countless others knew firsthand the rejection and fearful opposition and conflict that were first experienced by their Master and Lord. Now we are blessed by the outcome of their witness and ministry. Let us never forget their loneliness and fear, their rejection and suffering at the hands of those they came only to help and to save.

If they received the kind of ridicule and rejection that would have caused the weak spirited to turn away in silence, count on it—you as a bold and faithful witness will get more of the same.

Who, then, shall we fear? Or, more important, who can we trust? Who really sees all, knows all, and is in charge of all things living and dead?

It was a November day. Most of the leaves had fallen from the trees. In some strange kind of foolish analysis, I was wondering about how many leaves had fallen from a maple whose branches spread out across the sidewalk. Then my foot moved a leaf, and beneath it I saw the sparrow. It was dead. For how long, I could not know, nor did I care. Then I remembered the verse, "Two sparrows are sold for a penny. Yet not one of them will fall to the ground apart from the will of your Father. And even the very hairs of your head are all numbered. So don't be afraid; you are worth more than many sparrows."

If his eye is on the sparrow, I know he watches me. Yes, let us take counsel with fear. It is wise to do so. But the fear of God is the beginning of wisdom.

Two pastors stood outside the old German concentration camp where Bonhoeffer was held prisoner until he was hanged. This modern martyr for the faith had opposed Hitler, and, as a German citizen, was named a traitor and was sentenced to death. One pastor said to the other, "We must remember that there is no gospel without witness. And there can be no true witness without risk."

Suggestions for Worship

Call to Worship (Ps. 91:1-4):

PASTOR: You who live in the shelter of the Most High, who abide in the shadow of the Almighty,

PEOPLE: I will say to the LORD, "My refuge and my fortress; my God, in whom I trust."

PASTOR: For he will deliver you from the snare of the fowler and from the deadly pestilence;

PEOPLE: He will cover you with his pinions, and under his wings you will find refuge.

Act of Praise: Psalm 91:1-10.

Suggested Hymns: "Forward Through the Ages"; "Pass It On"; "I Am Thine, O Lord."

Opening Prayer: Lord Jesus Christ, enable us by the power of your love and grace to stand for you and with you in the trials of today. Bless and protect all those who bear witness to the gospel. Give us such a mighty awareness of your sovereignty that we will gain a righteous fear and bold confidence, and so lift high the cross of Christ. Amen.

Pastoral Prayer: Holy God, we are gathered today as a community of faith. We are all partakers of your grace and recipients of your love. Sometimes it comes to us in comforting words and gentle care. We are encouraged by your promises.

But sometimes your love makes a mighty claim and demands singular allegiance. Its challenge calls for an uncompromised commitment.

O God, be patient with us as we stand in tension between your call and our timidity; between who we are and who we are called to be. Let the strong example of Christ cause us to remain faithful.

In times when the days are evil, we need the power and inspirational fire of your Spirit.

Bring to the fearful a new confidence.
Bring to the anxious a steady peace.
Bring to the timid a holy boldness.
Bring to the lonely a sense of your nearness.
Bring to the beaten a healing of wounds.
Bind us all together in your watchful care and love.
In the strong name of Jesus Christ, we pray. Amen.

JUNE 27, 1993

□

Fourth Sunday After Pentecost

A prophet's reward is the subject of these lessons, which tell of the mixture of pain and blessing.

The Sunday Lessons

Genesis 32:22-32: Jacob was returning to the land of his father. (If one cannot bless his beginnings, he can never be truly blessed or become a blessing.) At Jabbok ford he wrestled with the divine. Maimed but unbeaten, he received a new blessing and a new name. One meaning of the name Israel is "God rules."

Romans 6:1-11: Baptism symbolizes death and burial with Christ. Being raised up from the waters symbolizes newness of life. Paul asks if we are to continue in sin, that grace may abound. "By no means!" (v. 2). The death we die we die to sin, but the life we live, we live for God.

Matthew 10:34-42: Discipleship requires that one be willing to be separated from every other devotion. A promise follows that those who lose their lives for Christ's sake will find them. Not only are the disciples rewarded, but also those who receive a righteous one.

Interpretation and Imagination

Most times, we believe that devotion to Christ and the cause of Christ will bring a blessing. We may even reason that the more one gives to Christ, the more one will be blessed.

The Gospel lesson speaks about the reward of the righteous, but it begins with a radical claim. One's foes will be from his or her own household. One who loves "father or mother more than me is not worthy of me" (Matt. 10:37).

Persons who seek a comfortable religion that will make no demands won't hear these words. Still, discipleship worthy of the name "Christian" means desiring Christ more than any other relationship, possession, honor, or position. Even family devotion is subordinate to devotion to Christ.

Suppose that a young man joins the Marine Corps with this reservation. "I'd still like to be a Marine, but I don't want to forsake my family. I want to be home for Christmas. I want to be there for the family reunion and for my mother's birthday."

That's simply not the way things are. The reality is that an insensitive and uncompromising drill sergeant demanding obedience tells new recruits, "I'm your mother and your father. I'm your brother and your sister. I'll tell you when to relax and when to stand tall. I'll tell you when to eat and when to sleep. And maybe when to die." If that demand sounds uncompromising, it only lasts four years for most recruits. And it's tame compared to the radical demand placed on any man or woman who joins the corporate structure and is required to put family matters second.

There is a reward to be had. A medical student intent on the research award for graduates said early on, "I intend to get it. I'll pay a higher price in time and effort than anyone else here." His singular purpose was rewarded. He won the award. (JKB)

THE NEW PERSON IN CHRIST

Romans 6:4

A SERMON BY WALLACE E. FISHER

Our text this morning is Romans 6:4. "By baptism we were buried with him, and lay dead, in order that, as Christ was raised from the dead in the splendour of the Father, so also we might set our feet upon the new path of life" (NEB). During fourteen of the Sundays in Pentecost this year the Epistle lessons come from Paul's letter to the Romans, chapters 5–14. Today we focus on the *Christian's new life in Christ.*

That phrase is used again and again in the church in America. In fact, many who have overheard it do not recognize its radical nature. The phrase glides across their consciousness without stirring them to critical thought, serious faith, or grateful participation in Christ's ministry in the world. Most Christians are hard put to say plainly who the new person in Christ is or to speak intelligently about one's "born-again" characteristics.

Many who belong to the church these days do not belong to Christ. They are too busy ushering, going to meetings, fiddling with new programs and parish structures, raising money to repair old church buildings or construct an addition to solid old ones.

It is not my intention to demean the institutional church or the members who engage in these necessary but secondary activities. I am simply describing the spiritual, biblical, and theological ignorance and shallowness of so many of its members. One can be in the church without being a new person in Christ. That is obvious. But it is not obvious to many these days that one cannot mature as a new person in Christ without becoming a full participant in the fellowship, the church. Here, if one is willing, Christ brings one's person to spiritual maturity through his or her disciplined response to the Redeemer in worship, prayer, meditation, and participation in Christ's ministry in the world.

What then are some of the characteristics of the new person in Christ? What does he or she look like?

First, new persons in Christ look like they did before they were born again of and by God's Spirit. Conversion, justification, and sanctification are not experiences that transform human beings from creaturehood into disembodied spirits who, wholly pure, praise God all day long. In Christ, through faith, we become *new* creatures; but we are still creatures—finite, fragile, erring. We still sin. We still fall prey and contribute to the demonic forces that mar society. And, like birds and beasts and redwood trees, we die. Serious Christ followers are saints (authentic believers) and sinners simultaneously throughout their time on earth. Being new in Christ is not human perfection. It is not a mystical experience. It is, for us mortals, an earthly affair, initiated by God and carried forward in responsive human beings.

What makes those who are "in Christ" different from others is that their sin is forgiven. They are enabled to recognize and hate their ego-centered life-styles, prompted and enabled to repent daily and renew their faith in Christ, motivated to serve Christ in the world, and enabled to face death without fear, grounded in Christ's promise that his victory is also the victory of his faithful followers. What makes the new people in Christ different from others is Christ, who is completing his good work in the midst of their sin-stained, hope-filled daily lives. In short, *his* mind becomes increasingly operative in each believer's person though never fully in this present life.

To become a new person in Christ is an ongoing, even costly affair for Christ and for us. It is not an out-of-this-world experience. Jesus of Nazareth lived in full union with his Father in heaven during his time here and now. To be in Christ is to journey inward daily to receive his gifts of forgiveness, inner renewal, and power, in order to journey outward daily to exercise our new creaturehood and to participate personally in Christ's ministry in and to the world. Either journey without the other warps spiritual formation in the individual.

Second, to be a new person in Christ is not a "hit and miss" affair that requires of us an hour or two now and again "for God." Spiritual formation in the biblical sense involves one's whole person in, with, and for Christ. In today's Gospel lesson Jesus frames his claim for the believer's whole person first in hard language and then paradoxically. He intends to get the need for his priority placed into our soft heads and hard hearts: "Do not think that I have come to bring peace to the earth; . . . Whoever loves father or mother . . . son or daughter more than me is not worthy of me; and whoever does not take up the cross and follow me is not worthy of me" (Matt. 10:34, 37-38).

Jesus' call to new personhood is not tentative, relative, or equivocal. It is absolute and unconditional. In Jesus God's first commandment, "I am the LORD your God" (Exod. 20:2), means that one cannot place anyone or anything—parent, mate, child, vocation, class, race, nation, denominational church or sect, or above all, one's own ego, ahead of God. The first commandment can be discussed, debated, and accommodated to one's culture. Jesus' *demonstration* of the first commandment and his simple, direct, focused statement of its essential meaning (today's Gospel lesson) gets under one's skin; it lodges in one's imagination. It requires the gift of sophistry to soften, ease, or confuse the meaning of Jesus' words. Of course, anyone can—and tens of thousands in the church do—ignore or reject outright Jesus' claim on one's whole person.

To be a new person in Christ is to recognize, accept, and respond affirmatively to his claim on your life. It involves one's whole person—body, mind, emotions, and will. God's Word addresses each person's private self, family self, and public self. Christ himself equips the private self to discern, accept, and fulfill its responsibilities to family, church, society, and God.

Third, the new person in Christ orients to the immediate and the ultimate, time and eternity. The serious Christ follower works for a more humane society for the sake of God's kingdom, partially present in Christ here and now, and waits patiently for its full coming in God's end time.

Many mainstream Protestant churches preach cheap grace, settle for shallow moralism, and in scores of other ways, depart from God's whole counsel. They preach and teach "half a Christ for tender minds." At the same time, however, there are also thousands of mainstream Protestant churches preaching and teaching the whole counsel of God (judgment and grace, law and gospel). But among these congregations there is substantial evidence that few emphasize the eschatological aspect of biblical faith, as well as its mundane aspects, in their preaching and teaching, in parish decisions, and in fashioning their prophetic witness in society. In this sense, ignoring as they do the immediate and ultimate implications of eschatology, they do not preach God's whole counsel. Many persist in this warped biblical approach in spite of the fact that the rediscovery of the importance of eschatology within the New Testament has been one of the outstanding achievements of historical theology in this century.

The new person in Christ simply cannot mature fully in the faith without learning scripture's double vision—time and eternity. Faith's double vision of God's kingdom partially present here and now in the abiding presence of Christ, and God's kingdom yet to come in its full righteousness, love, justice, and glory. God motivates the new person in Christ to evangelize the world *now* and to work for a more humane society *now*, for the sake of God's kingdom. These double-visioned new persons in Christ also look confidently to that day when Christ will complete the good work he has begun in them.

Most Christians agree with Origen, an early church father, that Christ *is* the kingdom of God, already present in his power to forgive and renew us here and now, even as he is the kingdom of God yet to come. To know him, affirm him, and accept his authority here and now will enable us to recognize him then and there when, in God's end time, we meet him in his full glory. It is then and there that Christ will deal with his followers in the same demanding yet gentle way he deals with them here and now: "Come, you that are blessed by my Father, inherit the kingdom prepared for you from the foundation of the world" (Matt. 25:34).

The new person in Christ also recognizes and accepts doubt, in its multiple guises, as the dark side of biblical faith. The Christian declares boldly, "I believe." The Christian also prays humbly, "Help me in my unbelief."

When Doctor William Rainey Harper, one-time president of the University of Chicago, lay dying, he asked plaintively, "Why didn't someone tell me I could become a Christian and settle the doubts later?" God's grace does cover our doubts, but the notion that Christians ever settle all their doubts on this side of heaven's line is not biblical. Paul, whose resilient faith inspires and intimidates us, acknowledged that his faith enabled him to see only a blurred reflection of reality.

When Jesus lived in a body like ours in this fallen world, he experienced days of doubt. His anguished cry, "Let this cup pass from me," at Gethsemane (Matt. 26:39), and his cry of despair on Golgotha, "My God, why have you forsaken me?" (Matt. 27:46), are the lonely cries of every Christian sometime, somewhere. Wherever faith is, doubt is never far removed. In the mystery of the Incarnation, God himself experienced the numbing impact of human doubt. It is the dark side of faith. It dogs all Christians until they join Christ in his kingdom. A thousand times a day in ever-changing situations, every Christian declares and demonstrates his or her faith in Christ. And just as often, day in, day out, he and she pray, "Lord, help me in my unbelief."

New persons in Christ are not starry-eyed idealists, religious sentimentalists, or whining cop-outs on the hard journey into biblical faith. They press on for the "high prize," Christ, praying daily, "Let the mind of Christ be in me." The triune God does not disappoint them.

Suggestions for Worship

Call to Worship (Ps. 17:6-7):

PASTOR: I call upon you, for you will answer me, O God;

PEOPLE: **Incline your ear to me, hear my words.**

PASTOR: Wondrously show your steadfast love,

PEOPLE: **O Savior of those who seek refuge from their adversaries at your right hand.**

Act of Praise: Psalm 17:1-7.

Suggested Hymns: "God of the Ages"; "America"; "Bread of the World."

Opening Prayer: Lord, give us stout hearts to bear our own burdens. Give us willing hearts to bear the burdens of others. Give us believing hearts to cast all our burdens upon Thee. Amen.

Pastoral Prayer: Gracious God, we thank you for your most precious gift to humanity, your only Son, Jesus Christ. In him—his life, teachings, death, resurrection, and abiding presence—you have opened to all who accept and affirm Christ as Lord and Savior your household of faith, the church, in which we, forgiven and renewed, share in Christ's ministry in the world now. We thank you for our place in this beachhead of your eternal kingdom of righteousness, justice, and love in our time and place.

We thank you for the privilege of worshiping you in beauty and truth. Give us ears that hear and eyes that see. Give us hearts and minds and wills that affirm and honor Christ's deed by acting daily on his commandments.

We pray for those who do not know your Son. We pray for those who are only mildly fond of him. We pray for those who deliberately live apart from him. We pray also for those, ourselves among them, who confess Christ in word yet neglect too often to do deeds that demonstrate his presence here and now.

Look mercifully on all people—and you know they are legion in this tangled world of sin—who hunger, live in poverty and pain, are oppressed, are without hope, are dying long and hard.

Strengthen them now and keep before them Christ's promise that in God's kingdom all tears will be wiped away, all injustices will be righted, hope will be fully realized, faith will be fulfilled, and God's love will prevail forever. All this we ask in Jesus' name. Amen.

July 4, 1993

□

Fifth Sunday After Pentecost

The strength of gentleness and the power of humility are the realities of these lessons that offer the invitation, "Come to me, all you that are weary" (Matt. 11:28).

The Sunday Lessons

Exodus 1:6-14, 22–2:10: A new king in Egypt oppressed the Israelites, but still they multiplied. Pharaoh ordered that every boy baby of the Hebrews be killed. When Moses was born, his mother hid him in a basket and floated it among the reeds. Pharaoh's daughter found him there and took him to rear. She named the child Moses because "I drew him out of the water" (2:10).
Romans 7:14-25*a*: Paul first writes, "I do not do what I want, but I do the very thing I hate" (v. 15). Then he asks, "Wretched man that I am! Who will rescue me from this body of death?" (v. 24). God's spirit, that raised Christ from the dead, can also conquer our sin.
Matthew 11:25-30: This passage in Matthew is akin to the thought found in John's Gospel: "All things have been handed over to me by my Father; and no one knows the Father except the Son and anyone to whom the Son chooses to reveal him" (v. 27). The teaching of the Law was often called "the yoke of the law." It was difficult. Christ's revelation is marked by gentleness.

Interpretation and Imagination

Augustine has written, "How often have I lashed at my will and cried, 'Leap now! Leap now!' and as I said it, it crouched for the leap, and it all but leapt; and yet it did not leap. And the life to which I was accustomed held me more than the life for which I really yearned."

The Apostle Paul wanted to keep the law. He tried constantly to do so, but without success. His experience is not strange to us. We, too, have often tried to be obedient to the highest and best we know. Our efforts at works righteousness have left us unfulfilled. For the most part, we know ourselves to be only half faithful or completely unfaithful.

The gift of Christ is an intimacy with God that comes to those who have encountered the living Christ. St. John of the Cross observed that anxious striving is not found in the lives of saints. Rather, there is tranquility, gentleness, and strength. This gentleness and humility and the rest belong to the citizens who give homage to the gentle king.

To all who have wearied of their efforts for goodness; to all who know the embarrassment of broken promises and the frustration of broken resolve; to the church that is disillusioned with bootstrap theology and efforts to lift the world's weight and its despair by what it thinks and says and does; the invitation of Christ is both comfort and promise, "Take my yoke. Learn from me" (Matt. 11:29). Whoever finds grace finds it by means of faith and zeal, not by zeal alone. (JKB)

THE CHRISTIAN—SAINT AND SINNER

Romans 7:14-25

A SERMON BY WALLACE E. FISHER

Last Sunday we identified some characteristics of the new person in Christ. Today, continuing our studies in Paul's letter to the Romans, we shall pursue the paradoxical character of the Christian as saint (authentic believer) and sinner simultaneously.

This theme lies at the center of the Christian faith. All Christ followers are forgiven sinners who still fall short of Christ's perfect righteousness on any and every day of their present life. Indeed, all Christians are acceptable to the righteous God only because Christ assumed the burden of their sin. Through faith in his deed, he makes us acceptable to God. Jesus—bone of our bone, flesh of our flesh, yet the "very God of very God"—has done for us and all people what no human can do for himself or herself: forgive their sins against God, self, and others; liberate them from the demonic powers in and around us; and protect their essential being against the oblivion of death. In today's lesson Paul acknowledges that he—committed to Christ through faith since his dramatic experience on the Damascus Road, and, responding to Christ's gifts of grace, maturing in his likeness—is still wrestling to let Christ cleanse him from the clinging dirt of sin that besmirches his best performances for God.

Admittedly, this Pauline view of salvation (justification and sanctification) is, as it was for many in the first century, a stumbling block for some and downright foolishness to others, inside and outside the church. Essentially, what Paul is saying is that the perfect level of good that he *wants* to do (Christ-inspired intention), he fails to manage; and the evil he abhors (as a new person in Christ) is what he often does instead. There is no hint of Christian perfectionism in Paul's faith. There is no suggestion that anyone deserves to be saved. There is no hint that faith is static—once saved, forever saved. Paul's cry, "Who can save me from this human condition that dogs me until I die" is every serious Christian's realistic plea. Paul's response to this day-in, day-out experience of sin is equally realistic: "Miserable creature that I am, only Christ can save me." This is the ground for every Christian's daily renewal of faith in Christ.

Paul, farther along in Christ's ministry than any other human being has gotten, confessed openly that he fell short of the glory of God in Christ every day. The Apostle, of course, was speaking about his spiritual condition. Instructed by his experience of new personhood in Christ, Paul made a clear distinction between God's providential gifts to his creatures (life, family, body, mind, spirit, freedom) and God's redemptive gifts in Christ to the people of faith (new life, reason corrected by revelation, freedom enlarged by discipline under Christ's Lordship). Paul does not demean God's providential gifts; he accepted and used the many he received responsibly during his whole life. When Paul calls himself a "miserable creature" he is looking at his inner person in the light of Christ's perfect, righteous person. In Christ's company, Paul recognizes that he is saint (authentic believer) and sinner at one and the same time. All serious Christians do.

The realistic linking of saint and sinner was not Luther's invention! That towering figure, striking at the medieval church's steady decline into a human conception of salvation (works righteousness) simply returned to Paul's Christocentric position, and said so plainly. Both men taught and exemplified the theology of the cross. Luther, struggling to make his life conform to his church's teaching (earned salvation, bought salvation, deserved salvation) fell into abysmal despair. It was God's Holy Spirit, working through Luther's studies in Romans, who brought the young Augustinian monk face to face with Paul's hard-worn understanding that "being in Christ" is to be a believer and sinner simultaneously. The cross of Christ is at the heart of God's new covenant with human beings. We sinners are justified by his grace through faith in his Son. Consequently, repentance and gospel faith are inseparable. Faith is dynamic, not static. Biblical repentance is a confession of one's need that leads to his or her acceptance, affirmation, and obedience to Christ day by day. That is what Paul is getting at in today's epistle lesson. But he, like Augustine and Luther, Wesley and Bonhoeffer, did not invent the doctrines of sin and grace. He studied the Old Covenant through Abraham, Jacob, Moses, and the ancient prophets; and he reflected diligently on the New Covenant in Christ, whom he recognized and accepted as the fulfillment of the Law and Prophets.

Turning now from our examination and declarative endorsement of Paul's theology of salvation, we need to point to several biblical stories among many that testify to God's indefatigable love for his "creatures," while they were, and are, still lost and victimized by sin.

The creation story in Genesis points to the God who, as Creator, loves his creatures even when they use their given freedom to rebel against him. The book of Exodus marks the first of God's great deeds of liberation. We see in the book of Jonah—if we free its nameless author from the whale and get to the heart of this inspired evangelical story—how God reveals to his exclusivist followers that he loves other people as well; in this case the people of Nineveh, roaring sinners. Through a reluctant, runaway prophet, he tells them so; they repent. Hosea, Isaiah, and Jeremiah also strike clear evangelical notes. The Old Covenant helped Paul appreciate God's second great act of liberation—Jesus' cross and resurrection.

Of course, the evangelical note becomes a finished symphony in the New Testament. Consider Jesus' parable of the Pharisee and the publican praying in the Temple. The Pharisee was not an evil man. Jesus presented him as a serious, religious man. You and I would value him as a neighbor. Most fathers would be glad to see their daughters marry such a decent, humane young man. Most mothers would rejoice in having sons who are as exemplary. In the parable, the Pharisee is presented as a man who is not only devoted to God's moral law, but also as a man who keeps it perfectly. There is no suggestion in the parable that he is a hypocrite who pretends to keep the Law; he does more than the Law requires. He fasts twice instead of once a week; he gives the tithe of his total income, more than the scribes said was necessary. This honorable, seriously religious fellow's basic fault, Jesus said, was that he held to a religion of law rather than a religion of grace. He accepted and honored the religious teaching that he could earn his salvation.

Now, look at the publican. He is not impressed with his own accomplishments. Instead, he is burdened by his sense of unworthiness before God. He threw himself on God's mercy. Jesus said the publican went from the temple justified. Why? Because he did not stand on his performance. He was not satisfied with himself. God, pleased with the publican's penitent plea for mercy, showered mercy on him even as he prayed. The suppliant was *ready* to be saved. Paul understood the thrust of this parable existentially. Setting out for Damascus, he was the Pharisee. Meeting and accepting Christ on the way to Damascus, Paul became, ever after, the publican. Like the penitent thief crucified beside Jesus, Paul's daily cry was, "Remember me, Lord, for I am a sinful man." That was Luther's stance, too. "We are all beggars," he said. "Only Christ can lift us from our poverty of spirit." Wesley, another of Paul's beneficiaries by way of Luther's preface to his lectures on Romans, "warmed his heart" daily in the study of, meditation on, and proclamation of God's searing, healing Word.

Another of Jesus' unforgettable parables about God and human beings—indeed his most memorable one—throws more light on Paul's doctrine of sin and grace. It is about a wayward, willful son and his patient, ever-loving, forgiving father. There is no need to retell the story here. But there is crying need in today's church to point up several of the eternal truth's in the parable that link repentance, gospel faith, and public witness.

The first truth is that the Christian God loves all of us wherever we are, in whatever condition. The prodigal son forgot his father for a season; the father never forgot his son for a moment. The father's generous, well-ordered household was blotted from the prodigal's memory by days and nights of gambling and drunken revelry. One day the wayward lad—his inheritance squandered, forsaken by his good-times friends, and reduced to eating husks in a pigpen—said to himself, "I don't have to live this way; the servants in my father's house have good food and safe shelter. I'll go home and ask to be a servant." He had come to his senses; he repented and went home. He got better than he deserved, better than being hired as a servant. He got the restoration of his sonship and a gala celebration! That's grace.

The second truth in this story is that God's love is structured by his righteousness. The father, however much he longed for his son, did not move his wholesome, well-ordered household half way to the pigsty to tempt his son to return. The father did not compromise his character. He loved the boy, but the youth had to return on the father's terms or not at all. Grace is costly to God. Cheap grace is rampant in cultural Christianity. It has no place in authentic Christianity. Cheap grace demeans Christ's awesome sacrifice on Calvary. Cheap grace attempts to compromise the righteous character of God. It denies the authority of his Word, obscures the deep-seated nature of human sin, and undermines the crucial nature of every person's freedom to accept or reject Christ's costly gift of faith.

Today's sermon has a single thrust: repentance and gospel faith go hand in hand. We cannot lay siege to the kingdom of God as the German army laid siege to Leningrad for nine hundred days. We cannot buy a seat in his kingdom as we buy an orchestra seat in a Broadway theater. We cannot earn a place in his kingdom as we earn a graduate degree from a front-rank university. We cannot count on a place in the kingdom of God as the German poet, Heine did, saying blithely, "It is God's business to forgive me." Nor can we count on our moral excellence to open the gates of the kingdom.

But we can, in every sense, count on Christ to give us a foretaste of God's kingdom already present in *him*, here and now in *his* church. Repenting *and* turning anew to Christ each day *and* joining him daily on the frontiers of human need, we can be confident that he will complete the good work he has begun in his sinner/saint followers—when he welcomes them as whole persons into God's full kingdom.

Suggestions for Worship

Call to Worship (Ps. 124:1-4, 8):

PASTOR:	If it had not been the LORD who was on our side—let Israel now say—
PEOPLE:	**If it had not been the LORD who was on our side, when enemies attacked us . . . when their anger was kindled against us;**
PASTOR:	Then the flood would have swept us away.
PEOPLE:	**Our help is in the name of the LORD, who made heaven and earth.**

Act of Praise: Psalm 124.

Suggested Hymns: "From All That Dwell Below the Skies"; "My Hope Is Built"; "O Happy Day, That Fixed My Choice."

Opening Prayer: Jesus, we have promised to serve thee to the end; O give us grace to follow, our Master and our Friend. Amen.

Pastoral Prayer: God, in whom we live, move, have our being, and apart from whom nothing of permanent good ever happens in the life of any one of us: we confess that we have sinned against you in thought, word, and deed; in ways we fully understand, partially understand, and do not understand at all. Like sheep, we have strayed from your presence; like the prodigal son, we have willfully fled your presence; like the prodigal's brother, we have angrily cut ourselves off from your presence. For all these offenses, and those that we do not recognize, we are heartily sorry and humbly ask forgiveness in your Son's saving name. Send your Holy Spirit to open us to your Son, Jesus Christ, that he may abide in us and we in him.

All that we ask for ourselves, we ask urgently and daily for our families, our neighbors, and all the people on this small, beautiful life-sustaining planet that you created and sustain.

Finally, on this July 4, help us to celebrate this as a holy day as well as a holiday. Remind us steadily that we Christians are called to be responsible, caring citizens. Keep ever before us that one of the Christian church's primary responsibilities is to remind the state that it is responsible to all its citizens *and to God.*

Hear our prayer for Jesus' sake. Amen.

(See page 447.)

July 11, 1993

□

Sixth Sunday After Pentecost

Seedtime is the image offered by these lessons. It suggests a time for confidence and hope. It's an important message that is often frustrated by poor response.

The Sunday Lessons

Exodus 2:11-22: Having killed an Egyptian who was beating a Hebrew, Moses fled to Midian. There at a well he met and aided the seven daughters of the priest of Midian. Welcomed to the tent and table of the priest, Moses married one of the daughters, Zipporah, who bore him a child. The boy was named Gershom, meaning "I have been an alien residing in a foreign land" (v. 22).
Romans 8:9-17: Contrasting life in the flesh with life in the Spirit, Paul says that we are in bondage, but not to flesh. Those led by the Spirit know that they are children of God, not slaves of God. The Spirit bears witness with our spirit that we are heirs of God and joint heirs with Christ.
Matthew 13:1-9, 18-23: The parable of the sower contrasts seed that falls in unproductive places with seed that grows and is fruitful. The explanation of the parable found in verses 18-23 is likely a later addition to the text, taken from the preaching of the early church. Unproductive seed is the emphasis of the explanation, while the great harvest is the emphasis of the parable.

Interpretation and Imagination

The Word of God will be preached in every city, town, and countryside this Sunday. It will be read and heard in churches all around the world. Week in and week out, the congregations that gather to hear the Word represent in the aggregate the largest gathering of persons in the Western world. In developing countries such as Africa, crowds attending Christian services are tremendous.

Do you think it makes any difference? Do you think it does any good? Is the world any better because of it?

It's not hard to lose hope in a world like this. Violence and vengeance are rampant. More crime is fought with more prisons. Wars and refugees, hunger and homelessness, dishonesty and greed, racism and bigotry, all join to suggest that for all the preaching and teaching of the centuries there is a meager harvest of righteousness.

Poor religion offers passivity, irresponsibility, and escape. It simply looks to heaven above and beyond all of this and neglects the call to seek justice and show love.

The church is ordained of God to be a people of hope. Hope is the thing to which these lessons call us. They ask us to decide against despair, to stand against oppression, and never to accept barrenness. (JKB)

HOW DOES GOD SPEAK TO US?

Romans 8:9-17

A SERMON BY ROBERT G. BRUCE, JR.

A small group of Christians in the Midwest had been meeting in the school cafeteria for over two years. Each week they brought their families and friends and gathered to worship God. They dreamed about the day when their new congregation would have a place where their mission could be expanded; a place to call *home*.

After much anticipation and planning, ground-breaking day finally came. One member, an old farmer from down the road brought his rusty one-bottom plow to the field where the church would be built. The members gathered and set the old plow down on the very spot where the altar would be placed a few months later. Then they attached a long rope and strung it out in front of the plow. When they finished praying, the members all joined their hands to the rope and began to pull. The faithful plow dug into the rich soil, the sod turned, and the new building was on its way.

The members were joined as they all had a hand in the ground breaking. Yet, none of this would have been possible had they not united their spirit with God's Spirit. Joined by his Spirit, they were also bound to one another as God's children. The members listened to the Holy Spirit and felt the presence of God. They knew that the power of the Holy Spirit was bearing witness that they were indeed children of the living God.

The eighth chapter of Romans is one of the finest chapters in the whole Bible. Some have called it the climax of this letter. This eighth chapter, from where we get today's text, is *the* great chapter on the Holy Spirit in all of Paul's writings. Paul says more concerning the Holy Spirit in this chapter than in any other of his letters. In fact, one could begin to develop his or her own doctrine of the Holy Spirit by putting together all that is said in this chapter. Paul concentrates on what the Spirit *does* rather than trying to explain *who* and *why* Spirit is. Paul speaks of the Holy Spirit, not as some vague and cloudy sort of being, but as a vital, personal power and presence.

There is still much confusion in the church today about the Holy Spirit and the various ways in which the Spirit functions in the lives of Christian disciples and in the life of the church. Many are unclear as to the function of the Holy Spirit and the many ways the Spirit speaks to those who will listen.

First, God speaks through his providence. Psalm 19 announces boldly, "The heavens are telling the glory of God; and the firmament proclaims his handiwork" (v. 1). The word *providence* means the care of benevolent guidance of God, but I would expand this definition to encompass all of God's creation. Through his providence, God speaks to his burdened people, comforts the sorrowful, and gives power to the weak. We human beings have made great strides in science and in medicine, but these do not begin to compare with the unexplainable miracles and blessings God sends to his people.

Years ago, it occurred to me that we human beings *do* pride ourselves greatly in our accomplishments. Little do we realize that all we are really doing is uncovering, combining, and recombining what is already here. For example, consider the fact that human beings have not *created* anything new. We have done a great job using what is already here, but we have not *created* anything. I have a vision of God watching over us, and at each new historic discovery or technical advance saying, "Yes, that's right. I made it that way, I put it there. Now, keep looking." "It is that very Spirit bearing witness with our spirit that we are children of God" (Rom. 8:16). The Holy Spirit speaks to us through providence.

Second, God speaks through prayer. God speaks to us when we pray. When we fellowship with him in prayer, we sense his presence and his peace. Psalm 91:15 reminds us, "When they call to me, and I will answer them, I will be with them in trouble, I will rescue them and honor them." God speaks to us through the presence of the Holy Spirit in moments of quiet meditation and in worship. We are taught in Scriptures to "pray without ceasing" (I Thess. 5:17). How many of us can honestly say we live up to that standard? So often the complaint is that we do not know how to pray. Jesus gave us the Lord's Prayer as a model for prayer. Use this prayer as an outline—not just repeating the words, but as an outline, and enlarge upon each section and petition in your own thoughts and words. Be still and listen. Also be encouraged by these words of Paul later on in chapter 8, verses 26-27, where Paul teaches us that even when we do not know what to say, when we have "sighs too deep for words," the Spirit intercedes on our behalf. The desire to pray is at the heart of prayer itself. When we pray "it is that very Spirit bearing witness with our spirit that we are children of God." The Holy Spirit speaks to us through prayer.

Third, God speaks through the promises of Scripture. Skeptics have ridiculed the Scriptures for centuries, but the Word of God has never been outmoded, outmaneuvered, or destroyed. It offers permanent hope for humankind. The Bible is the Word of God; it is his message to his people. Through his Word we receive the promise of salvation, sustenance, and stability. The Bible contains promises for every need. We must read them, reread them, remember them, and rely on them. God speaks to us through his eternal Word.

When we are in the presence of the Word of God either, in private, personal devotional time or in the context of divine worship, the Scriptures "are that very Spirit bearing witness with our spirit that we are children of God." The Holy Spirit speaks to us through the Scripture.

Fourth, God speaks through other people. God's Word was written by holy men and women, and proclaimed by the same. God spoke through his preachers of the past—Abraham, Moses, Esther, Peter, Paul, Lydia, Priscilla, Luther, Wesley, Brooks, Moody, Sunday. God speaks through totally committed messengers today. God's word is alive, dynamic, ever changing, ever relevant—*always, always* relevant! How many times have we been at the point of despair, when it seemed that we were at the end of our rope, and God sent an angel of mercy into our presence with a divine word of compassion that brought healing and hope? Those times, for certain, are the work of the Holy Spirit, bearing witness with our spirit that we are children of God. The Holy Spirit speaks to us through other persons.

God speaks to us through providence, through prayer, through the Scripture, and through others, but it surely is the Holy Spirit that guides them all.

Henry M. Steinmeyer reminds us that, "the way to experience God's Holy Spirit begins in the heart of every Christian. It begins with a commitment of our entire *being* to a new way of life. That is really what Paul is trying to express in the eighth chapter of Romans. Paul was a man who was once totally committed to a life of Law. He knew it through and through. He taught it, he could quote it backwards and forwards. Paul discovered that God in Christ did something for him the law could never do . . . it set him free."

To experience and grow in the Spirit of God, we cannot limit our commitment, for God's Spirit goes far beyond anything we can feel. It surpasses our intellect or understanding. It sets us free. It gives us new life! Paul discovered the power through the Holy Spirit, and we can discover it also.

The Spirit of God speaks to us in various ways in all of our experiences. It speaks to us through providence, through the Bible, through prayer and worship, through music, and through the love of our family and friends. It even speaks to us through that "still small voice" that makes our hearts "strangely warm." It is time for us to listen!

Suggestions for Worship

Call to Worship (Ps. 69:13-14):

PASTOR: My prayer is to you, O LORD.

PEOPLE: At an acceptable time, O God,

PASTOR: In the abundance of your steadfast love, answer me.

PEOPLE: With your faithful help rescue me.

Act of Praise: Psalm 69:6-15.

Suggested Hymns: "My Faith Looks Up to Thee"; "Trust and Obey"; "Come, Sinners, to the Gospel Feast."

Opening Prayer: Almighty God, we confess before you and one another that our lives are so full of distractions, that often we do not hear your Spirit speaking to ours. Through our worship today, guide us to a new understanding of the various ways you communicate to your people through your Spirit. Forgive us for our busyness and our lack of awareness of your presence. Give us honest sorrow for our sins and a desire for new life that we may hear your saving word today. In Christ's name we pray. Amen.

Pastoral Prayer: Today, as we gather for worship, we give thanks to you, O Lord, and glorify your name, Almighty God. You have consistently and continuously shown us your lovingkindness and your faithfulness. We praise you and glorify you for your mighty wisdom which created all things. We bless you and praise you for raising your Son, Jesus Christ, from the grave and for providing us a place in heaven, an eternal home. We thank you for sending your Holy Spirit among us that we might hear and respond to your call through Jesus Christ.

Lord, we confess that we have no merit of our own, and we are totally dependent upon you. We confess that we have been negligent toward the task of sowing the seed of your Word so that your church would increase. We have failed to be a blessing when we are so immensely blessed. We have failed to hear your Spirit when you speak to us through your providence, through your word, through the messages of others, and even through our own personal prayers.

God, restore our sense of your presence and your power from on high, that we may gain renewed zeal for the gospel and a revitalized determination to spread the seeds of your Word. Revive our vision that we may see and respond to the myriad needs that are around us at all times.

Give strength to the weak, a sense of your presence to the lonely, hope for healing to those who are sick, and a purpose for life for those who may be discouraged or defeated. We pray that you will bless our nation with peace, that we may lead the nations of the world in seeking your divine will for an eternal peace. We pray in the name of your Son, our Lord and Savior, Jesus Christ. Amen.

JULY 18, 1993

□

Seventh Sunday After Pentecost

The kingdom of God is both persistent and patient. It will not force, yet it does not yield. "Let both of them grow together until the harvest" (Matt. 13:30).

The Sunday Lessons

Exodus 3:1-12: While herding sheep in Midian, Moses turned aside to see a bush that was burning but not consumed. The God of his fathers spoke from the bush and called him to deliver his chosen people. Moses debated this call saying, "Who am I that I should to go Pharaoh" (v. 11). God's promise was, "I will be with you" (v. 12).

Romans 8:18-25: Present sufferings do not begin to compare with future fulfillment and glory. All creation shares in the stress and suffering of the temporary which so soon decays in futility. Those who have the Spirit also "groan" but wait for adoption. "In hope we were saved" (v. 24).

Matthew 13:24-30: Three parables about the Kingdom speak to the issues of mixed quality and meager growth. The Kingdom, as we know it, contains the bad as well as the good. The parable of the weeds among the wheat teaches patience and tolerance. "Let both of them grow together until the harvest" (v. 30).

Interpretation and Imagination

Impatience and intolerance are characteristic of our self-righteous ways. When our efforts to serve the kingdom of God are met by indifference, stubborn resistance, and evils that are the very opposite of Christ's goodness and mercy, we are inclined to root them out.

Luther once said, "If I were the Lord God and the world had treated me as it has treated him, I would have kicked the wretched thing to pieces."

We who are always in need of mercy can be glad that

forbearance and patience are at the very center of the universe. When we recall the obstinate wills of some persons who later became saints, we thank God for his gentle and persistent ways. When we recall the recalcitrance of our own stubborn hearts, we again thank God.

Emerson once noted that the work of John Brown against slavery was not "a plot of two years or of twenty years," but, as Brown himself said, his devotion to the cause was in response to an oath made to heaven forty-seven years before. Emerson uses an eternal perspective when he writes that the decision was much older. "This was all settled millions of years before the world was made."

The finest qualities of human personality, like the greatest values of modern civilization, are the products of many slow hesitating steps, some of which are ages apart. From mere creature hungers and survival instincts have emerged the instinctive goodness, noble desires, and visionary insights of the twentieth century Christian man and woman. The end is not yet. (JKB)

GENTLE ENOUGH TO BE STRONG

Matthew 13:24-30

A SERMON BY JOHN K. BERGLAND

The little sower stands resolutely on the campus of Duke University. He has been there for a half century, seed bag on his shoulder, his broad right hand scattering the life-giving promise of blessed seed.

This statue came from the New Jersey estate of James B. Duke, along with the gift of money and stocks that created the Duke Endowment and Duke University. Miniature reproductions of the sower have become the cherished memento of those who gain membership in the Founder's Society of the university. What a fitting symbol it is. The sower, boldly and generously scattering his seed, reminding persons who want to leave their mark in the world through a permanent gift to the university, that some seeds falls on good ground and produces eighty- or a hundredfold.

The parable of the sower is an encouragement to the

witnessing community and certainly to this church, reminding us that our message and testimony will be rewarded with an increase of faith and love. If you cannot see any immediate response, be reminded that the seeds grow in gentle and unseen ways. If the evidences of evil are embarrassingly present, take comfort in the parable of the weeds among the wheat. Let both grow together until harvest.

Where should we begin to best find ourselves in the parable of sower, seed, and soils? Is one more important than the other? Should we center our thoughts on the quality of the soil—the hearers? Should we concentrate primarily on the seed and its miraculous, life-giving power—the Christian gospel? Or should we focus our attention on the sower—the witnessing church? All of these emphases have integrity and are apparent in the text, but this morning I invite you to turn away from seed, soil, and sower to consider what is being said about the kingdom of God and the nature of the God revealed by Jesus Christ.

Notice first that our God, whose kingdom is portrayed by seed and sower, is *strong enough to be gentle.* You've seen them just as I have—bulldozers, locomotives, explosives, storms, and earthquakes. I've felt the powerful thrust of jet engines that propelled an aircraft with its tons of steel and cargo down a long runway and then into flight. I've stood among the marshes of Cape Canaveral and watched the brilliant flash of rockets firing, sending a spacecraft into orbit. I've stood on the granite cliffs of the Pacific Ocean and felt waves, forty feet high, break against the rocky shore that trembled beneath my feet. That's power! I've seen how lightning split a mighty live oak tree from top to bottom in a single burst. That's power! I've seen a mountain blown away and whole forests leveled when the volcano of Mount St. Helens erupted. I've seen a city leveled by a hurricane. That's power!

But none of this begins to compare with the life-giving power of vital seed and fertile soil, of blessing rains and warming sun. Every devastation is soon covered by the greening grass. Every ruthless, brutal, aggressive expression of destructive power pales in comparison to the vigorous and vibrant powers of life. Our God is like that. He is strong enough to be gentle.

Come further, then, and note that God is *lasting enough to be patient.* Our world has become increasingly rushed. We want an immediate response and quick results. Long-term consequences are disregarded if quarterly dividends are large. Weekly paychecks have replaced annual harvests. We are the people who buy instance rice and instant pudding. We are also the people whose lives evidence the temporary.

An assertive and impatient mother was enrolling her son in a college preparatory school. Wanting some assurance that her investment in quality education would bring dividends for her son, she asked, "Why does this educational process take so long and cost so much?" The headmaster pondered her question, and patiently answered, "Have you ever noticed that one can grow a squash in six weeks, and that it's gone before fall? It takes a life-time to grow a great tree, especially one whose leaves do not wither. We want your son to be like a mighty oak tree."

Our God was before the beginning, and he will last beyond the end of time. He set the stars in their courses. He sees a thousand years and calls it one day. Our God is lasting enough to be patient. He waits for seed to grow.

Notice also that our God is *righteous enough to be tolerant.* When one is uncertain about his or her own character, the tendency is to be critical and judgmental. Insecure persons are pathetically negative. But when one knows a right relationship with God and neighbor, a remarkable grace attends every confrontation. Jesus revealed a God of grace, a God good enough to be tolerant. He would let weeds grow together with the wheat.

A pilgrim sat in a shaded place and meditated as the waters of a broad river lapped against the shoreline. Near the water's edge he noticed a scorpion that had fallen into the water from a banyon tree. It tried again and again to climb out onto the roots of the tree, but each time it reached a safe place another wave would wash it back into the water. The pilgrim, who reverenced all of life, went to the scorpion intending to save it. He reached down to lift it from the water, but the scorpion stung him. Drawing back his hand he thought, "Perhaps if I lift it more gently." But again the scorpion stung him. Then he reasoned, "Perhaps if I lift it out quickly." The scorpion stung him a third time. A cynical man watching this, laughed at the pilgrim and asked, "Why do you try to help a thing that only wants to hurt you?"

It's the old, old question. Why would God want to love those who hated him; why would Christ forgive those who crucified him? The pilgrim answered righteously, "It is the scorpion's nature to sting. It is my nature to save." Our God is like that—good enough to withstand wrong, righteous enough to tolerate evil. The weeds and the wheat will grow together.

And finally note that this parable reveals a God who has *resources enough to be extravagant.* A five-year-old boy was helping his grandmother plant a garden. The rows were not long, but the carrot seeds were very small. "Plant them very carefully or you won't have enough," cautioned the grandmother. But the little boy was unimpressed. Carefree and careless, as little boys can be, he poured and scattered the seeds recklessly. But his resources didn't match his extravagance. He was out of seed before he reached the halfway point of the row.

Life's like that for most of us too. We run out of money, run out of energy, run out of ideas, run out of time, run out of space. Our limitations and our needs teach us to conserve. We soon learn to measure and count and carefully calculate our resources in almost every circumstance.

I don't understand God's ways, do you? If I could make a cherry tree, beautiful and fragrant in full bloom, I think I'd try to make it last longer than a week or ten days before the flowers fade. If I could take all the wonder and mystery of life and put it in little brown seeds, I wouldn't scatter it among weeds and waste it in rocky ground. I surely wouldn't use it for bird food. But the endless resources of God are evident in his extravagance. He scatters the seed. The cattle on a thousand hills are his. So is the morning and the evening. Both seed time and harvest belong to him. That's why he could take heaven's very best, his only begotten son, and let him die on a cross in a garbage dump outside Jerusalem. Our God has resources enough to be extravagant.

I'm glad it's that way aren't you? If you're lonely and need a friend; if you are poor and need a helper; if you are sick and need God's healing; if you have sinned and need God's mercy; rejoice in this—Jesus Christ has revealed a king and a kingdom strong enough to be gentle, lasting enough to be patient, good enough to be tolerant, and with resources enough to give his very best for your greatest hunger and deepest need.

Suggestions for Worship

Call to Worship (Rom. 8:22-24):

PASTOR: We know that the whole creation has been groaning in labor pains until now;

PEOPLE: And not only the creation, but we ourselves, who have the first fruits of the Spirit, groan inwardly while we wait for adoption,

PASTOR: The redemption of our bodies.

PEOPLE: For in hope we were saved.

Act of Praise: Psalm 103:1-13.

Suggested Hymns: "How Great Thou Art"; "Go Down, Moses"; "Just As I Am, Without One Plea."

Opening Prayer: O Lord our God, your patience and gentleness are revealed to us in the growing seed and the greening grass. Your word teaches that your mercy will not always last, nor will your wrath continue forever. Give us such confidence in your steadfast mercy that we may trust ourselves and everything that is dear to us to your saving and keeping power, through Jesus Christ our Lord. Amen.

Pastoral Prayer: Almighty and everlasting God, help and defend us we pray. Set free those who are oppressed. Let your love and mercy reach out, especially to the least of us. Raise up those who have fallen. Reveal your presence to the lonely. Feed the hungry. Help the weak to stand. Heal the sick. Bring back to the safety of your fold those who have gone astray.

We thank you, O God, for seasonable weather, good harvests, and peaceful and plentiful times. We praise you for seed and soil, for blessed sun and blessed rain. We rejoice in your faithfulness and pray that when Christ returns he shall find faith among us. Help the children have faith, we pray.

We pray for this Christian community; for those who are present, and for those who are absent; for those who are gathered to the very center of its warmth and love, and for those who only gather at the outside edges; for those whose lives are well ordered and fruitful, and for those who have known failure, embarrassment, and all of the accompanying poverty. We all need your power and love. So guard the church we pray. Watch over and protect us all. Nourish every one of us with your loving care and save your people for the sake of your dear son, our Lord Jesus Christ. Amen.

JULY 25, 1993

□

Eighth Sunday After Pentecost

The kingdom of God is something better, something infinitely more valuable than what we now have. Two parables speak of this—the treasure in the field and the pearl of great price.

The Sunday Lessons

Exodus 3:13-20: Moses' second objection to his call was that he didn't know God's name. How could he answer if asked, "Who sent you?" "Say I AM has sent me to you," God answered (v. 14). This verb form of "to be" suggests *I will be what I will be; I cause to be all that is.* It indicates God's presence, purpose, and power.
Romans 8:26-30: The Father's plan of love intends for us "to be conformed to the image of his Son" (v. 29). Paul writes, "We know that all things work together for good for those who love God, who are called according to his purpose" (v. 28). Those who are called by God are formed by the Spirit into the likeness of Christ.
Matthew 13:44-52: The last three parables concerning the Kingdom refer to a treasure hidden in a field, a pearl of great value, and a dragnet that gathers fish of every kind. The first two make the same point. The Kingdom is of more value than anything you now possess. The dragnet parable speaks of mixed values—some good, some bad—and of the sorting out at the close of the age.

Interpretation and Imagination

The Gospel of Luke speaks of the worth of every person. Parables tell of one lost sheep that is of such worth that the shepherd leaves ninety-nine in the fold to go and find it. A woman sweeps the house in search of a lost coin, and the father waits for the return of a lost son. These parables speak of the worth of one soul.

A woman who had come to believe that she was unworthy, a

worm in the sight of God, was reading these parables from Matthew 13. Suddenly she said, "I'm the pearl of great price. God has given the best that he has, even his own Son, for me."

In Matthew's Gospel, the parable of the treasure hidden in the field and the parable of the pearl of great price are interpreted to mean that the kingdom of God is of such value, that those seeking to be citizens will forsake every other value in order to have the best.

In the larger context of the gospel, one may see how it goes both ways. We love because he first loved us.

If we believe that the God who is the only true God is goodness and steadfast love—a parent who knows us, loves us, thinks of us, provides for us and seeks us—and the one who has sent an only Son to reveal his love, will we not turn away from any other affection and choose a God who saves and heals?

We know that we are faced with thousands of choices in today's world. Confronted with so many opportunities, we tend to value all things equally. We have become increasingly casual about the uniqueness of Christ. The lesson calls for us to put all that we are and all that we have in one heap, and store and willingly surrender it in devotion to Christ. (JKB)

OUT OF OUR CONTROL

Romans 8:26-30

A SERMON BY JERRY LOWRY

It is often difficult for us to admit that there are some things in life over which we have no control. Some of them are very basic. As children we could not choose our parents. We could not choose our gender. We could not choose the color of our skin, hair, or eyes. We could not choose the country in which we were born. So, how does it feel to be in skin you can't shed or a body you can't get rid of?

Some things in life are beyond our control. Imagine a daughter who has planned an outdoor wedding. On the day of the wedding mom and dad are hoping for sunshine. But the darkest clouds of the summer roll in, and the rain begins pouring an hour before the wedding. Or consider the baby's first birthday. Parents have been waiting for a year to video this special occasion. They grab the video camera and switch it on, but it does not work. It fails precisely at that moment.

A more tragic example, Junior is sailing down the street on his sixteenth birthday. This is the first time he has driven a car on his own. He takes his eyes off the road for just a moment to look at a young girl. At that moment, a truck backs into the street in his lane. Instant tragedy! No matter how disciplined, intelligent, or hardworking we are, there are some things in life beyond our control.

Some of our efforts to control the uncontrollable are ludicrous. Many persons today are resorting to forms of superstition, such as lucky charms, rituals of signs, root-working, and palm reading. Believe it or not, athletes are notoriously superstitious. For example, Minnie Minoso, a former baseball star, was hitless in five at-bats during a doubleheader. Between games he took a shower in his uniform, claiming he was washing away the evil spirits. Everybody laughed, but the second game Minnie got three hits. After the game, eight players took showers with their uniforms on. Ludicrous, wouldn't you say?

Superstition is growing in our nation. According to a 1978 Gallup poll 19 percent of American teenagers believed in witches, 28 percent in astrologers. By 1988, 29 percent of the teenagers polled believed in witchcraft and 58 percent in astrology.

Would you believe that superstition has even crept into our Christian faith?

There is a common practice among Christians called "lucky dipping." What is "lucky dipping"? It is a method of Bible study in which a person prays for divine guidance and then lets the Bible fall randomly open to wherever it will. Then, with eyes shut, the person dips his finger onto the page and gets his answer from God wherever the finger lands.

For example, most of us have heard the story about the man who lucky dipped the Scripture and his finger fell on the verse, "And Judas went out and hanged himself." Trying again, his finger fell on another verse, "Go thou and do likewise." This is not sound use of the Bible. The Holy Spirit would not lead us to such foolishness.

Not only do we try the varied forms of superstitions, but many of us have tried prayer to control the uncontrollable at some time. Have you ever thought what a bind it would put God in if he tried to answer all our prayers?

Let's face it, there are areas of our lives beyond our control, and this is good. Aren't you glad you can't control God? With our finite minds, we could never order a perfect world. We will never have enough knowledge or enough wisdom to perfectly determine what would be best for our lives.

Suppose God would give any one of us his all-poweredness (omnipotence) for twenty-four hours. We would change a lot of things in this world. But what if God gave us his wisdom with his all-poweredness? I believe we would leave things as they are. Aren't you glad God is in control, and that some things are out of our control.

There is one more thing that needs to be said: The Christian relies not on superstitions or upon luck, but upon faith in a wise, all-knowing and loving God. It was this God who inspired St. Paul to write, "We know that all things work together for good for those who love God, who are called according to his purpose" (v. 28).

If we live obedient lives, loving God and our neighbor, God will be able to work everything that happens to us for our good. However, we must belong to God. This is the gospel! Good news! If this doesn't fill our rationalistic view of the universe, then it makes a mockery of our dependence upon charms, good luck, and astrologers. But it is the gospel. In everything, God is working for *good* for those who love him. God can't work for our good if we do not love him.

Is God in control, controlling the uncontrollable? How can we get our minds around this great truth, that God works in everything for good to those who love him?

Beloved, what in your life are you trying to control that you can't control? Is your faith gone? Does it seem your prayers never help? Are you trying to control your son or daughter? Are you trying to control their destiny? Or are you allowing God to have his way in your life and in these matters?

Unsaved, why should you control any longer? Let God have his way with you. For God works for goodness in everything for those who love him and who are called according to his purposes. God is saying "Trust me, for you are my child. You are an heir of God and joint heirs with Christ." Problems, suffering, and chaos are part of life. But do not be afraid, for God searches our hearts and God knows what we need. And we know that in all things God works for the good if we will just love.

In closing, I recall hearing the story of the late Reverend Maltbie Babcock, a Presbyterian pastor. He frequented a hill daily to view God's beautiful creation. Upon his return one morning, God inspired the writing of a hymn that all of God's people have learned to love, "This Is My Father's World." Hear the words:

This is my Father's world.
O let me ne'er forget
That though the wrong seems oft so strong,
God is the ruler yet.
This is my Father's world:
why should my heart be sad?
The Lord is King; let the heavens ring!
God reigns; let the earth be glad!

Amen. Oh yes, it is true there are some things we cannot change. It is true we often try the ludicrous to control the uncontrollable. So, as Christians, we must rely on our faith in God who is still "ruler yet." God still reigns. Let us rejoice and be glad.

Suggestions for Worship

Call to Worship (Ps. 105:1-3):

PASTOR: O give thanks to the LORD, call on his name,

PEOPLE: Make known his deeds among the peoples.

PASTOR: Sing to him, sing praise to him; tell of all his wonderful works.

PEOPLE: Glory in his holy name; let the hearts of those who seek the LORD rejoice.

Act of Praise: Psalm 105:1-11.

Suggested Hymns: "Stand Up and Bless the Lord"; "Source

and Sovereign, Rock and Cloud" (Hymn tune "Jesus Loves Me"); "I Know Whom I Have Believed."

Opening Prayer: Dear gracious God, you come to us to reveal yourself in many ways, and we believe that as we worship together this day that you will come to us in new ways revealing more fully who you are. You reveal yourself to us best of all through your Son, Jesus, who is the love of God incarnate. His Spirit is present with us as a gathered community of faith, to reveal even deeper things of your love for us and for the world. Give us receptive hearts to know who you are for our lives this very hour. In Jesus' name we pray. Amen.

Pastoral Prayer: O great God of love, who we know best through your Son, Jesus Christ, we come to you this day with the assurance of Jesus Christ as our intercessor as we make our requests known to you. His love for our lives gives us this assurance. His willingness to be born into a world of woe and his willingness to leave a life of splendor to become as us, he who knew no sin, that we might be made right and reconciled to God. To see his compassion as he ministered and continues to minister to persons reveals to us even greater depths of love that he has for us. His willingness to die on the cross for the sins of the whole world is no less than perfect love. So with great thanksgiving, we pray knowing that kind of love pleads for us as we confess our sins, and knowing they are forgiven. To make our request known with faith brings a consolation that can be found in no other place.

Through Jesus' resurrection we know he is very much alive and in our presence as the church of the Lord Jesus Christ. Thank you, O God, for the gift of your Son and for the presence of his Spirit with us now and forever. Thank you for making him our Savior, Lord, and Redeemer. Thank you for allowing him to continue to teach us and to prepare an eternal place for us in mansions he is now preparing.

We simply want to say, O God, thank you for Jesus, who loved the world so much that he gave all that he had and all that he was to the world.

So we understand why you, O God, have given him a name which is above every name—the name of Jesus. With praise and honor we pray in his name. Amen.

August 1, 1993

□

Ninth Sunday After Pentecost

Bread is basic to life. Whether a sandwich in a brown bag, manna in the wilderness, multiplied loaves by the Sea of Galilee, or the bread of the Holy Supper, it is that which speaks of God's steadfast love.

The Sunday Lessons

Exodus 12:1-14: The feast of the Passover has roots in an ancient nomadic festival of spring that Israel reinterpreted as a reminder of their deliverance from slavery in Egypt. A year-old lamb, without spot or blemish, was slaughtered, roasted, and eaten by everyone in the house. Blood, deity's portion, was smeared on the doorposts. The Passover was eaten with sandals on and staff in hand, ready for the march. The Israelites recalled how the Lord passed over the blood-marked houses during the firstborn death plague.
Romans 8:31-39: "If God is for us, who is against us?" (v. 31). Here the question is not whether we side with God or not, but rather, if God sides with us. Proof that God is "for us" is that, "He . . . did not withhold his own Son" (v. 32). Nothing created can separate us from this love.
Matthew 14:13-21: "They need not go away" (v. 16). The disciples had only five loaves and two fish, and the crowd numbered five thousand men plus women and children. Yet after the crowd had been fed, twelve baskets full of broken pieces were left over. Matthew sees this miraculous bread as the new food of the Messiah, who, like Moses, leads God's people to the promised land flowing with milk and honey.

Interpretation and Imagination

When the disciples were faced with hungry multitudes in a place too poor to feed them, they wanted to send them away. In modern America, an isle of affluence in a poor world, we simply keep them out. When we consider millions of destitute and hungry persons gathering at our ports of entry, we, like the disciples, are inclined to send them away.

In such a context, our Lord's, "You give them something to eat" (v. 16) and "Bring [what you have] to me" (v. 18), take on compelling significance. The church continues its efforts to be obedient to Christ's command to feed the hungry and welcome the stranger. We dare to do it because of our faith in Christ, who can and will supply all that is needed.

There are words in these lessons that have become the cherished words of ritual at the Lord's Supper—"took the loaves . . . blessed . . . broke . . . gave" (v. 19). They remind us of the one who said, "My body is broken for you"; one who is vision, challenge, and strength for the church. (JKB)

HOW TO HANDLE THE HUNGER

Matthew 14:13-21

A SERMON BY JAMES R. McCORMICK

This account from the Gospel of Matthew is about hunger. But even before the story gets to the obvious bodily hunger that Jesus satisfied with loaves and fish, we see another hunger. Large numbers of people, driven by hungers of the heart, followed Jesus across the lake to a wilderness. They stayed there all day, receiving his words, seeking his touch.

They were probably not aware of Jesus' needs. Jesus had just been told of John's death. Perhaps he was concerned for his own life, not yet ready to openly confront his opposition. No doubt he was grieving for his cousin and friend, and for the kind of world that would do such a thing to a man like John. Certainly, he was physically tired, needing a time of refreshment and rest. But, oblivious to Jesus' needs, the crowd pressed on, calling for him, reaching out to him.

And, as always, Jesus had compassion for them. Setting aside his own needs for the moment, he healed those who were sick, he spoke with them, he gave himself to them. That's what compassion is. It's feeling with others, so that their hurts become our hurts, their needs our needs. Read through the Gospels and you will discover that when Jesus healed people or fed people or spent time helping people, he was never showing off or attempting to prove anything about his identity or power. Always it was an act of compassion, because he really cared about people.

And his caring was for the whole person. Distorted Christianity tends to divide people into parts and to focus attention upon either the salvation of the soul or upon meeting the needs of the body or the mind. Jesus never did that. Human beings cannot be pulled apart like tinker toys. We come as a package, with all the parts connected. Knowing that, Jesus ministered to the whole person. He fed the hungry, healed the sick, spent time with the lonely, filled the spiritually empty, redirected the lost—where would the list end? In whatever ways people were in need, Jesus sought to meet those needs because of his compassion.

That's why, when the people began to be hungry, Jesus wanted them to be fed. The disciples assumed that they would have to go into the villages to buy food. As usual, they underestimated Jesus. And, as a consequence, they underestimated themselves.

Do you see yourself in this story? The Bible will never be God's enlivening word to us unless it becomes a mirror in which we see ourselves. Certainly I am there. In the face of a problem, it is tempting to concentrate upon what I do not have, what I cannot do, instead of focusing upon what I do have and what I can do. A poet has written:

> It's not what you'd do with a million
> If riches should be your lot,
> But what are you doing today
> with the dollar and a quarter you've got?

The disciples focused upon their inadequacy and were ready to send the people away. Instead, Jesus asked them to take inventory of their resources. They said, "We have nothing here but five loaves and two fish" (v. 17). There were over five thousand people there, and the disciples had only five loaves and two fish. Does that sound familiar? Such great need, such paltry resources. So much to do, so little with which to do it. It's easy to become overwhelmed in our kind of world. It's tempting, with such a seeming imbalance between need and resources, to simply give up, turn off the compassion switch, send the people away, and look after number one.

That's the very thing Jesus refused to do. That's the thing Jesus always refused to do. Just as human beings are whole persons, needing to be ministered to as whole persons, so the human family is an unbroken whole. It is never enough to see to it that the needs of one, or the needs of a few are met, not if we belong to Christ. In fact, it may well be that the most accurate test of our Christian commitment is the size of our circle of compassion. We must never be content as long as there are those in need.

It is true that, at first glance, our resources seem woefully inadequate. "We have nothing here but five loaves and two fish." But look at what Jesus did with that. He said, confidently, "Bring them here to me" (v. 18). Jesus did not berate them for not having more. He did not ask them, nor does he ask us, for more than we have to give. (Neither does he ask for less.) But when we give it in love and trust, we discover that our all is enough. After receiving the food they brought, he asked the people to sit down on the grass. Doesn't that form a picture of confidence and peace? They weren't panicking or clamoring for food. They were sitting on the grass, waiting expectantly. Then Jesus blessed the food, broke it, gave it to his disciples, and they gave it to the crowds. The text says then that "all ate and were filled" (v. 20).

Look at the gracious way in which Jesus ministers to people's needs. He could have done it all himself. But he chose to let his disciples have a part in it. He took what they had brought, blessed it, and then allowed them to distribute it to the people. What they had brought was not enough without what Jesus did with it. Our resources alone never are. But what an honor Jesus gave to his disciples! And what an honor he gives to us, to allow us to share in the compassionate ministry of Christ, feeding the hungry, clothing the naked, visiting the sick and the imprisoned, telling the story of God's love made known in Christ. When we understand it, such responsibility is not a burden, but an honor. It is our privilege to be called by the name of Christ and to be used by him in distributing gifts of his grace!

One cannot hear this account from Matthew's Gospel without being reminded of the Lord's Supper. They did it that day much like the first-century Christians celebrated the Sacrament. Jesus blessed the food, probably using the traditional Jewish prayer, "Blessed art thou, O Lord our God, king of the world, who has brought forth bread from the earth." Then, he broke the bread and asked the disciples to give it to the crowds (as the deacons did in the church) and to gather up the fragments afterward. No doubt, Matthew was making the connection between the way Jesus fed the five thousand and the way he feeds us at the Lord's Table. There is also a connection here with the Messianic Banquet to be held at the end of history. There all the faithful will sit down with the Messiah at the victory banquet in the kingdom of God. There all hungers will be fed. All hurts will be healed. All needs will be met.

In Matthew's story, there, on that hillside in the grass, a miracle took place. And I don't particularly care how you understand that miracle. It could be that Jesus used the power of prayer to increase the amount of food. It could be that through the loving example of the few who were willing to share what little they had with the many, others in the group began to take out of hiding the food they had stashed away for themselves. (Jews carried small baskets with them containing kosher food for those times when it was otherwise unavailable.) Or, it could be that in this sacramental moment, when everyone was so moved by the loving presence of Jesus and the unselfish sharing of the group, each one took only a small fragment of the food and was content with the spiritual nourishment. It doesn't really matter how you understand it, the fact is, a miracle took place that day.

I also see in this account a metaphor for the living of life. I see in it the best way—no, let me make it stronger—I see in it the *only* way to handle the hunger of life. When we take what we have and bring it to Christ, when he blesses it, adds his power to it, and gives it back, then, it is enough. Above all else, this story is about the sufficiency of God's grace. Everything we need in life is available to us as a gift of God's grace. Not always everything we want, but everything we need is available.

Jesus took the food and blessed it. And in the blessing, he acknowledged that every good gift is from God. We may think that what we have is inadequate. But there is more where that came from. God's abundance is greater than all our need. When we trust that, and live our lives in that security, life becomes the good gift that God intends for it to be.

In the New Testament, the opposite of faith is not unbelief. The opposite of faith is fear. That's why, again and again in the Bible, the announcement of good news is preceded by the words, "Fear not"; "Do not be anxious"; "Let not your hearts be troubled"; "Don't be afraid." Then there is an announcement of what God has done for us in Christ, or of what God will yet do by the Spirit. That's why we don't have to be afraid—because of God!

But life without faith is a life of fear. The person without faith fears that there will never be enough of the things he needs. I tell you, to live in such fear is to live in hell. Whatever we acquire, it is not enough. Whatever we achieve, it is not enough. No matter how much we are loved by family and friends, it is not enough. People without faith are like bottomless pits of need. The emptiness remains because anything you put into it falls through the bottom. That's life without faith. At our deepest place there is a haunting fear that there will never be enough of what we need. That's why some people feel compelled to live a grasping life, a life lived over against their neighbor. That's why some people feel that they've got to hang on to whatever they have instead of sharing it, because they are afraid there isn't enough to go around. Do you sense the fear in that?

By contrast, the life of faith is one that trusts God to provide for all our needs. The gift of grace is the assurance that God's abundance is greater than all our need. Do you hear the good news? God has riches we can't overdraw. God has resources we can't exhaust. God's abundance is always greater than our need.

So, after we have been moved by Christ to do what we can and share what we have, we don't have to be afraid. We can just sit down on the grass in confidence and peace. Because after Jesus has blessed it and added his power to it, it will be enough. In fact, there will be twelve baskets more than enough! That, finally, is how to handle the hunger of life. In trust, you bring it to Christ.

Suggestions for Worship

Call to Worship (Ps. 143:1, 5-6):

PASTOR: Hear my prayer, O LORD; give ear to my supplications in your faithfulness;

PEOPLE: **Answer me in your righteousness.**

PASTOR: I remember the days of old, I think about all your deeds, I meditate on the works of your hands.

PEOPLE: **I stretch out my hands to you; my soul thirsts for you like a parched land.**

Act of Praise: Psalm 143:1-10.

Suggested Hymns: "Glorious Things of Thee Are Spoken"; "Break Thou the Bread of Life"; "Guide Me, O Thou Great Jehovah."

Opening Prayer: Gracious God, we come to you today conscious of our need. Each day we are reminded, that, apart from your enlivening presence, our resources are inadequate for the demands of life. But we trust that your grace is greater than all our need, and that you delight in providing for us. So, come to us now and give us what a loving God knows how to give his family. In the name of Christ we pray. Amen.

Pastoral Prayer: Loving God, we are grateful that we are coming to One in prayer who is never too busy for us, always ready to listen, always willing to love us and forgive us, always able to give us what we need. We are not deserving of such gracious care, but we need it, and we are so very grateful for it. And, when we are at our best, we sense that our best hope in life is in reaching into your storehouse of love and allowing you to give us the gifts you are so anxious to give.

Father, we are grateful for the way in which your love has already blessed our lives. You have called us into being and given us a good world in which to live. You have touched us by the caring concern of families, teachers, and friends. You have ministered to us through your church. You have guided us when we were confused, forgiven us when we failed, comforted us when we were hurting, come to us when we were alone, strengthened us when we were faltering, and again and again loved us into new life. We know, when we are thinking clearly, that all we are and all we ever hope to be, we owe to you and the generosity of your great love.

Help us now to share that love with others. Help us to know that it spoils and loses its power when we try to hoard it selfishly. Help us to trust that the more love we give away, the more we receive from you, and there is no limit to your supply. Give us the spirit of our Lord, who loved the unlovely, forgave the undeserving, helped the helpless, and reached out to those considered untouchable. Give us a love big enough to love all those you love, and thus help to bring new life to this hurting world.

Use this service to do something good for us and to prepare us for service in your world. For we pray in the name of Christ, who loved the world so much that he gave his life for it. Amen.

August 8, 1993

□

Tenth Sunday After Pentecost

Solitude and prayer (Elijah in the mountain cave, Jesus on the mountain alone), and the overwhelming power of nature's violence, are brought together in Gospel and Old Testament lessons that encourage faith.

The Sunday Lessons

Exodus 14:19-31: A shining pillar of cloud, the power of Moses' rod, and the parting of the waters, tell of God's deliverance at the Red Sea. Natural phenomena—a strong east wind that made the sea dry land and Egyptian chariot wheels clogged with mud—are also part of the miracle. When Israel saw the great work that the Lord did they feared and believed.
Romans 9:1-5: In Romans 9–11, Paul agonizes over the Jews' rejection of Jesus as Messiah. He does not separate himself from them but longs for their conversion to faith in Christ. Paul would gladly be "cut off from Christ for the sake of my own people" (v. 3).
Matthew 14:22-33: The disciples' boat was far from land, "battered by the waves," and "the wind was against them" (v. 24). Jesus came to them walking on the storm tossed waters. Peter went to meet him, but his faith turned to fear "when he noticed the strong wind" (v. 30). "You of little faith, why did you doubt?" (v. 31).

Interpretation and Imagination

Scholars note that the early church, suffering persecution and inclined to fear, allegorized the story of Jesus walking on the water to encourage faith. The disciples are in a small boat (the church) that is beaten by the waves (persecution). Even Peter, the disciple known as "the rock," was afraid. Jesus came to them in the midst of the storm and rescued Peter. In one voice the disciples confessed, "Truly you are the Son of God" (Matt. 14:33).

George Herbert, a seventeenth-century poet, suggested that

if you want to learn to pray, you should go to sea. When confronted by a storm at sea, by hurricanes and tornadoes, earthquakes, floods or fires, we pray. Such prayers are prompted by fear rather than faith. Frightened by the natural powers of this world, one need not be taught to cry out like Peter, "Lord save me!" (v. 30). Fear prompts such prayer.

The opposite of faith is not simply doubt; it is mostly fear. People who do not wholly understand God's goodness and faithfulness by personal experience are often intimidated and afraid. If you doubt God's power and love, you have little to lose in putting it to the test.

In the Gospel lesson the emphasis centers more on the confession of faith than on the miracle. Thus one may conclude that the story is told not to prompt a desire for miracles—fear does that—but to give us faith. "Truly you are God" is the affirmation that the sermon must proclaim. (JKB)

FIXING THE FOCUS

Matthew 14:22-33

A SERMON BY JAMES R. McCORMICK

There is nothing more important for us than to fix the focus of our lives. What is central for us? What is foundational for us? What is it that shapes our identity, our perceptions, our values, our decisions? What is the core reality at the center of our lives out of which everything else flows? Have you given serious thought to that?

Probably, most people do not think about it very much. Most of us live from moment to moment, making the immediate decisions, attending to matters of necessity or matters of enjoyment, without giving much thought to the overarching meaning of it all. Of course, at any given moment, there is something we value at the center of our lives, causing us to think what we think, decide what we decide, and act as we act. At one moment it may be one thing, at another moment it may be something else. But at every moment, there is something that prompts us and motivates us. We do not have a choice as to whether or not there is something at the center of our lives. Our only choice is about what it will be.

It is essential to know what we have placed at the center. The decision about the focus of our lives must not be a matter of expediency or of following the course of least resistance. It must be a serious decision and a studied decision, because not just any center of meaning will do. Life will be good or life will be less than good depending upon what we place at the center of life. And the Gospel makes it clear that only the God made known in Christ is worthy of that position!

We see that point made several times in our scripture from the Gospel of Matthew. Just after Jesus fed the crowd with the loaves and fish, he sent the disciples across the lake by boat. Finally, he was alone. You will remember that his original intent in crossing the lake was to spend some time recharging his own physical and spiritual batteries. The crowds had followed him and, of course, he had compassion on them and ministered to their needs. But now, he was alone, and again took up his original intent. He went up on the mountain to pray.

Please don't see Jesus' prayer time as a digression from the real story, a momentary pause before the action begins again. When we read the Gospels with eyes and hearts wide open, we see that, for Jesus, prayer *is* the real story, and everything else is the overflow of that. Whoever else he was, Jesus was a man of prayer. God was the focus of his life and prayer was the time of fixing that focus. Jesus repeatedly affirmed that God was the source of all goodness and power in his life. So, moment by moment, day by day, Jesus sent his roots deep into the greatness of God. There was a healthy rhythm to his life, not unlike breathing in and breathing out. He spent time in prayer and then spent time in servant ministry. There was time with God and then time with God's people.

So, in this account from the Gospel of Matthew, Jesus had sent the disciples ahead by boat, and he was spending time alone with God, breathing deeply of God's grace and strength. In the meantime, a storm had formed on the lake. And the disciples were in trouble. They were being buffeted by a wind and tossed about by the waves. They had grown weary from their struggle with the storm, using all their strength to row in futility against the wind.

I have no difficulty seeing myself in the boat with the disciples. If you think of the storms and the winds tossing you around right now, you can probably see yourself there, too. The boat is large enough. All of us can join the disciples there. The fact is, life carries with it the likelihood of difficulty. If you live for any length of time, you will experience it. It has been suggested that we could send a form letter to the entire human race, saying, "I'm thinking of you in your time of difficulty." They may wonder how we found out about them, but every person would know what we are talking about! Of course, we are not promised otherwise. In fact, Jesus told his disciples honestly: "In the world you will have tribulation" (John 16:33 NKJV). That's the way it is.

When Jesus saw that the disciples were in trouble, he came to them. Even before they called out to him, he was on his way to help them. Do you hear the implied promise in that? No matter what our difficulty in life, no matter what storms are threatening to engulf us, we are never alone. Even before we call, Christ reaches out to us. So, Jesus came to the disciples and said, "Take heart, it is I; do not be afraid" (v. 27).

There is a promise in those words. It is the promise of his presence. It is another sounding of that best and most reassuring of Jesus' promises, "I am with you always, to the end of the age" (Matt. 28:20). No matter where we are, no matter what we are experiencing, Christ is there. We are never forsaken, never abandoned. Even when we are not aware of it, Christ is there.

As I have said, there is a promise in Jesus' words, the promise of his presence. But there is also a choice there. Jesus says, "Do not be afraid." The choice being offered by Jesus may well be the basic choice in life: faith or fear. As I said in last week's sermon, in the New Testament the opposite of faith is not unbelief; the opposite of faith is fear.

When Peter was invited to come to Jesus across the water, he opted for faith. In this narrative we get a good picture of what faith is. It is more than belief (an intellectual agreement with a set of ideas), although belief is certainly a part of faith. Faith is trust, the willingness to risk and to act on the basis of our core belief. It is the willingness to live our lives as if God is, and as if God is like, Jesus, the Christ. If we have such faith, we are secure and life basically is good. If we do not have faith, we are fearful and insecure, no matter what else we have. Peter believed and Peter trusted. So, in faith, he stepped out of the boat to go to Jesus.

For me, the most intense drama of the story is provided by the distracting storm. As long as Peter was focused upon Jesus, all was well. It was when he became conscious of the storm and took his eyes off Jesus that he began to sink. That is a very suggestive image. And it reminds us again of the importance of fixing our focus. The mind cannot concentrate on more than one thing at a time. Either the storm of Jesus; either fear or faith. We cannot concentrate on both. And the outcome is always determined by what is at the center of our mind and heart. Thus the importance of focus.

I probably don't have to remind any of us of the storms of life, nor of the innumerable distractions that tempt us to take our eyes off Christ. The details may vary from person to person, but every one of us has known too many times of fear and failure, and too few times of buoyant faith. No, we don't have to be reminded of the storms nor of the distractions. But we must be reminded again and again that faith alone is a sufficient foundation for life. Nothing else will sustain us.

In the *Disciple* Bible study series, we are told that there is a recurring theme throughout the Bible: that life must be arranged according to a "right order of things." That has been a central theme in my preaching for years. Again and again I have said that we are living in a world designed to function in a God-centered way. God planned it. God created it. And God structured it so that all the component parts will function properly only if God is at the center of it. Put anything else at the center, and life goes wrong. We can learn that early and easily, or we can learn that late and painfully. But this world was designed to function in a God-centered way.

And, if I understand *salvation* correctly, salvation means *wholeness*. It means having life made whole by gathering all the fragmented parts and ordering them around their proper center, God. It is fixing our focus upon the God made known in Christ, and then having our lives graciously affirmed by that experience, having our values shaped by that experience, having our resolve strengthened by that experience, and then having all our actions directed by that experience. So, the Christian life is life with God at the center and with everything else flowing out of that central, focused reality.

Returning to our scriptural story, when Peter was overcome by his fear of the storm and lost his focus on Jesus, he began to sink beneath the waves. He cried out, "Lord, save me!" (v. 30). It is a sad commentary on human nature that we tend to have wandering eyes and itching ears when things are going well for us and we seem to have little need for faith. Prosperity is far more difficult to manage than adversity. It is when the storms come and we begin to drown that we turn to Christ for help. But hear the good news: he is so gracious and forgiving that he will take us even on such ignoble terms!

When Peter cried out for help, Jesus reached out and took him by the hand. Looking now at Jesus, he could no longer look at the storm. Filled now with faith, he was no longer overcome by fear. And the Scripture says that when the two of them got into the boat, the storm subsided.

Perhaps it is too much to say that all the storms of life subside when, by faith, we get into the boat with Jesus. But it is not too much to say that some storms do. And even the lingering storms lose much of their terror and become manageable when we take hold of faith. I believe that. What's more, I have experienced that!

So when the storms of life come—no, we don't want to wait for that—every day, as we seek to fix the focus of our lives, let's faithfully get into the boat with Jesus, and let's hear him say, "Take heart, it is I; do not be afraid."

Suggestions for Worship

Call to Worship (Matt. 14:30-31, 33):

PASTOR: When he noticed the strong wind; he became frightened, and beginning to sink, he cried out, "Lord, save me!"

PEOPLE: Jesus immediately reached out his hand and caught him, saying to him,

PASTOR: "You of little faith, why did you doubt?"

PEOPLE: And those who were in the boat worshiped him, saying, "Truly you are the Son of God."

Act of Praise: Psalm 106:4-12.

Suggested Hymns: "Great Is Thy Faithfulness"; "Standing on the Promises"; "Stand by Me."

Opening Prayer: Almighty God, we gather in this place as your people to acknowledge that you are the creator of life and the source of all meaning in life. We confess that sometimes we forget. With all the temptations and distractions that call to us each day, sometimes we forget that you are the one in whom we live and move and have our being. Help us today to remember. Enable us to focus upon you as life's source and meaning. In Jesus' name we ask it. Amen.

Pastoral Prayer: Come, Holy Spirit, come. We sense your presence. We acknowledge you to be God close to us, God within us, God present with us to give us love and power. Move among us during this service of worship. Speak to each of us where we are. Give us the gifts you have prepared for our every need. And make us responsible to the urgings of your Spirit.

On this day set aside and made holy as a day of worship, we count it a privilege to gather with our church family in this place of praise. There are so many gifts of love that we receive from you each day. We could not begin to count them, so many of them there are. But especially today, we want to thank you for creation and providence. You have gifted us with life and with all the good things of life. Everything that is exists because you have spoken the word of creation. We are indebted to you for life itself. But not only do you give life, you are at work night and day to sustain life and to make it good. We do not take any breath without your enabling power. We do not live even for one moment without your sustaining presence. We do not have any life experience without your being there, working for our good and for that of all your children. Whatever it is that makes life good for us, we can trace it to your loving concern for us. So, for all your providential care, we give you thanks!

It is your love at work in us that makes us want to reach out to others with our concern and help and prayers. So hear us now, Father, as we pray for others. You know far better than we what is needed. So, whether the need is for comfort, for healing, for guidance, or for strength, that is what we pray for, trusting in the all-sufficiency of your grace.

Now hear us as we pray for this service of worship. As we present our gifts, sing our hymns, and listen to your word, may we sense your presence. When this hour is over and we leave this place, make us to know that we have been in the presence of God and that we have been touched by your amazing grace. In the name of Christ we pray. Amen.

AUGUST 15, 1993

□

Eleventh Sunday After Pentecost

The walls of hostility that divide those who see themselves as God's favorites from those they consider outcasts are broken down by Christ. God's special call and special gifts are *not* revoked by a salvation that is for everyone.

The Sunday Lessons

Exodus 16:2-15: Israel's constant murmuring in the wilderness—"You have brought us out into this wilderness to kill this whole assembly with hunger" (v. 3)—was answered with God's providence. In the evening quail came and covered the camp. In the morning, a fine, flake-like substance appeared—manna, "the bread that the LORD has given you to eat" (v. 15).

Romans 11:13-16, 29-32: Paul concludes his discussion of the salvation of Jews and Gentiles. The apostle expects his ministry to pagans to provoke jealousy among Jews "and thus save some of them" (v. 14). The key verse is "the gifts and the calling of God are irrevocable" (v. 29).

Matthew 15:21-28: The faith of a Gentile woman whose daughter was ill is the central theme of this miracle story. "It is not fair to take the children's food and throw it to the dogs," Jesus said (v. 26). The "children" are God's people, the Jews. The "dogs" are the pagan Gentiles. The Canaanite woman answers, "Yet even the dogs eat the crumbs" (v. 27). The bread symbolizes salvation. Salvation is by faith alone.

Interpretation and Imagination

A department store invited "a few select customers" to an after-hours sale. A mail-order promotion noted that "this offer is being made to only a few persons like yourself." A real estate development firm sent a certificate that could be redeemed for cash or prizes because "you have been chosen to receive this unique offer."

In every case, the appeal was made to our desire to be special or to enjoy some favored position. We are that way. Imagine that there is only a little bread to be had. Do we not reason that our particular family should have it? If there are only a few barrels of oil to be had, should not Americans get them? In matters of religion, such a spirit produces an exclusive, selfish, and elitist church.

These lessons make us wrestle with dilemma. God's gifts are particular and special for nations and individuals, yet God's salvation is for all people. The tension is important, for if we are totally universal, we deny the reality of inequality and the importance of that which is unique. If we are in any way exclusive, bigotry and superiority will lead to the kind of evil expressed in the Holocaust, religious wars, and the Palestinian problem. (JKB)

BREAD FOR THE WORLD

Matthew 15:21-28

A SERMON BY DONALD WILLIAM DOTTERER

In Garrison Keillor's best-selling book about the mythical town of Lake Wobegon, there is a chapter entitled, simply, "Protestant." In it the narrator tells of his years as a boy growing up in that small community.

He says that in that town, where everyone was either a Lutheran or a Catholic, his family was neither. They were "Sanctified Brethren," a church so small that nobody but the members and God knew about it. When the other kids asked what religion he was, he just said that he was "Protestant." Being a member of the Sanctified Brethren was too much to explain; it was sort of "like having six toes. You would rather keep your shoes on." (Keillor, *Lake Wobegon Days* [Thorndike, ME: Thorndike Press, 1985] 205-206.)

The boy from Lake Wobegon discovered early in life that folks who call themselves Christians are not all the same, that they, in fact, may do things very differently. Christians are all divided up into Catholics and Protestants, and then the Protestants are further separated into Lutherans and Methodists and a host of other well-known denominations.

How often we forget that despite our denominational labels, despite our nationalities, we who have faith are all equal in the eyes of God. God's grace revealed to us in Jesus Christ is open to all who are willing to call him Lord in faith and in love. As Paul reminds us, "There is no longer Jew or Greek, there is no longer slave or free, there is no longer male and female; for all of you are one in Christ Jesus" (Gal. 3:28).

Divisions among religious people who believe in the same Savior are not limited to life in the twentieth century. Our Gospel lesson for the morning concerns that extraordinary encounter between Jesus and a person who is known to our tradition as "the Canaanite woman." We read that Jesus had just left Galilee and moved north, crossing the boundary of Israel and entering into a foreign territory populated by non-Jews. Some translators call this woman a Phoenician.

New Testament scholars have never known quite what to do with the verbal exchange between Jesus and this woman. This mother was obviously aware of Jesus' reputation as a healer, and she cried to him for help in cleansing her daughter of a vicious demon, saying "Have mercy on me, Lord, Son of David" (v. 22). We are told by Matthew that Jesus paused in silence, as if to consider what he must do.

On the other hand, his disciples did not hesitate a moment; they simply demanded that Jesus send this foreign woman away. After all, what right did she have to ask for healing from the one who had come to save the people of Israel? Their comment reveals an attitude of racial superiority, a problem we still have nearly 2,000 years later.

Jesus, perhaps at this point struggling with his own identity as the Jewish Messiah, answered softly, saying that he had been sent only to the lost sheep of Israel. Mark's version of this story makes the issue a little clearer for us, telling us that Jesus said the children of Israel must be fed "first" (Mark 7:27).

But this woman was persistent. She demanded that Jesus take her seriously and be in relationship with her. Again, she said to Jesus, "Lord, help me" (v. 25). Jesus then gave a response that constitutes one of the most difficult and perplexing sayings in Scripture: "It is not fair to take the children's food and throw it to the dogs" (v. 26). "Dogs" was a derogatory term often applied to Gentiles by the Jews. Jesus took the bite out of the insult by using a diminutive form of the word in Greek, so its meaning was more like "puppies." He was quite possibly quoting an old Jewish proverb.

But once again the woman was persistent in her request. We can imagine her kneeling before Jesus, looking him straight in the eye, her voice touched with motherly concern for her daughter, as she says: "Yes, Lord, yet even the dogs eat the crumbs that fall from their masters' table" (v. 27).

Jesus, apparently overwhelmed by this woman's trust and confidence in his power, responded, "Woman, great is your faith!" (v. 28). Great is your faith! The child was then healed instantly. Jesus had shared "bread" with this foreign woman.

As in the case of the healing of the Roman centurion's slave (Matt. 8:5-13), a Gentile's trust and confidence had compelled Jesus to widen his ministry and mission to persons who were considered outsiders. It is also interesting to note that the girl was healed *from a distance,* which was also the case in the healing of the centurion's slave. This is testimony to the confidence that these Gentiles had in Jesus' healing and saving power. How great indeed was the faith of this woman and this man who were outside of Jesus' cultural religious constituency. Sometimes it does take an outsider to see the truth which is invisible to those on the inside.

Civil rights leader Martin Luther King, Jr., in his famous "Letter from Birmingham Jail," responded to criticisms of prominent Birmingham, Alabama clergy who charged that he was an "outside agitator" who was stirring up trouble away from his home community. He wrote these words from his city jail cell:

> I am cognizant of the interrelatedness of all communities and states. I cannot sit idly by in Atlanta and not be concerned about what happens in Birmingham. Injustice anywhere is a threat to injustice everywhere. We are caught in an inescapable network of mutuality, tied in a single garment of destiny. Whatever affects one directly, affects all indirectly. (King, "Letter From Birmingham Jail," in *The Norton Reader,* 5th ed. [New York: W. W. Norton & Co., 1980], 853.)

So it is that we rob ourselves of insight and relationship when we begin to draw lines between us, to label people as insiders and outsiders, nationals and foreigners. The most important aspect of the story of the Canaanite woman for people of all generations is the way in which Jesus was able, personally and spiritually, to overcome cultural prejudice in order to minister to the woman as a human being. Since Jesus was able to break through racial and religious barriers and create a new basis for unity, should we as disciples of Christ not attempt to do likewise?

But how difficult it is for us to accept all persons as equals! We allow differences in religion, skin color, nationality, and personal income to separate us from other people who have been created by God to be fellow citizens on this earth.

Like these disciples, because of deep-rooted prejudices, we fail to see people as people, identifying them only as persons who are unlike us. And also like the disciples, we may miss opportunities for ministry and relationship because deeply ingrained prejudices leave us unable to think on our own.

The American playwright Arthur Miller visited the black townships outside of Cape Town, South Africa. He encountered a concrete wall hiding the view of a wretched shantytown from the public. Miller said of South Africa's white minority, "There's a sense that simply their eyes stop seeing" (quoted by Christopher Wren, *Austin-American Standard*, 6 December 1990).

That is what we do when we allow ourselves to be divided from other people whom we do not know and therefore cannot understand. How many of us condemn whole groups of people without ever having had a relationship with even one person from that group? When we see poverty and suffering on our streets and in our neighborhoods, we may look, but we do not see, simply because those people are not like us.

When we do this, we are like the disciples who only saw a woman of a different race coming to Jesus, disturbing their little circle of accepted persons. What they did *not* see was a mother whose little girl was being ravaged by what must have been a terrible illness. An important aspect of genuine faith is this ability to look, and to really see, all people as human beings.

The story of Jesus and the Canaanite woman is a preview of the whole history of Christianity. In opening the covenant with Israel to all the peoples of the world, Jesus offers forgiveness and salvation to all who will call him Lord. This is where Jesus first makes it known that he is bread for all the world, not just the Jewish people.

Let us then praise God that Jesus Christ is bread for all the world, and that through him we can overcome our differences with others, and learn to live together in peace and harmony. Let our prayer this day be that we may live together in the unity of the Spirit, which makes us one in Christ.

Suggestions for Worship

Call to Worship (Ps. 78:1-4):

PASTOR: Give ear, O my people, to my teaching; incline your ears to the words of my mouth. I will utter dark sayings from of old,

PEOPLE: Things that we have heard and known, that our ancestors have told us.

PASTOR: We will not hide them from their children;

PEOPLE: We will tell to the coming generation the glorious deeds of the LORD.

Act of Praise: Psalm 78:1-3, 10-20.

Suggested Hymns: "O Worship the King"; "I Stand Amazed in the Presence"; "God Will Take Care of You."

Opening Prayer: God of all that is precious and good in our lives, we pray that in these moments you will come to us in a new and powerful way. Set us free from all that would keep us from dwelling in peace and harmony with our brothers and sisters. Empower us through worship to become men and women who have the strength to live every day in faith and obedience. Through Jesus Christ we pray. Amen.

Pastoral Prayer: O God of all that is and all that will ever be, we come to you in prayer seeking healing in our lives. We confess that we have been people who have not always accepted others as our equals. We have ranked persons above and below us, forgetting that in your eyes, the eyes of our Creator, we are all loved and accepted without any worldly distinctions. We have denied other people relationships with us simply because they are different in one way or another.

We pray that you will bring us together so that people from every race and every nation may live in peace and harmony. Take from us any fear and distrust that we have of one another. Grant us eyes to see all people as human beings, created and loved by you, the one God who is the Creator and Sustainer of all living things.

We pray for all those throughout the world who struggle for justice in a cruel and unjust world. Strengthen your soldiers of faith with righteousness, as they fight battles against prejudice and injustice both near and far. May we become of one mind and spirit as we confront evil wherever it is found. Lord, make us instruments of your peace in a troubled world.

O God, hear now the prayers of your people this day. In the wonderful name of Jesus we pray. Amen.

AUGUST 22, 1993

□

Twelfth Sunday After Pentecost

An old gospel hymn refers to Jesus as the rock in a weary land. Peter's faith, the rock on which the church is built, and Israel's faithlessness at the rock of Horeb are contrasted in these lessons.

The Sunday Lessons

Exodus 17:1-7: At Rephidim there was no water for the people to drink. Again they complained, "Why did you bring us out of Egypt, to kill us and our children and livestock with thirst?" (v. 3). At God's command, Moses took his rod and struck the rock at Horeb. Water came forth so that the people could drink. Massah means to test. Meribah means to find fault. Together they named the place where Israel's faithlessness would always be remembered.
Romans 11:33-36: Paul concludes his discussion of salvation of Jews and Gentiles with a doxology. "O the depth of the riches and wisdom and knowledge of God! . . . To him be the glory forever" (vv. 33, 36).
Matthew 16:13-20: When our Lord asked his disciples, "But who do you say that I am?" (v. 15), Simon Peter made the first confession of faith: "You are the Christ" (v. 16 RSV). Simon, son of Jonah, was given a new name, "You are Peter, and on this rock I will build my church. . . . I will give you the keys of the kingdom of heaven" (vv. 18-19).

Interpretation and Imagination

Caesarea Philippi is known as a pagan site where many beliefs had shrines. Legend told that the Greek god Pan was born in a cave on the hillside. A shrine to Pan stood there. The altars of Baal were present everywhere. On the day that Jesus walked that road, Phillip was king. His kingdom was symbolized by the gleaming marble palace he had built and dedicated to Caesar. Everyone who passed by would call Caesar his lord.

On the road that day, Jesus asked, "Who do people say that the Son of Man is?" (v. 13). Then coming close to the nerve, he asked, "But who do you say that I am?"

Ancient exegeses of this important passage focus on the keys to the Kingdom. Peter, the first bishop of the church, and all who succeed him in that office, are honored as those who have been given authority. Protestant exegeses lift up faith as the authority in matters of faith and conduct.

In the Wesleyan tradition, faith is not understood to mean only privilege. Keys are accompanied by responsibility. Commitment, discipline, and service are a part of the obedience that follows faith in Christ. (JKB)

PETER'S MIDTERM EXAM

Matthew 16:13-20

A SERMON BY DONALD WILLIAM DOTTERER

Elie Wiesel, in his book *A Jew Today,* tells a Hasidic story of a man named Israel of Kozhenitz, who was known for saintliness and compassion. This man loved his fellow humans, and they loved him. Everyone who came to see him asked him for his intercession in heaven, for it was believed that nothing was denied him there.

Israel once had a visit from a poor and unhappy woman. "Help me, pray for me," she said. "My husband and I are lonely; we would like a son; intercede on our behalf. God will hear your prayer even if He closes His ear to ours," the woman said as she cried.

"You must not cry," said the Rebbe of Kozhenitz. "My mother, of blessed memory, had the same problem. For years she wanted a son, and God refused to let her have him." Israel told the woman how his mother and father recited psalms all day long, and how they had visited rabbis and miracle makers. But it was all in vain.

Then one day the mother learned that a Rebbe Israel Baal Shem Tov was expected in the village. The woman took heart, because she believed that surely this man could deliver her from despair.

On the day he arrived, she went to see the famous teacher. As she wept, she told him of her grief. Rebbe Tov told the woman, "Don't cry, I don't want your tears. . . . On the other hand I should like it very much if you were to present me with a caftan. . . ." Rebbe Israel then said that his mother went out immediately to a tailor and bought this long gown and brought it to the Rebbe. "One year later she had a son. Me."

"Is that all?" cried the woman, her face suddenly radiant with joy. "Thank you Rebbe. Thank you for the remedy. I shall go home and buy you the most beautiful caftan, the costliest one."

Rebbe Israel of Kozhenitz interrupted her, smiling. "It would do you no good. The formula is not valid for everyone. My mother, you see, did not know this story" (Wiesel, *A Jew Today* [New York: Random House, 1978] 107-108).

The message to us in this tale is that if we know the story of the miracle, we will probably not be blessed in the same way, for seldom does God work the same miracle twice. That is why we should not expect God to do for us what he has done for somebody else. The God we worship in this place is a God who surprises us.

Perhaps the most difficult aspect of living in our time is that so often we do not know how or where God will act. We do not know just how God might help us. In other words, God may be a constant source of strength for those who take time to pray, but his movement in our lives cannot be accurately predicted by human minds.

The inability to predict God's movement may leave us very frustrated at times. It has led people to curse the name of God because he did not appear to work a miracle when self or friends or relatives suffered. Even Jesus cried from the cross, "My God, my God, why have you forsaken me?" (Matt. 27:46).

Our lesson from the Gospel of Matthew gets to the heart of this issue because it deals with the problem of not receiving that which is desired or expected in life. Our disappointment is great when we do not get what we want or hope to receive.

Such was the predicament of the disciples and many others who had chosen to follow Jesus. This conversation of Jesus with his disciples marks a critical point in his ministry. For many months, Jesus had traveled throughout the land, healing the sick, feeding the hungry, teaching parables, and preaching the good news of the love of God for humanity.

The ministry of Jesus could have been judged highly successful at this point. Large crowds came to hear him preach; many followed him about seeking healing. It would not be long now before he would turn his face towards Jerusalem and his final destiny.

Despite his success, we sense that Jesus had a troubled heart. His anguish was rooted in the dilemma caused by his realization that he was not the kind of messiah the people wanted and expected him to be. The people of Galilee had failed to understand his purpose.

The Jewish hope was that the Messiah would reestablish the supremacy of Israel among nations, as the reign of God was established. The assumption was that this would be done in a violent and vengeful manner, overthrowing ruling powers.

Jesus, therefore, had to communicate to the disciples and others that what he was offering was something completely different from that which they expected. They did not understand that messiahship meant sacrifice, suffering, and death. No, Jesus could not be what the people wanted him to be.

So Jesus gathered together his disciples on the slope of beautiful Mount Hermon, close to the sources of the River Jordan, to rest and find some peace. He came to this place of seclusion to prepare for the difficult days that lay ahead of him. It was also time for him to evaluate his ministry. Was he really accomplishing his divine purpose? Had anyone figured out who he was?

Perhaps around a campfire, Jesus asked his friends a question that he had never asked them before: "Who do people say that the Son of Man is?" The disciples told him that some thought he was John the Baptist resurrected, which was the belief of Herod who had executed the outspoken prophet. Some said he was Elijah, the prophet who was to return before the final Day of Judgment. Still others said he was Jeremiah, the fearless spokesman for God.

Then Jesus asked the disciples directly the question to which he had to know the answer: "But who do *you* say that I am?" (emphasis added). And Peter responded with those famous words of faith: "You are the Christ, the Son of the living God" (v. 16 RSV). With this response, Jesus blessed Peter and bestowed upon him a special leadership role in the ministry of the soon-to-be-established church.

Why have I titled this sermon "Peter's Midterm Exam"? Because Peter was a man who had several tests throughout his ministry with Jesus. Like many beginning students, who do not know what is expected of them or have not developed proper study habits, Peter was not ready for that first exam. You will remember the story of when the disciples were in the boat on the sea of Galilee in a storm, and they saw Jesus walking on the water (Matt. 14:22-33).

The Lord called to Peter to walk out on the lake and meet him, which Peter started to do. But then he saw the wind, became afraid, and began to sink into the water. Jesus, in his disappointment, had to say to him, "You of little faith, why did you doubt?" (Matt. 14:31). Peter had failed his first test of faith.

But Jesus the teacher always gives us another chance, which is what he did with Peter. And this time Peter answers correctly, affirming Jesus as Lord and Savior, as the long awaited Messiah.

Peter passed his midterm exam. However, we must not forget that he failed the next test, denying that he knew Jesus three times during the time of his Passion. Yet in the end, Peter fulfilled his calling and became the leader of the early church in Jerusalem. This man and his faith became the rock upon which Jesus built his church.

So my friends in Christ, how will it be for us? How will we answer that question from Scripture that is directed to each and every one of us who calls himself or herself a Christian: "Who do *you* say that I am, and what difference do I make in your life?"

We do believe that people are "born again," that men and women can have a faith experience of Jesus Christ that changes their lives. However, the life of Peter demonstrates that we must affirm that faith repeatedly throughout the course of our lives. We are put to the test again and again. We have early, middle, and final exams in faith. It would be useful for us, every once in a while, to do a study and review of where we have been and where we are going on our journey of faith.

We may not always get what we want or expect in life. However, if in the end we have a rock-solid faith like that of Peter, we will find the way through Christ to find peace and salvation. All that we must do is say with Peter, "You are the

Christ, the Son of the living God," and then live in that trust and obedience that our tradition calls *faith*.

Let our prayer this day be, then, that we may find Christ and have him shine through us in all that we do. May we see Jesus now and always.

Suggestions for Worship

Call to Worship (Ps. 95:1-3, 6):

PASTOR: O come, let us sing to the LORD; let us make a joyful noise to the rock of our salvation!

PEOPLE: Let us come into his presence with thanksgiving; let us make a joyful noise to the songs of praise!

PASTOR: For the LORD is a great God, and a great King above all gods.

PEOPLE: O come, let us worship and bow down, let us kneel before the LORD, our Maker!

Act of Praise: Psalm 95.

Suggested Hymns: "Ye Servants of God"; "Of the Father's Love Begotten"; "Fairest Lord Jesus."

Opening Prayer: Come to us, Almighty God, in this hour, so that we may be freed by your power from any doubt and hesitation in our faith. Cleanse us now from the sin of false expectations. Instill in us the love of Jesus Christ that enables us to live in peace with those around us. Grant us strength and courage to serve you in all that we do. Through Jesus Christ our Lord, we pray. Amen.

Pastoral Prayer: Gracious and everliving God, we come to you this day in search of your will and your way for our lives. How often we have wanted and expected things which, had we received them, would have been disastrous for us. Help us instead to appreciate the many gifts and opportunities which you have so graciously bestowed upon us in your love and mercy. Save us, we pray, from the sin of desiring that which we cannot or should not have.

In these moments we open our hearts to you, hoping to experience your love and mercy in a new and inspiring way. We thank you for your holy Son, Jesus, who has shown us the way to live in peace and happiness. Let us say with assurance to Jesus when he calls to us, "You are the Christ, the Son of the living God."

We remember all those who are in need, both near and far. We pray for those who are ill; may your healing power and presence be upon their bodies and their minds. We pray today and always for peace in your world; may that peace begin with each one of us.

All this we pray for in the name of the one named Christ who is with us and for us always. Amen.

August 29, 1993

□

Thirteenth Sunday After Pentecost

Jesus told his disciples that he would suffer and die. "Take up [your] cross and follow," he said (Matt. 16:24). If you try to save your life, you will lose it.

The Sunday Lessons

Exodus 19:1-9: Sinai was a sacred mountain for Israel, and the place of meeting and covenant between God and Moses. God initiates everything. God is the chief actor. "Thus you will say . . . I bore you on eagles' wings and brought you to myself" (v. 4). God's covenant is not negotiable, but it is conditional—"if you obey my voice and keep my covenant" (v. 5).
Romans 12:1-13: "Present your bodies as a living sacrifice, holy and acceptable to God" (v. 1). The word *therefore* is significant. For eleven chapters Paul has written about salvation that is a gift. Now, he appeals for an ethical response. It is a "therefore" ethic that begins with being "transformed by the renewal of your minds" (v. 2).
Matthew 16:21-28: When Jesus predicted his suffering and death, Peter said, "God forbid it, Lord! This must never happen to you" (v. 22). The Lord rebuked Peter, "Get behind me, Satan!" (v. 23). He told his disciples, "If any want to become my followers, let them deny themselves and take up their cross and follow me" (v. 24). The promise of resurrection and life is central to the passage, "And those who lose their life for my sake will find it" (v. 25).

Interpretation and Imagination

There is a careful style of life that avoids confrontations and accommodates almost any abuse in indifferent and cowardly ways. It is called "playing it safe." Relationships are kept at superficial levels and are so shallow that differences never spark conflict and nothing matters much.

An old story tells of a youth who was going to leave the safety of family, church, and community to work in a logging camp for the summer. His pastor warned him that he would likely face some ridicule from roughnecks because of his Christian standards.

When he returned home in the fall, the pastor asked, "How did it go. Were you teased and tormented for being a Christian?" "No, not at all," the young man replied. "They never found out."

Yet for some men and women, there comes a day when their uninvolved and casual approach to life is changed. Call it a new revelation, if you will. Perhaps it comes through great sorrow. Perhaps it results from a new-found joy. Perhaps it grows from a new vision of reality or new responsibilities. On that day you get a new sense of who you are and with it new values, a new style, and a new awareness of the reality of a cross.

The cost of discipleship was made painfully clear to Jesus' disciples. "Anyone who wants to be a follower of mine," he said, "should expect to bear the cross." He never tried to soften it or compromise the radical demand.

Have you ever wondered why no one, no one at all, at Golgotha broke through the lines of guards shouting, "I'm his disciple. I am with him. I want to die with him." The Gospels record that they all forsook him and fled.

The resurrection faith of the New Testament church changed all of that. The disciples' timidity and confusion of spirit was transformed into a Christlike courage and obedience. There were crosses, and still there are more crosses. Thanks be to God for those saints who take up their cross to follow. (JKB)

A CLOUD, A CROSS

Exodus 19:1-9

A SERMON BY ROBERT ERIC BERGLAND

An advertisement that made the rounds a few years ago pictured a well tanned, muscular, very handsome man. "Hi! I'm Jake. You can look this way too." Then he went on to tell about a gym and tanning salon. The name of the place was compelling—it was called, "Shaped by Jake."

That seems a little trite and sounds like something most people would pass over. But it's sobering to realize that that ad caused many people to make an appointment to be "shaped by Jake."

And the shaping would not be easy. Persons would fast, sweat, hurt, and work hard to be "shaped by Jake," and to achieve the kind of beautiful body they wanted to have.

Shaping is not an unusual thing. We are all shaped by outside influence. Thousands of things intend to shape our lives: our physical health, our appearance, our clothing, the places we live, the schools our children attend, the food we eat, the places we go, our entertainment. These things also shape our destiny and our very souls.

The book of Exodus records that the children of Israel were shaped by a covenant; a promise made between Moses (on their behalf) and the Lord God. On Mt. Sinai, Moses met with God, and God said to Moses, "Thus you shall say to the house of Jacob, and tell the Israelites: You have seen what I did to the Egyptians, and how I bore you on eagles' wings and brought you to myself. Now therefore, if you obey my voice and keep my covenant, you shall be my treasured possessions out of all the peoples. Indeed, the whole earth is mine, but you shall be for me a priestly kingdom and a holy nation" (vv. 3-6).

The text goes on to say that Moses came down to the children of Israel and told them everything that God had said to him. They replied together in unison, "Everything that the LORD has spoken we will do" (v. 8).

They heard the word of the Lord God through Moses. They listened and covenanted together to do what God had said. They were shaped as a covenant people; a people chosen by God; a nation blessed with the promise of being the very possession of God.

Now, in those times God seemed very far away, and when he spoke to the children of Israel, it was always through Moses. Then came the frightening moment when God decided to make his presence known, so that his own possessions and people would believe Moses "forever." So God came to them in a heavy cloud. From this thick cloud, through which no one could see, he spoke. They were again being shaped and formed by God, not for their benefit, but that God might be glorified.

We know the rest of this story. The children of Israel, the chosen people of God, journeyed through the wilderness, and so soon forgot their covenant to obey all that the Lord had spoken. They forsook their relationship with God, and disobeyed his commandments. They turned away, worshiped idols, and failed to keep the Sabbath. They let foreign gods influence and shape their lives.

Then Jesus of Nazareth came preaching a gospel of judgment and mercy; a gospel of love and forgiveness; a gospel of obedience and service.

But people were not so ready to hear the words that this Nazarene spoke, so they arrested him and tried him; they crucified and buried him. But he rose from the grave and is living still.

That's the power and person that is shaping each of us today.

The resurrection of Jesus Christ has shaped our destiny, for on that cross he bore the sins of all people. He died once and for all, for each of us, that we might be saved from sin and death. And in his rising, Jesus Christ opened the door to everlasting life.

Today, Jesus Christ continues to hold the power and love that can shape you and shape me. He shapes us into a people of faith and hope, a people of love and service. Through the power of the Holy Spirit, Christ shapes us into his likeness, and he calls us to turn from those things that divide us and destroy the unity of the Body of Christ, the church. He calls us to become obedient to the shaping of his will. He calls us to make covenant with him and to forsake those things of the world that desire to shape us by their values and style.

The Apostle Paul wrote in Romans 12:2, "Do not be conformed to this world, but be transformed by the renewal of your minds, so that you may discern what is the will of God—what is good and acceptable and perfect."

Jesus Christ says to us, "If any want to become my followers let them deny themselves and take up their cross and follow me. For those who want to save their life will lose it, and those who lose their life for my sake will find it" (Matt. 16:24-25).

What shapes you today, my friend? Don't give yourself over to those things that cannot save and will not last. Listen, "What will it profit [a person], if they gain the whole world but forfeit their life?" (Matt. 16:26).

Let your life be shaped by Christ.

Suggestions for Worship

Call to Worship (Rom. 12:1-2, 12):

PASTOR: I appeal to you therefore, brothers and sisters, by the mercies of God, to present your bodies as a living sacrifice, holy and acceptable to God, which is your spiritual worship.

PEOPLE: Do not be conformed to this world.

PASTOR: But be transformed by the renewing of your minds,

PEOPLE: So that you may discern what is the will of God—what is good and acceptable and perfect.

PASTOR: Rejoice in hope, be patient in affliction,

PEOPLE: Persevere in prayer.

Act of Praise: Psalm 114.

Suggested Hymns: "Take Time to Be Holy"; "Alas! and Did My Saviour Bleed"; "Must Jesus Bear the Cross Alone."

Opening Prayer: Almighty God, you are Lord, and there is no other. You form the light and create darkness. You make prosperity and create woe. Shower, O heavens above, and let the skies rain down sovereignty and grace. Let the earth open, that salvation may sprout forth, and let your righteousness spring up and grow among us, for you, O Lord, have created it. Amen.

Pastoral Prayer: All-merciful God, hear, we pray, the prayers of your rebellious people. Like offspring of Adam and Eve, we have been defiant and disobedient, following too much the self-centered fears and selfish desires of our own hearts. But now we cry to you from this land of exile.

The evil and darkness of this wilderness world have confused our values and claimed our loyalties, and they are wasting our children. Our streets are filled with violence; our schools are plagued with disorder; our homes are fated with brokenness. Your eyes have seen, O God, the chemical addiction, the unwanted pregnancies, the child abuse, the destruction of war, the dishonesty of government, the white-collar crime. You know, O God, the emptiness of our hollow lives and our lonely desperation that has even made death attractive.

For too long we have followed false values, which like thieves come only to kill, steal, and destroy. O Christ, good shepherd of the sheep, turn your eyes of mercy toward us. Bless the household of each one here today. Enfold them and all dear to them in the healing and safety of your almighty arms. Lead us in the paths of righteousness; be our guardian and deliverer; defend us from evil's power; and be our gracious advocate in the courts of the Almighty. Lord Jesus Christ, have mercy on us. Amen.

September 5, 1993

□

Fourteenth Sunday After Pentecost

The day is past when members of Methodist societies would expect a class leader or preacher to rebuke an individual's sins and discipline members of the societies. But this is still an important question: "To whom will I submit myself for correction?"

The Sunday Lessons

Exodus 19:16-24: Moses brought the people out of camp to meet God. The Almighty came down from heaven for this meeting with humankind. He came like earthquake, wind, and fire. The awesome holiness and otherness of God are manifest in the account. Moses was sent back to the people with words of warning lest they "break through to the LORD to look" (v. 21). He was to bring only Aaron back to the holy mountain.
Romans 12:9–13:10: Following his discussion of God's love for us, Paul now writes about our love for others. All of the commandments are summed up in this sentence, "Love your neighbor as yourself" (13:9). With regard to submitting oneself to authority, Paul writes, "One must be subject, not only because of wrath but also because of conscience" (13:5).
Matthew 18:15-20: "If another member of the church sins against you, go and point out the fault" (v. 15). This lesson, a part of the sermon to the church, follows the parable of the sheep gone astray. The emphasis is not on forgiveness but on correction. "If the member listens to you, you have regained that one" (v. 15). Those who do not heed will be outside the fellowship of the church. The judgment of the church will be final. "Whatever you bind on earth will be bound in heaven" (v. 18).

Interpretation and Imagination

There has been a total breakdown of any kind of church discipline in Protestantism. While the church continues to make ethical demands upon society; calls for investigation of dishonest government leaders; and desires integrity, virtue, and accountability in political arenas; there is little evidence of any serious effort to correct a brother or sister who sins.

It has not always been so. John Wesley asked his preachers regularly, "What sins have you committed since last we met?" One of the responsibilities assigned to classes and prayer bands was a watchful concern for any who may tend to go astray. One of the rubrics of the annual report was "reclamations," which referred to "backsliders" who had been restored to the fellowship of the church.

The fact that there is now little discipline in the church does not mean that it is not desirable and helpful. I was blessed on the day that a colleague said, "My friendship won't mean much to you if I don't tell you the truth as I see it, will it?" Then he proceeded to offer a gentle rebuke, and I knew that he cared.

Alcoholics Anonymous, Weight Watchers, and the like, implore members to encourage one another to forsake old habits and indulgences. If a parent never corrects a child, it is not likely that the absence of discipline will be seen as evidence of great love. Rather, we are likely to say, "They simply do not care." (JKB)

MENDING FENCES

Matthew 18:15-20

A SERMON BY ROBERT ERIC BERGLAND

Robert Frost, the brilliant American poet of this century, wrote of a man going out in the Spring to help his neighbor repair a broken-down stone fence. There is an unforgettable line: "Good fences make good neighbors."

When I imagine the repairing of broken-down fences, I am reminded that it is an easier task when there is another to help. The task of carrying fence materials for the work is easier when there are two or more. In laying off the fence line it is easier when there is one to sight the line and one to set the line. There is one to steady the post and hold it straight as another tamps it in. There is one to stretch the wire as the other drives the staples. And when the task is finished, there is shared joy in a job well done.

In the Gospel of Matthew we find a passage that gives biblical scholars reason to question its historical integrity. It just doesn't sound like Jesus, who ate and associated with tax collectors and sinners. It doesn't sound like the same Jesus who said that tax collectors and harlots will enter the Kingdom before the orthodox religious people of that time. It sounds more like a set of rules and regulations set up by some ecclesiastical committee.

Some scholars suggest that this passage needs to be recognized as something not from the time of the "historical" Jesus, when he actually lived, but rather from a time after the church came into being; a time following the first Easter. These sayings suggest the existence of congregations that gather from time to time to settle disputes and offenses among members.

In spite of all this, I believe we can be sure that this teaching relates to something Jesus did say. Perhaps it was something like, "If anyone sins against you, spare no effort to make that person admit their fault so that things will be right between you again."

Basically, what this passage says to us is this: "Never tolerate any situation in which there is a breach of a personal relationship between you and another member of the community of faith."

Each one of us here today has been wronged, either in reality or in our own imagination, by some other person. There are frequent times when the person who wronged us, spoke falsely against us, spread rumors, made threats, and destroyed a friendship has been a professing Christian, one who honors his or her baptism. When that happens, we are hurt and confused by what has taken place. Too often we want to retaliate with hurt and vengeance. Sometimes we become bitter and resentful. At last we may become so cynical and hardened that we no longer feel anything for anyone. But Jesus says, "If another member of the church sins against you . . ."

This passage is intended for the offended person. He or she is the one called upon to take the initiative and right the relationship. But for so many of us that is very difficult, if not impossible.

There is no room in the teachings of Jesus or in the conduct of the Christian life for people to sit around, licking their wounds sighing, "poor me." None of us can avoid becoming a victim of wrong. But we can avoid "victim mentality." We can refute that blame-and-shame kind of thinking that labels someone or something as responsible for our lot in life.

Still, that's more easily said than done. I recall a tense situation in which a person was wronged in a treacherous way by another member of her church. It began at a rather normal church meeting. There was misunderstanding followed by misinterpretation, and then gossip, and finally the spreading of a vicious rumor. Cutting remarks and hostile telephone calls passed between several members of the church.

I will always admire the strength and goodness of that woman who, with tears flowing down her cheeks, confronted the one who started it all. The tears were not tears of anger or tears of hate. They were shed out of a deep sense of loss and a sincere desire to make the friendship whole once again. As the two of them sat down together, they spoke of the misunderstanding, the hurt, the sadness. Though it was not easy, the relationship was restored, and with some fence mending, a friendship was saved.

Does that not reflect the teaching of Jesus, "If another member of the church sins against you, go and point out the fault when the two of you are alone. If the member listens to you, you have regained that one" (v. 15).

The lesson Christ teaches us today is this: When we find ourselves offended by a member of the community of faith, the church, the primary concern is one of respect, both for the offender and for the unity of the Body of Christ. The matter must therefore be settled privately, if possible. If not, then in the presence of only one or two others. This teaching of having one or two witnesses goes back to the Old Testament teaching from Deuteronomy 19:15: "A single witness shall not suffice to convict a person of any crime or wrongdoing in connection with any offense that may be committed. Only on the evidence of two or three witnesses shall a charge be sustained."

If this second step fails, then the entire congregation is to gather to hear and to resolve the dispute. This teaching assumes a small gathering of Christians who are pure in motive and objectively fair in judgment. Not all congregations can be described that way.

How many times have we sadly heard of people being brought before the church with the result being a split in the congregation. Reconciliation and the restoration of broken relationships is the goal; not vindication.

In the early days of the Methodist Society meetings, members gathered not only for prayer, but to build each other up in the faith and to evaluate their progress in living a holy life. If a person was struggling, others helped to strengthen them. If a person was failing, they were confronted with their failure. And if they made no effort to change to a holy life, they were banished from the society.

It was harsher than the way we United Methodists do things today. At Annual Conferences when the clergy members gather, the presiding bishop always asks about the conduct of the preachers. Each district superintendent is expected, if there are any charges, to make them known. The answer is almost always, "Nothing against them, Bishop."

My sisters and brothers, there is a very good way to handle disputes among Christians. It is offered by Christ himself. First confront the source of the dispute, one on one, with respect and gentleness. Don't be party to any kind of self-righteous judgment. The goal is forgiveness of sin and the righting of the wrong.

Moses is remembered as the prophet of law, yet he spoke judgment upon the children of Israel through tears. He did not leave them, not even when they turned away from God. He rebuked them through tears and went with them to wander in the wilderness.

The Apostle Paul displayed the mercy of Christ when he pleaded for the salvation of the Jews, willing to be damned himself so they might be saved.

Peter said, "Lord . . . how often should I forgive? As many as seven times?" (v. 21).

That seems to give an offender more than enough chance to repent. We rarely give anyone seven chances. Two is about my limit: "I'll give you one more chance, then, watch out!"

But Jesus answered Peter, "Not seven times, but, seventy-seven times" (v. 22).

We must ask this question today, Is there anyone here who is without sin? Is there anyone among us who has not wronged in some way a sister or brother? Are there any persons here today who are without sin? All we like sheep have gone astray.

And we have all prayed, "Forgive us our trespasses, as we

forgive those who trespass against us." God forbid that anyone here today will lack forgiveness in his or her heart.

Let this be the time when all those things that separate us from one another, that keep us from truly being the loving and united community Christ desires, can be laid aside. Let it be fence-mending time, a time of reconciliation and peace. Better yet, let us begin to tear down every dividing wall, that we might be bound together in the love of Jesus Christ. Amen.

Suggestions for Worship

Call to Worship (Ps. 115:1, 3, 11):

PASTOR: Not to us, O LORD, not to us, but to your name give glory,

PEOPLE: For the sake of your steadfast love and your faithfulness.

PASTOR: Our God is in the heavens; he does whatever he pleases.

PEOPLE: You who fear the LORD, trust in the LORD! He is their help and their shield.

Act of Praise: Psalm 115:1-11.

Suggested Hymns: "Forward Through the Ages"; "Lord, I Want to Be a Christian"; "Where Charity and Love Prevail."

Opening Prayer: Holy and merciful God, you are the author and finisher of faith. You are strength for the weak and rest for the weary. You are savior for the sinful and home for the wanderer. You are healing for the sick and comfort for the sorrowful. You are our refuge and fortress. Increase our faith through Jesus Christ our Lord and Savior. Amen.

Pastoral Prayer: O saving God, Father of our Lord Jesus Christ, your word has gone forth to the ends of the earth, and you have declared that it shall not return void. Every knee shall bow and every tongue confess that Christ is Lord. Only in him can we find our righteousness and strength.

Let all who have worshiped false gods bow before you and be ashamed. Let all who will honor you, O God, declare your triumphant power, your steadfast mercy, and your everlasting glory. Amen.

(See page 447.)

September 12, 1993

□

Fifteenth Sunday After Pentecost

Forgiveness is central in the teaching of Christ. Through the Lord's prayer, we are taught to say, "Forgive us our debts, as we also have forgiven our debtors" (Matt. 6:12). One who harbors resentment does not know the mercy of God.

The Sunday Lessons

Exodus 20:1-20: The Ten Commandments are the highest and best requirements of duties toward God and neighbor. The first four relate to God—no other gods, no idols, no misuse of God's name, keeping the sabbath. The last six relate to neighbor—honor your father and mother, do not kill, do not commit adultery, do not steal, do not bear false witness, do not covet.
Romans 14:5-12: Some members of the church had "weak" consciences. Others were more particular about ethical demands and religious observance. Paul asks, "Why do you pass judgment on your brother or sister? . . . For we will all stand before the judgment seat of God" (v. 10).
Matthew 18:21-35: Peter asks, "How often should I forgive?" Jesus answered, "Not seven times, but . . . seventy-seven times" (vv. 21-22). The parable of the unforgiving servant follows. "I forgave you all that debt because you pleaded with me. Should you not have had mercy on your fellow slave, as I had mercy on you?" (vv. 32-33). The unmerciful man was handed over to the jailers.

Interpretation and Imagination

"I just can't find it in my heart to forgive her," she said, and I understood why. Her only son had married a beautiful, but thoroughly selfish, young woman who had no sense of obligation to any vow or to any other person. Not only did she take without giving, but she lied, cheated, ridiculed, and betrayed. The young husband loved her and tried desperately to save their marriage. On the day that he was notified of her divorce proceedings against him, he took his own life.

Now, a grieving and bitter mother was saying, "I hate her. I just can't find it in my heart to forgive. Not after how she hurt and destroyed him."

True forgiveness that can heal is not a trite and hasty thing that can be easily spoken. Some things aren't okay. Some things cannot be overlooked or quickly forgotten.

The gospel takes seriously the alienation caused by sin. It does not deny the pain or gloss over the failure. But it does insist on forgiveness as the way of Christ. It recalls his words spoken from the cross, "Father, forgive them" (Mark 23:34). The beginning place is when we learn to pray, "Forgive us . . . as we have forgiven our debtors" (Matt. 5;12).

The parable of the unmerciful servant speaks of a debt impossible to pay, "ten thousand talents" (v. 24). At that time it took more than fifteen years for a laborer to earn one talent. The debt the servant would not forgive was a mere "hundred denarii" (v. 28), which could be worked off in one summer. We tend to view our sins as significant, but consider sins against us monstrous. (JKB)

THE CASE PENDING IN COURT

Romans 14:10c

A SERMON BY MILFORD OXENDINE, JR.

Have you ever been in a courtroom when a trial of a very serious nature was in process? On occasion, I have watched such a scene, as the solicitor questioned and examined a witness. Ultimately, he would give his final argument in behalf of his client to the jury. I have watched and listened also as the counsel or attorney for the defense followed suit and did as the prosecuting attorney did.

In every case, I was moved to some degree with compassion as I tried to identify myself with the person who was on trial. I have watched certain ones in various cases as they sweated and wrung their hands, as their anxiety turned to despair. Some even became very angry. I have noted the great anxiety and suffering of the person on trial while awaiting the verdict. I have seen a jury bring in a verdict of guilty and watched some sink into an oblivion of sadness when the verdict was announced. They would drop their heads and cry as their judges sentenced them. All trials that we see in court should move us and cause us to think, especially those in which life or death hang in the balance.

Whether we know it or not, every one of us has a case pending in court. One day each of us shall stand before a judge. We are soberly reminded in Romans 14:10, "We will all stand before the judgment seat of God." Every one of us shall give an account of ourself to God. Our case, however, will be decided by the just and perfect judge—God—who created us and the world in which we live. When God hands down his decision, there will be no appeal. God's judgment will be final.

With these thoughts in mind, have we made or are we making preparations for our case, which is pending in court? Do you have an attorney, counselor, or someone to represent you? Or will you stand alone?

Judgment is mentioned more than one thousand times in the Bible: all authorities, vigorous youth, the old or aged with slow-moving and stumbling feet, the poor without adequate clothing and insufficient food, the rich with their lavish possessions. All are moving toward judgment. All of us, no matter what our status in life, must appear before the judgment seat of Christ.

But how, or on what basis, will we be judged? By what we have done about Christ—deciding for or against him. Throughout our lives, we are faced with numerous questions, but we never face a question more important than the one raised by Pontius Pilate when Christ was before him. "Then what should I do with Jesus who is called the Messiah?" (Matt. 27:22). Sooner or later, each of us will come to the judgment seat of God, and the question will be, What will Jesus do with me? Will he send me into everlasting joy or everlasting torment? This will be determined by how we have lived in this life.

What are we doing for our fellow human beings? There is far more to being a Christian than simply being a good, moral person. Doubtless the priest and Levite in the parable of the good Samaritan were good, moral men, who hurt no one. They were condemned by Christ, however, because they proved to be good for nothing when faced by a fellow human being in need of their help and their goodness.

This can be the story of our lives. Christ is deeply interested in what we are doing to help our neighbors. What is your relationship to your neighbor? Don't let your answer be, "Lord, when was it that we saw you hungry or thirsty or a stranger or naked or sick or in prison, and did not take care of you?" (Matt. 25:44). How we treat our neighbors and deal with them is how we treat the Master.

One of the greatest minds and greatest speakers of all times was Daniel Webster. On one occasion, when he had finished an after-dinner speech and the applause had somewhat subsided, the toastmaster thanked him and asked, "I wonder, Mr. Webster, if you could tell us what is the greatest question that has ever crossed your mind?" Mr. Webster hesitated a moment and answered, "Gentlemen, the greatest question that has ever crossed my mind is my personal accountability to God." What greater question could anyone ever grapple with than that? The Bible teaches that God will judge not only words and acts or deeds, but even the secrets of our inner hearts.

Facing this fact, who among us feels comfortable? We have not always done what we should. Many times we have knowingly done what we should not have done. The Bible states that all have sinned and fallen short of the glory of God. All of us know this is true. When our case is tried in court, however, it makes all the difference in the world if we know the judge, and the judge knows us. In the Gospel of John, Jesus said, "Anyone who hears my word and believes him who sent me has eternal life" (5:24). Jesus is saying that such a person will not be condemned.

God has designed a plan of pardon for every condemned person who will accept his offer. It is not God's will that anyone should perish, but rather that all should have eternal life. However, the solemn fact remains that one who knows the will of the Father, and does not do it, will be held accountable.

It is God's will to save all who will accept his grace. Salvation always comes by grace and grace alone; we can never earn it. If we could, it would not be sovereign grace. Just as Noah found grace in the eyes of the Lord, so can we.

The Bible teaches that at the moment Christ died, there was an earthquake and the great veil of the Temple in Jerusalem was torn from top to bottom (Matt. 27:5). Legend tells this story of the crucifixion: It was the hour of the evening sacrifice. The priest in the Temple was in the act of offering a lamb as a sacrifice. He may have been terrified by the shake of the earthquake, and as a result, the knife dropped from his hand, and the little lamb ran away, escaping what would have been certain death.

Why did all this happen? Because the Lamb of God who takes away the sins of the world had given himself as God's payment and offering for our sins. By accepting that Lamb of God and believing his Word, we can know that we, too, have passed from death into life. And thus he blots out the record of our sins on the judgment books. We are set free from the penalty of sin—eternal death and torment. God holds Christ accountable for our sins, that we may be found "not guilty," and be set free.

And how are we set free? God has an appointed day of judgment, but he has a counselor for us—Christ himself. On that day he will intervene for us, as God did for the ancient Hebrews who brought their offerings to the door of the sanctuary. After the Priest had sacrificed an offering, they could return to their homes forgiven of the committed sins. But the person who failed to come, and thus made no confession of sin, was cut off. One's sins went before, while the other's sins followed after. In the same way, we exclude ourselves from grace by our refusal to accept the Savior, who is our expiator. Thus God will reject those who refuse to confess and forsake their sins.

In Revelation 3:5, God's word says, "If you conquer, you will be clothed like them in white robes, and I will not blot your name out of the book of life; I will confess your name before my Father and before his angels." Jesus is ready to save right now. Why not confess your sins and be forgiven, before you bring judgment upon yourself?

A father carried his youngest son to the pet shop to pick out a puppy for a birthday gift. The lad looked all the puppies over very carefully, but was especially interested in one that kept wagging its tail. It stood out from all the other dogs. When asked which one he wanted, the boy replied, "The one with the happy ending." Do you want a happy ending, or perhaps I should ask, a happy beginning?

Then come to Jesus Christ right now. Make him your Lord and

Savior. Let him be your Counselor in God's judgment court. He and he alone can win your case today. He has never lost!

Opening Prayer: Lord, prepare us for the facing of this hour. As your spirit descends on us, allow each one of us to make divine preparations for the supreme event in history. Amen.

Pastoral Prayer: O God, our Redeemer, we have heard about a coming day when we will be judged after a better fashion than we can judge. How dare we travesty your great assize by mounting the throne ourselves. Forgive us for intruding into the prerogative of Christ.

Lord, we know your judgment will be universal. It will be for the strong and the weak. No elevation in piety will exclude us, and no weakness will serve as an excuse. The person of one and the person of ten talents must alike be reckoned with. What a motley throng will gather in that court of all nations and peoples and tongues!

Prepare us to stand alone. Cause us to look more into the hearings of our life. Teach us not to live a life of haphazardness, but one with wisdom and thoughtfulness. Amen.

ON HOARDING FORGIVENESS

Matthew 18:21-35

A SERMON BY THOMAS H. TROEGER

The man's debt was equal to 150,000 years of wages.

10,000 talents is the way Matthew puts it.

A note in my Bible explains that one talent equals 15 years of wages so I figure 15 × 10,000 = 150,000.

150,000 years of wages!

Talk about a spending binge, talk about living beyond your means, talk about compulsive buying.

What did the man do?

Order the contents of every catalogue that arrived in the mail every day?

Did he pay the minimum amount on his Visa, Mastercard, and American Express, and never read the fine print?

The day of reckoning finally comes.

He walks into the commercial trust building and finds the door marked "Collections."

On the manager's desk sits a stack of bank card statements thicker than *Webster's International Dictionary.*

The manager taps the stack with his forefinger and announces: "We want payment in full. Today!"

Maybe the man could get an advance on next week's paycheck.

But the debt is for 150,000 years of wages, which adds up to 7,800,000 weekly paychecks.

Sweat rolls down the debtor's face.

Although he doubts there is any chance of mercy, he swallows hard and cries out in desperation,

"Have patience with me, and I will pay you everything."

The debtor waits for the manager to pick up the phone and ask the secretary to call for the police.

The debtor imagines the sound of a siren, the click of handcuffs, a steel door being closed and locked.

Instead, the manager picks up the stack of statements and drops them into the wastecan beside the desk.

They hit the bottom of the can with the force of a brick.

Then the officer announces the debt is entirely forgiven.

Entirely forgiven?

Yes, entirely forgiven.

The manager shows the forgiven debtor to the door.

On his way out the man sees a friend who owes him a personal debt.

It adds up to about a hundred days wages.

A million times less than the debt that has just been cancelled.

The forgiven debtor grabs the man and shouts,

"Pay what you owe."

The receptionist runs and brings out the manager who listens to the whole story.

Then the manager retrieves the stack of bank statements from the wastecan, shakes them in the debtor's face and says,

"How wicked can you get? I forgave you all that debt

because you pleaded with me. Should you not have had mercy on this person as I had mercy on you?"

The receptionist calls the police.

The siren whines.

The handcuffs click.

The steel door bangs shut.

"And in anger his lord handed him over to be tortured until he would pay his entire debt. So my heavenly Father will also do to every one of you, if you do not forgive your brother or sister from your heart."

Forgive or be tortured!

It is as if Matthew, in reporting Jesus' parable,
gets so frustrated with human nature that he decides to force people into being gracious and forgiving.

That is not untypical of Matthew.

He often tacks a violent ending onto Jesus' parables.

Matthew wants passionately to straighten out the church's community life.

His Gospel is filled with instructions about living together as Christians.

How to settle disputes.

How to forgive.

How to treat one another.

Matthew tells all these things to a church that is having a difficult time.

Jesus has not returned as expected.

The reign of God appears to be losing out to Roman violence.

The strain of keeping the faith while the church is under attack is taking a toll.

People are becoming less forgiving.

Less gracious.

They are parceling out their deeds of goodness.

The evidence of Christ in their lives is withering.

In desperation, Matthew raises his voice and drives his point home: those who fail to forgive their brothers and sisters "from the heart" will be "tortured."

Perhaps Matthew once believed that if people only knew how gracious God was to them, they would be gracious to others.

But when grace did not work as easily as he hoped, Matthew

turned up the pressure with a threat:
Forgive or be tortured.
I do not like Matthew's ending to Jesus' parable.
A torturing Father God does not inspire grace.
A torturing Father God easily becomes a rationale for abusive behavior.
A torturing Father God may compel our outward compliance but will never win us over to the cause of love.
Putting the debtor on the rack will extract neither money nor forgiveness!
And yet Matthew is onto something of extraordinary importance in this severe parable.
The melodrama spells out the point of the story in capital letters: WE ARE NOT TO HOARD GOD'S FORGIVENESS FOR OURSELVES.
Since we have been forgiven an enormous debt,
God expects us
to extend the same spirit of grace to others.
But the melodrama of the story also reveals a subtler truth:
how difficult it is to reach the human heart,
to transform our patterns of calculated goodness.
Even an act of extravagant forgiveness may leave the heart unchanged.
That is what Matthew's church was discovering.
It was not enough to preach about Christ's love and grace.
It was not enough to point out how much they have been forgiven.
It was not enough to contrast the boundless mercy of God with the constricted limits of human pardon.
People needed day by day to persist in forgiving each other.
Matthew makes that plain with the verses that precede the parable:

"Then Peter came and said to [Jesus], 'Lord if another member of the church sins against me, how often should I forgive? As many as seven times?' Jesus said to him,
'Not seven times,
but, I tell you, seventy-seven times.' "

Only persistent grace.
Only persistent mercy.
Only persistent forgiveness.

Only persistent love brings the transformation of the human heart.

I think of all the endless debates I've heard about the correct theological understanding of Christ's death.

I think of all the times I have heard the words that God loves me, God forgives me.

True words, important words.

But what has convinced me of their truth?

What moves me to forgive my brother and my sister "from the heart?"

Is it words? Is it the threat of violence?

No.

It is rather the experience of persistent grace, of living with my wife, who day by day embodies the spirit of the gospel.

It is the experience of working with my friends and colleagues who persistently put up with my foibles and make allowances for my weaknesses.

It is the experience of people who have not kept track of my failings, but who have forgiven me seven times seven, who have forgiven me past all counting and calculation.

At his best, Matthew knows this truth.

He names the principle of persistent grace when he reports Jesus' answer to Peter's question about how many times he should forgive another person:

"Not seven times, but, I tell you, seventy-seven times."

God is not a torturing Father.

God is the one who in Christ invites us to forgive each other day by day until all our numbered acts of mercy blend as one with the eternal flood of grace.

Opening Prayer:

Fountain of love, Well of mercy,
who provides every essential gift of life,
rain and sun, food and air,
grace and truth, meaning and beauty,
awaken in us such thanks for your generosity
that we may give up all stinginess of spirit
and be extravagant in our compassion and care
of this earth and all its inhabitants.
For Christ's sake, Amen.

Pastoral Prayer:

Holy Judge, source of wisdom and justice,
We acknowledge that our lives are a thick and tangled wood, and we are lost in the shadow of moral confusion.
Speak again those clear commandments which enlighten the heart and make wise the simple.
When we misorder our priorities, let us hear once more the thunder at Sinai:
"You shall have no other gods before me."
When we are caught up in the frantic busyness of life,
call us back to "Remember the Sabbath and keep it holy."
When we are tempted to get ahead of others at the expense of truth, remind us, "You shall not bear false witness against your neighbor."
Let us keep your law with a gracious spirit so that all we do and say may be acceptable in your sight. Amen.

Suggestions for Worship

Call to Worship (Ps. 19:7):

PASTOR: The law of the LORD is perfect, reviving the soul;

PEOPLE: The decrees of the LORD are sure, making wise the simple;

PASTOR: The precepts of the LORD are right, rejoicing the heart;

PEOPLE: The commandment of the LORD is clear, enlightening the eyes;

PASTOR: The fear of the LORD is pure, enduring forever;

PEOPLE: The ordinances of the LORD are true and righteous altogether.

Act of Praise: Psalm 19:7-14.

Suggested Hymns: "Grace Greater Than Our Sin"; "Tell Me the Stories of Jesus"; "Amazing Grace."

SEPTEMBER 19, 1993

□

Sixteenth Sunday After Pentecost

Mercy does not give us what we deserve. Instead, it gives us what we need. Our Lord treats sinners with the same mercy that he has for those who have "borne the burden" of righteousness.

The Sunday Lessons

Exodus 32:1-14: When Moses was delayed in coming down from Sinai, the people turned to Aaron as a spiritual leader. Collecting their rings of gold he fashioned a golden calf, built an altar, and proclaimed a feast. God's wrath was kindled and would have consumed them. But Moses interceded. "And the LORD changed his mind about the disaster that he planned to bring on his people" (v. 14).
Philippians 1:21-27: Paul writes from prison at a time when he faces a martyr's death. He does not complain about his circumstances or seek another reward. Rather, he encourages "the saints in Christ Jesus who are at Philippi" (v. 1), that their "love may overflow more and more" (v. 9). He wants to be with Christ, "For to me, living is Christ and dying is gain" (v. 21).
Matthew 20:1-16: Laborers who had worked from early morning to late evening are paid the same as those who worked only the last hour of the day. The first workers expected to receive more and complained, "You have made them equal to us" (v. 12). The householder answered, "I choose to give to this last the same as I give to you. . . . Are you envious because I am generous?" (vv. 14-15). The parable speaks to the controversy with the Pharisees over inviting tax collectors and prostitutes into the kingdom.

Interpretation and Imagination

Toward the end of the semester, a student stood in my office saying, "It bothers me that students who do just enough to get by get the same amount of credit for the course that I do, when I exceed every requirement. Once I shared my notes and helped a student prepare for an exam. He got a better grade in the course than I did."

It bothers me that persons who are indifferent to the claims of Christ receive the same mercy and can expect the same steadfast love as the saints. That they may finally enjoy the same heaven just doesn't seem fair.

The parable of the laborers in the vineyard doesn't reflect careful economics, nor is it an example of equal justice for all. We have come to expect a fair wage for the hours we work. If we work more than another laborer, we expect to be paid more. If there are bonuses paid, some good formula is employed that will protect the morale of the whole group. The parable ignores such things. "I choose to give," are the key words. Wages are earned. Gifts are freely given.

The parable is difficult for those who view work as demanding and confining—a kind of heavy, unhappy chore that one does only for the sake of a paycheck. It is also difficult for those impressed by works-righteousness. Some people work with no thought of reward. Benedictine monks have that view and teach, "To work is to pray." They do not work for a reward, but for the sheer joy of it.

The apostle Paul wrote to the Philippians about this "higher way" and about the fruits of righteousness that are "union with Christ." (JKB)

TURN! REPENT!

Exodus 32:1-14

A SERMON BY THOMAS H. TROEGER

Moses talks to God the way preachers talk to sinners:
"*Turn* from thy fierce wrath, and *repent* of this evil against thy people."
The words *turn* and *repent* are the same words that the Bible uses to call wayward people back to God.
Jeremiah calls Israel to "turn" to God.
Job confesses, "I despise myself," and "repent in dust and ashes."

Hosea pleads, "by the help of your God turn back, hold fast to love and justice, and wait continually for your God."
But in this passage from Exodus, the roles are reversed.
It is not God who asks us to turn and repent.
It is Moses who asks God to turn and repent.
The audacity of it.
Telling God to turn.
Telling God to repent.
Speaking to God the way God speaks to us.
"*Turn* from thy fierce wrath, and *repent* of this evil against thy people."
At first, the idea of calling God to turn and repent may strike us as sacrilegious.
Who are we, mere human beings, that we should talk so brashly to God?
Besides, we may think, God does not need to change.
God is by nature constant and changeless.
There are places in the Bible that support such a view.
Samuel, for example, tells King Saul, "The Glory of Israel will not lie or repent; for he is not a man, that he should repent."
And the letter of James describes God as one "with whom there is no variation or shadow due to change."
Eternal, changeless, immutable God.
We bend to God, God does not bend to us.
That image of God has sustained many believers through the crises and upheavals of this world.
But it is not the way Moses relates to God.
There is a fierce give and take between the two of them.
From the moment God calls him,
Moses argues back and speaks
his mind freely to God.
He does not mince words with the Almighty:
"*Turn* from thy fierce wrath, and *repent* of this evil against thy people."
These are strong words, but strong words are needed.
God has had it with the Hebrews.
They have moaned and groaned in the wilderness, and now they have made the golden calf.
A direct violation of the first commandment.

God is furious and wants to wreak revenge upon the ingrates: "I have seen this people, and, behold, it is a stiff-necked people: Now therefore let me alone, that my wrath may wax hot against them, and I may consume them, and I will make of thee a great nation."

Moses is still in God's good graces.
God tells him, "of you I will make a great nation."
Moses is not facing destruction.
The rebellious Hebrews are the target of God's anger.
So when Moses tells God, "*Turn* from thy fierce wrath, and *repent* of this evil against thy people," Moses is not out to save his own neck.
He is interceding on behalf of others.
By asking God to repent, Moses helps God to be as gracious as God intends.
Through his courageous prayer,
Moses calls God back to being a God of mercy rather than vengeance.
God's love is drawn forth by human love.
This may sound like blasphemy, but it is not.
The Bible says, "And the Lord repented of the evil which he thought to do his people."
What kind of God is this that would listen to a human being and turn and repent?
It is a God who refuses to become an unchanging idol.
For that is exactly what God would be if God said to Moses:
"No, my first decision was to consume the people. I'm God.
I don't have to turn and repent."
Such a God would be no more bending,
no more responsive than
the golden calf.
But God turns and repents from evil.
God acknowledges having willed a violent end for the people.
We say we are made in the image of God.
We say salvation is claiming that image and letting it shine forth in our lives.
But sometimes we reduce God's image only to its gentlest, most attractive qualities:
Tenderness, grace, compassion.

Of course, we want these qualities of God's image to be apparent in our lives.
But if we are honest, there is also a deep and frightening violence within our hearts.
In the name of God we often deny this, feeling that such passions are incompatible with the image of God.
But in this story from Exodus, God does not deny the violence in God's own heart:
"Now therefore let me alone, that my wrath may wax hot against them, and that I may consume them."
God is not without violent desires.
But, unlike us, God acknowledges them openly and thereby becomes open to the call to "turn" and "repent."
Thus the way to let God's image shine more fully in us
is not to deny the violence in our hearts,
but to follow God's example,
to confess our violence
so that we may then turn and repent.
Notice that before repenting,
God tells Moses, "Let me alone, that my wrath may wax hot against them."
But Moses refuses to let God "alone."
Moses does not allow God to break off their communication.
Moses argues that for God to wipe out the people would contradict God's original purpose in freeing them:
"Wherefore should the Egyptians speak, and say, "For mischief did [God] bring them out, to slay them in the mountains, and to
consume them from the face of the earth?"
Moses pleads. Moses bargains. Moses argues.
Moses takes God too seriously to let God get away with being less than divinely merciful and compassionate.
Such an understanding of God may upset many of us.
It does not seem reverent or respectful enough.
But I believe we should follow the example of Moses.
It is in the Bible.
And it is in the Bible for good reason:
because a God we can argue with,
a God we can tell to repent
is a God we can keep relating to.

How long do we keep talking to people who never respond,
never change,
never admit to our impact on them,
and never acknowledge their feelings?
Not very long.
We might as well talk to a statue or a golden calf.
But someone who will listen to our pleas,
someone who will even turn and repent,
that is someone whose company we will seek and honor and value and celebrate.
"*Turn* from thy fierce wrath, and *repent* of this evil against thy people."
Start speaking to God the way Moses did and see what happens to yourself as well as to God.
Tell God, "Turn from your fierce wrath,"
and listen for how your words sound in your own ears.
Tell God, "Repent of your evil,"
and listen for how your words affect your own desires.
Speak your heart to God
and God will speak to your heart.
Call forth God's love from God
and it will come forth in you.
Live this bravely in the presence of God,
and you will have no desires for a golden calf.
No desires for any idol.
No desires for any God except the dynamic, living, changing God whom Moses knew.
The God humble enough to turn and repent of evil.
The God humble enough to come to us in Jesus Christ
that we might turn and repent of our own evil.

Opening Prayer:

O Christ, whose life is life itself to us,
beat in our hearts,
breathe through our breath,
speak through our speech,
and move through our actions
until all we are and all we say and all we do
declares that you are risen

and still seeking the lost,
still feeding the poor,
still healing the sick,
still freeing the imprisoned,
still bringing in the reign of God. Amen.

Pastoral Prayer:

Ancient of Days, Alpha and Omega, Beginning and End,
we, like the Israelites, have short memories.
By dawn we forget that you brought us through the night.
By noon we forget the promise of the morning.
By evening we forget you sustained us through the day.
In grief we forget the peace you brought us in the past.
In transition we forget that you have been
our dwelling place in all generations.
Renew our memories of your grace so that recalling the past
we may hear you calling us into the future,
and may be filled with the courage of Jesus Christ,
who has gone before us and in whose name we pray. Amen.

CHRISTIAN LABORERS RECEIVE THE SAME PAY

Matthew 20:14

A SERMON BY MILFORD OXENDINE, JR.

In today's Gospel reading, we find the story of a landowner hiring people from the marketplace to work in his vineyard. Every three hours the landowner returns to hire more workers. At the end of the day, all the workers are paid. When working in the secular environment, different workers receive different wages. This isn't the case for those who work in God's vineyard. Those who were hired at the eleventh hour received the same pay as those who were hired at sunrise. The amount of pay was one day's wage. It was just enough money to purchase the family's food for one day.

Labor is the human activity that puts a roof over our heads, food to nourish our bodies into our grocery bags, and clothes on our backs. Farmers, doctors, lawyers, and owners of large businesses are usually self-employed. But only about 10 percent of working people in the United States are self-employed. Most of us work for other people, and receive compensation for our efforts in the form of wages and salaries.

In a true democracy, we are free to choose our life's work. No one can force us to take jobs or work for an employer if we do not wish to. If we are not paid enough or fail to receive a deserved pay raise, we can quit and look for another job. In a totalitarian society, people do not enjoy that kind of freedom. The political system makes people less important than the state. The state dictates the terms and conditions of employment and sets the minimum wages for those who work.

But this isn't the case in God's church. Some Christians disagree with God's terms. Others feel that he isn't justified in making the pay equal for all laborers. However, one must keep in mind that God, through Jesus, is the one hiring the vineyard laborers. He is the one who has set the level of pay. This can be seen as the small churches are put on the same wage scale as the large churches. Both churches have the same goal—to provide workers for God's vineyard. Therefore, God shows no partiality as he pays all of us with grace.

The parable states a basic fact of Christianity in very simple terms. It declares that if someone starts work in God's vineyard at the eleventh hour, they will receive more than they could ever hope. This person may fear entering the vineyard under a disadvantage at the eleventh or twelfth hour, but the parable says that one can and will be given pay equal to that of those who started working at sunrise. "The parable cannot indicate the secret, but it names the fact, that often those repenting late may overtake those who started long before in goodness and service" (Herbert Lockyer, *All the Parables of the Bible* [Grand Rapids, Michigan: Zondervan Publishing House, 1963] 220).

The parable reaffirms that it isn't the length of time one labors in the vineyard. Rather, it is the quality of service one puts into the vineyard. Discontentment can set in among the laborers, however. It usually comes from the workers who have labored the hardest and the longest. They become angry because they receive no more wages than those who started working later.

They feel angry because they have rendered a longer service. They demand a greater reward. This mood mars discipleship with a lot of discontent.

Let's recall the story of the prodigal son and his elder brother. The elder brother fits in quite well with those who complained to the landowner about working longer hours (vv. 11-12). What the laborers and the elder brother failed to realize is that they agreed to work for the landowner for the wages they were paid. The landowner and son's father, being just, know what each worker has agreed to work for. Therefore, the early workers' and older son's discontent over their pay is unwarranted. All of us who enter the vineyard must enter it with the full persuasion that our labor for the landowner will not be in vain.

The landowner of the vineyard has the sovereign right to claim and to do whatever he wills, especially in his own affairs (v. 15). As laborers in his vineyard, we cannot question the amount of reward he pays each worker. Why? Because he shows no partiality. He acts fairly to everyone.

Here in the parable, we find the *generosity* of God. The laborers did not do the same amount of work. Yet, they received the same pay. There are two important lessons here. First, all service is recognized and rewarded by God. It isn't the amount of service given, but it is the love with which we labor that matters. Nor is it God's intention to look on the amount of our service. What matters is what we have to give. Thus God will recompense all services equally, and will provide a fitting reward.

The second lesson is perhaps even more important than the first. All that God gives is a full measure of grace. We cannot earn what he pays us. Why? Because no matter what the wages, they are far greater than we rightfully deserve. "All have sinned and fall short of the glory of God" (Rom. 3:23). What God gives to the laborers in his vineyard comes from the goodness of his heart. What God gives is not really wages. It is a gift. It isn't a reward, but an overwhelming measure of grace.

The supreme lesson of the parable is that "the whole point of work is the spirit in which it is done" (William Barclay, *The Gospel of Matthew* [Philadelphia: The Westminster Press, 1975], 226). The laborers are split into two classes. The first laborers had an agreement and a contract with the landowner.

They simply said, "We are willing to work, if the pay is right." When it came time to be paid for their labor, they wanted more pay than they had originally bargained for, more than what was given to those who came to work at the eleventh hour. But the latter laborers had made no contract. All they wanted was the opportunity to work. They were willing to let the landowner decide what their just wages should be.

Can any of us be mature Christians if our first concern is how God will reward us? Christians work for the joy of serving God and offering love to others.

The Scripture tells us to "strive first for the kingdom of God" and everything else will be given to us as well. Many of those who have earned great rewards in life will have a very low place in God's kingdom. Why? Because they have worked only for a reward. Conversely, those we count as poor will be the greatest in God's kingdom, because as they worked in God's vineyard, rewards were not on their minds. Instead, they went out to work for the joy of serving. Thus they will be the ones to fulfill the paradox of Christian living—the one who aims at reward will indeed lose it, and those who forget the rewards will find them working in God's vineyard. There one will find grace, hope, and peace of mind.

Suggestions for Worship

Call to Worship (Matt. 18:19-20):

PASTOR: Jesus said, "I tell you, if two of you agree on earth about anything you ask,

PEOPLE: It will be done for you by my Father in heaven.

PASTOR: For where two or three are gathered in my name,

PEOPLE: I am there among them."

Act of Praise: Psalm 106:7-8, 19-23.

Suggested Hymns: "All Praise to Thee, for Thou, O King

Divine"; "Leaning on the Everlasting Arms"; "My God, I Love Thee."

Opening Prayer: Lord, we desire to be in your arms of safety. We seek your glory. We need rest from our labor. Put us in your center of quiet peace and love during this sacred hour. Amen.

Pastoral Prayer: Dear Lord, there are few words that have more powerful influence over human affairs than gain. It is the folly and the sin of humankind that we do not often extend our search for gain to the realm of the spirit. Blessed are those who can recognize where real gains, real rewards, and real treasures lie in this life. How wonderful does this appear when we consider that our gains, rewards, and treasures are found in love. Give us strength that will allow us to continue working in your kingdom until it is time for us to enter your eternal vineyard. True, at death, one loses all that is most precious to one in life upon earth. But all one loses here compared with what one gains in heaven is as the surrender of a little homestead to gain a kingdom and a crown, or parting with a single farthing for the acquisition of a princely revenue. Yes, dear Lord, let us not forget that our labors bring reward. They are the fruits of joy, grace, and peace. For all of your goodness, we thank you. May we lift our labors to you. Thank you. Amen.

September 26, 1993

□

Seventeenth Sunday After Pentecost

It is relatively easy and painless to make promises. To promise loyalty and service to Christ and his church costs little. It is quite another thing to do it.

The Sunday Lessons

Exodus 33:12-23: God had revealed to Moses his ways. Now Moses boldly asks to see his visible glory—God's face. But no man can see God and live. Placed behind a rock and covered there by God's hand, Moses was allowed to see God's back as he passed by. Even though God's presence is known, his being, very personal and much more than person, is hidden.
Philippians 2:1-13: Paul encourages Philippian Christians to have "the same mind," "the same love" as Christ (v. 2). Humility and a concern for others are marks of this oneness with Christ, who "humbled himself and became obedient to the point of death—even death on a cross" (v. 8).
Matthew 21:28-32: Speaking in the Temple in Jerusalem, Jesus said, "Tax collectors and prostitutes are going into the kingdom of God ahead of you" (v. 31). He had told the parable of two sons. One said, "I go sir," but he did not go (v. 30). Jesus told the parable to show the difference between saying and doing. Matthew uses the parable to contrast the rabble who responded to John the Baptist's message, to the Pharisees who did not.

Interpretation and Imagination

The place where most of us make bold statements about our allegiance to Christ is in church on Sunday morning. We say it in our hymns. "Jesus I my cross have taken, All to leave and follow thee." We say it in our creeds. "I believe in Jesus Christ, his only son, our Lord." We say it in our prayers. "Thy kingdom come, thy will be done." We say it in prayers that dedicate our offerings. "With these gifts we offer our very selves to thee."

Is it not true, for most of us, that our promises in church surpass our ability to serve our Lord. Our commitments through hymns and creeds often don't change anything about the way we spend our days, conduct our personal lives, and manage our institutions. Yet, we go out of church believing we are loyal sons and daughters of the divine parent.

Plato offered the famous doctrine of "idea." He taught that every concrete reality exists first of all as an idea in the divine mind. Yet he failed to explain in any satisfactory way how the idea becomes a concrete reality.

Jesus did not address problems philosophically, but rather, had a quality of character that involved him in actual relationships and actions. In the final analysis, he taught more by what he was and what he did than through mere words.

There is a sobering word in these lessons that suggests drunks and whores may have a better time of it at the judgment seat of God than those who promise love and loyalty but do not live it out. In every spiritual pilgrimage, and in any effort to live life in ways that will add up to fulfillment, the next step is obedience. (JKB)

THE PARABOLIC LOVE OF GOD

Philippians 2:1-13

A SERMON BY MARJORIE J. THOMPSON

There is a Jewish legend that tells of two farmer brothers. One was married and had children; the other lived alone. One day, the single brother said to himself, "Why should I keep all the harvest for myself? I am one and my needs are few, while my brother has a wife and children to feed. What I will do is take a sack of grain each night from my storehouse to his. Then he will have more to feed his family." At the same time, the married brother said to himself, "Why should I keep all the harvest for my own family? I have children to help me farm and to take care of me when I am old, while my brother has no one. What I will do is take a sack of grain each night from my storehouse to his. Then he can sell the surplus and provide for his future." The brothers proceeded in their secret charity for many years. Each wondered that his own grain store was never diminished, until one night they met. When each learned what the other was doing, they embraced in gratitude. And God, seeing, wept tears of joy.

This story may bring tears to our eyes as well. Yet how unlike our own experience it probably seems! My early memories include plenty of sibling rivalry—quarrels over whom that treasured possession belonged to, arguments over who was right or wrong, competition for the attention and approval of our parents. I suspect most of us continue, with a thin veil of adult sophistication, to act out of self-interest with relatives, colleagues, and friends. It seems natural to claim, "This is *my* possession, *my* original thought, *my* special prerogative, *my* unique role."

The world rewards us for standing out from the crowd, so we quickly learn to lay claim to something we can call "mine." It may be a particular "style," a joke for every occasion, a spotless home, a high-status job, "insider" information, or an honorable title. Some of us find the most effective way to gain attention is negatively; the most pugnacious, outrageous, or obnoxious person in a group still earns a distinctive reputation!

When our primary focus is on maintaining an image; when we feel a need to win out over others; when our sense of identity and security lies in special status, privilege, or approval, our relationships with others become distorted. We find ourselves competitors, broadsiding each other out of our chosen paths to acclaim. Rivalry and retaliation become weapons of choice, and it seems impossible to place the other person's concerns before our own.

Paul, writing to the young and inexperienced church at Philippi, knows this perfectly well. He knows that in his absence, some are preaching Christ from envy and rivalry with him (1:15-17). He knows that his beloved co-laborers in Christ, Euodia and Syntyche, have been quarreling over some matter (4:2). And he knows that internal church divisions born of personal ambition and vanity can only weaken the witness of the church against its true opponents—Judaizers who preach circumcision (3:2-3) and unbelievers who persecute the church (1:27-30).

Paul understands that what is needed is a radically different way of thinking about ourselves in relation to others—a way that places us in cooperation rather than competition; a way that sets us free from self-absorption so we can respond to the needs and concerns of others. It is the mind and spirit of Christ that enables our attitudes and behaviors toward one another to change. Accordingly, Paul urges his Philippian flock to take their union with Christ seriously, saying, in essence: "If union with Christ means anything to you, if the love of Christ has any power to move you, if you are sharing in the reality of Christ's Spirit, then show yourselves to belong to him. Live together in harmony, for Christ gives you one mind and one spirit. If you dwell in his attitude, you will act with humility!"

The apostle then places before his converts the most incontrovertible evidence possible for a Christian: the living example of Jesus. He borrows a liturgical hymn from the early church, called by scholars the *Carmen Christi* (Song of Christ) or Hymn of Christ. It is perhaps the most potent poetic reflection on the nature and mission of Jesus preserved for us in Scripture. Embedded in its cadences we find not only the spiritual core of Paul's message in Philippians 2, but the very heart of Christian faith and confession.

Within the space of six verses (6-11), we are given a panoramic view of the sweep of salvation history. It begins with the Christ of divine pre-existence. Here is one who possesses the very form of God and enjoys the glory of divine status. Yet he does not consider his heritage a possession to be clutched or a privilege to be grasped for personal gain. Instead, he lets go his equality with God, relinquishing divine glory for the status of a human creature. He is the marvel of Christ's self-emptying humility.

Paul gives us three deepening phases in the self-emptying of Christ. First, the Incarnation itself—God becoming human. The Greek makes clear how profound is the condescension of this humility. Christ moves from the "form of God" *(morphe theou)* to the "form of a slave" *(morphe doulos)*—from the status of divinity to the status of one in bondage, the very image of powerlessness.

As if this were not sufficiently shocking, the text continues, "having assumed human form, he humbled himself *still further*, and became obedient to death." Doesn't death simply come with the territory? we might well ask. R. P. Martin, in his book *Carmen Christi*, argues that Jesus did not simply die, as others must. For ordinary human beings, death is a *necessity;* for Jesus it was an *obedience* freely accepted in voluntary submission to God's redemptive design. Indeed, the "victory" of death was possible only because Christ consented to submit to its power.

In the original hymn, identification with death marked the low point in the drama of Christ's descent from heaven to earth. But Paul purposely points out a final and yet deeper dimension in the self-emptying process: "*even* death on a cross!" The death Jesus freely consented to was not from natural causes, nor from a single mortal blow. His was a form of public execution reserved for the worst criminals—a lingering, agonizing death-by-inches in the blazing sun. The cross was a crude instrument of torture. By adding this brief phrase to the hymn, Paul reveals the full extent of Jesus' humility—the complete and utter surrender of divine love to the very worst the world could dish up.

By the end of verse 8, we have come to the lowest point in what one scholar calls "the dramatic parabola" drawn by this hymn. "These three verses lead, in one great sweep, from the highest height to the deepest depth." From this point, the curve of the parabola carries us swiftly upward. The reversal of Jesus' abasement is equally dramatic. On account of his complete obedience and humility, God has lifted him to the loftiest height, in abundant contrast to his ignominious death. God has bestowed on Jesus a new name, revealing the fullness of his identity: Kyrios, Lord. Every spiritual power in the created cosmos will recognize and acclaim the sovereignty of the humiliated and exalted One, confessing his rightful dominion and adoring his name.

Yet his humility remains, even in Christ's exalted state. The worship of Jesus as Lord is not usurpation of the throne of God. The utter absence of rivalry between Father and Son was made clear when Christ refused to "cling to his equality with God," willingly entering the human state. The purpose of Jesus' life on earth was not his glory, but God's. He drew people to himself in order to draw them to the heart of God. As the Father was honored in Christ's voluntary humility and obedience, so God is glorified in Jesus' exaltation.

Moreover, our Lord did not calculate that the high yield would ultimately make his self-sacrifice a smart investment; his self-renunciation flowed from divine love. Nor was Jesus' exaltation an automatic reward to make up for his suffering; it was a gift of grace. "Whoever exalts himself will be humbled, and whoever humbles himself will be exalted" (Matt. 23:12) simply expresses the way of God's love—the natural outcome of our chosen attitudes in God's realm. The Incarnation reveals that God's way turns our worldly understanding inside out. God's power is manifest in what we consider weak. Wisdom and compassion constrain God to the power of persuasion, not the power of force. Have we yet discovered that the most persuasive power on earth is love? This is the very basis of Paul's appeal: "If the fact that you are in Christ has any power to influence you, if love has any persuasive power to move you . . ." (Barclay).

It is not merely Jesus' *example* of selfless humility that Paul sets before us. We cannot *imitate* One who took human form from pre-existent celestial equality with God! Paul invites us, rather, to *participate* in the life and spirit Christ has made available to us through union with him. When Paul urges his flock to "have for one another that attitude which you have *in* Christ Jesus" (v. 5), he is saying, "Allow the vital union between you and Christ to be expressed in harmonious and humble relationships with one another." Is it not so much a matter of imitating Jesus as participating in the new creation he embodies.

Thinking of others' interests before our own, as the brothers of the Jewish legend do, does not come naturally to us. Self-interest, petty jealousy, and personal ambition are more familiar. How are we released from living in concentric circles around our own egos? Is it not by realizing that we do not belong to ourselves, but to Another—to One who has loved us from the beginning with tenderness, passion, humor, and freedom? Here, indeed, is a love that willingly flings itself down from highest heaven, right into the sordid depths of human cruelty and suffering, even the bowels of hell itself; yet because love endures all things, it gathers into its orbit every fragment of human experience, lifting up all as it ascends again into the realm of healing, purifying light. The parabolic love of God in Christ Jesus throws a net wide and deep enough to embrace the whole creation.

When we know ourselves to be cradled in this love, we can participate in it with joy! The gift of salvation has been given! Our task is to "work it out" (v. 12) in our daily lives and relationships, to bring to completion the new life God has offered us in Christ.

Humble service to one another, unity in spirit, willingness to think of the "least" among us more highly than ourselves is how we realize the new creation in our midst.

Paul ends with one final and indispensable word of encouragement: Bringing the gift of new life to fruition is possible because "God is already at work within us, giving us both the will and the power to achieve God's purpose" (v. 13). Without this promise, our efforts would be doomed. With it, how can they fail?

Suggestions for Worship

Call to Worship (Ps. 99:1-2, 5):

PASTOR: The LORD is king; let the peoples tremble!

PEOPLE: He sits enthroned upon the cherubim; let the earth quake!

PASTOR: The LORD is great in Zion; he is exalted over all the peoples.

PEOPLE: Extol the LORD our God; worship at his footstool. Holy is he!

Act of Praise: Psalm 99.

Suggested Hymns: "I Love Thy Kingdom, Lord"; "Am I a Soldier of the Cross"; "O Day of God, Draw Nigh."

Opening Prayer: All-loving and ever-living God, we confess that our lives are self-absorbed; we are motivated by self-interest, seeking the rewards of the world rather than those of your kingdom. Power, privilege, status, and approval have too much hold on our hearts. The need to be right, to be well thought of, to be accepted by others often takes a terrible toll on our integrity. Lead us out of our prison of self-centeredness and into a new life in Jesus Christ. Amen.

Pastoral Prayer: God, whose power is revealed in humble

service, as you release us from the grip of our own concerns, may we see more and more how you call us to be for others, as you are for us in Christ. Open our eyes to the needs of those around us in our families, our schools, our cities, our nation—indeed, in all the world's nations who are one family in your eyes. Teach us to listen for your voice in those whose lives and thoughts are different from ours; teach us to obey your command to love one another as you have loved us, remembering that Jesus' humility and sacrifice are the final measure of your love.

These prayers, and all the silent pleas of your Spirit in our hearts, we lift to you in trust and thanks; in the name of Jesus Christ, your Incarnate Word and our exalted Lord! Amen.

October 3, 1993

□

Eighteenth Sunday After Pentecost

Self-centered people and self-serving tenants can only be set aside. The vineyard provides the image. Worthless vines are burned. Wicked tenants are thrown out.

The Sunday Lessons

Numbers 27:12-23: Moses was commanded to go into the hilly region of Abarim where Mount Nebo is located. From there he could see the land of promise, but he would never walk there. God commanded that Joshua son of Nun be commissioned to succeed Moses. The sacred lots (Urim), cast by Eleazar the priest, would confirm his choice.
Philippians 3:12-21: Wanting spiritual maturity for the converts at Philippi, Paul speaks of perfection. "I press on to make it my own, because Christ Jesus has made me his own" (v. 12). He writes about those who live as enemies of the cross of Christ (v. 18). Selfish appetites had become their God. The upward call of God is the controlling theme.
Matthew 21:33-43: Jesus told Jewish leaders the parable of the wicked tenants. A landowner sent servants to collect his share of the grape harvest. They were beaten, stoned, and killed. Finally, he sent his son, and the heir to the vineyard was killed. Jesus asked, "How do you think he (the owner of the vineyard) will deal with those tenants?" They answered, "[He will] lease the vineyard to other tenants who will give him the produce at the harvest time" (v. 41).

Interpretation and Imagination

It's a sobering thought, yet it must not be dismissed. We can forfeit our place in the cause of Christ and be set aside in God's plan for things.

The parable was directed at the Pharisees and the priests. They knew it and wanted Jesus arrested. When anyone's place and power in the scheme of things is challenged—or worse, shown to be counterfeit and temporary—that person will try to dismiss the true authority, even the authority of God.

More than fifty years have passed since German Christianity was at the forefront of biblical and theological leadership in the Christian world. Then came Hitler's rise to power, World War II, the Holocaust. Christian pastors like Bonhoeffer, Niemöller, and Thielicke spoke out against the injustice and were jailed. Bonhoeffer was hanged. The prophets were silenced.

But many German Christians were silent. One German pastor, reflecting on the absence of a strong Christian witness in those times, said, "There is not gospel without witness and there is not witness without risk." It has been noted that the German church lost credibility and leadership through it all. "One is still hesitant to speak up as a German Christian," was the sad lament of one German theologian.

The truth is evident in so many places. Athletes who do not perform well know they will be benched. Industrial leaders who fail to produce will be replaced. Unfaithful stewards will be relieved of all responsibility.

Wesley taught that we could fall from grace. Those who follow their own desires and ignore the might and right of God will be set aside. Others will take their place.

The question asked is, What will the landowner (God) do? The question implied is, What must we do? Obedience is always the next step in discipleship. (JKB)

STOLEN FRUIT

Matthew 21:33-43

A SERMON BY BARBARA BATE

Landlord-tenant problems have been around for a long time. In apartment complexes, tenants complain that their leases give the landlord all the rights and the tenant all the obligations. But landlords often say that tenants do damage, fail to pay the rent on time, and make noise that wakes the neighbors.

This parable in Matthew—also told in Mark and Luke—is enough to make any landlord give up renting property forever.

The landlord seems to have been more than fair. He planted the vineyard himself. He put a fence around it to protect it. He dug a hole for a wine press. He built a watchtower to keep an eye out for intruders. And only then did he lease this much-improved property to tenants and leave for another country. This man could hardly be called uncaring and uninterested. He paid as much attention to developing the land he owned as some people pay to members of their own family.

Thus far the story sounds almost too good to be true. How could anyone fail to be grateful and cooperative toward such a generous and responsible host? As you know from the story, such ingrates seem to exist, at least in the world of the parable. The tenants in this vineyard made themselves comfortable on the land until harvest time. Then they proceeded to beat, stone, or kill two different groups of the landlord's servants who had come to collect his share of the produce. Why in the world would they do this? The story suggests that greed might have been a motive. When the landlord finally sent his son to talk with the tenants, they said to each other, "This is the heir; let's kill him and get his inheritance." (Does this sound like the plot of a television miniseries?) They seized the son and killed him, but first they threw him out of "their" vineyard.

It is quite possible for me to believe in human greed sufficient to be the motive for murder. The trials of rich families fighting over a will, and unethical stock traders fighting to keep their millions, make this an easy scenario to believe. But somehow I am inclined to think that more is going in this parable than the sheer desire of a few tenant farmers to hang on to more of their crops. I wonder whether these people were incapable of experiencing gratitude. I wonder whether they were so eager to control their own lives and circumstances that they could not look a true benefactor in the eye.

Matthew's version of this parable has Jesus asking rather than telling his listeners what they think the owner will do to the tenants who have killed his son. (In contrast, Mark and Luke have Jesus report the end of the tale himself.) The listeners, full of the spirit of vengeance, answer confidently that the owner will "put those wretches to a miserable death and lease the vineyard to other tenants"—presumably tenants who will know how to behave.

Put yourself in the group in front of Jesus as he told this

parable. I know that I, for one, would choose to be the landowner, the servants, or perhaps the son. All of these are on the right side of the story. The tenants are clearly the villains. But as we see so often in the Gospels, Jesus turns the spotlight on his listeners. "You" listeners, you ungrateful tenants, will see the kingdom of God given to another people—people with the capacity and the honesty to bring forth "the fruits of the kingdom."

Who are "you" in this case? The audience probably included both religious leaders and the general followers of Jesus, who are often referred to as "the crowd." Jesus often divided his listeners by his style of speaking into allies and enemies. This time the targets knew who they were. The chief priests and Pharisees were stung by the prophecy that the kingdom of God will be given to another people. Full of the spirit of vengeance, they were ready to kill Jesus.

But the "you" in this passage seems to float off the text and into the crowd—our crowd. This little pronoun invites anyone present to ask, "Does this mean me?" Apparently tenants can be store clerks, homemakers, business managers, teachers—even pastors.

For a number of years I have worked on preaching issues with seminary students and pastors of local churches. I have never met a pastor who did not want to preach well. I have, however, met many pastors who feel pressured in the pursuit of all their pastoral tasks. Ministering to the sick, managing programs, mollifying the troublemakers, and even maintaining buildings can eat up all the time they had hoped to spend on study, devotions, and preaching preparation. Pastors in Christ's church are tenants in a large and fertile vineyard. While the opportunity for producing fruit has never been greater, the size and complexity of the task and the possibility of being judged a failure can be daunting to the most dedicated of pastors.

As a preacher myself, I have sometimes heard whispered in my ear one of two messages coming from an unseen tempter. The first says, "If you preach very well, others will want to preach like you." The other message is, "You don't have to worry about spending hours on preaching; someone else has already done a well-crafted message that you can use in your own pulpit." In the first case, my desire for recognition and praise tempts me to view the preaching act as a personal tour de force, instead of being a response to God and a gift from a faith community. In the second case, the temptation to borrow another's words for my own community leads me to treat the preaching event not as a living celebration with specific people but as a generic reading of secondhand words.

Both messages are pernicious. They make pastors into tenants who are likely to lack both gratitude for the vineyard and the stamina to produce live fruit themselves. In a culture in which both ambition and laziness are fostered, these messages proliferate outside as well as inside the church.

The parable of the vineyard is harsh in both its language and its plot. The tenants kill the son, and they are punished by being killed themselves. They are prevented from ever getting a glimpse of God's kingdom. The connection between this first-century parable and the inappropriate production and use of generic sermons in modern pulpits may seem distant and tenuous at best. But while no preacher in my acquaintance is likely to be charged with "killing the son" because of reading words borrowed silently from another writer, many preachers are charged by their own congregations with reading words that are lifeless. Even when the eyes look periodically at the worshipers or the arms move in a regular rhythm, the voice of the preacher tends to reveal whether the preacher's own experience of the gospel is included in the words that are spoken. The Word becomes flesh only when the words come from the life of the speaker and the lives of those sharing in worship.

The parable of the tenants reaches off the page and beyond its original community. It calls to anyone who considers claiming the vineyard without working for its harvest and returning its fruits. Jesus asks each of us—clergy and laypersons alike—simply to show gratitude for God's vineyard and to listen to the voice of its real owner.

Suggestions for Worship

Call to Worship (Phil. 3:12-14):

PASTOR: I press on to make it my own because Christ Jesus has made me his own.

PEOPLE:	**I do not consider that I have made it my own; but one thing I do:**
PASTOR:	Forgetting what lies behind and straining forward to what lies ahead,
PEOPLE:	**I press on toward the goal for the prize of the heavenly call of God in Christ Jesus.**

Act of Praise: Psalm 81:1-10.

Suggested Hymns: "In Christ There Is No East or West"; "He's Got the Whole World in His Hands"; "Let Us Break Bread Together."

Opening Prayer: Holy One, who has entrusted us with a rich and complex world, full of magnificent fruits and attractive temptations; bring us this day to a new awareness of your trust in our stewardship of life itself. Enable us to celebrate the fact that we owe to you everything that we are and all that we accomplish. In the name of the One who is the first fruits of your creation, amen.

Pastoral Prayer: O God of justice and risktaking love, you have placed each of us in situations in which choices must be made. We are asked to choose whether to accept the demands of a covenant relationship with you, or to seize control of our time and our resources. We are invited to see and hear and feel life in your presence, rather than allowing the voices of death to rule in us. We are permitted to decide our own priorities and to discover for ourselves whether those priorities foster lives of celebration or of cynicism.

Dear God, be with each person who has decided that the wider culture is right and that personal ambitions are of ultimate worth. Be with each of us who becomes consumed with envy toward the very people who have made choices we say we find unacceptable. Be with each person who gives up personal control in favor of trusting another individual or a group, allowing them to address a task in their own way. Help those of us who are trusted by another, that we may be grateful, confident, and faithful.

Finally, be present to your church. Help preachers to deal with their pressures; help critics to recognize their self-righteousness in judging pastors; and help parishioners to know their own powers as listeners to and proclaimers of your Word.

We pray in the name of the one who came to us in the spirit of loving justice, Jesus Christ. Amen.

October 10, 1993

□

Nineteenth Sunday After Pentecost

Isaiah speaks of a feast. Paul writes about God's providence that supplies every need. The parable invites many to the wedding and compels others to come. Though many are called, few are chosen.

The Sunday Lessons

Deuteronomy 34:1-12: Moses climbed Mount Nebo to the very top of Pisgah. From there he could see all the land the Lord had promised to Abraham. "This is the land of which I swore to Abraham, to Isaac, and to Jacob" (v. 4). Moses died there, and was buried in the land of Moab, but no one knows the place of burial. "Never since has there arisen a prophet in Israel like Moses, whom the LORD knew face to face" (v. 10).

Philippians 4:1-9: "Rejoice always," Paul says (v. 4). The New English Bible translates the verse, "All joy be yours. Let your magnanimity be manifest to all" (vv. 4-5). Anxiety is set aside by thoughts of all that is true, honorable, just, pure, lovely, and gracious. Paul thanks the Philippians for their gift, but intends to be free from the concerns of poverty as well as plenty. "I can do all things through [Christ]. . . . My God will fully satisfy every need of yours" (vv. 13, 19).

Matthew 22:1-14: Two lessons are taught in this parable centered on a wedding feast. The first is of those who would not come. "They made light of it and went away, one to his farm, another to his business" (v. 5). The rejection of Jesus as Messiah is Matthew's point. The parable goes on to say that the angry king commands, "Go therefore into the main streets, and invite everyone you find to the wedding banquet" (v. 9). The second lesson is about a guest who is not dressed in a wedding garment. "Throw him into the outer darkness" (v. 13). Both judgment and grace are seen in the parable.

Interpretation and Imagination

Those called and those chosen are puzzling distinctions. The parable provides helpful insights. This is an allegory in two parts. The first refers to religious leaders—Pharisees, Sadducees, and priests—whom one would expect to be attentive to God's revelation. They rejected Christ and ridiculed his kingdom.

Persons who were at first thought to be worthy of an invitation to attend the wedding feast given by the king ignored and ridiculed the invitation. They simply went about their own affairs. They are pronounced unworthy because they failed to honor the king's hospitality.

The second part of the parable tells of those who were not invited, but compelled to come. The poor, the outcasts, those considered to be sinners, were persons who received Christ and his teaching. Driven by their oppression and misery, they were ready for the good news. Yet one of the men from the street showed up without a wedding garment. He had no explanation for this lack of protocol, and the king had him thrown out.

Bishop William R. Cannon, commenting on this parable writes, "The kingdom of heaven has its standards. The king expects those at the wedding of his son to show proper respect. Sinners cannot remain sinners and be citizens of this new order. Those never worthy of an invitation to the king's palace, must be made worthy" (*The Gospel of Matthew*, p. 97).

Last Sunday was Worldwide Communion Sunday, and many heard the invitation "Ye that do truly and earnestly repent of your sins . . . come." The Book of Common Prayer warns of "the great peril of the unworthy receiving." It continues, "Come holy and clean to such a heavenly feast, in the marriage garment required by God." (JKB)

YOU ARE INVITED

Matthew 22:1-14

A SERMON BY HERMAN S. WINBERRY

Ready or not, here comes Jesus with an invitation. The kingdom of God is at hand. You are invited to enter. Your name is on the invitation list. The new order of existence, where God rules the human heart by love, confronts us in Jesus. Membership in the kingdom of heaven is opened by him. The invitation is for everybody; no one is excluded from the guest list. The invitation is as deep as the grace of God and as wide as the peace of God.

The invitation is crucial because it demands a response. So many of the invitations of Jesus have this aspect of decisive confrontation. You can view it as a threat or an opportunity, but there is no way to escape the invitation of God. Let's not think that we want to do so.

Let us consider the opportunity we are afforded in this invitation of Jesus. The kingdom of God is like a king who gave a feast for his son. The king sent his servants out to deliver personal invitations to those on the guest list. Some accepted and some rejected the gracious invitation. The king enlarges the guest list time after time. The banquet hall is still not full so the king sent the servants out to invite every Tom, Dick, and Harry; every Mary, Jane, and Carol they can find; everyone was invited. The invitation was sent everywhere, into the broad avenues and the narrow streets, to all the people of the land. The good, the bad, and the indifferent were graciously offered a place at the table of the wedding feast.

The new community Jesus came to establish does not include only the pure. Aren't you glad? The "down and outs" and the "up and outs" are invited. Moreover, Jesus calls and urges the multitudes to enter. Many are called. Come to the celebration. Come to the feast. All is ready. Jesus bids you enter. In this parable, an invitation is extended to the indifferent and uncaring, in the hope that there will be a readiness discovered in their hearts to respond, "yes." God is relentless in his aggressive goodwill to share the life of the kingdom of heaven with all. The food is ready. The plates are hot. Come!

What a day it was for Peter when he understood that the good news of the kingdom of God was for everyone! Peter tells us in Acts 10 "that God shows no partiality, but in every nation anyone who fears him and does what is right is acceptable to him" (vv. 34-35).

So I return. The invitation of God to enter the kingdom of Heaven has gone out to the ends of the earth, and not only to one country or one color or one community or one church. We United Methodists hear Charles Wesley, who would have us sing,

> Come, sinners, to the gospel feast;
> Let every soul be Jesus' guest.
> Ye need not one be left behind,
> For God hath bid all humankind.
> ("Come, Sinners, to the Gospel Feast")

The old legend relates that God looked down from heaven on humankind's predicament and was moved to tears. A council was called in high heaven and the heavenly beings were assembled; the Holy Trinity, the cherubims and seraphim, the archangels, the angels, and some of the saints. Who would go to earth and rescue men and women from their sad plight? A saint offered to go. But God said, "No, you yourself had to be redeemed; your arms are too short to save." One of the archangels volunteered, but God said, "No, you have never known sin and sorrow, you would not understand human sin and guilt." Then, the only Son of God, the Eternal Christ spoke, "I will go to earth, be born of the virgin, and take my place with the sorrowing men and women on earth. I will become one of them, I will be clothed in mortal flesh. I will work, suffer, and die for every person. And after my resurrection, I will return to heaven with saved humanity as my trophy to present at your feet." And God said, "This is the remedy; let is be so."

And so, the parable of the wedding feast, given by the king for his son, confronts us with an invitation that demands a response.

In stark contrast to the wide and broad invitation to participate in this new community of love, our response to the invitation is limited—Yes or No. Accept or reject. Jesus comes straight at us with this invitation and our response is crucial. So much is at stake in our choice. What response will we make? The decision to accept or reject the call of Jesus to enter the kingdom of heaven is ours, but we must remember that the consequences of our choice are not ours to determine.

The King sends his servants to bid those invited to come to the feast given for his Son. One group simply ignores the invitation. Indifference is their response. Those who reject Jesus by their indifference have made a choice, and are tied to an inferior life, not worthy of the kingdom of God.

A second group of servants are sent to deliver a more pressing and personal invitation, "Come to the feast, the food is on the table." These are not indifferent, but they reject the invitation. Some say, this is not important to me. Others say, I am over extended and cannot put the kingdom of heaven first on my agenda. Still others resent the invitation as their life-style is threatened by it. They understand at least this much about the new Kingdom. Their response is swift and sure. They lash out harshly at those who deliver the invitation and slay them on the spot. Such rejection of Jesus and his Kingdom results in tragedy. "The wedding is ready, but those invited were not worthy" (v. 8). Could we put it this way: Acceptance of Jesus and his invitation makes us worthy; rejection of Jesus and his invitation keeps us unworthy?

One more time the King says to his servants, "Go out and invite anybody you can find. Go everywhere and invite everybody." They do, and the wedding hall is filled.

Sometimes I hear a line of thought that runs something like this: God is so gracious and so loving and so powerful and so caring for all persons, that sooner or later, in this world or the next, all men and women will come to the Messianic feast and be blessed in the presence of God. The King of Heaven will eventually rule in love over all. I confess, this appeals to me. But, dearly beloved, I do not find this in the parable told by Jesus, comparing the kingdom of God to a marriage feast given by a king for his son. Even those who accept the invitation to participate in the kingdom feast must do more than show up at the table. We are to be clothed with God's righteousness. The man in the parable who was not outfitted with garments of God's righteousness was considered an intruder and cast out. The fate of those who reject Jesus is theirs by right of refusal.

There is good news in this parable of the kingdom of heaven—good news about a new life that can be compared to the abundance, laughing, singing, and joy of a feast. In the wedding feast, we see the hope of new beginnings. All are invited; Jesus has come. All of us want to know he has come, don't we? When we respond to God's seeking love with an everlasting, "yes," we are clothed by God and outfitted by him with righteousness. We do not enter because we are perfect. Such good news! Jesus invites us to lay aside, with his help, the old garments that are flawed by sin and selfishness and pride. Old behaviors and old attitudes unworthy of his kingdom are traded for a new life. E. Stanley Jones once said, "Jesus came not only to get men and women out of hell, but to get hell out of men and women; he came not only to get men and women into heaven, he came to get heaven into men and women."

It is possible to reject the call of Jesus to live in the kingdom of God. That freedom is given to us by God. But Jesus has come, and he does not want to let us go. To refuse to go in to the feast is to be left outside in an inferior life, and to experience life's disappointments with the fellowship of the miserable, in a life apart from Jesus Christ. To accept the invitation of Jesus to be his disciple and enter his Kingdom is to be made worthy by him, to be given his Spirit, to live in his friendship, and to mingle with others who love him.

One of life's immeasurables is the grace of God coming to us in the invitation of Jesus to believe the good news and enter the kingdom of heaven. The feast is ready. Come now. The door is wide open! Jesus will outfit you with the garment of the King. You can say with joy, "This is my outfit. Here is where I belong."

Dr. Reginald Mallet, a British Methodist pastor and a doctor of medicine, tells a story from the early days of the Salvation Army in England. William and Catherine Booth, the co-founders of the Salvation Army, have died, and their son, Bramwell Booth, had become Captain of the Army. He carried on the work of his parents, he held meetings and preached, he sought out the needy, he played the accordion in the Salvation Army band. He had a way with those persons who had mental retardation or developmental disabilities, and always had them sit on the front rows when he held a service or an outdoor meeting. They understood little of what he was saying in the sermon, but they knew his compassion and love.

One day, a soldier in the army came to Bramwell Booth and said, "One of your boys is ill. It's Reggie." Captain Booth went at once to a very poor section of London, to a dimly lit basement room, and there on an old bed, with a tattered and worn blanket, was Reggie. He was ill with tuberculosis. In those days there was no known cure.

Captain Booth knelt down by the bed and said "Reggie, I'm here." Reggie was weak, but could talk. He said, "Captain Booth, look in the top drawer of the desk." When Captain Booth opened the drawer of the old battered chest, he found a new Salvation Army uniform. It had never been worn. He turned back and said, "Reggie, I don't understand. Why haven't you worn your uniform?" There it was, with the stripe down the trouser leg, the coat, the tunic. Reggie said, "Captain, I saved my money for a long time and bought the uniform. You know when I march with the Army and go to meetings, sometimes people say things about me. They say I am not too bright. I didn't want to wear the uniform and have people say anything that would shame it." Then Reggie said, "Captain, when I am promoted, I want to be buried in my uniform." Captain Booth assured Reggie it would be so.

Not many days afterward, Reggie died. Captain Booth sent word far and wide for the soldiers to come to the east end of London. He gathered the largest Salvation Army band some people had ever seen. They marched through the streets in a procession to the cemetery. They carried the white pennants and banners. They wore not black, but white arm bands, signifying the Resurrection. People on the streets saw the procession and wondered, "Who died? It must be somebody *big*." To some, just a mentally retarded boy had died. But in the kingdom of God, a young prince of glory had come to the heavenly banquet, to feast with all the saints of God and receive the welcome of Jesus Christ.

Jesus invites us to come to the feast and enter the joy of the kingdom of God. He holds the door open and beckons us. What will you do with his invitation?

Suggestions for Worship

Call to Worship (Philippians 4:4-7):

PASTOR: Rejoice in the Lord always; again I will say, Rejoice.

PEOPLE: Let your gentleness be known to everyone. The Lord is near.

PASTOR: Do not worry about anything, but in everything by prayer and supplication with thanksgiving let your requests be made known to God

PEOPLE: And the peace of God, which surpasses all understanding, will guard your hearts and your minds in Christ Jesus.

Act of Praise: Psalm 135:1-14.

Suggested Hymns: "Rejoice in God's Saints"; "Shall We Gather at the River"; "Marching to Zion."

Opening Prayer: Almighty and eternal God, who has invited us to participate in the kingdom of heaven in the arrival of thy son Jesus Christ, grant us the grace to respond to that invitation with wholehearted discipleship, and clothe us with the garment of praise, that we may feast at the Kingdom banquet in the friendship of Jesus Christ forever, and mingle in the fellowship of joy with all who love him. Amen.

Pastoral Prayer: Almighty and eternal God, the Father of our Lord Jesus Christ and our Father, evoke from us today worship and praise that will be pleasing in your sight. We thank you for the privilege of prayer and that we can come to your house and mingle with others who love you in this blessed communion. We gladly confess that when we turn to you in prayer and praise, we know you have prompted us and called us into your presence. Our Father, we ask you for a deeper, truer, stronger life of prayer. Keep within us a hunger to be men and women of prayer and a desire to be a praying church.

We admit to you and before you our sins, our selfishness, and our pride. Forgive us and free us from the penalty and power of sin, O Divine Redeemer. We pray again this week, cleanse our inner life and renew a right spirit within us.

Our Father, we thank you for the blessings of home and family life. So much of our happiness clusters around our loved ones. Help us to put our best foot forward in the home, and free us from hurtful attitudes and acts in the family. Raise up, O God, a generation of families who will be in the vanguard of a new movement for widespread Christian family living.

We thank you, O Sovereign Lord, for the measure of peace we enjoy in the world today. We ask that, more and more, discord and strife may be brought to an end. Guide the rulers and leaders of the nations with divine counsel, give to them a mind set on peace, that the passions of men and women may be restrained from bloodshed and death. We even dare to pray because you have taught us to pray, "Thy Kingdom come on earth." O Jesus, our cities are filled with human tears, and in prayer we realize that you weep over the cities. Let thine alabaster cities be undimmed by human tears. Yes, we pray, "Thy Kingdom come."

Pour out thy Holy Spirit upon us and upon all flesh. Bring the full victory of thine Eternal Kingdom. As your church, we pray, establish thou the work of our hands, establish thou it. And let the beauty of the Lord our God be upon us.

In the matchless name of Jesus Christ, our Living Lord, we pray. Amen.

OCTOBER 17, 1993

□

Twentieth Sunday After Pentecost

How should the people of God relate to a secular and pagan state? The relationship of nations to the sovereignty of God, and one's allegiance to both, is the issue.

The Sunday Lessons

Ruth 1:1-19*a*: Ruth, a foreign woman from Moab, had married a Hebrew. When he died, she chose to go with her mother-in-law, Naomi, to Judah, rather than enjoy the security of her own people. Urged once and then again to turn back, Ruth spoke those cherished words, "Entreat me not to leave you, or to turn back from following after you . . ." (v. 16 NKJV).

I Thessalonians 1:1-10: Faced by persecutions, the Thessalonians remained faithful. Paul gives thanks for "your work of faith and labor of love and steadfastness of hope in our Lord Jesus Christ" (v. 3). He is confident that God has chosen them, because the gospel came to them, "Not in words only, but also in power and in the Holy Spirit and with full conviction" (v. 5).

Matthew 22:15-22: Pharisees, seeking to trap Jesus, asked, "Is it lawful to pay taxes to the emperor, or not?" (v. 17). Jews who supported Herod collaborated with the Romans. The Zealots refused to pay. Jesus answers, "Show me the coin. . . . Whose head is this, and whose title?" (vv. 19-20). The emperor's inscription implies that it is the emperor's money. "Give therefore to the emperor the things that are the emperor's, and to God the things that are God's" (v. 21).

Interpretation and Imagination

In his book *Modern Rivals to the Christian Faith,* Cornelius Loew names two idols that challenge Christian loyalty—democracy and this nation. He writes, "Democracy is the measure . . ." "The nation is the measure . . ." The prophets of Israel constantly challenged the tendency of their people to believe that God was always for them and never against them. They declared that judgment would overtake any nation that exalted itself as the ultimate kingdom. Even if that nation was Israel, God's chosen, it would be brought down. The test is to ask the question, Is it more important to be a citizen of a democracy than a citizen in the kingdom of God? Is it more important to be an American than it is to be a Christian? Loew writes, "The greatest service Christians can render their country is to become actively concerned about the distinctive community and destiny of the church over against American society." Churches should not be viewed as a part of the American landscape, or any national scene. The church is a "colony of heaven."

Preachers have sometimes argued that the words, "Render unto Caesar that which is Caesar's," mean that a Christian is duty-bound to love America, right or wrong. The questions of civil disobedience are complex. The reality of the church's involvement in revolutions around the world is apparent.

The text is sometimes used to encourage an absolute distinction between church and state. "Don't become involved in politics," is the message taken from the text. Any faithful reading of the whole biblical witness will point to the error of this.

The message is straightforward. Give to God all that is God's. Pay to Caesar only what is Caesar's. (JKB)

WHAT IS YOUR CHURCH'S REPUTATION?

I Thessalonians 1:1-10

A SERMON BY HERMAN S. WINBERRY

I wish to begin this sermon with a question. This is a time-honored method for preachers and teachers, to begin with a question. But even this method is not entirely safe. I heard the story of a nine-year-old girl who returned from Sunday school, and as her father was sitting down with the newspaper after a delicious Sunday noon meal, she asked him some questions. "Father, why did God make all the leaves green?" He thought a moment and replied, "I don't know." Then she asked, "What did God do before he made the world?" Again he said, "I don't know." She asked another one: "Father, how did Noah catch two snakes and put them in the ark?" He put the paper down and said, "I don't know." The little girl sensed her father was a bit restless, so she asked, "Do you mind if I ask you questions?" He replied, "Not at all. How are you going to learn anything if you don't ask questions?"

I wish to ask a question and I trust we can do a bit better than our nine year old. The question is, "What is your church's reputation?" What image pops into people's minds when they hear the name of your church? What reports sound forth about your church?

There is a church in Washington, D.C., well-known because of the many presidents who have attended it. There is a church in a town where I once lived known for having the highest steeple of any church in town. Mention the name of a certain church, and right away you get reports of a strong and successful youth program. Still another church is held in high esteem because of its music and choir programs. What is your church's reputation?

At the time Paul writes this letter to the Thessalonians, he is receiving reports about them from many sources. Paul had founded the church and his pastoral heart is evident in the letter. Paul, the pastor, could not remain with the church at Thessalonica, but he is so concerned about their welfare, he sends Timothy to assist them and bring back a report on how they are faring. Timothy has returned to Paul at Corinth with good news. The members were standing firm. The church was growing and getting a strong reputation. People said to one another, "Have you heard about those Christians at Thessalonica?" Paul writes "Your faith in God has gone forth everywhere" (v. 8 RSV).

What a reputation! Dear men and women of God, if the United Methodist churches worldwide could be known for the things Paul writes about this church at Thessalonica, we would more nearly be the church God has in mind for us. We would be strong where we need to be strong. I am not about to pour gloom and doom on you and our church. Rather, this is a call to strengthen our discipleship and witness by considering the character of the Thessalonian church as seen through the eyes of the apostle Paul.

First, Paul says, we have heard of your faith in God. We have heard of your faith in Christ Jesus. Throughout chapter one and the entire letter Paul writes over and over, we have heard of your sure faith in Jesus Christ. How basic can you get? Paul sends word to this small membership church, "Every time I hear of your church I hear about your faith."

Dear men and women, what we believe and do and say about Jesus Christ is central to all else in the church. "The church's one foundation is Jesus Christ her Lord."

I read of a thirty-story building in a large city, built some years ago. It was written up because the thirty stories were built and completed in a matter of weeks. It was quite a feat. But the project manager was asked about this building, and he told of the weeks it took to build the foundation. He said that the taller the building, the deeper the foundation. So with the church. The one foundation is Jesus Christ. May the word sound forth about our church, "You can come here and get to know Jesus Christ as Savior."

We of the ordained ministry have been set aside by our church to preach and teach and have been given a high place in the church; but we are not the objects of your faith. The Kingdom seems at times to falter because we are stingy with the church; yet our budget had best not be our chief reputation. Methodism, since its beginning, has been a lay movement. I have known some wonderful Christian men and women, stalwarts in the church of God; yet the name of Jesus is above every name. We United Methodists have been known for social concerns, an evangelistic thrust, and a catholic spirit; and all this is well, so long as it is rooted in a living faith in Christ Jesus.

What if the post office in your town received a letter addressed "To the church in God the Father and the Lord Jesus Christ." Which church would receive the letter? Paul says, We have heard of your faith in Christ Jesus. What a reputation!

> My hope is built on nothing less
> Than Jesus' blood and righteousness. . . .
> All other ground is sinking sand.
> ("My Hope Is Built")

Second, the church was a caring fellowship. They cared for each other, and they reached out to others not yet in their fellowship. People talked: "Have you heard about those new Christians at Thessalonica? They have taken to the faith with enthusiasm. They really care for each other. And they are reaching out to share the gospel with others."

This small group of believers loved each other. They experienced the communion and fellowship of the Holy Spirit. This preacher is sure that people are looking for a church where people care, where love is given and received, a place where they feel they belong. We have heard about your church. You love each other.

Some persons refer to our time as the "age of loneliness." There are so many lonely people. Friendliness is not the same as love, but it can be the first step in introducing a person to a church fellowship where love can be experienced.

A mature woman went to a pharmacy every day. She had a prescription for pills, and she was to take three each day. She would not buy a whole bottle but would come each day to the pharmacist and buy three pills. Sometimes she would have to wait in line. The pharmacist would greet her by name, ask how she was doing, and wish her a pleasant day. One day the pharmacist said to her, "Why don't you let me fill the whole bottle for you? Then you would not have to stand in line and wait." But no, the next day she was right back in line, waiting her turn. After two or three more such days, the pharmacist greeted her and said, "You remember what I told you about filling the prescription." She replied, "I appreciate your offer." Then she continued, "I don't have to come here every day, and I could get the whole prescription filled at once. But if I sat that large bottle of pills on my table, it would never greet me or call me by name or wish me a happy day."

Persons are lonely. One man said he was seeking a fellowship that would help him get through the week so he would not have to tough it out alone. Loneliness is an invisible virus. Paul wrote about this church, saying, We have heard of the love you have for each other, of how you reach out to care for others.

I heard of a poll that was taken a few years ago. We are big on polls in this country. This one was designed to find out, Who are the loneliest persons in our society? The results of this poll surprised a great many people. The loneliest persons were:

1. College students
2. High School students

3. Single-again women with children
4. The elderly

How about your church? Is all the machinery of the church, from the smallest committee to the largest congregational gathering, characterized by the fellowship of love? Are all the organizations of the church lubricated with the oil of caring love?

One Sunday morning I went to a small membership church. It was many years ago, but I still remember the prayer of one of the laymen in that small church. He was a plain main of the earth, a farmer. One sentence in his prayer went like this, "We thank you, Lord Jesus Christ, that we can come up to this house of worship and mingle with others who love you." I have had a deeper appreciation for Christian fellowship ever since I heard that prayer. O Church, you have a reputation: "See how those Christians love one another."

Third, the church had a steadfast hope. Paul said, I hear about you Thessalonians from so many places, and people tell of your hope in our Lord Jesus Christ. The church was characterized by its hope. One of the dominant notes in this group of believers was their expectancy of the second coming of Christ. Paul says, We remember you Thessalonians in our prayers, we remember your "steadfastness of hope in our Lord Jesus Christ" (v. 3). We hear your hope is not in the things of earth, but is laid up for you in heaven. Those who have a vision of the heavenly city are the ones who will be able to build here on earth after the master plan of the kingdom of God. When we envision in our Christian hope the eternal city whose builder and maker is God, we can be used to build the alabaster cities undimmed by human tears. These believers held on to their hope and their hope held on to them.

These early Christians in Thessalonica were watching and waiting and longing for the return of the Lord. They expected Jesus to come soon. They were disappointed in their expectancy of the immediate return of Christ, but they were not disappointed in their hope. They were so right in seeing all of human life in the light of the reality of the resurrection. This small group of Christians at Thessalonica was to be tried and tested and persecuted, but they remained steadfast in their hope in Christ Jesus. Their hope was firmly based on the centrality of our holy faith, the resurrection of Jesus Christ. The stone was rolled away from the tomb, not so Jesus could get out, but so you and I could get in on life eternal.

I heard of a high school that had a different way of sending report cards home. This school would seal the report card in an envelope and the students would take it home to be opened by the parents. One student, on report card day, would slip into the kitchen, steam the envelope open and look at the report card. If it was good, he would seal it and hand it to his father that evening. The father would be pleased. But on those occasions when the marks were not so high, when the teachers failed to discern his capabilities, he would reseal the envelope and give it to his mother. She would open it and express concern. She would then cook a delicious meal and afterwards present the report card to the father so it would be seen in its best light.

One day our report card will be opened in heaven. The marks will not all be good. But we have an Advocate, the Lord Jesus Christ, who will plead for us. What a blessed assurance and hope we have! What is your church's reputation?

Suggestions for Worship

Call to Worship (Ps. 146:1-2, 10):

PASTOR: Praise the LORD!

PEOPLE: Praise the LORD, O my soul!

PASTOR: I will praise the LORD as long as I live;

PEOPLE: I will sing praises to my God all my life long.

PASTOR: The LORD will reign forever, your God, O Zion, for all generations.

PEOPLE: Praise the LORD!

Act of Praise: Psalm 146.

Suggested Hymns: "Holy God, We Praise Thy Name"; "I Surrender All"; "Have Thine Own Way, Lord."

Opening Prayer: Almighty and everlasting God, our Father, all the day long you have stretched out your hand to bless and to forgive, to save and to renew. Grant that we may see your church in its greatness, glory, and beauty, and enable us to serve in it with devoted hearts as your adopted sons and daughters. In the matchless name of your only Son, Jesus Christ, Amen.

Pastoral Prayer: Almighty and everlasting God, our Father and the Father of our Lord Jesus Christ, we praise and worship your holy name. We love this place, O Christ, and pray you to send light and peace into this sanctuary. We thank you that we can enter here to worship and pray, and be with others who love you. O generous and giving God, we thank you for simple and plain blessings. We thank you for our measure of health, for the faculty of reverence before the beauty of the good earth, for the ability to hear children laughing and see the faces of our loved ones, for the gladness of a home and family. Do not let us take any of these things for granted. Rather, inspire us to express gratitude for the simple pleasures of life.

O God, you are so personal in your care of us. We thank you for those individual and particular instances of your goodness. We have had those high moments when they came from you, O God, a special token of your love and goodness. We thank you, O loving Father.

Lord Jesus Christ, some are here today with heartaches and defeats, we ask for them your perfect ministry of mercy and strength. Some are here today, Lord, with joy and victories, we rejoice with them before you.

Holy Father, we give thanks to you for the supreme gift, the unspeakable gift of your only Son, Jesus Christ. O crucified, resurrected, and living Christ, in whose keeping there is power and life, look upon your church with favor, your church here and throughout the world. May those of us gathered here in worship learn to trust more and more in the working of your power and endless grace, that will bring forth the salvation of men and women.

Lord Jesus Christ, we feel the need to bring before you some things we have talked over with you often. We come stained by sin, weakened by our lack of obedience, flawed by evil. Do now evoke from us a true penitence, that we may be cleansed and freed from the penalty and power of sin.

As your children through faith, you know our cares and sorrows. We turn these over to you and seek the peace that you give. Keep us steadfast in faith, that your name may be lifted up and exalted in the world. We pray in your resurrected and matchless name. Amen.

OCTOBER 24, 1993

□

Twenty-first Sunday After Pentecost

A rabbi was challenged to explain the whole law of Judaism while balancing on one foot. The wise and gentle Hillel responded, "Thou shalt love thy neighbor as thyself."

The Sunday Lessons

Ruth 2:1-13: Boaz, a wealthy farmer and a kinsman of Naomi, instructed Ruth to glean in his fields and ordered that she not be molested. "Why have I found favor in your sight, that you should take notice of me, when I am a foreigner?" Ruth asked (v. 10). Her faithfulness to her widowed mother-in-law would not go unrewarded. "May the LORD reward you for your deeds" (v. 12).

I Thessalonians 2:1-8: Paul continues to recall his preaching and ministry among the Thessalonians. "We had courage in our God to declare to you the gospel of God. . . . our appeal does not spring from deceit . . . not to please mortals. . . . we never came with words of flattery or with a pretext for greed" (vv. 2-5). Not only the gospel was shared "but our own selves" (v. 8). We were "like a nurse tenderly caring for her own children" (v. 7).

Matthew 22:34-46: The Jews asked another question to test Jesus: "Which commandment in the law is the greatest?" (v. 36). He answered, "You shall love the Lord your God with all your heart, and with all your soul, and with all your mind. . . . Love your neighbor as yourself" (vv. 37, 39). This summary of the law is also found in Deuteronomy 6:5 and Leviticus 19:18. "On these two commandments hang all the law and the prophets" (v. 40).

Interpretation and Imagination

Is there one duty, greater than any other, that should claim our lives? What is the greatest commandment? Although their motives were poor, the question of the Pharisees was a good one.

Their question implies yet another. Is there a highest value from which all realities and actions derive true worth?

Any effort to write a perfect formula for living and prescribe an absolute style for loving is absurd. Filled with ethical demand, the great commandment is more, much more, than an absolute. Our desire for absolutes, like that of the Pharisees, will never be realized.

The God that Christ reveals is a living God. The God to whom we pray saying, "Our Father," is not some impersonal cosmic force or first cause that we recognize and define. Christ is not abstract truth or manifest beauty. Christian love is not just moral goodness. God is not the supreme mystery we come to know and understand through secret stories and teachings of initiation. The God revealed by Jesus Christ is a God who lives; a God who is more than person not less; a God who loves and desires first of all to be loved with whole heart, whole soul, whole mind.

Can we make that real? As real as a $20 bill and team loyalties and computer data? To love God with a whole heart means to desire him more than any other possession or any other person. Loving God with soul means to adore him with devotion and abandon. Loving God with one's whole mind means to think of him constantly, deeply, seriously.

How does one show love to neighbors? By giving to them; giving the things they need that we possess. By doing for them; helping them and promoting their welfare in every way possible. By suffering with them; sharing their burdens and doing all in our power to lift the heaviness that weighs them down. (JKB)

WHAT THINK YE OF CHRIST?

Matthew 22:41-46

A SERMON BY JERRY LOWRY

There are many misconceptions of Jesus. Some think of Jesus as a *divine bellhop*, always at their service for every little whim; at the snap of a finger he is there to serve. Some think of Jesus as a *puppet;* you pull him any way and anywhere you want. Some think of Jesus as so *holy*, that one could never really please him; so why try. Some think of Jesus as a *dispenser of cheap grace;* it's okay to do as you please. He died for our sins, so all one has to do is keep on repenting and enjoy life. Some think of him as *totally divine;* nothing human about him at all, so you can't relate to him. Still others think of him as *totally human;* a good man who taught good values and morals, but not of God, so not important. Remember it was said of him, "How can anything good come out of Nazareth?"

Yes, we often talk about Jesus; sing about him, think about him, offer prayers in his name, and some even serve him. But do we really know him?

What do you think of Christ? Whose son is he? This question came from the very lips of Jesus! Just as he asked it of the religious folk in his day, so we ask it of the church today.

This question must be an important one. Why? Because Jesus knew the crowd, as well as the religious leaders, did not know who he was. He had said to all persons that he was the Messiah, God's anointed one. This agitated the Pharisees, scribes, chief priest, and others, so they sought a way to arrest him. But they could not because of the love of the multitude.

As he taught in parable, the religious people knew he was talking about them. So they came to him, attempting to trap him in some way. First they asked, if it was right to pay taxes to Caesar. He asked, "whose picture is on the coin? "Caesar" they replied. Jesus said, "Render unto" Caesar what is his and unto God what is his" (Matt. 21:15-22, paraphrased). Amazed by his answer, they left him immediately.

Then the Sadducees came. They did not believe in the resurrection. They came to challenge him, stating the law of Moses. If a man dies and his wife is left barren, it is the responsibility of the next of kin, a brother, to marry his widow. The children they have are considered the deceased husband's children. Now, there were seven brothers. All of them married their brother's widow, and still she was barren. Finally, she died. Now, they asked, "Whose wife will she be in heaven?" Jesus replied, "You do not know the way or have the power of God. At the resurrection, marriage won't matter. For all persons will be like angels. God is not the God of the dead but the living" (22:23-32, paraphrased).

Then the Pharisees returned again. This time they selected the wisest of them, an expert in the law. He came to test Jesus and asked, "Teacher, which is the greatest commandment?"

Jesus said, " 'Love God with your heart, soul, and mind' is the first. The second is like it, 'Love your neighbor as yourself.' This fulfills the law and prophets" (22:34-40, paraphrased).

Now Jesus turns the tables. It is his turn. He asked the Pharisees, "What think ye of Christ? Whose son is he?" (v. 42). They answered, "He is the son of David." "How is it," Jesus replied, "that David calls him Lord if he is his son. For David said the LORD said to my Lord, Sit at my right hand until I put your enemies under your feet." Then Scripture says what no one could answer him, nor would they ask him any more questions.

"What think ye of Christ?" is a profound and pressing question! If we search out the scripture, we will find what many persons thought of Jesus. They state emphatically how they feel.

People often ask us what we think of certain individuals: Bush, Gorbachev, Nelson Mandela, Saddam Hussein, etc. We usually respond very quickly as to what we think of these persons, because our minds are already made up. We know what we think and believe about them.

In a similar manner, why don't we make up our minds about what we think of Christ? The way we live says what we think. We stand for him or against him. We should let it be known where we stand in certain terms, because there is no neutral stand one can take concerning Jesus.

Who do you think Jesus is? One day, sooner or later, we will answer this question.

- Is he the Messiah, God's anointed one?
- Is he the one the prophet declared would come to deliver us?
- Is he our Savior, Lord, and Redeemer?

Well, let's look at his life. What do you think of him as a *teacher* and a *preacher?* We see his enemies send their men to arrest him, but when they heard him, they said, "Never has anyone spoken like this" (John 7:46). Jesus was able to look at the shepherds of the field, sheep, flowers, trees, almost anything, and place such eternal truths upon them, no one would ever forget them. We have heard great preachers and teachers, but Christ is unsurpassed. His lessons were so simple that little children loved them; yet, the wisest persons of our day could never discern the great truths imparted. What think ye of him as a *teacher and a preacher?*

What think ye of him as a *doctor?* Dr. Jesus? See him giving sight to those who were blind, lifting up those who were lame. At his word, any disease or ailment had to flee from the victim. Today we have our great cancer institutes and our institutions for incurable diseases. But Jesus never found a disease he could not heal. The perfect doctor! What think ye of him as Dr. Jesus?

What think ye of him as *Comforter?* Follow him up and down the Gospels, and see him driving out sorrow and bringing in joy and hope. See him as he becomes a father to the fatherless; rest for the weary; a friend and companion to the widow, the lonely, the outcast. What think ye of him as Comforter?

What think ye of him as *Redeemer?* Peter—impetuous, blundering, clumsy Peter, who could not witness to a little girl. Yet on the day of Pentecost, three thousand souls were saved under his preaching. James and John—Sons of Thunder, bringing down fire from heaven. They desired for themselves the best seats in the Kingdom. Nathaniel—day dreamer. Thomas—the doubter, the believer. Out of such raw material, Jesus brought the awesome power of God that turned the world upside down. What think ye of him as Redeemer?

Well, let's ask Pontius Pilate—What think ye? "After I examined him, someone handed me a note from my wife. She warned, 'Have nothing to do . . .' I find no fault in him."

The centurion at the foot of the cross: "Truly this man was God's Son! John the Baptist: "Behold, the Lamb of God." Matthew—Royal King. Mark—Suffering Servant. Luke—Son of Man. John—Work of God.

Paul, what do you think of Christ? "He appeared to me as one untimely born, a persecutor of his followers. Then on the road to Damascus, Jesus appeared to me and I was blinded for three days. But he sent Ananias with his healing touch, and I was filled with the Holy Spirit. God has given Jesus a name which is above every name."

Peter—"You are the Christ, the Son of the Living God. Let all the house of Israel know assuredly, that this same Jesus whom you crucified, God has made Lord and Christ."

Finally, let's ask his Father—What do you think? "This is my Son, the Beloved, with whom I am well pleased" (Matt. 3:17).

O dear ones, if God is well pleased with him, so should we be. Say to him, in all sincerity: I am pleased with you, I will accept you, I will hear and obey you. The moment you do that, you will be wed to him. For to hear him is to accept him, love, and obey him. Confess with your mouth the Lord Jesus Christ. Believe in him with your heart by faith, and thou shalt be saved.

Suggestions for Worship

Call to Worship (Matthew 22:37-39):

PASTOR: Jesus said, "You shall love the Lord your God with all your heart, and with all your soul, and with all your mind.

PEOPLE: This is the greatest and first commandment.

PASTOR: And a second is like it:

PEOPLE: You shall love your neighbor as yourself."

Act of Praise: Psalm 128.

Suggested Hymns: "All Creatures of Our God and King"; "Open My Eyes, That I May See"; "I Am Thine, O Lord."

Opening Prayer: Eternal God, this is the beginning of another beautiful day that you have made. All things are still working together for the good. We are here to celebrate your love in the midst of our lives as your followers. Some things have been out of our control, but not out of yours. Allow your Spirit to increase our faith in this time of worship. In the name of Christ we pray. Amen.

Pastoral Prayer: O Gracious God, what would we do without you? In our times of loneliness, you have been our companion. In our times of temptation, you have a way of escape. In our times of sorrow, you have brought comfort and joy. In our times of weakness, you have been our strength. O Lord, what would we do without you? You have reconciled us to yourself through the gift of your Son, Jesus Christ. You have proven your love through the continual presence of the Holy Spirit, as we face the mountains that are too high to climb. Even in our valleys of despair, you have been there. O God, what would we do without you?

Continue to be our control in our world, in the church, and in the life of every believer. Hear our prayer, O Lord. In Christ's name, Amen.

October 31, 1993

□

Twenty-second Sunday After Pentecost

The Gospel lesson portrays self-centered religious leaders who do not truly believe and do not care for others. This message, addressed to the church, urges us to prefer God's final approval to prestige in the present.

The Sunday Lessons

Ruth 4:7-17: At the gate of the city, the usual place for transacting legal business, Boaz told Naomi's nearest male relative that he cannot inherit family property, which had belonged to Elimelech, unless he also marries Ruth. When he chose not to redeem it for himself, Boaz bought the land of Elimelech and formally took Ruth as his wife. Ruth's son was named Obed; he was the father of Jesse, the father of King David.
I Thessalonians 2:9-13, 17-20: The ministry of Paul reflects a deep pastoral concern. Recalling his missionary efforts at Thessalonica he wrote to his converts, "We determined to share with you not only the gospel of God but also our own selves, because you have become very dear to us" (v. 8). The apostle made demands, but he was gentle, "like a nurse tenderly caring for her own children" (v. 7).
Matthew 23:1-12: Jesus warned against the teaching of the scribes and the Pharisees. They did not practice what they preached. They fashioned heavy burdens with their laws, but were not willing to help bear the weight of them. They sought places of honor for themselves and loved to be called "rabbi." Jesus called for humble service as the true mark of greatness. "The greatest among you will be called servant. All who exalt themselves will be humbled, and all who humble themselves will be exalted" (vv. 11-12).

Interpretation and Imagination

The radio preacher got my attention when he began to describe the apostasy and sins of Methodist ministers. With a holy boldness that almost passed for real authority, he ranted about our atheism, and our compromising and self-satisfied ways. He warned that we would go to hell and take many unsuspecting folks along with us.

I turned him off and reasoned that he was trying to make himself look good by making others look bad, that he was trying to make his message ring true; not by preaching truth, but by denouncing the hypocrisy of other confessed Christians. But it gave me little comfort. I remembered that the prophets and evangelists also declared woe and warning when they cried out against the hypocrisy of religious leaders.

In his commentary on Matthew, J. C. Fenton writes, "Experts on the Judaism of the first century tells us that the scribes and Pharisees have been considerably caricatured here; they were not all like this picture of them, indeed many were extremely loving and holy men." No doubt the description of scribes and Pharisees in Matthew 23 misrepresents many faithful religious leaders in first-century Judaism. The radio preacher surely misrepresented many dedicated Christian pastors serving Christ through the United Methodist Church. Professor Fenton defends Matthew's use of the caricature by repeating the words of the prophet Nathan, "You are the man" (II Sam. 12:7).

Every evidence of sham, pretense, and hypocrisy should send us to our knees before the altar of God. Knowing that final judgment belongs to God, will one dare to masquerade as God's messenger? Knowing that the only honor that finally matters comes from God, will one be satisfied with an elected office, or a good appointment and the praise of peers?

True greatness, the kind that lasts when our temples are torn down, begins with humility, and is established through service. (JKB)

AN INVITATION TO HUMILITY

Matthew 23:1-12

A SERMON BY DONNA SCHAPER

If all we had ever heard from Jesus were these twelve verses, we would not like him very much. These are twelve angry verses expressed by an angry and disappointed man in public.

What he does here would be like my making fun of our town council and what they wear and how they look in what they wear. Or saying that the presidents of the banks were using us to bear their burdens. Or that the local postmaster was a shyster, appearing to be something that he was not.

Pretty soon the question would have to arise: Who do you think you are, if all you can say is bad things about everyone else? If all we had ever heard from Jesus were these twelve verses, we would not like him very much. He would be just another one of those men who couldn't move out of the county of anger, who could never face himself deeply enough to face others in love.

Fortunately we know a lot more about Jesus than these twelve verses. We know that he did move out of the county of anger into the county of love; that he knew the trouble of his anger and he knew how to practice what he preached. He spent his life loving those who had nothing to give in return. He attributed any goodness in himself to a source beyond himself. And he paid the price of his judgment against the Pharisees.

This text is an invitation to humility. It comes to us in harsh words, harsher than almost any Jesus speaks. They are the words that caused him to be killed. No Pharisee can stand up long to this exposure. Mind you, Jesus did not get killed because he was angry. He got killed because the Pharisees could not bear his anger.

Nor can we. This tirade against Pharisees is a tirade against the Pharisee in each one of us—that part that doesn't just give money to start a community garden but asks that a sign be erected saying that we have done so; that part that doesn't just serve Communion at church but wants to be thanked for it; that part of us that hopes we are being seen when we are doing good.

There is enough Pharisee to go around. This text can mean as much today as it did 2,000 years ago.

But standing alone it cannot. It has to be a piece of our gospel memory. We have to know who is inviting us to be humble. And we have to know that he spoke not only in these "woe" verses but also in the verses of blessing. If, he will tell us elsewhere, we can get a handle on our anger and our disappointment, we can be happy. We can be peaceful.

Here we get only the woes—twelve full verses. The Pharisees are bad because they don't practice what they preach. They put heavy burdens on others, and they don't carry them. A better complaint against a preacher I can't imagine.

The Pharisees like only the better tables. They make their garments look ridiculous by their ornaments. They get hung up on their titles. Any one verse is an accusation sufficient to skewer all by itself.

Elsewhere in the Gospels Jesus escapes the stream of woe long enough to tell us that there is not only punishment but also reward in humility. If we live only in the county of anger, only in the land where nobody is worthy of respect, we soon eat the ashes of our own disappointment for breakfast, lunch, and dinner. But if we learn the way of humility, we can find the road out of the county of anger into the county of peace.

This text shows us the way. It is not just a diatribe against pride but also an invitation to humility. It reminds us of nothing so much as the matter of roofs—the things we put on top of ourselves to provide shelter. For thousands of years, the problem of shelter was a problem of roofs. The Greeks, though good poets and potters, were, with their clay-topped temples, among the worst roof-builders in history. It wasn't until the Middle Ages that the revolutionary roof truss, a simple A-shaped frame, was developed. Allowing a roof's outward thrust to be directed downward led to thinner walls, bigger windows, and eventually to making possible the great cathedrals.

This structural concept is a good spiritual concept as well. Life may be nothing more than learning how to handle our outward thrust, how to manage our pride. If we can let it be directed downward, toward an inner peace, an inner strength, then we can risk the flights of pride. If we can only go higher and higher, only make ourselves more and more visible, only ascend and ascend, never descend or descend—you see the problem. We fall down.

Jesus tells us what to do with our pride: Direct it downward, into servanthood, into love, into self-examination. That way we can move out of the county of anger into the county of peace.

Jesus invites us to humility. Don't worry about what other people think or see or do. Worry about yourself, what you think and say and do. Examine yourself with the intensity you examine others and see what happens.

Recently I have become quite obsessed with anger toward

someone I used to love. I'm angry at what she said about me. It was so true—in its parts. I can't forgive her for seeing me so well so partially. Nor, therefore, can I forgive myself for being something of the person she said I was. Before God can enter this picture, some pride has to be released. I have to let drop the pride that stings. I have to accept the part of me that was seen even though it wasn't a part that I had on display.

How do you know when you've gotten onto one of these back roads in the county of anger? You find yourself walking around giving replies, making excuses, explaining, talking to some known or unknown assailant about how you couldn't have done any better. You let your tassels hang down long, focusing on what you wear outside and how you look rather than what is going on inside.

Did you ever notice how many people focus on cleaning up the clutter in the living rooms while allowing their inner rooms to experience messy build-up? I am certainly one. I indulge the fantasy that if things can just look good, we can convince each other that they are good. This is the Pharisee trick. And, as Jesus exposes, it doesn't work. It's not just that it is a woe and a failure that we are part Pharisee and part human being. It is not just a matter of getting free of accusation.

There is also a reward, a blessing. The invitation to humility is an invitation to a good life, a better life, one richer than the world of shaded, graded appearance. We are blessed by humility, not just condemned by pride.

Think again of the problem of the roof. It goes down to ascend. It reaches for support so that it can stand up straight. It respects its inner life as much as its outer reaches.

Think with me about the joy we experience when a "Pharisee" falls. Donald Trump comes to mind. Whenever the big topple, the little people clap. But then look more closely. What if we heard tomorrow—God forbid—that Trump had a brain tumor? Or that he had a terrible car accident and hurt someone? What if he was brought low? Would we still be laughing? I don't think so. Beneath our enormous capacity for anger, there is also an even larger capacity for love. Beneath our enormous disappointment that not one of us is who we think we should be, there is also hope that we might yet be the people we want to be.

Think of my friend. I am hurt by her only because I love her.

She is criticizing me only because she loves me, too. I hope we won't need tragedy to come together. Humility would indulge the hope that we can return to each other without tragedy; that we could do so by choice—by the choice of blessing for our lives rather than the avoidance of woe.

Or think of the bitterness in our own diatribes against the Pharisees of our own time. Hear our woe: "You can't trust politicians. They're in it only for their own good." Ouch. And yet these words are some of the most commonly spoken in the county of anger today.

What if we followed the lesson in the invitation to humility? What if we focus on ourselves and our political participation, not that of others? A leader is only as good as his or her people. When we put down the political Pharisees of our day, are we not also putting down our own record as democratic citizens?

Or we can follow the invitation to humility in our personal hurts. Rather than changing the behavior of those who hurt us, we can and should change our own. Other people will be able to accept our faults if we can. And we can if we let God in and let pride out. We don't have excuses to make to other people about who we are. We have depths within to travel. To go up again, we must go down. Not in the ridiculous way that the mighty fall, but in the mighty thrust of a cathedral, capable of that thrust only because it has respected the true physics of up and down. To go up, you must go down. To be raised from the dead, you must go down to the cross.

Humility is a blessing that allows us to stand tall. Pride is a woe that trips us up and makes us fall. If the Pharisees had just understood these spiritual physics, they might have enjoyed their own lives. Instead they never left the county of anger, even to the point that they had to raise their hand against Jesus. They had nowhere else to go.

Or as the Scripture puts it, humility exalts and exaltation humbles.

Suggestions for Worship

Call to Worship (Ps. 127:1-2):

PASTOR: Unless the LORD builds the house,

PEOPLE: **Those who build it labor in vain.**

PASTOR: Unless the LORD guards the city,

PEOPLE: **The guard keeps watch in vain.**

PASTOR: It is in vain that you rise up early and go late to rest, eating the bread of anxious toil;

PEOPLE: **For he gives sleep to his beloved.**

Act of Praise: Psalm 127.

Suggested Hymns: "For All the Saints"; "Ask Ye What Great Thing I Know"; "When I Survey the Wondrous Cross."

Opening Prayer: Almighty God, in whom we live and move and have our being, draw near and humble us. Dress us with the inner glow of peace and let our costumes go unnoticed. Adorn us with enough love for this day, and grant that appearances would not prevail. Grant us enough humility to allow others to trust our love for them, and keep us out of our own way as we go through this day. Through Jesus Christ our Lord, Amen.

Pastoral Prayer: Spirit of the living God, we know that there is a little bit of Pharisee in each one of us. We know that we are quick to see the faults of others and slow to see our own. We know that we tolerate spiritual clutter while making our surfaces look smooth. And we know that we are angry at our failures, lost on the back roads of this anger, and hungry for a return to grace. Forgive us, deepen us, direct us inward so that we may lead more blessed lives, and grant us your peace.

For humility in politics, we pray. For humility in our church, we pray. For humility in our homes, we pray. Wherever we are sure that we are right and others are wrong, pause us and require reflection. Exalt us by deepening within us the practice of humility. Show us the many ways that pride has held us captive, and grant a new direction this day, one that doesn't make us look silly but rather grants forgiveness to the waste of our pride. For the way our pride has hurt the poor, we repent. For the way our pride has hurt our children, we repent. For the way our pride has hurt those we love, we repent. And for the way it has hurt the earth, we repent. Come now, Holy Spirit, and fill us with repentance that we may care beyond pride in a new, less hurtful way. Thanks be to you, O God. Amen.

November 7, 1993

□

Twenty-third Sunday After Pentecost

End times and final judgment are the themes of lessons assigned to the last Sundays of the church year. We are not given a time schedule; only the warning, "Watch therefore."

The Sunday Lessons

Amos 5:18-24: Knowing that folks looked forward to holidays, with their feasts and festivities, Amos warned, "Alas to you who desire the day of the Lord!" (v. 18). Holy days are judgment as well as blessing and hold some surprises, as if one escaped from a lion only to meet a bear. The day of the Lord "is darkness, not light" (v. 18).
I Thessalonians 4:13-18: Paul's converts had come to believe that Christ's return would be immediate or at least in their lifetime. But Christ had not come and some of their number had died. What would become of these dead? Paul answers, "God will bring with him those who died" (v. 14). The eschatological imagery "caught up in the clouds together" (v. 17) is hard to realize in twentieth century thought forms. It was meant to encourage faith in the fact that "We will be with the Lord forever" (v. 17).
Matthew 25:1-13: The parable of the ten bridesmaids follows a discussion of end times and teaches, "Keep awake therefore, for you know neither the day nor the hour" (v. 12). Ten girls waited at night for the bridegroom to arrive so that they could go with him to the bride's home, then to his house, where the wedding ceremony would be held. Five had enough oil for their lamps. Five did not. Finally, arriving late and asking to be let in, the five foolish maidens were told, "I do not know you" (v. 12).

Interpretation and Imagination

"Then we will know." The idea of separation of good from evil pervades the preceding chapter in Matthew. The Greek word *tote* (then) is used often and suggests a final decision. "Then" one will be taken; one will be left. There's an urgency conveyed by the thought. Many students have been moved to all-night cram courses before finals, aware that "then" we will know who has mastered the material and who has not.

Have you ever had to say, "I'm not ready yet"? Have you ever had to wait for someone? It happens so often in our daily lives that we may have become immune to finalities. Scheduled arrivals are often delayed. Is there anyone who has not waited at a terminal? Court hearings are often postponed on a motion to delay.

The text suggests that one cannot forestall the day of the Lord. There are some things that happen whether we want them to or not; whether or not we are ready for them. The wise will embrace the uncertainties, acknowledge their lack of control over finalities, and be ready and watching.

I was a duly-appointed member of the committee and knew the time and place of the meeting. But I was late. When I knocked on the door, hating to interrupt but wanting to get in, someone inside asked, "Who is it?" "John Bergland," I answered. "Never heard of him. We don't know you," they teased. It's a foolish anecdote, but may serve to emphasize the heavy words of the parable, "I do not know you."

Missed opportunities are often followed by "There will be another time." The final moment of truth comes when one hears, "It's too late now. I don't know you." (JKB)

BE PREPARED

Matthew 25:1-13

A SERMON BY JOHN B. PETERS

One of my most vivid memories of my experiences as a Boy Scout was when our Troop 21 went on a camping trip in James City County. We were nearing the time for the Boy Scout Jamboree, and our troop wanted to have some unique displays for that event. A number of the scouts in our troop decided we should do a wildlife exhibit. We wanted to be able to describe how certain animals lived in the wild, what their habits were, and what they ate. It was our plan to capture a few creatures from the woods, display them at the Jamboree, and later, turn them loose.

While on the camping trip, we hunted for wildlife. We were successful in finding and catching a tortoise, a lizard, and a chipmunk. But it was my hope to find a snake. When you're a Boy Scout, there's something kind of exciting about snakes. There's the danger of them, and they cause mothers and sisters to shiver. Boys like that! Our troop scoured the woods for a couple of hours. Then all of a sudden, several of us saw one slithering across some rocks in our path. I concluded this was my big opportunity. I had seen on television how one could grab a snake behind its head and hold it securely and be in no danger. I was prepared to go into action, or so I thought. We recognized that this was a black snake. I sneaked up on him, ready to put into practice the techniques I had learned on television. I grabbed him near his head. I thought he was mine. However, this clever little black snake slithered through my grip, turned its head, and bit me on my bony finger. This was *not* the way it was supposed to happen! The man on television hadn't gotten bitten. In my fear and surprise, I threw the snake down. Actually, I think I cursed him too. Not surprisingly, he got away, and we had no black snake at the Jamboree that year.

I was not hurt from the snake bite, although my pride was bruised. You see the motto of a Boy Scout is "Be prepared." The truth is, I was not prepared. I should have used a snare to hold the snake and brought along a bag to put him in. I had not made adequate preparation, and so I lost my big opportunity and was a failure at my first and last occasion for snake handling.

The parable of the Ten Bridesmaids is about being prepared. Five bridesmaids were prepared and five were not. Five brought enough oil for their lamps; five did not.

In the Palestinian culture of Jesus' day, the role of the bridesmaid was simply to be ready for the coming of the bridegroom. Whenever he arrived, the bridesmaids would quickly move into the procession to escort the bride and the groom to the wedding festivities. These festivities might last an entire week. There would be feasting and dancing and singing. It was the highlight of social life in Palestine. No one wanted to miss it. There was no specific time at which the bridegroom would come. The bridesmaids simply had to be prepared for his coming at any moment.

A Boy Scout is prepared by acquiring knowledge from the experience of earning merit badges. He learns practical and emergency measures like first aid, or skills in the woods that will enable him to handle a particular situation.

What kind of preparedness do we demonstrate on a spiritual plane? The parable of the ten bridesmaids is about the coming of the kingdom of God. How does one prepare for such an event? The nation of Israel's entire history was for the purpose of being ready for the Messiah's initiating of the Kingdom. Yet, the people of Israel failed to recognize him. They were not prepared when Jesus came, and thus they missed him.

There is surely a sense, as the theologian Bultmann would remind us, in which the kingdom of God is not solely a future event that will only occur with Christ's second coming, but is also a present reality. When we are about the sharing of our faith, the proclaiming of the good news of Christ with urgency—the ministering to the needs of God's people and the lifting of the concerns of our world in prayer—there is a sense in which the Kingdom comes and Christ is already among us.

Being prepared for his kingdom is found in carrying out these spiritual disciplines: sharing and living by faith, praying for others, reading and studying the Scripture, obeying the teachings of Christ, and ministering to God's people. A bridesmaid's duty in Palestine was to be ready to begin the procession upon the arrival of the bridegroom. A Christian's duty is to live one's entire life prepared to give an accounting to Christ. It is both doing and being. Being prepared doesn't happen at the last second. It is a way of life. Yes, this parable would first remind us to be prepared.

Secondly, this parable speaks to us about remaining expectant. An indication of the fact that five of the bridesmaids were expectant was demonstrated by their bringing extra oil for their lamps. Perhaps the other five had given up hope that the bridegroom would really come. A child who knows his birthday is near is exceedingly expectant. There is the assurance that soon his or her special day will arrive. There will be gifts and a celebration and cake and ice cream. The prisoner of war who remains confident that his country is making every effort to secure his release is expectant; anticipating his ultimate freedom, certain that day will come.

Even though the five wise bridesmaids slept while waiting, they were still confident in the bridegroom's coming. They rested, assured the wedding would occur. Perhaps Jesus is saying to us through this parable that God's kingdom is sure. No one knows the day or the hour of the fulfillment of the kingdom, but just as surely as day follows night, the kingdom will come. Therefore, we should live with that kind of expectancy, confident in Jesus' words, "Thy Kingdom come. Thy will be done in earth, as it is in heaven" (Matt. 6:10 KJV). Christian people are expectant people, confident that the will of God will ultimately prevail, and his kingdom will come upon the earth.

We may be disturbed by the portion of the parable in which the five wise bridesmaids don't share their oil when asked. Not only does such action seem uncharitable, it seems absolutely unchristian to us. We are taught to share with the have-nots, those who are less fortunate. However, it's just possible that there are some things you can't really share; some things another can't receive from you. For instance, how can someone else take your faith? Faith is something we have to develop for ourselves. It is something that is cultivated over time. Ultimately, we can't live on someone else's faith. Maybe you've heard someone say, "I'm getting to heaven on my spouse's coattails." It just doesn't happen that way. We need our own faith, our own prayer life, our own worship and study. The reminder we have from this parable is that the oil in the lamp is eventually burned up. Our lamps need replenishing, as do our spirits. We must be about the development and nurturing of our own spiritual lives. We can't rely on the spiritual life of someone else.

We can't rely on someone else's faith, nor can we rely upon another's character. Can we give to another a guilt-free conscience? Can we give to another a righteous life? No, a person must live in such a way that these things are developed. We can seek to emulate another's life, but we can't take another's character. So faith and character can't be given away, they must be cultivated individually. The five wise bridesmaids had their faith and their character intact, perhaps the other five did not. Five were ready for the coming of the bridegroom, five were not.

Perhaps the harshest portion of this parable is when the five foolish maidens finally arrived at the wedding festival, only to find the door was locked and they could not enter. In truth, this is an accurate description of what occurs at a Palestinian wedding. After the procession arrives, all the guests enter the hall together and no one else is allowed in.

What is the point of the parable? Isn't it true that there will come a time when the door to the Kingdom is closed and one is no longer able to enter? If one fills one's life with nothing but self-serving and personal pleasures, no time or interest in the way of Christ, and a hardness of heart to the Spirit's direction, then the door to the Kingdom may be finally closed. It is not so much the fact that God closes the door as the fact that we do not avail ourselves of its openness. Thus we fail to share in the great festivities and joy God has in store for us in his kingdom.

Perhaps the door is closed for those not prepared to enter; those who would miss the opportunity. When Albert Schweitzer was in the middle years of life he had already achieved phenomenal success. He was a renowned concert organist throughout Europe and was at the top of his field as a biblical scholar, theologian, and lecturer. However, Schweitzer came to recognize his real opportunity when he was made aware of the needs of people in Africa. He seized what he saw as his opportunity and became a medical missionary there, throwing away any interest in attaining wealth and stature. After his first successful operation performed in Africa, Schweitzer said, "I wish my friends everywhere but knew the exquisite joy of an hour like this." Perhaps Albert Sweitzer was one who lived a life in preparation for the kingdom of God.

The duty of the bridesmaids was to be prepared for the bridegroom's coming, so they might share in the wedding celebration. And our duty? God calls us to be spiritually prepared throughout our lives, so we might be ready to share in his kingdom. "Keep awake, therefore, for you know neither the day nor the hour."

Suggestions for Worship

Call to Worship (Ps. 50:14-15):

PASTOR: Offer to God a sacrifice of thanksgiving,

PEOPLE:	**Pay your vows to the Most High.**
PASTOR:	Call on me in the day of trouble;
PEOPLE:	**I will deliver you, and you shall glorify me.**

Act of Praise: Psalm 50:7-15.

Suggested Hymns: "Come, We That Love the Lord"; "Soon and Very Soon"; "I Love Thy Kingdom, Lord."

Opening Prayer: Lord, we hunger for signs of your presence. We live in a world that worships at many different altars, and beckons to different gods. Give us a keen eye and a receptive spirit, that we might surely know you and be prepared to receive you when you meet us along life's way. Amen.

Pastoral Prayer: O God we come in a spirit of thanksgiving to worship you and praise you. You are the God who provided manna in the wilderness for the Jews, and you offer your manna still. We are tempted to proclaim our own self-sufficiency; we are tempted to congratulate ourselves for all we have accomplished and all we have created. Bring us to our senses, Lord. Remind us that all we have and all we are is due to your grace. Shame us for our unwarranted pride. Enable us to recognize the source of all goodness is from your hand.

Lord, use us in avenues of service to others. We see a world around us that is hungry for good news. There is so much pain and suffering. We see poverty, homelessness, hunger, and disease. We see lives destroyed by drug and alcohol abuse. We see nations involved in armed struggles. Remind us that the gospel brings hope and healing to all. Your Son, Jesus Christ, came to initiate your kingdom. Sometimes we fear we are a long way from that kingdom's fulfillment, Lord. We know that only you can bring the kingdom to fruition; but enable us to be agents of your kingdom, proclaiming the hope, building the bridges, and strengthening relationships. May we live our lives in such faithfulness that we would anticipate the kingdom. Keep us at your work that we might always be in a state of preparedness for your coming. For we offer our prayer in the name of your Son, who taught us to pray diligently that your kingdom might come. Amen.

November 14, 1993

□

Twenty-fourth Sunday After Pentecost

Faithfulness is rewarded. Failure to use the gifts of God results in punishment. One can be a loser. Everyone is held accountable.

The Sunday Lessons

Proverbs 31:10-13, 19-20, 30-31 ***or*** **Zephaniah 1:7, 12-18:** The lesson from Proverbs describes a virtuous woman who is a wife and mother. It describes her faithfulness and the fulfillment that follows. "[She] works with willing hands. . . . Give her a share in the fruit of her hands, and let her works praise her" (vv. 13, 31). The lesson from Zephaniah speaks of disappointment rather than fulfillment. "Though they build houses, they shall not inhabit them" (v. 13).

I Thessalonians 5:1-11: Considering "times and seasons" the question is asked, When will the day of the Lord come? Paul raises a more important issue—the way in which we wait for it. The day will be a surprise. "[It] will come like a thief in the night" (v. 2). His counsel is to be awake and sober; to be armed with the breastplate of faith and love, and the helmet of hope.

Matthew 25:14-30: This parable tells of three servants entrusted with talents. A talent was the highest denomination of currency. "To one he gave five talents, to another two, to another one" (v. 15). The lesson focuses on reward and punishment for faithfulness or the lack of it. When accounts were finally settled, those who had been good stewards were entrusted with more. "Faithful over a few things, I will make you ruler over many things" (v. 21 NKJV). Those who fail to take advantage of opportunities will be left with nothing. "Take the talent from him. . . . Cast the unprofitable servant into the outer darkness" (vv. 28, 30 NKJV).

Interpretation and Imagination

Often one's religious life centers only on teaching, discussion, and reflections. It is a matter of ideas that seek to settle the final issues intellectually. The result is theoretic religion that has little power to help and none to save.

The important questions in life are not thought out. They are worked out, loved out, fought out, lived out. Understanding the scheme of things is not very important if one lacks the power to live. The one-talent man knew the way of it—a hard master who reaped harvests where he had scattered no seed—but he lacked the courage and initiative to do anything in that kind of world.

Life is not fair. We do not get equal opportunities. Life is hard. The sooner we learn that, the easier it becomes. Life is not casual. Those who respond faithfully to its challenge will be rewarded. Those who do not will discover that in anything or everything one can be a loser. One applicant gets the job; another does not. One player wins the tournament; many do not. One nominee receives the award; others do not.

Our culture encourages us to value life in material and temporal ways. It suggests that these are the realities which will finally prevail. Christ would have us cherish the spiritual and the eternal; and this not in thought only, but also in word and deed.

P. T. Forsyth, in his timeless book *Positive Preaching and the Modern Mind,* wrote that the church suffers from three things: triviality, uncertainty, and self-satisfaction. To cure these, he suggests a new note of greatness, a new note of reality, and a new note of judgment. (JKB)

USE IT OR LOSE IT

Matthew 25:14-30

A SERMON BY JOHN B. PETERS

Our forefathers who framed the Declaration of Independence penned the words, "We hold these truths to be self-evident, that all men are created equal, that they are endowed by their Creator with certain inalienable Rights." It may well be that our creator has endowed us with inalienable rights. We may receive a great deal of discussion, however, as to whether or not we are created equal. Our experience would indicate that we were not created equal, for each of us have vastly different gifts.

Which one of us would claim to have the statesmanship of an

Abraham Lincoln, the creativity of a Michelangelo, the voice of a Caruso, or the intellect of an Albert Einstein? We see these persons as five-talent people. The parable of the talents reminds us that endowments are given unequally. One man received five talents, another two, another one.

I enjoyed watching the World Series in the fall of 1990. One of the players, Jose Canseco, was considered to be unusually talented, and he had the salary to match his credentials. Everyone expected big things from him. However, when the time came for him to perform in the Series, his performance was rather mediocre. There were those who thought he certainly had not lived up to his billing. There were fans who were angry because he had not done what he seemed capable of doing.

We would say, "to whom much is given, much is required." No doubt, the master who gave the five talents to the one expected much from him. Perhaps we would agree that of the work done in the world, most is accomplished by the two-talent or the one-talent persons. Maybe we feel more comfortable with the idea anyway, and see ourselves as the person with one or two talents.

In the book *Nicholas and Alexandra*, the author suggests that had Czar Nicholas lived in a different era, he might have been fully capable of handling his position. However, Nicholas lived during the era of the Bolsheviks and the Russian Revolution. He was a rather ordinary man living in extraordinary times. Perhaps he was a man of one or two talents, yet the circumstances called for far more.

It would appear that, indeed, we are not equally endowed; God has given to different persons different talents. Some seem to have far more than others. Perhaps what we can conclude is that God would expect each of us to use the same energy, and the same effort, in cultivating the talent that we have been given.

In reading this parable, it may surprise some of us to find what God gives as the reward for doing our work well. Recall the words of the master in the parable. The man with five talents and the man with two talents came to the master and the master said to them, "Well done, good and faithful servant; you have been faithful over a few things, I will make you ruler over many things. Enter into the joy of your lord" (v. 23 NKJV). On the one hand, the master gives his fellowship to those who have done their work well. On the other hand, he gives them more work to do.

Now that may not be exactly what we had hoped to hear. Perhaps as we do the Lord's work well, we would like to hear that a load is removed from us and the burden ceases. We would like a reprieve, a rest from all of the work. But it appears that is not the way God works with us. Instead, he gives us more responsibility. When we look at the making of steel, we find that steel has to be tempered to reach its greatest strength. It may be the same with human beings. The talents that we have must be tested, refined, and well used if we are to be fully equipped. They must be completely developed. God counts on those who have done that work well to do more. Perhaps that is not an easy word to hear but it is the way God works through us.

Surely the real emphasis of this parable is on the man with one talent. Maybe we feel a certain empathy for this man. Is what he did so bad? He simply took the talent that he was given and buried it in the ground. He knew the master was a rather harsh man; one who had great expectations of him. He put the talent away so that he could give it back upon the master's return. He wasn't like the dishonest steward in another parable who stole from the master and padded his pockets at the absent landlord's expense. He didn't do that. The one-talent man simply played it safe.

Some years ago, I went with a group of Senior Citizens to Tangier Island, Virginia. Maybe some of you have been there; it's an interesting place. I was told by a number of the fishermen there that many of them don't use banks. They simply take their earnings and stick them under the bed and leave them there until they need something. Well, that kind of reminds me of the man with one talent who takes his silver, sticks it in the ground, and leaves it until the master's return. No interest is earned. No risk is taken. In this particular parable, it may be that Jesus was referring to the scribes and Pharisees of his day. They had been given the law. In a sense, that was their talent. They also hid it away in the ground. They refused to hear anything more from God after the law. They closed their ears to the fact that Jesus might be the Messiah. Thus the law did not bear fruit.

What's wrong with hiding away a talent? What did the one talent man do that was so bad? He simply failed to take a risk. He played it safe. God has not called us, in the course of this life, to play it safe. God calls us to risks. I wonder what the state of aviation would be today if Orville and Wilbur Wright had not been willing to take some risks. They certainly had their bumps and their crack-ups before they finally flew a plane. Suppose the apostle Paul, in the face of Jewish opposition, had concluded it would probably be better not to speak of the gospel of Jesus Christ. Had he not done so, I would imagine the missionary movement of Christianity would not be nearly so far along. We are called to be willing to take risks.

We've heard the expression, "use it or lose it." It seems to be ever so true. Here is an olympic champion in the 100-meter dash who decides to run again in another Olympics. However, he remembers all the practice and all the training it took to achieve what he achieved. So he concludes, "I'll not train like that this next time. I'll simply wait until the time of the trials and then run my first race." What does he find? The speed he once had he has no longer. Or here is a concert pianist who has played all over Europe. She decides she's tired of the constant practice, and so she does not practice for an entire year. When the time for another concert arrives, she finds the skills that she once had at the keyboard have diminished significantly. Use it or lose it.

So, it would seem that if we hide away the talent we have been given, it will never be cultivated. Perhaps we can understand this as a parable of the Christian faith. Maybe we can recognize that God has given to each of us the talent of the gospel. Yet some will say, "I cannot teach Sunday school, I can't sing in the choir, I'm uneasy about sharing the faith with a neighbor. It is best for me to do nothing." What happens then to the gospel? What happens to the church that no longer feels a sense of urgency about sharing the good news of Jesus Christ? Does it not begin to die?

Years ago it was the practice after surgery to keep patients in their hospital bed for two weeks at a time, or longer. Then they would be assisted in attempting to walk. What did they find? Their muscles had lost nearly all of their strength; they could hardly walk at all. It was like learning to walk all over again. We find that if muscles are not exercised they atrophy and lose the strength they have. And so it is with all God-given talents. Those that go unused deteriorate. Talents are not to be placed on a shelf like some museum pieces to be admired from a distance. It was Charlotte Brontë who said, "Better to try all things and find all empty than to try nothing and leave your life blank."

According to the parable, what God condemns is our unwillingness to try. The unused faculty becomes extinct. If the workers of Christ cease to work, then Christ's work will never be done. Edward Everett Hale once said, "I am only one, but still I am one. I cannot do everything, but I can do something; and because I cannot do everything I will not refuse to do the something that I can do. I will not let what I cannot do interfere with what I can do." What kind of stewards shall we be with talents given by God? Use it or lose it.

Suggestions for Worship

Call to Worship (Ps. 76:1-3, 5-6, 8, 11):

PASTOR: In Judah God is known, his name is great in Israel. His abode has been established in Salem, his dwelling place in Zion.

PEOPLE: There he broke the flashing arrows, the shield, the sword, and the weapons of war.

PASTOR: The stouthearted were stripped of their spoil; they sank into sleep;

PEOPLE: At your rebuke, O God of Jacob, both rider and horse lay stunned.

PASTOR: From the heavens you uttered judgment; the earth feared and was still.

PEOPLE: Make vows to the LORD your God, and perform them.

Act of Praise: Psalm 76.

Suggested Hymns: "Stand Up, Stand Up for Jesus"; "Rescue the Perishing"; "Faith of Our Fathers."

Opening Prayer: O Lord God, giver of all gifts and graces, grant that we might be faithful stewards of all that you have bestowed upon us. Use us that our words, our actions, our whole lives might offer praise and glory to the one in whom we believe. Amen.

Pastoral Prayer: God of rain and wind, sun and moon, God whose hand is evident in all creation; we praise you for your wondrous works. We marvel at your universe that we have not made, but shudder when we realize how our actions and insensitivities have threatened its beauty and stability. Lord, cause us to treasure the world's resources over which you have given us dominion. Your gifts are so bounteous. We give you thanks for the sunrise, for salt spray from an ocean wave, and for the smell of wild flowers. Lord you have painted a landscape upon this earth that we could not have even fathomed. Help us to cherish our earth, even as the people of Israel cherished the promised land. May our efforts of right stewardship help to make it possible for all future generations to also rejoice in the earth's grandeur.

O God, as you have made the world beautiful, make our lives beautiful. We are too often tempted to accept that which cheapens life. We confess our prejudice, ill will, lust, and hunger for power. Lead us away from that which would rob life of beauty and grace. We marvel at the life and example of your son, Jesus Christ. Remind us that Christ's spirit has been set free among us. Enable us to listen to that still small voice of the Spirit. May we be so led that our faith would be strengthened and our lives would proclaim the one whose life was the most beautifully lived, Jesus Christ. Amen.

November 21, 1993

□

Last Sunday of Pentecost (Christ the King)

The Old Testament lesson refers to the Lord God as a shepherd. The New Testament lesson refers to Christ the King as a shepherd who separates the sheep from the goats. All things are subject to Him.

The Sunday Lessons

Ezekiel 34:11-17, 23-24: Ezekiel, prophesying during the Babylonian exile, condemned the pre-exilic kings as shepherds who fed only themselves. Now God proclaims, "I myself will search for my sheep and will seek them out" (v. 11). Like a shepherd, God will separate the sheep from the goats. Sheep and goats grazed together, but were separated each evening. Sheep were of more value.

I Corinthians 15:20-28: "God has put all things in subjection under his feet" (v. 27). The resurrection of the dead, the relationship of Adam and Christ, the order in which the dead will rise, and Paul's conclusion, "Then comes the end, when he hands over the kingdom to God the Father, after he has destroyed every ruler and every authority and power. . . . that God may be all in all" (vv. 24, 28).

Matthew 25:31-46: "When the Son of Man comes in his glory . . . he will sit on the throne of his glory. All the nations will be gathered before him, and he will separate people one from another as a shepherd separates the sheep from the goats" (vv. 31-32). Those who have accepted and served Christ the King through acceptance and service to "the least of these who are members of my family" will hear, "Come, you that are blessed by my Father, inherit the kingdom" (v. 34). Those who reject the poor dying Christ and neglect "the humble brother" (NEB) will hear, "You that are accursed, depart from me" (v. 41).

Interpretation and Imagination

If the preacher centers on the criteria by which God's judgments are made, he or she will speak of caring for the hungry, the thirsty, the stranger, the naked, the sick, and those in prison. This familiar passage is often used to call the church to serve, in very practical ways, "the least of them."

To whom does Matthew refer when he speaks of "the least of these who are members of my family"? Many scholars agree that it refers to the disciples and those who serve in the cause of Christ. Often preachers use the text to emphasize the needs of all who are oppressed. The text is explicit: Those who show mercy to the oppressed are rewarded; those who do not are punished.

If one emphasizes "the least of these," he or she will need to guard against moralizing. H. Grady Davis describes a familiar mode of preaching as the "imperative." It is summed up as *"You ought to:"* feed the hungry, clothe the naked, and so forth. This mode encourages works righteousness.

The dominant idea of the text declares that Christ the King is both Judge and Redeemer. Everyone and everything is subject to his sovereignty. This Shepherd King seeks no solace for himself, but receives the kindness shown to "the least of them" as though it were done for him.

When Bishop William R. Cannon retired, he was presented with a check for $25,000. Donations, intended as personal gifts for him, were given by churches and individuals. He would not keep the money for himself saying, "When David was engaged in battle with his enemy, he expressed a wish that he might have a drink of water from the spring at Bethlehem. Three of his friends risked their lives to get it for him. When they returned with the water he poured it on the ground because to him it represented their blood." The bishop went on to say, "You have given me a generous gift. I want to leave it here with you in the form of a scholarship fund. I can gain more pleasure and satisfaction from that than from spending the money on myself."

Christ the King, Christ the Shepherd seeks no benefit for himself. But God who shows mercy demands mercy. (JKB)

Note: The lections for Thanksgiving Day are Deuteronomy 8:7-18; II Corinthians 9:6-15; Luke 17:11-19; Psalm 65.

NOVEMBER 21

THE THANKFUL HEART—A NARRATIVE

Luke 17:11-19

A SERMON BY MICHAEL C. WOLFRAM

This didn't really happen, but it could have . . .

It began so many years ago that he could hardly remember what it was like. But there had been a day. A day when he laughed and played with the other boys in town, a day when his heart was filled with optimism and hope, a day of youthful pleasures and fantasies.

Then came *that* day, a day he will never forget.

At first hardly anyone noticed. He didn't seem to have the energy he used to enjoy. While many of his friends wanted to play, he sat down to rest and watch. He wasn't sure, but he just didn't feel right. "You're growing up," they would say. "You're becoming a man!" He wasn't convinced.

It was the sore that he discovered that caused anxiety. His parents shared his concern. "We must take him to the priest."

As he ascended the steps to the visit the priest he was bewildered. "Why are they taking me here? I want to see the doctor. What is going on?"

The priest was a kind, older gentleman. This was not a new sight to him. He carefully examined the open sore on the boy's body. Yes, the hair in the sore spot had turned white, but the disease appeared to be no deeper than the skin. Perhaps there was hope. "Come back in seven days, I want to examine this again."

The next seven days proved to be some of the most anxious days of his life. He was confined to his house, isolated from his friends. By now he realized that this was a serious matter. What could it mean?

As he and his parents walked back to see the priest, he broke into a cold sweat. He was scared. The priest examined the sore again. By now, more sores had appeared. There was no denying the diagnosis.

The priest sat back in his chair, and in as gentle a way as was possible, tried to explain the situation. But only one word was heard. Only one word rang through the chamber. Only one word would be remembered. *Leprosy!*

At first he tried to deny the diagnosis. "This can't be happening to me! Other people get leprosy. Leprosy is for those people no one cares about; you know, those living in the colony outside of town. No one in my family ever had leprosy. You didn't look close enough!"

Anger then swept through his body and his knuckles turned white from his clenched fists as he thrust them to the heavens, "Why me, God?"

For now he realized that all of his dreams had been shattered, as a clay pot explodes when dropped to the ground. Pools of tears filled his eyes as he thought of the carpenter shop that he and his father were going to set up. They were both going to specialize in different aspects of carpentry in order to make their shop the most versatile in town. He had already thought of where he would establish his home, within walking distance of the shop. And the girl he was going to marry. Now she would marry someone else. She would bear someone else's children. And someone else's family would fill that house with laughter and love.

His life would be a life spent in a leper colony. He would never again approach another person without crying out, "Unclean." He had heard about those who went to the colony. Eventually paralysis sets in, and then death.

His parents tried to be supportive, but even they wanted to keep their distance.

Loneliness. . . . Isolation. . . . Despair. . . . Rejection. . . . *Leprosy!*

As he walked to the outskirts of town on *that* day he turned for one last look into the village. There were his friends, playing in the street. They were having so much fun, it looked as if they didn't even miss him. How could they? Didn't they understand? Can't they see what they have? They have their health. They have their families. They will have a warm meal tonight and a family to go home to. Aren't they thankful for what they have, or do they take it all for granted?

The clopping of hooves alerted him to the fact that someone was coming. Turning, he saw a farmer whistling as he brought his harvest into the open market. Jumping to the side of the road, he shouted "Unclean!" How strange the word sounded.

The boy recognized the farmer as he guided his cart by. He

had bought food from him in the market. It seemed the man was always complaining. It was either too hot or too cold, too wet or too dry. Just having the crop was not good enough, it had to be sold in order to realize a profit, and then the prices he got were not keeping up with inflation.

"Why can't these people see what they have?" thought the boy. But hanging his head, he realized that he had been just like them until he had his visit with the priest. And on *that* day he vowed never again to take the ordinary things for granted, but to be thankful for all God had given to him. Yes, even in the leper colony he would find reason to give thanks.

The years in the leper colony were years of growing for the boy, now a young man. He contemplated God's goodness and his unworthiness.

Then, one day, he and his new friends heard of one coming. Jesus was his name. Some said he was the Messiah. Could this be? They had heard that he was able to perform miracles.

They left the colony hoping by chance to get a glimpse of this famed rabbi. When they approached a gathering of people, they were sure they had found him. "Jesus, Master, have mercy on us," the young man cried, but the leprosy had weakened his voice so that no one heard. Together, they cried in unison, "Jesus, Master, have mercy on us."

He turned, looked, and said, "Go show yourselves to the priests."

Did they hear right? Why would he send them to the priests? The priests had already diagnosed their leprosy. Obediently they followed his order.

On the way, the gray death that covered their bodies began to vanish right before their eyes! He had heard their prayer! "We must run to the priest!" They hurried their steps as they ran, not to be diagnosed, but to be declared clean!

All but one, that is. The young man stopped in his tracks. He looked back, but it was too late to stop his friends. He would not be unthankful. He would go back to the one who gave him healing.

He started to run as the words of the psalmist provided cadence for his feet as they pounded the path. "Oh give thanks unto the Lord for he is good, for his mercy endures forever." Faster and faster came the words as his pace quickened, "Oh, give thanks to the LORD, for He is good! For His mercy endures forever."

And arriving, he knelt at his Master's feet.

"Rise and go your way, your faith has made you well."

A feeling he had never experienced filled him as he rose. He had been healed, not only physically, but spiritually as well. Not only had his leprosy left, but he had found the Savior.

That occurred years ago, and now, as he thought again of *that* day and of another day of God's goodness, he silently spoke the words he had used as his prayer to close every day since. Yes, he had so much to be thankful for, he would never again take the ordinary things for granted. "O, give thanks to the LORD for He is good! For His mercy endures forever."

A satisfied smile appeared on his face as he lay down his head and drifted off to sleep.

My Christian friends, as we consider what God so graciously and daily gives to us, let us give thanks to the Lord, for he is good. For his mercy endures forever.

Suggestions for Worship

Call to Worship (I Corinthians 15:24-26, 28):

PASTOR: Then comes the end, when he hands over the kingdom to God the Father,

PEOPLE: After he has destroyed every ruler and every authority and power.

PASTOR: For he must reign until he has put all his enemies under his feet.

PEOPLE: The last enemy to be destroyed is death. . . . so that God may be all in all.

Act of Praise: Psalm 23.

Suggested Hymns: "All hail the Power of Jesus' Name"; "Jesus Shall Reign"; "Rejoice, the Lord Is King."

Opening Prayer: Good Father of us all, you watch over your creatures with unfailing care. Great is your faithfulness. We have gathered to praise you and to know your presence. Now surround us with the far-reaching embrace of your love that we may have, through Christ our Lord, the help we long for. Amen.

Pastoral Prayer: Almighty God, you have created us by a word spoken. You have shaped our lives by your wisdom and designed our days according to your plan. You have sustained us by your providence and kept us by your love. And only you can make our hearts truly glad.

Help us to be grateful and to give thanks at all times and in all seasons. When we are awake, give us eyes to see your mercies on every hand; give us ears to hear the whisper of your guiding truth and your call to serve the needs of others. As children of the light, help us to watch and pray.

Watch over us when we sleep. In the quietness of night let us rest in the assurance of your nearness. Let us rest in the peace of Christ. Be for us shelter and safety and home. And at last receive us and the ones we love into the dwelling place that has been prepared for us. Sleeping and waking, our journey is to our Father's house.

On this day of sabbath rest, refresh us and renew us in body and soul. Let Christ rule our hearts. Let the word of Christ in all its fullness dwell in us. Keep strong the ties that bind us to one another, and then lead us to new friends so that your children everywhere will give you thanks and praise through Jesus Christ our Lord. Amen.

November 28, 1993

□

First Sunday of Advent

Waiting expectantly, even longing for the intervening power and splendor that will cause every eye to see, the church speaks its advent message once again. "Watch!"

The Sunday Lessons

Mark 13:32-37: "From the fig tree learn its lesson: as soon as its branch becomes tender and puts forth its leaves, you know that summer is near" (v. 28). Warned about the approaching end, the disciples asked, "When will this be?" (13:4). Darkened sun and falling stars suggest end times. The Son of Man, coming in great glory, is, "at the very gates" (v. 29). Exact time schedules are unknown. The parable of the servant who does not know when his master will return warns all to stay awake. "About that day or hour no one knows. . . . Keep alert" (vv. 32-33).
Isaiah 63:16–64:8: The prophet returned to Jerusalem and found the city in ruins and the temple destroyed. He cried, "We have long been like those whom you do not rule, like those not called by your name" (63:19). Acknowledging that "no eye has seen any God besides you, who works for those who wait for him" (64:4), and confessing the sins of the people, he pleads, "Do not be exceedingly angry, O Lord" (64:9).
I Corinthians 1:3-9: The greeting is found in each of Paul's letters to the churches. "Grace to you and peace from God our Father and the Lord Jesus Christ" (v. 3). Giving thanks for all the gifts God has bestowed on the Corinthians, the apostle still writes about waiting expectantly. "He will also strengthen you to the end. . . . God is faithful; by him you were called into the fellowship of his Son, Jesus Christ our Lord" (vv. 8-9).

Interpretation and Imagination

Sometimes we wait in line or wait our turn. That kind of waiting is mostly passive. Sometimes we wait for a verdict, a decision on our application, or a diagnosis. That kind of waiting is filled with anxiety. Sometimes we wait for pain or death—the prick of the needle, the separation, the last heartbeat. Then we wait with dread and fear. What is the mood with which we await the coming of Christ this advent?

The apostle Paul writes about "waiting expectantly." The prophet Isaiah, acknowledging the sins of his people, longs for God's intervention and believes it will be for good to those who wait for him. The gospel urges one to watch for the coming of the Son of Man in awe before his power and glory.

But most of us don't expect anything big to happen today. At least not in the realm of Christianity. We might sing, "Come, Thou Long-Expected Jesus," but we don't expect any sudden interruptions. Bakers will watch the rising dough, brokers will watch the market reports, and bored worshipers will watch their watches. Does anyone, anyone at all, watch for the coming of Christ in power—the kind of power we have come to know as the power of the cross, power made perfect in weakness?

Phillips Brooks said it well in his Bethlehem carol, "How silently, how silently, the wondrous gift is given; so God imparts to human hearts the blessings of his heaven." (JKB)

THE SILENCE OF THE LAMBS

Mark 13:32-37

A SERMON BY CARLA SCANLAN

In this passage of Mark we are reminded that the day and the hour are unknown. We do not know when God is planning to deliver us from this world and this time. Yet as human persons, we desire to know God's plan and movement in the contemporary era.

Some friends of mine were traveling through Europe on their vacation. Stopping in Copenhagen, they decided to tour the wonderful Hans Jensen clock near the central part of the city. Housed in a building, the clock itself is huge and the workings are open so that you may walk the length of the house around it. There are many gears and parts which move so minutely they are almost hypnotic. After spending nearly half an hour caught up in the awe of this mighty timepiece (which loses less than a second every 500 years), my friends began to tire. Absentmindedly, the wife inquired "Honey, what time is it?" to which the spouse replied, "I really don't have any idea!" Captured by the fascination of the big machinery, they laughed as they realized the profundity of their error! So often it is that we are so close to the fine details, we simply fail to see and understand the larger plan.

Yet as people of faith we keep asking the question "Why?" If a woman is told she is pregnant, she wants to know when she will be delivered. What is the date and time? How long must she wait?

Stephen Kurtz, in his book *The Art of Unknowing*, speaks of the human need for connection with time as part of connection with the culture. Kurtz believes "to be cast out of time is to be cast out of society." Social existence functions from rules which add structure to people's lives. He suggests that Michael Tournier's novel *Friday*, based on Defoe's *Robinson Crusoe*, describes the process of separation from society and the attempt to regain a sense of order and structure.

Robinson writes in his journal that, "insofar as I live from day to day, I let myself drift; time slips through my fingers and in losing time I lose myself. When I began a calendar I regained possession of myself." Robinson constructs a water clock and later a calendar which enables him to come to himself. Later Robinson meets Friday, who accidentally detonates a powder keg, destroying Robinson's calendar and clock. The structure of time is lost and Robinson begins to live in a new order—experiencing the natural rhythm of the island and his impulses as not chaotic. He learns to live in the endless present.

The AIDS patient on receiving the diagnosis asks the doctor, "How long do I have?" The doctor says, "I don't know. It could be days or years." The AIDS patient is like Robinson Crusoe. His reality has changed and he begins to live in the long reality of the present.

What we offer this person is not an ineffective false assurance, but the awareness of the deeply experienced moment-by-moment presence of life. When will I be delivered, Lord? Nobody knows the day or the hour.

The human fear of death is the basis for all our claims of faith. As young people, if our fear is the end of life, in our middle years the challenge is to gaze into the potential of that void and find meaning. Learning to wait, to be patient, to relinquish the urge to control what cannot be controlled are acquired capacities.

We ask the question *why?* because we want somehow to be in charge, in control, on top of the situation. This is a symptom of the narcissism of the age.

A colleague of mine was counseling with a very disturbed patient. The man had delusions and no one could help him move out of his ill state. My friend spent many hours just listening and accepting the sick man's delusions. Gradually, through the love and acceptance of the therapist, the man began to be more and more lucid. One day, he was able to sit calmly in his chair during the therapy hour, look straight at my friend and say wistfully, "I want to be God, and I am not God." Within weeks of that confession he was able to return to his family and friends. Had my colleague challenged the man directly he might still be separated from reality. What the therapist did was to give the client a place to be, a holding environment for all the chaos and confusion that no one had heard before. He gave the man a place and time in which to be, and so the sick man became a self returned from exile.

In therapy, part of the cure rests with the therapist's ability to remain silent. It is the real test of therapeutic maturity to allow the client to talk and project all the hurt, loneliness, and confusion of life at the person of the therapist, while the therapist remains calm and steady.

Kurtz writes of a brilliant but desperately lost client, Lydia. Her conversation is sprinkled with delusions, remnants of several languages, and a cacophony of historic and artistic imagery. Just reading his recitation of her conversations makes one feel dizzy. As the young psychotherapist struggled to be present in a nonjudgmental way for his client, patiently sorting through the confusing verbiage, she informed him in one of the sessions, in theological terms, "God does not want to be understood, God wants to be loved." For Kurtz, Lydia's recovery is not only of a lucid mind, but is also a recovery of her ultimate destiny. Lydia became a prophetess of her age, winning converts to the vision of God within her. In some ways she has become his guide into a deeper understanding of the mystery of life. Here is a marvelous reversal in the healing process. The client, in the best of therapy, heals the therapist is some deep way.

Like Kurtz, we ask when will Lydia be delivered from this burden of life. Like Kurtz, we stand in silent amazement at the ability of God to heal through passive relationship. It is not the therapist who heals through understanding, it is the God who heals through love. The therapist's silent acceptance opens the door for the grace of healing, the deliverance of the captive into freedom, and in Lydia's special case, her ultimate destiny as a child of God able to be in harmony and community with the real world.

Silence imposes no demands on the subject but gives the client a space and a time to reconstruct a reality. Like the good therapist, God gives us a sense of time and place, but leaves us the silence so that our defenses are eroded away. Finally, like hungry children, we seek a word of acknowledgment and with one word, God feeds us like children.

There is an Indian tribe near Medellin, Colombia; natives of the rain forest. While primitive by western standards, they have a highly evolved sense of order which includes the belief in nonstriving and noncompetition. When a member of the tribe dies, the other members of the community come to the grieving family, hanging their heads in silence. After embracing their grieving friends, they remain silent, saying quietly, "Somas nada . . . Somas nada." The translation is quite profound, it means "We are nothing . . . We are nothing."

When the great shepherd leads the sheep, the sheep follow best when they let the shepherd lead. In the silence of the lambs, God's voice is heard. If the lambs could speak they would say, "Somas nada . . . Somas nada."

Suggestions for Worship

Call to Worship (Ps. 80:1-3):

PASTOR: Give ear, O Shepherd of Israel, you who lead Joseph like a flock!

PEOPLE: You who are enthroned upon the cherubim, shine forth.

PASTOR: Stir up your might, and come to save us!

PEOPLE: Restore us, O God; let your face shine, that we may be saved.

Act of Praise: Psalm 80:1-7.

Suggested Hymns: "Lift Up Your Heads, Ye Mighty Gates"; "Come, Thou Long-Expected Jesus"; "People, Look East."

Opening Prayer: Almighty God, be attentive to the cry of each heart. You know us better than we know ourselves. You know what we need. Help us to find in your Son our Lord comfort in our distress, certainly in our doubt, courage in our fear, and confidence in the victory he has already won. Amen.

Pastoral Prayer: God of the living, God of the dead, we who die the death of our humanity have thought that we are as wise as God. No secret seems completely hidden to us. We have gotten wealth and planned for security. We have gained power and desired control.

In our hearts we are proud. We have pretended to sit in the seat of gods. Yet in the hour of our death we will not say, "I am a god." Before all that can wound us, and in the presence of what will slay us, we dare not say, "We are gods." On the last day, we will not say, "We are Gods."

Therefore, manifest your glory in our midst and among all humanity. Let us know again that you are Lord—God of the living, God of the dead. Let everything that lives and breathes know that you are the Lord their God. Amen.

December 5, 1993

□

Second Sunday of Advent

Preparation for Christ's coming is the theme for this Sunday in Advent.

The Sunday Lessons

Mark 1:1-8: "The beginning of the good news" (v. 1). This is Mark's equivalent to the prologue of John and the birth narratives of Matthew and Luke. He begins with John the Baptist, a lone prophet who confronted the apostasy of Israel with a message of repentance and waters of purification. The words of Isaiah, "Prepare the way of the Lord, make his paths straight" (v. 3), introduce the Baptist's declaration, "The one who is more powerful than I is coming after me" (v. 7). Messianic hope wanted heaven to open and God's spirit to pour over his people. The waters of repentance poured over sinners is a prologue to that mighty happening.

Isaiah 40:1-11: There is to be a new journey through the desert—not into exile, but back to the Holy City. "Comfort, O comfort my people" (v. 1), are the first words followed by the cry, "prepare the way . . . make straight in the desert a highway" (v. 3). *The Messiah* by Handel has acquainted us with the text, "And the Glory of the Lord shall be revealed and all flesh shall see it together." Flesh, like grass of the field, withers and its beauty fades like a flower, but "The word of our God will stand forever" (v. 8). The "herald of good tidings" (v. 9) brings good news to the cities of Judah.

II Peter 3:8-15*a*: The expected return of Christ had not come about. Scoffers ridiculed. Peter responded with warnings and wisdom. "With the Lord one day is like a thousand years" (v. 8). The delay provides time for repentance. Don't be caught by surprise like people were at the Flood. The text explicitly states, "The earth . . . will be burned up" (v. 10 RSV). (This idea found its way into Jewish apocalyptic thought from eastern pagan traditions.) "We wait for new heavens and a new earth" (v. 13).

Interpretation and Imagination

The philosopher ponders and guesses, analyzes and debates. "Will the reign of truth and goodness come because we diligently prepare?" Or, "Will the Kingdom arrive (in its good time) in spite of anything we do or don't do?" Should we get ready so that Christ will come to us, or must we get ready because, ready or not, he's going to come?

The prophet just looks and listens, lives and speaks. With the compelling language of firsthand experience, Isaiah shouts, "Prepare the way of the Lord." John the Baptist proclaims, "Repent and be baptized. One greater is coming." Preparation for God's coming among us is their common theme.

What is the shape of that preparation in Advent 1993? It's still the same as it was for John the Baptist, in meaning if not in symbol. Repentance and baptism. Repentance means being so sorry for sin that we stop sinning. The baptism of repentance (the purifying rite of John the Baptist) means that we seek to be cleansed from the stain and every intimidating memory of our disobedience.

The apostasy addressed by John the Baptist in first-century Jerusalem is not what you face in twentieth-century America. Every preacher should be specific from his or her own pastoral experience. Some suggestions: We have other gods—science, technology, materialism, pleasure. We don't care about the poor if we are not one of them. We mortgage our children's future for our well-being today. We risk all of life in our war games and armaments. We look only to the familiar and ordinary and fail to pray and get ready. (JKB)

PATIENT FAITH IN AN IMPATIENT WORLD

Mark 1:1-8

A SERMON BY JAMES A. HARNISH

One of our daughters would ask the question every time we pulled out of the driveway for a long trip: "Are we there yet,

Daddy?" It went back to the time my wife's family moved from Florida to California. They were less than 30 miles from home when their five-year-old daughter began asking, "Are we there yet, Daddy?" She kept asking it, all the way to California!

I get that feeling during Advent. As we travel toward Bethlehem, I find myself asking, "Are we there yet, God?" Are we any closer to the fulfillment of the Kingdom which Jesus described? Are we closer to the time when "love and faithfulness will meet; righteousness and peace will kiss" (Ps. 85:10)? Are we near the place where valleys are exalted and mountains are made low, the rough places plane and the crooked straight, and the glory of the Lord is revealed? Are we within earshot of the promise of peace on earth and good will to all people? Are we there yet, God?

You don't have to be a biblical scholar to feel that longing. A few years ago, *My Weekly Reader* asked 45,000 elementary school students what they would like to tell the President. The most common responses were: "The whole world should be at peace." "We should learn to take care of nature." "Everyone should get along with each other." "Candy bars shouldn't cost so much."

Three of the four reflect the deepest longings of biblical faith. But when we hold those visions up against the mirror of the daily newspaper, we know that the promise of Bethlehem is a long way off. We are a long way from God's intention for us.

This kind of longing lingers in the shadows behind the epistle of Peter. It was written to second-generation skeptics. Their parents were first-generation Christians who expected that Jesus would return to fulfill the promise of the Kingdom any day; next week at the latest. But years have passed. The first-generation Christians died. Now, their heirs are asking, "Where is the promise of the coming of the Lord? Our fathers have all died and the world is still the same as it has always been. Where is the new heaven and new earth, the place where justice will be at home?" (II Pet. 3:4, 13, paraphrase).

The apostle's answer is patience, which is tough, because I'm an impatient person in an impatient world. I am a product of a microwave society, where we expect everything to be completed instantly, right now.

Robert Schuller tells of a frantic man who came running down the ramp waving to the ferry, which was just a few feet away from the dock. He jumped from the pier onto the ferry and said, "Wow, I made it!" The boatman on the ferry replied, "Yep, but if you had waited one more minute we would have pulled right up to the dock."

Sometimes we're all like that. We get so busy trying to accomplish everything at once that we lose our sense of perspective or direction. We need to hear Peter say, "the first thing you must remember is this, that a thousand years in the Lord's sight is like a day and a day is like a thousand years" (II Pet. 3:8, paraphrase). Patient faith comes from a long view of God's work in human history.

We forget that the God in whom we place our faith is the God who took a thousand years to grow a sequoia, who took millions of years to carve the Grand Canyon, who took a thousand years to prepare the way for the Son to be born. God isn't in a hurry. A thousand years are like a day.

A Methodist bishop told the story of a hunting trip into northern Maine in the fall of 1896. His fellow hunters included a geologist and an astronomer. They were guided by an old north Maine woodsman who had never been outside the forest; a rock-ribbed Republican, who was absolutely petrified at the prospect that a Democrat like William Jennings Bryan might actually be elected to the White House that fall.

Around the campfire one night, the astronomer looked up into the sky and talked about the size of the galaxy and the distance to the nearest star. The geologist picked up a rock and talked about its formation during the Ice Age. The guide had never heard anything like it before. He listened in amazement, and when the bishop asked what he thought of all this, the guide scratched his head and said, "Well, if all that's true, then I guess it wouldn't be too bad if Bryan was elected."

I am not suggesting that it doesn't matter who picks up the mail at 1600 Pennsylvania Avenue. Choices shape our destinies, and we are responsible for their consequences. But we need to see our strutting and fretting on the stage against the backdrop of God's eternity, the God to whom a day is like a thousand years.

But this passage is not about our patience with God; it is about God's patience with us.

> The Lord is not slow to do what he has promised. . . . Instead, he is patient with you, because he does not want anyone to be destroyed, but wants all to turn away from their sins. (II Pet. 3:9 GNB)

God will accomplish his purpose. The kingdom will come. The question has to do with us: Will we be faithful to the kingdom vision? Will we be a part of the fulfillment of God's redemptive purpose in human history?

Which brings us to John the Baptist, the wilderness prophet in his rough hair coat, eating his honey and wild locust, offering his stern call to repentance. He's not exactly the guy you invite to Christmas dinner! He is here to prepare the way for the coming of Christ. He calls us to be road builders for the coming King; men and women who clear the path and pave the highway for God.

The prophets of Advent remind us that the point of life is not to see who gets to Bethlehem first, but to be on the journey, to prepare the way for God's kingdom to come and God's will to be done on earth as it is in heaven. Martin Luther described it in these powerful words:

> This life is not righteousness but growth in righteousness, not health but healing, not being but becoming, not rest but exercise. We are not yet what we shall be but we are growing toward it. The process is not yet finished but it is still going on. This is not the end, this is the road. All does not yet gleam in glory but all is being purified.

"Are we there yet, Daddy?" The answer is, No, we aren't there yet, not by a long shot. But the Lord is very patient because he does not want any to be lost, but for all of us to come to repentance along the road that leads to Bethlehem.

Suggestions for Worship

Call to Worship (Ps. 85:8-9, 11, 13):

PASTOR: Let me hear what God the LORD will speak, for he will speak peace to his people.

PEOPLE: Surely his salvation is at hand for those who fear him.

PASTOR: Faithfulness will spring up from the ground.

PEOPLE: Righteousness will go before him, and will make a path for his steps.

Act of Praise: Psalm 85:8-13.

Suggested Hymns: "Hail to the Lord's Anointed"; "Blessed Be the God of Israel"; "There's a Song in the Air."

Opening Prayer: O eternal God, the timeless one whose Spirit flows through all creation, give us that patient faith which lives and works in the expectation of the coming of your Kingdom, through Christ our Lord. Amen.

Pastoral Prayer: Deliver us, O Lord, from the foolishness of impatience. Let us not be in such a hurry as to run on without Thee. We know that it takes a lifetime to make a tree; we know that fruit does not ripen in an afternoon, and Thou Thyself didst take a week to make the universe.

May we remember that it takes time to build the nation that can truly be called God's own country. It takes time to work out the kind of peace that will endure. It takes time to find out what we should do; what is right and what is best.

Slow us down, O Lord, that we may take time to think, time to pray, and time to find out Thy will. Then give us the sense and courage to do it, for the glory of Thy name. Amen (Peter Marshall, Prayer in the U.S. Senate, 22 January 1947).

(See page 447.)

December 12, 1993

□

Third Sunday of Advent

John bears witness that the Light has come. Christ brings peace and joy.

The Sunday Lessons

John 1:6-8, 19-28: The prologue to the Gospel of John presents a cosmic Christ in the context of eternity. The hymn is interrupted with the words, "There was a man sent from God, whose name was John" (v. 6). His ministry was more than preaching repentance and baptizing; he came as a witness to the light. "He himself was not the light, but he came to testify to the light" (v. 8). When asked by a deputation from Jerusalem if he was the Messiah, or Elijah, or the awaited prophet, he answered, "I am the voice of one crying out in the wilderness, Make straight the way of the Lord' " (v. 23).
Isaiah 61:1-4, 8-11: The new Jerusalem rejoices, following the exile, in songs of salvation and "a garland instead of ashes, the oil of gladness instead of mourning . . . repair [of] the ruined cities" (vv. 3-4). Jesus described his ministry with the words of this text. "The Lord has anointed me; he has sent me to bring good news to the oppressed, to bind up the brokenhearted, to proclaim liberty to the captives, and release to the prisoners" (v. 1). The messianic age (Spirit upon me), prophetic vocation (anointed) and the year of jubilee (prisoners set free) are evident in the text.
I Thessalonians 5:16-24: Paul asks the Thessalonians to "respect those who . . . have charge of you in the Lord" (v. 12). Esteem and affection are their due. Paul teaches "Be at peace among yourselves" (v. 13), but then goes on to say, "admonish, encourage, help, be patient" (v. 14). Negative restrictions and a catalogue of "don'ts" are not characteristic of the Christian life. Joy, thanksgiving, and prayer are.

DECEMBER 12

Interpretation and Imagination

Peace and joy are not qualities that I easily associate with John the Baptist. There's joy in the Jerusalem Isaiah describes. Both peace and joy are prescribed by the Thessalonian text. Can it be seen in the Baptizer? He lives in wilderness without creature comforts. He's a testy prophet and a frightening voice confronting people with their sins. If one made a movie with John the Baptist as chief actor, there would be little laughter and no songs of joy.

Oswald Chambers noted that the joy of Jesus was the absolute self-surrender and self-sacrifice of himself to his Father. The thing that will hinder this kind of joy is the captious irritation of thinking too much about our own well being. It follows, then, that John's self-understanding—"I'm not the light. I bear witness to the light"—is an example of contentment and true joy. Perhaps John the Baptist knew all about real joy.

One of the best statements regarding Christian joy that I have read is found in Tom Langford's book *The Harvest of the Spirit*. He writes, "Joy is a freedom from ourselves and our own small, artificially-limited world. Among human beings, saints soar because they think lightly of themselves. So joy comes from large vision, from a vision of far horizons."

Self-conscious and self-centered narcissism is a common sin and sickness in our society. Assertiveness training, self-realization programs, health spas, glamour magazines, and such, encourage it. Narcissists get very little enjoyment from life other than the accolades they receive from others or from their grandiose fantasies. They feel restless and bored when the external glitter wears off.

True joy is a gift. It is not the giddiness of laughter, the mere gratification of emotion; it is not fulfilled ambition or an honored position. "My delight is in the Lord."

If this Advent will be Jubilee when our prisons are opened; if light will shine in our darkness; if this will be a season of peace and joy, it will be because someone—a few, many, but at least someone—bears witness to the Light. (JKB)

IMAGINE THAT!

John 1:6-8, 19-28

A SERMON BY JAMES A. HARNISH

A sentence from the writings of Albert Einstein snagged my thinking recently: "Imagination is more important than knowledge."

Imagination. The Advent-Christmas season is loaded with it! Just imagine, a penny-pinching, nasty old coot named Ebenezer Scrooge, being transformed into a laughing, generous, gift-giving uncle.

Imagine a Grinch, trying with all his might to steal Christmas, only to discover that Christmas comes anyway. He couldn't stop it if he tried.

Imagine shepherds hearing angels sing, wise men following a star, and a stable becoming the birthplace of the Prince of Peace.

Imagine, Isaiah said, good news preached to the poor, broken hearts mended, captives released, and the year of the favor of the Lord fulfilled.

Imagine a day when people who mourn will wear a garland instead of ashes, a mantle of praise instead of a faint spirit.

Imagine ruined cities being repaired, and destitute people decked out in wedding clothing.

Imagine righteousness and praise springing up like new shoots in the garden.

Imagine, John the Baptist said, one coming who is so great that I'm not worthy to carry his sandals.

Imagine one who will baptize you, soak you, saturate your life and your world with the Holy Spirit of God.

Perhaps imagination *is* better than knowledge.

Old Testament scholar, Walter Brueggemann writes that "the task of prophetic imagination is to cut through the numbness, to penetrate the self-deception, so that the God of endings is confessed as Lord." Our task during Advent is to allow the prophetic imagination which comes from Isaiah and John the Baptist to cut through the numbness of our lives, so that the God who comes to us in Bethlehem's stable can become our Lord.

Let's face it: We know the experience of spiritual numbness. Because of the wear and tear of the world in which we live, because of the pressure and tension we experience, because of the pain and disappointment we suffer, our souls can become insensitive and unfeeling. We can become convinced that there are no new possibilities for us or for our world. All too easily, we become uncaring, anesthetized by the incessant chatter of the world, unresponsive to the Spirit of God, unfeeling toward those who are closest to us.

But one day, when we least expect it, we run into someone like John the Baptist—someone who, by their words and their life, bears unmistakable witness to the possibility of a new light shining in the darkness. Somewhere along the road toward Bethlehem we hear a baby cry and it cuts through the numbness of our lives. Out on some quiet, barren plain, we feel the flutter of angel wings or catch a glimpse of an Eastern star. Some gift of imagination cuts through the numbness of our souls, and suddenly we envision new possibilities for our lives and our world.

Broken-hearted people can be healed.

Imprisoned folks can be set free.

Selfish people can become generous.

Takers can be transformed into givers.

The sorrowing can find joy.

Nations who have lived on the assumption of war can begin to live in peace.

On my desk is a small chunk of the Berlin Wall, chipped out with a screwdriver by a newspaper correspondent who was there when the gates were opened. Who imagined it? All the "knowledge" people were so preoccupied with the political and military assumptions of the Cold War era, that it took them totally by surprise. When we least expected it, the light of divine imagination cut through our political numbness and gave us a new way of seeing the world.

On a more personal level, I'm sure you've heard them this season: those Salvation Army bells. I've heard them all my life, and I must confess that I have been known to hustle by, avoiding eye contact with the ringer of the bell.

But I remember a particular day when I heard that bell as if for the first time. Amid the bustle of rushing through the pre-Christmas sales, it penetrated my numbness and reminded me of all those people who—far from worrying about trees and gifts—were wondering what they would eat, where they would find a diaper for the baby, and where they would spend the night. I vowed that day that I would never again pass one of those kettles without emptying the change from my pocket into it. The point is not the size of the gift. I help more people through my check to the church than I do through my change in the kettle. The point is that I am allowing the sound of that bell to cut through the numbness of my own soul and give me a Christlike compassion for the people around me.

Our Advent task is to allow the prophetic imagination to cut through our numbness, to penetrate our self-deception, so that the God who is revealed in the Jesus of Bethlehem becomes Lord in our lives and our world. That kind of imagination is better than knowledge.

Suggestions for Worship

Call to Worship (Luke 1:47-50):

PASTOR: My soul magnifies the Lord,

PEOPLE: And my spirit rejoices in God my Savior,

PASTOR: For the Mighty One has done great things for me, and holy is his name.

PEOPLE: His mercy is for those who fear him from generation to generation.

Act of Praise: Luke 1:46-55.

Suggested Hymns: "O Come, All Ye Faithful"; "O Come, O Come, Emmanuel"; "Angels We Have Heard on High."

Opening Prayer: Eternal God, out of whose divine imagination all creation came into being, as we prepare to celebrate the Word made flesh in Jesus, we pray that you will penetrate the numbness of our souls with the gift of divine imagination, that we might become part of your new creation. In the name and spirit of Jesus Christ, Amen.

Pastoral Prayer: Give to us open minds, O God, minds ready to receive and to welcome such new light of knowledge as it is Thy will to reveal. Let not the past ever be so dear to us as to set a limit to the future. Give us the courage to change our minds, when that is needed. Let us be tolerant of the thoughts of others, for we never know in what voice Thou wilt speak.

Wilt Thou keep our ears open to Thy voice, and make us a little more deaf to whispers of those who would persuade us from our duty, for we know in our hearts that only in Thy will is our peace. Amen (Peter Marshall, Prayer in the U.S. Senate, 28 February 1947).

DECEMBER 19, 1993

□

Fourth Sunday of Advent

God is present in reality no matter what illusions our practices and secularism imply.

The Sunday Lessons

Luke 1:26-38: The birth of Jesus was foretold by the angel Gabriel. Mary, greatly troubled by this strange visit, was told, "Do not be afraid, Mary, for you have found favor. . . . You will . . . bear a son, and you will name him Jesus. . . . God will give to him the throne of his ancestor David. . . . and of his kingdom there will be no end" (vv. 30-33). The virgin, too young and too unmarried, at first questioned, "How can this be?" Elizabeth, too old and too barren, had also conceived. With God, nothing is impossible. "I [am] the servant of the Lord; let it be with me according to your word" (v. 38).
II Samuel 7:8-16: God spoke with David through the prophet Nathan. "I took you from herding sheep, I have been with you, I have cut off your enemies." A promise was made. "I will appoint you a place, raise up offspring, establish your kingdom, Your offspring will build a house for my name, I will establish the throne forever." The words "establish the throne of his kingdom forever" (v. 13) declare the permanence of the throne of David.
Romans 16:25-27: Paul concludes his letter to the Romans with a doxology. It begins, "Now to God who is able to strengthen you . . ." (v. 25). Mysteries, unknown for ages, were revealed in Christ. The final praise is "to the only wise God, through Jesus Christ, to whom be the glory forever!" (v. 27).

Interpretation and Imagination

Forever is a very long time. Does anything last forever? Will the throne of David, foretold by a minor Jewish prophet now long dead, last forever? Is the kingdom, introduced by Mary's son, really more eternal than the sun?

Things like virginity, barrenness, offspring, a child who will rule, are landmark events in our lives. They are the stuff that make up vital statistics in the long history of mankind. A people, a throne, a nation, a temple are historic realities that are described as "established." But can we ever really believe Gabriel's prophecy—"of his kingdom there will be no end" (v. 33)?

Solomon's temple didn't last. Only the western wall of Herod's temple still stands. More wars have been fought at the gates of Jerusalem than at any city on this earth. The destruction has filled valleys and leveled hills. "David . . . died and was buried, and his tomb is with us to this day" (Acts 2:29). Indeed, David's tomb is an important pilgrimage for Christians and Jews even today. Scholars doubt that the site on a southwestern hill of Jerusalem is the King's true burial place, but that's not vitally important, is it?

What finally matters in this story, and the compelling truth that will ultimately hold us, is this: "Nothing will be impossible" (v. 37); "I [am] the servant of the Lord; let it be" (v. 38); and this, "To the only wise God . . . be glory forever" (Rom. 16:27). (JKB)

HOW CAN THIS BE?

Luke 1:26-38

A SERMON BY EMERSON S. COLAW

Years ago there was a Canadian evangelist by the name of Chuck Templeton. He had been a television personality, was converted, felt the call to evangelism, and began conducting city-wide crusades. Later, he left the ministry and returned to television. I happened to hear him when he appeared as a guest on a late-night show. He was asked, "Why did you leave the ministry?" He responded with candor: "I ceased to believe in the divinity of Christ."

Advent is about something more than the birth of a baby. Everyday there are thousands of births. Not all children are welcome. A newspaper article, reporting rising sexual activity among teenagers, said that young people worry more about pregnancy than they do about AIDS and other diseases (*USA Today*, 5 March 1991). Advent is a celebration of a unique child and one evidence of this distinctiveness, the lesson reminds us, is that Jesus was born of a virgin. When the angel Gabriel concluded the announcement that Mary would conceive and bear a son, she asked a perfectly natural question: "How can this be, since I am a virgin?" And the angel said to her, "The Holy Spirit will come upon you" (vv. 34-35).

The virgin birth is one of the controversial doctrines of the Christian faith. On one hand, this passage in Luke, as well as Matthew 1:18-25, clearly states that Jesus was to be born of Mary, without a human father. But the genealogies of Jesus, both in Luke and in Matthew, trace the genealogy of Jesus through Joseph, which is strange if Joseph was not his real father. And the rest of the New Testament does not make any reference to the Virgin Birth. But the fact that it is mentioned in two of the Gospels should suffice.

Professor William Barclay, in his commentary, leaves the decision to the individual. In a beautiful statement, he writes, "It may well be that the New Testament stories of the birth of Jesus are lovely, poetical ways of saying that, even if He had a human father, the Holy Spirit was operative in His birth in the most unique and special way. In this matter we may make our own decision" (William Barclay, *Daily Study Bible* "Gospel of Luke" [Philadelphia: Westminster Press, 1953], 7).

But the fact remains that unless the church finds a way of affirming the uniqueness of Jesus Christ, there is no tenable foundation for the Christian faith. I heard a theologian trying to counteract the current emphasis of some televangelists on the "Gospel of Success." He said that the story of Jesus was not a success story; it ended on a cross. And I thought, as I listened, if that were true there would be no Christians. Through the centuries there have been thousands of martyrs who have died for causes in which they believed. And while their courage may inspire us, we can't build a religion on it. Without the resurrection there would be no Christian faith. And without some evidence that the Christ is truly human and truly divine, the doctrine of salvation, as we know it, is without foundation.

The early church struggled with the idea that Jesus was both human and divine. Their Jewish legacy was monotheistic and the notion of Jesus being divine suggested two Gods. Furthermore, they were influenced by Greek philosophical tradition which taught that the divine cannot suffer. As all this suggests, there were many reasons why early Christian thinkers had difficulty seeing Jesus as both human and divine. But they finally hammered it out and said in the Creed, "We believe . . . in Jesus Christ, his only Son, our Lord, who was conceived by the Holy Spirit, born of the Virgin Mary, suffered under Pontius Pilate . . ." It was their way of affirming that he was indeed both human and divine.

Let's acknowledge that we are dealing with a mystery. On a recent Saturday afternoon I was mowing the lawn, and a neighbor came over for a brief visit. He asked if my sermon for Sunday was finished. My response was noncommittal. Then he asked about the subject of my sermon and I told him I was trying to answer the question, "Who is Jesus?" and gave him a thirty-second summary. His response was, "He's pretty complex, isn't he?"

Most parishioners know Jesus as a presence, as a friend, as a teacher and guide, and do not need clergy to confuse personal faith with needless questions. I have heard that on a seminary bulletin board there was this clipping: "Jesus said to them, 'Who do you say that I am?' and they replied, 'You are the eschatological manifestation of the ground of our being, the kerygma in which we find the ultimate meaning of our interpersonal relationship.' And Jesus said, 'What?' "

But the question of the uniqueness of Jesus is relevant. On one occasion I asked the leader of the Islamic community in the city where I live what the Islamic faith believes about Jesus. He replied that he is respected as a teacher, he is a prophet among many prophets, but he is not unique.

That's the point. If we did not believe he was unique, we would not be Christians. Some years ago I was invited to dialogue with a visiting Anglican bishop, who was on tour with the choir from his English cathedral. Because he had spent time in Africa and Iran, someone in the group asked for his reflections on interfaith dialogue. In response, he used an interesting phrase: "All of us have irreducible jealousies, things so precious we can't let them go." For those of us who are Christian, that irreducible jealousy, something we simply cannot let go, is a conviction about the uniqueness, the divinity, the deity of Jesus the Christ.

Yet, having said this, we must also affirm his humanity, as did the early church. His followers took his humanity for granted. His body was a normal human body like our own; familiar with weariness, hunger, thirst, pleasure, suffering, and death. I find that comforting. I have the assurance that he understands my every care and need.

I tend to believe his mental life was also like ours. Some insist that from childhood he knew his divine mission, and remind us that as a child in the temple he said, "Did you not know that I must be in my Father's house?" (Luke 2:49). But that could have been said by any Jewish boy reared in a devout home.

Of more importance for our purpose is the humanness of Jesus' spiritual life. He prayed as any struggling person might pray—sometimes in triumph, as on the Mount of Transfiguration; at other times in grief, as in Gethsemane. He lived his life in humble, filial dependence on God, and faced his temptation in the spirit of simple, childlike trust.

Yet I believe in the divinity of Christ. I believe because the early church, and those closest to Jesus, were so convinced, that they said when God chose to make a special entry into the world, he did so in a special way. They gave us the doctrine of the virgin birth.

I believe in the divinity of Christ because he revealed what God is like. Jesus was the vessel in which God revealed his own nature. The early church records Jesus saying, "Whoever has seen me has seen the Father" (John 14:9). Those early believers went out into the Roman Empire with a thrilling message: God was like Jesus!

A parent once asked me what she should have said when her four year old asked, as they were entering the church, "Does Jesus live here?" I said the proper answer would be, "No." The child was not thinking abstractly. Had the mother said yes, the child would want to see the apartment. Most of us are rather childlike when it comes to dealing with abstractions. "God is Spirit," yes; but we want the "Word made flesh." Jesus said, "Whoever has seen me has seen the Father."

I believe in the divinity of Christ because of the quality of his life. There was in him moral and spiritual superiority. I've always been glad saints are in stained glass windows and we don't have to live with them. Shakespeare had a sense of this when Iago said of Cassio, "He hath a daily beauty . . . that makes me feel ugly." We often feel uncomfortable in the presence of someone who is obviously morally and spiritually superior. Peter reveals something of this when he said, "Go away from me, Lord, for I am a sinful man!" (Luke 5:8). Yet when Jesus confronted the disciples with the question, "Who do you say that I am?" (Matt. 16:15 RSV), Simon Peter replied, "You are the Christ, the Son of the living God." At that moment, there were no creeds to tell them that. They knew it from the quality of life he lived in their midst.

Finally, I believe in the divinity of Christ because of what he can do for me and all of humankind. But if he was only a good man, while he might tower above the rest of us, he could not save us from our sins nor promise eternal life. I am glad Jesus was truly human, but it is his divinity that enables him to redeem us mortals. As the carol, "Good Christian Friends, Rejoice," says:

He hath opened heaven's door,
And ye are blest forevermore.
Christ was born for this . . .
Christ was born to save!

Mary asked, "How can this be, since I am a virgin?" and the reply was "the child to be born will be holy . . . the Son of God." And thus we celebrate at this holy season the birth of one who because he was truly human and truly divine is the Savior of the world!

In the forties, the premier preacher in this country was Harry Emerson Fosdick. He once said, "Of all foolish things, I can think of nothing more foolish, when looking back over our race's history and discerning amid its tragedy and trouble this loveliest, strongest, spiritual life that has visited the earth, than to try to minimize it. Upon the contrary, exalt him. If you cannot discover the divine in that life, then I do not see how you can discover it anywhere."

Suggestions for Worship

Call to Worship (Ps. 89:1-2, 5):

PASTOR: I will sing of your steadfast love, O LORD, forever;

PEOPLE: **With my mouth I will proclaim your faithfulness to all generations.**

PASTOR: I declare that your steadfast love is established forever; your faithfulness is as firm as the heavens.

PEOPLE: **Let the heavens praise your wonders, O LORD, your faithfulness in the assembly of the holy ones.**

Act of Praise: Psalm 89:1-4, 19-24.

Suggested Hymns: "Joy to the World"; "O Little Town of Bethlehem"; "Silent Night, Holy Night."

Opening Prayer: Almighty God, everlasting in time and eternal in being, glory to you in the highest. On earth let there be peace among those with whom you are pleased, and number us here with the builders and the makers. Beget in us ennobling aspirations, kindle in us healing resolutions, nurture in us kindly virtues. Purge us of hatred. Imbue us with love. Through Jesus Christ our Lord. Amen (Roy Pearson, *Prayers for All Occasions* [Valley Forge, Pa.: Judson Press, 1990], 25).

Pastoral Prayer: O mighty, glorious, loving God, we come to praise you. Through all time you constantly search for a people prepared to receive your great gift of love, personified in your Son, Jesus Christ. In this blessed season of expectancy, prepare our hearts to receive your gift anew . . . the wondrous gift of your incarnation. Let our lives evidence the incarnation of Christ in us. Relieve our minds of the conflicting message of the world's understanding of this season, by restoring to us the thrill of singing, "O come, O come, Emmanuel"—God with us!

May your church experience new life, rekindling its devotion to Christ and your kingdom. May we eliminate our preoccupation with "things" filled with nothingness, so that our energies can be used toward sharing the things that matter most—faith, hope, love, justice, and mercy toward all your children.

Hear our prayers in the name of the Christ, whose coming we symbolically await in this season of expectancy. Amen (Adapted from a prayer by Richard Pope, *Contemporary Altar Prayers*, vol. 8 [Lima, Ohio: C. S. S. Publishing Col., 1988], 10).

DECEMBER 26, 1993

□

First Sunday After Christmas

The signs of salvation are cherished in every generation. What are they today?

The Sunday Lessons

Luke 2:22-40: The Nunc Dimittis: "Now lettest thou thy servant depart in peace . . . for mine eyes have seen thy salvation" (vv. 29-30 KJV). The infant Jesus was presented in the temple and brought hope to Simeon, a devout and righteous man. But he spoke of controversy and conflict, "the falling and the rising of many in Israel" (v. 34). The devout prophetess Anna, who had spent a lifetime in the temple, was moved to rejoicing that day. "The favor of God was upon him" (v. 40).
Isaiah 61:10–62:3: The passage refers to righteousness throughout all nations. "The Lord GOD will cause righteousness and praise to spring up before all the nations" (61:11). Zion will be restored. "The nations shall see your vindication, and all the kings your glory" (62:2). Her deliverance will be like a blazing torch.
Galatians 4:4-7: "[Through God] you are no longer a slave but a child." Describing our relationship to God as either a slave or God's own child, Paul writes that we were enslaved, but then, in the fullness of time, the preexistent Christ was sent from God to be born of a woman. The Son came to redeem those under the law. The Spirit came to make our hearts cry "Abba! Father!" (v. 6).

Interpretation and Imagination

The signs of death and resurrection are often more visible, and thus more threatening, than the signs of life. Any reading of today's newspaper will reflect continuing violence and terror, nations that neglect human rights, crowded populations and hungry children, the idolization of technology, flagrant racism and sexism, ruthless grasping for power and manipulation of persons, a loss of personal morality, a domination of Third World nations by superpowers, reliance upon military power and arms. We may see the signs of death in our neighbors and families; in personal loneliness, apathy and despair; in alienation and broken relationships; in cynicism and spiritual dullness.

Can the same eyes that see the signs of death see signs of deliverance and salvation? The signs of salvation are seen when lives are transformed through an encounter with the living Christ; when people who belong to Christ gladly bear his name, his style, his values.

Signs of salvation appear whenever persons long for more humane life, struggle for liberation, and oppose any system that oppresses. Signs of salvation appear in our midst when the church becomes a pilgrim people, guided by the transcending love of God. Signs of salvation appear in the church when individual Christians reflect their deep concern for sharing the Christ, for mutual care, for costlier commitment, for genuine unity.

Signs of salvation are the new garments of baptism—compassion, kindness, patience, and especially, love. Begin with the Word of God and tell us what you've seen and heard today. (JKB)

WHAT TO DO UNTIL THE MESSIAH COMES

Luke 2:25

A SERMON BY EMERSON S. COLAW

Yesterday was Christmas. In the church where I have an office, the parishioners write devotionals for an Advent and Christmastide booklet. One person included this prayer: "Dear God, every year I get so excited about Christmas and so tired of shopping and so concerned about how the money is holding out. This is a fun season, but it is also a holy season. Help me remember that." I saw a cartoon which showed a man saying, "Of course, I'm depressed; 'tis the season to be jolly."

Another person shared this parable from an anonymous source. "It was late Christmas Eve. The night watchman of a large department store, now closed until after Christmas, was setting out on his usual rounds. Floor after floor presented the same wild disorder: piles of mixed-up goods; boxes and cartons of all shapes and sizes; indeed, a minor cyclone could not have left a worse jumble behind. But a bigger shock awaited the security guard, when, under one of the counters, he found a man who had apparently been pushed aside and trampled in the mad rush of shoppers. The man was an absolute stranger, and no item of his clothing provided a single clue to his identity. But when his body was examined, nail prints were found in the palms of his hands."

I share this, not to encourage any feelings of guilt about the way we observed the season. Most of us have doubts already. We know how easy it is to miss the true significance of Christmas. One magazine carried a two-page ad. On one side, in beautiful color, was a bottle of Scotch whiskey. On the other was this message: "Go ahead, spend the extra money. It's Christmas, isn't it?" Obviously, from the Christian perspective, that isn't what the Mass of Christ is all about! And that is, after all, the source of the word *Christmas*.

We're not the first to encounter this problem. The early church faced the Roman pagan celebration of the winter festival. One reason December 25 was chosen to celebrate the birth of Christ was to provide a religious festival for the Christians at a time when the pagans were having their winter orgies!

As the church grew in strength it tried hard to root out the vestiges of the Yule festival that remained in the Mass of Christ. That it was not totally successful is readily apparent. In common practice, Yule and Christmas came to be combined. But rather than lamenting this, I think we should acknowledge that much of what has come from the Yule festival is good. Christmas trees come from pre-Christian times, but in a day when families frequently move, children get a sense of continuity from seeing the same ornaments on the tree.

Santa Claus is a corruption of the Dutch St. Nicholas. But much of us need a reason for offering a gift. And it can be a practical way of expressing love.

We are also aware that for some the holiday season is a time of sadness and depression. There are youngsters, and possibly adults, who get overexcited and exhausted, and the holiday is experienced as a letdown. Some people are separated from loved ones and ruin their holiday by dwelling on the separation. Others are saddened because the holiday is linked with loved ones now deceased.

Nevertheless, for most people this is a time of lift and exhilaration. Studies suggest that more sick people get better at Christmas than at other times. Some even decide to live a little longer because they want to see the holly and the mistletoe again; they want to receive gifts and to give to their friends. There are fewer divorces than at any other time of the year. It's a time for getting families together. It provides a reason to maintain friendships or reestablish them. Recently I received a letter from someone I have not seen for a long time. He began by saying, "As Christmas came, I decided it was time to renew a cherished friendship."

It's one thing to have a celebration. It's another to know why we celebrate. One of the carols we sang during the Advent season was "Joy to the world; the Lord is come." In the lesson from Luke, Simeon rejoiced because "Mine eyes have seen thy salvation" (2:30), and Anna spoke of him to all who were "looking for the redemption of Jerusalem" (2:38). These, however, were expressions of hope. The baby was born but the messianic promise was yet to be fulfilled.

In the lesson there is a suggestion that Simeon had been waiting for the coming of the Lord's Christ, the Messiah, who would provide for the "consolation of Israel" (v. 25), the "redemption of Jerusalem." For the Jew, the coming of the Messiah was tinged with nationalism. The Messiah, born from the line of David, would lead the people of Israel to power and rule them brilliantly. That was their vision of the Messiah. In other words, the Jewish expectation of the Messiah was shaped by the failures of some of their kings and the burdens the people experienced under the oppression of foreign armies. The Messiah would bring peace, justice, deliverance, and happiness.

When we, as Christians, affirm that the Messiah has come, our Jewish friends ask how we can say that! Justice does not run down as waters. Nations have not beaten their swords into plowshares. The lion does not lie down with the lamb. Cain still lifts his hand against his brother. Suffering and pain are still here. The poor are still oppressed. Since Jewish literature is rich with promises of peace and prosperity when the Messiah comes, how can we celebrate that fact that he has come?

Our answer, of course, is that Christ's promised kingdom is inward and spiritual. The New Testament Messiah is more spiritual than material. He came to reveal the suffering love of God. He came to forgive our sins and empower us to live lives of faithfulness and courage. Matthew tells us that when John the Baptizer was preaching in the wilderness, he said, "Repent. . . . Prepare the way of the Lord. . . . I baptize you with water. . . . He will baptize you with the Holy Spirit" (Matt. 3:2, 11).

We also believe that the New Testament affirms, although not with the clarity we would wish, that Christ shall return and do many of the things the Old Testament ascribes to the Messiah. He will appear as judge of the world. He will destroy the hostile world power. The dead shall be resurrected and judged. The kingdoms of this world shall become the kingdom of our Lord. The Messiah has come, and the Messiah is coming.

The early church, of course, had the strong conviction that the return of Jesus (known as the Second Coming) would be immediate. Many of the teachings of the apostle Paul must be interpreted in the light of this expectation. It was the Apostle's belief that Christ would return soon, usher in the millennium, and draw this age of apostasy and sin to a close. Thus, he faced with those new Christians this question: What shall we do until the Messiah comes?

We sing and celebrate because the Christ child was born. But the Messiah, who will bring in a new world order, is yet to come. How do we prepare ourselves for this coming?

First, we can let the love of God so fill our hearts that we overcome greed. The world was tense during the fall and winter of 1990–91 because of the Iraqi invasion of Kuwait. Historians will discuss for years why this event happened. It seems, however, that greed was a major factor. Our lesson for the day tells us that Simeon rejoiced when he saw the child, Jesus. The next time Jesus was in the temple was when, at the age of twelve, he was talking with the learned teachers of the Law. The final time was when he cleansed the temple of those who were defiling it with their greed.

Greed is at the heart of so many of our problems. The newspaper is filled with stories of politicians, financial leaders, and even clergy who, because of greed, destroy the trust required to have a sound communal life and responsible society. In almost every state we support lotteries, which means I hope to become rich at the expense of thousands of people who lost.

The Christmas story reminds us that God so loved, he gave! The cancer of greed is destroyed when we give. Even children derive satisfaction from giving. Just watch how a child's eyes will glisten as the parent opens the gift the youngster made at school.

Second, we prepare ourselves for his coming by giving time to the Scriptures. It is of interest that Bible Sunday comes during Advent. It is in the Bible that we discover the story of the birth, life, teachings, death, and resurrection of the Messiah. It is in the Bible that we come in touch with the expectation of the early church as to the "coming again," rich with promise.

Third, we prepare ourselves for his coming by living as though the Messiah may come today! Years ago I was a guest preacher in Pennsylvania. Following the service, the host pastor, shared a personal experience while driving me to the airport. He had served some years in a mining town. One day he received a call to conduct the funeral service for a famous actress who had been killed in an accident. She had attended the Sunday school at his church as a child, and that is why he was called, though he did not know the family.

When he entered the parlor at the funeral home, only a few people were there, and none from the entertainment world except the man with whom the actress had been living. Her mother was the first to greet him, and after a few moments of visiting she asked, "Reverend, tell me. Is my little girl in heaven?" How should he answer? Here was a young woman who had been reared in austere, difficult circumstances in a coal-mining town. Because of her natural beauty, she had received attention, and had been commercially exploited. She had been on drugs. She had moved from bedroom to bedroom. Perhaps she had been more sinned against than she had sinned. "Is my little girl in heaven?" Here is a mother waiting for an answer. What should he say? "Your daughter," he replied "is in the hands of God who knows the secrets of our hearts and whose mercy is everlasting. That's all we need to know."

Here was a young woman whose life had been taken in a moment of time. Then the anxious question: "Is my little girl in heaven?" We prepare for the Messiah by living as though he may come at any moment. It is not enough that the Christ was born in history. He must be born in you and me. As the children's song says, "Come into my heart, Lord Jesus. Come in today, come in to stay. Come into my heart, Lord Jesus."

A sincere believer once asked me, "Are you saved?" I replied, "I have been saved; I am being saved; I shall be saved."

Has the Messiah come? We answer the Messiah has come, the Messiah is here right now as a living presence in the hearts of believers, and the Messiah will come, bringing justice, peace, and hope. "Let every heart prepare him room."

Suggestions for Worship

Call to Worship (Ps. 111:2-4, 6, 9-10):

PASTOR: Great are the works of the LORD,

PEOPLE: Full of honor and majesty is his work,

PASTOR: The LORD is gracious and merciful.

PEOPLE: He has shown his people the power of his works,

PASTOR: He sent redemption to his people; he has commanded his covenant forever.

PEOPLE: Holy and awesome is his name. His praise endures forever.

Act of Praise: Psalm 111.

Suggested Hymns: "Joy to the World"; "It Came Upon the Midnight Clear"; "What Child Is This."

Opening Prayer: O God, during the Christmas season, we heard the story of Jesus' birth; we saw beauty in simple and profound places; we celebrated the wondrous gift of eternal love. Move us to keep these things through all the coming days and ponder them in our hearts. Don't let us slip too quickly into the mundane, but keep the glow of what we have experienced brightly burning through the year to come. Through Jesus Christ our Lord. Amen.

Pastoral Prayer: God of glory, you have made us to experience mystery, wonder, and all the amazing joy that surrounds the celebration of Jesus' birth. From silent night to Sunday morning, we continue to ponder the wonder of Your glory, in the birth of Jesus, the Word made flesh, the Incarnation.

We sing our songs of celebration, for the gift of Your Light to the world, the gift of your Love to us, the gift of Your Life to all who believe.

Turn us to translating our celebration into service, the Christmas hope into hopeful actions, Christmas peace into peacemaking, Christmas joy into continuing gladness, Christmas goodwill into acts of goodness, Christmas greetings into constant caring, that Your Word may take flesh in us, Your love be made manifest through us.

In our celebrations we pray for those who have circumstances depriving them of Christmas joy: the hungry who must think constantly of finding food for their body, the lonely who sense their aloneness more in this season than at any other time, the grieving who feel the depth of loss as they remember past Christmases shared with others, the unemployed who are denied the opportunity to give in this season of giving.

As we continue in our worship, keep a healthy tension in us, of both celebrating the good news of Christmas, and confessing our failure to care for those for whom we can be good news. Amen. (A prayer by Larry L. Hard, *Contemporary Altar Prayers*, vol. 8 [Lima, Ohio: C. S. S. Publishing Co., 1988], 16).

Section II

□

SERMON RESOURCES

LESSON GUIDE
BASED ON THE COMMON LECTIONARY (1983), Cycle A

Sunday	Season	First Lesson	O.T. Theme	Second Lesson	Epistle Theme	Gospel Lesson	Gospel Theme	Psalm
1/3/93	2nd After Christmas	Isa. 60:1-6	Your light has come	Eph. 3:1-12	The mystery made known	Matt. 2:1-12	The visit of the Magi	Ps.72:1-14
1/10/93	Epiphany 1	Isa. 42:1-9	The Servant of the Lord	Acts 10:34-43	Peter's sermon at Cornelius' house	Matt. 3:13-17	The Baptism of Jesus	Ps. 29
1/17/93	Epiphany 2	Isa. 49:1-7	The Servant of the Lord will restore	I Cor. 1:1-9	God's grace has enriched you in every way.	John 1:29-34	Jesus the Lamb of God	Ps. 40:1-11
1/24/93	Epiphany 3	Isa. 9:1-4	A light has dawned	I Cor. 1:10-17	Divisions in the church	Matt. 4:12-23	Jesus begins to preach and calls disciples.	Ps. 27:1-6
1/31/93	Epiphany 4	Micah 6:1-8	What does the Lord require?	I Cor. 1:18-31	Chose the weak to shame the strong	Matt. 5:1-12	The Beatitudes	Ps. 37:1-11

2/7/93	Epiphany 5	Isa. 58:3-9*a*	True fasting—share, provide, clothe	I Cor. 2:1-11	Wisdom from the Spirit	Matt. 5:13-16	Salt of the Earth, Light of the World	Ps. 112:4-9
2/14/93	Epiphany 6	Deut. 30:15-20	Prosperity after turning to the Lord	I Cor. 3:1-9	I planted, Apollos watered, God made it grow	Matt. 5:17-26	Righteous-ness that surpasses the law	Ps. 119:1-8 (Response 3)
2/21/93	Last of Epiphany (Trans-figuration)	Exod. 24:12-18	Moses went up on the mountain	II Pet. 1:16-21	He received honor and glory from God	Matt. 17:1-9	The trans-figuration	Ps. 2:6-11
2/28/93	Lent 1	Gen. 2:4*b*-9, 15-17, 25; 3:1-7	The fall of man	Rom. 5:12-19	Death through Adam, life through Christ	Matt. 4:1-11	The temp-tation of Jesus	Ps. 130
3/7/93	Lent 2	Gen. 12:1-4*a* (4*b*-8)	The call of Abram	Rom. 4:1-5 (6-12) 13-17	Abraham justified by faith	John 3:1-17	Jesus teaches Nicodemus	Ps. 33:18-22
3/14/93	Lent 3	Exod. 17:3-7	Water from the rock	Rom. 5:1-11	Justified through faith we have peace	John 4:5-26 (27-42)	Samaritan woman at the well	Ps. 95
3/21/93	Lent 4	I Sam. 16:1-13	Not outward appearance, but the heart	Eph. 5:8-14	Once as in darkness, now in light	John 9:1-41	Jesus heals a man born blind	Ps. 23

3/28/93	Lent 5	Ezek. 37:1-14	The valley of dry bones	Rom. 8:6-11	Not controlled by a sinful nature	John 11:17-45	Jesus raises Lazarus	Ps. 116:1-9
4/4/93	Lent 6 Passion/Palm Sunday	Isa. 50:4-9*a*	Offered my back to smiters	Phil. 2:5-11	Obedient to the cross	Matt. 21:1-11	The triumphal entry	Ps. 118:19-29
						Matt. 26:14–27:66 or Matt 27:11-54	Betrayed, arrested, tried, crucified	Ps. 31:9-16
4/11/93	Easter Sunday	Acts 10:34-43	Ate and drank with risen Christ	Col. 3:1-4	Look for the things of heaven	John 20:1-18	Mary found the empty tomb	Ps. 118:14-24
4/18/93	Easter 2	Acts 2:14*a*, 22-32	Peter's sermon/But God raised him	I Pet. 1:3-9	Though you have not seen him, you love him	John 20:19-31	Thomas says, Unless I see	Ps. 16:5-11
4/25/93	Easter 3	Acts 2:14*a*, 36-41	Peter preaches, Repent, be baptized	I Pet. 1:17-23	Born of imperishable seed	Luke 24:13-35	Road to Emmaus appearance	Ps. 116:12-29
5/2/93	Easter 4	Acts 2:42-47	Fellowship of believers	I Pet. 2:19-25	Like sheep gone astray	John 10:1-10	Shepherd and flock	Ps. 23
5/9/93	Easter 5	Acts 7:55-60	Stoning of Stephen	I Pet. 2:2-10	Living stone, chosen people	John 14:1-14	Father's house, many rooms	Ps. 31:1-8
5/16/93	Easter 6	Acts 17:22-31	Paul in Athens; to unknown god	I Pet. 3:13-22	Baptism saves through resurrection	John 14:15-21	Another counselor, Holy Spirit	Ps. 66:8-20

5/23/93	Easter 7	Acts 1:6-14	You shall receive power	I Pet. 4:12-14; 5:6-11	Cast all cares on him	John 17:1-11	Jesus' high priestly prayer	Ps. 68:1-10
5/30/93	Pentecost Sunday	Isa. 44:1-8	Israel the chosen	I Cor. 12:3*b*-13	About spiritual gifts	John 7:37-39	Risen Christ breathed Holy Spirit	Ps. 104:24-34
6/6/93	Trinity Sunday	Deut. 4:32-40	By his presence and great strength	II Cor. 13:5-14	Love of God, Grace of Christ, Fellowship Spirit	Matt. 28:16-20	Baptizing in the name, Father, Son Holy Spirit	Ps. 33:1-12
6/13/93	2nd After Pentecost	Gen. 25:19-34	Twins born to Rebekah	Rom. 5:6-11	God demonstrates his love	Matt. 9:35–10:8	The workers are few	Ps. 46
6/20/93	3rd After Pentecost	Gen. 28:10-17	Jacob's ladder dream at Bethel	Rom. 5:12-19	Life through Christ	Matt. 10:24-33	Servant like his master	Ps. 91:1-10
6/27/93	4th After Pentecost	Gen. 32:22-32	Jacob is named Israel	Rom. 6:3-11	Newness of life	Matt. 10:34-42	To set one against own family	Ps. 17:1-7
7/4/93	5th After Pentecost	Ex. 1:6-14, 22; 2:1-10	The birth of Moses	Rom. 7:14-25*a*	Struggling with sin	Matt. 11:25-30	My yoke is easy	Ps. 124
7/11/93	6th After Pentecost	Ex. 2:11-22	Moses flees to Midian	Rom. 8:9-17	Controlled by the Spirit	Matt. 13:1-9, 18-23	Parable of the Sower	Ps. 69:6-15
7/18/93	7th After Pentecost	Ex. 3:1-12	Moses and the burning bush	Rom. 8:18-25	Future glory	Matt. 13:24-30	Parable of the Weeds	Ps. 103:1-13

7/25/93	8th After Pentecost	Ex. 3:13-20	I AM has sent you	Rom. 8:26-30	All things work together for good	Matt. 13:44-52	Parables of the Treasure, Pearl and Net	Ps. 105:1-11
8/1/93	9th After Pentecost	Ex. 12:1-14	The Passover	Rom. 8:31-39	More than conquerors	Matt. 14:13-21	Feeding the five thousand	Ps. 143:1-10
8/8/93	10th After Pentecost	Ex. 14:19-31	Crossing the Red Sea	Rom. 9:1-5	God's chosen people	Matt. 14:22-33	Jesus walks on the water	Ps. 106:4-12
8/15/93	11th After Pentecost	Ex. 16:2-15	Manna and Quail	Rom. 11:13-16, 29-32	God's gifts and call are irrevocable	Matt. 15:21-28	Faith of the Canaanite Woman	Ps. 78:1-3, 10-20
8/22/93	12th After Pentecost	Ex. 17:1-7	Water from the rock	Rom. 11:33-36	The depths of the riches, wisdom, and knowledge	Matt. 16:13-20	Peter's Confession at Caesarea Philippi	Ps. 95
8/29/93	13th After Pentecost	Ex. 19:1-9	God's promise from Mount Sinai	Rom. 12:1-13	Bodies as living sacrifices	Matt. 16:21-28	Jesus predicts his death	Ps. 114
9/5/93	14th After Pentecost	Ex. 19:16-24	God's warning from Mount Sinai	Rom. 13:1-10	Submission to authorities	Matt. 18:15-20	If one sins against you	Ps. 115:1-11
9/12/93	15th After Pentecost	Ex. 20:1-20	The Ten Command-ments	Rom. 14:5-12	We live to the Lord	Matt. 18:21-35	Parable of the unmer-ciful servant	Ps. 19:7-14
9/19/93	16th After Pentecost	Ex. 32:1-14	The golden calf	Phil. 1:21-27	To live is Christ, to die is gain	Matt. 20:1-16	Parable of workers in the vineyard	Ps. 106:7-8, 19-23

9/26/93	17th After Pentecost	Ex. 33:12-23	Moses and the glory of the Lord	Phil. 2:1-13	Imitating Christ's humility	Matt. 21:28-32	Parable of two sons asked to work	Ps. 99
10/3/93	18th After Pentecost	Num. 27:12-23	Joshua to succeed Moses	Phil. 3:12-21	Pressing on toward the goal	Matt. 21:33-43	Parable of rebellious tenants	Ps. 81:1-10
10/10/93	19th After Pentecost	Deut. 34:1-12	The death of Moses	Phil. 4:1-9	Rejoice always; think nobly, rightly, purely	Matt. 22:1-14	Parable of the banquet and refused invitations	Ps. 135:1-14
10/17/93	20th After Pentecost	Ruth 1:1-19*a*	Where you go I will go	I Thess. 1:1-10	The Thessa-lonians' faith	Matt. 22:15-22	Paying taxes to Caesar	Ps. 146
10/24/93	21st After Pentecost	Ruth 2:1-13	Ruth meets Boaz	I Thess. 2:1-8	Not to please men but God	Matt. 22:34-46	The greatest command-ment	Ps. 128
10/31/93	22nd After Pentecost	Ruth 4:7-17	Boaz marries Ruth	I Thess. 2:9-13, 17-20	Message re-received as word of God	Matt. 23:1-12	Seven woes	Ps. 127
11/7/93	23rd After Pentecost	Amos 5:18-24	The day of the Lord	I Thess. 4:13-18	The coming of the Lord	Matt. 25:1-13	Parable of wise and foolish virgins	Ps. 50:7-15
11/14/93	24th After Pentecost	Zeph. 1:7, 12-18	The great day of the Lord	I Thess. 5:1-11	Like a thief in the night	Matt. 25:14-30	Parable of the talents	Ps. 76

11/21/93	Last of Pentecost (Christ the King)	Ezek. 34:11-16, 20-24	Judging between sheep	I Cor. 15:20-28	Everything put under his feet	Matt. 25:31-46	The sheep and the goats	Ps. 23
11/28/93	Advent 1	Isa. 63:16–64:8	Rend the heavens and come down	I Cor. 1:3-9	Blameless on the day of the Lord	Mark 13:32-37	The day and hour unknown	Ps. 80:1-7
12/5/93	Advent 2	Isa. 40:1-11	Comfort for God's people	II Pet. 3:8-15*a*	One day like a thousand years	Mark 1:1-8	John the Baptist preparing the way	Ps. 85:8-13
12/12/93	Advent 3	Isa. 61:1-4, 8-11	Year of the Lord's favor	I Thess. 5:16-24	May the God of peace sanctify you	John 1:6-8, 19-28	A witness to the true light	Luke 1:46*b*-55
12/19/93	Advent 4	II Sam. 7:8-16	God's promise to David	Rom. 16:25-27	Mystery now revealed	Luke 1:26-38	Birth of Jesus foretold	Ps. 89:1-4, 19-24
12/26/93	1st After Christmas	Isa. 61:10–62:3	Clothed with garments of salvation	Gal. 4:4-7	God's son, born of a woman	Luke 2:22-40	"My eyes have beheld salvation." Simeon	Ps. 111

TEXT GUIDE
THE REVISED COMMON LECTIONARY (1992), CYCLE A

Sunday	Gospel Lesson	First Lesson	Second Lesson	Psalm
1/3/93	Matt. 2:1-12	Isa. 60:1-6	Eph. 3:1-12	Ps. 72:1-7, 10-14
1/10/93	Matt. 3:13-17	Isa. 42:1-19	Acts 10:34-43	Ps. 29
1/17/93	John 1:29-42	Isa. 49:1-17	I Cor. 1:1-9	Ps. 40:1-11
1/24/93	Matt. 4:12-23	Isa. 9:1-4	I Cor. 1:10-18	Ps. 27:1, 4-9
1/31/93	Matt. 5:1-12	Micah 6:1-8	I Cor. 1:18-31	Ps. 15
2/7/93	Matt. 5:13-16	Isa. 58:1-9*a* (9*b*-12)	I Cor. 2:1-12 (13-16)	Ps. 112:1-10
2/14/93	Matt. 5:21-37	Deut. 30:15-20	I Cor. 3:1-9	Ps. 119:1-8
2/21/93	Matt. 17:1-9	Exod. 24:12-18	II Pet. 1:16-21	Ps. 99
2/28/93	Matt. 4:1-11	Gen. 2:15-17; 3:1-7	Rom. 5:12-19	Ps. 32
3/7/93	John 3:1-7	Gen. 12:1-4*a*	Rom. 4:1-5, 13-17	Ps. 121
3/14/93	John 4:5-42	Exod. 17:1-7	Rom. 5:1-11	Ps. 95
3/21/93	John 9:1-41	I Sam. 16:1-13	Eph. 5:8-14	Ps. 23
3/28/93	John 11:1-45	Ezek. 37:1-14	Rom. 8:6-11	Ps. 130
4/4/93	Matt. 21:1-11; 26:14–27:66 or Matt. 27:11-54	Isa. 50:4-9*a*	Phil. 2:5-11	Ps. 31:9-16; 118:1-2, 19-29
4/11/93	John 20:1-18 or Matt. 28:1-10	Acts 10:34-43	Col. 3:1-4	Ps. 118:1-2, 14-24

4/18/93	John 20:19-31	Acts 2:14*a*, 22-32	I Pet. 1:3-9	Ps. 16
4/25/93	Luke 24:13-35	Acts 2:14*a*, 36-41	I Pet. 1:17-23	Ps. 116:1-2, 12-19
5/2/93	John 10:1-10	Acts 2:42-47	I Pet. 2:19-25	Ps. 23
5/9/93	John 14:1-14	Acts 7:55-60	I Pet. 2:2-10	Ps. 31:1-5, 15-16
5/16/93	John 14:15-21	Acts 17:22-31	I Pet. 3:13-22	Ps. 66:8-20
5/23/93	John 17:1-11	Acts 1:6-14	I Pet. 4:12-14; 5:6-11	Ps. 68:1-10, 32-35
5/30/93	John 7:37-39	Acts 2:1-21	I Cor. 12:3*b*-13	Ps. 104:24-34, 35*b*
6/6/93	Matt. 28:16-20	Gen. 1:1–2:4*a*	II Cor. 13:11-13	Ps. 8
6/13/93	Matt. 9:35–10:8 (9-23)	Gen. 18:1-15	Rom. 5:1-8	Ps. 116:1-2, 12-19
6/20/93	Matt. 10:24-39	Gen. 21:8-21	Rom. 6:1*b*-11	Ps. 86:1-10, 16-17 *or* Ps. 17
6/27/93	Matt. 10:40-42	Gen. 22:1-14	Rom. 6:12-23	Ps. 13
7/4/93	Matt. 11:16-19, 25-30	Gen. 24:34-38, 42-49, 58-67	Rom. 7:15-25*a*	Ps. 45:10-17, *or* Ps. 72
7/11/93	Matt. 13:1-9, 18-23	Gen. 25:19-34	Rom. 8:1-11	Ps. 119:105-112 *or* Ps. 25
7/18/93	Matt. 13:24-30, 36-43	Gen. 28:10-19*a*	Rom. 8:12-25	Ps. 139:1-12, 23-24
7/25/93	Matt. 13:31-33, 44-52	Gen. 29:15-28	Rom. 8:26-39	Ps. 105:1-11, 45*b*
8/1/93	Matt. 14:13-21	Gen. 32:22-31	Rom. 9:1-5	Ps. 17:1-7, 15
8/8/93	Matt. 14:22-33	Gen. 37:1-4, 12-28	Rom. 10:5-15	Ps. 105:1-6, 16-22, 45*b*

8/15/93	Matt. 15:(10-20) 21-28	Gen. 45:1-15	Rom. 11:1-2*a*, 29-32	Ps. 133
8/22/93	Matt. 16:13-20	Exod. 1:8–2:10	Rom. 12:1-8	Ps. 124
8/29/93	Matt. 16:21-28	Exod. 3;1-15	Rom. 12:9-21	Ps. 105:1-6, 23-26, 45*b*
9/5/93	Matt. 18:15-20	Exod. 12:1-14	Rom. 13:8-14	Ps. 149
9/12/93	Matt. 18-21-35	Exod. 14:19-31	Rom. 14:1-12	Exod. 15:1*b*-11, 20-21
9/19/93	Matt. 20:1-16	Exod. 16:2-15	Phil. 1:21-30	Ps. 105:1-6, 37-45
9/26/93	Matt. 21:23-32	Exod. 17:1-7	Phil. 2:1-13	Ps. 78:1-4, 12-16
10/3/93	Matt. 21:33-43	Exod. 20:1-4, 7-9, 12-20	Phil. 3:4*b*-14	Ps. 19
10/10/93	Matt. 22:1-14	Exod. 32:1-14	Phil. 4:1-9	Ps. 106:1-6, 16-23
10/17/93	Matt. 22:15-22	Exod. 33:12-23	I Thess. 1:1-10	Ps. 99
10/24/93	Matt. 22:34-46	Deut. 34:1-12	I Thess. 2:1-8	Ps. 90:1-6, 13-17
10/31/93	Matt. 23:1-12	Josh. 3:7-17	I Thess. 2:9-13	Ps. 107:1-7, 33-37
11/7/93	Matt. 25:1-13	Josh. 24:1-3*a*, 14-25	I Thess. 4:13-18	Ps. 78:1-7
11/14/93	Matt. 25:14-30	Judg. 4:1-7	I Thess. 5:1-11	Ps. 123 *or* Ps. 76
11/21/93	Matt. 25:31-46	Ezek. 34:11-16, 20-24	Eph. 1:15-23	Ps. 100
11/28/93	Mark 13:24-37	Isa. 64:1-9	I Cor. 1:3-9	Ps. 80:1-7, 17-19
12/5/93	Mark 1:1-8	Isa. 40:1-11	II Pet. 3:8-15*a*	Ps. 85:1-2, 8-13
12/12/93	John 1:6-8, 19-28	Isa. 61:1-4, 8-11	I Thess. 5:16-24	Ps. 126
12/19/93	Luke 1:26-38	II Sam. 7:1-11, 16	Rom. 16:25-27	Luke 1:47-55
12/26/93	Luke 2:22-40	Isa. 61:10–62:3	Gal. 4:4-7	Ps. 148

Children's Sermons

□

Louise Stowe Johns

There are varied ways one can include children in the worshiping community. The most familiar, but also the most difficult, is a children's sermon. Included in this book are ten children's sermons, briefly stated. There is one for each month, omitting July and August. The lectionary is used, making them congruent with other elements in the service. The sermons do not fall on a consistent Sunday of the month; only one is on the first Sunday due to that being the most likely Sunday for Communion.

Here are guidelines for developing and delivering children's sermons:

1. Be concrete; most children are not able to think abstractly. Avoid "why" questions (an abstraction). "What" questions are more within their thinking. Use techniques and images that appeal to the senses.
2. Stay away from object lessons; they rarely communicate the intended message. When your sermon is dependent on saying that some thing is *like* something else, you've probably lost them.
3. Don't use the children's sermon to preach to the adults.
4. Keep it simple. It is not possible to deal with the full range of a theological issue. However, simple is not the same as shallow.
5. Remember that calling the children forward, sitting with them, knowing names, praying together are all elements in the sermon.
6. Stories work extremely well. Any lection that is a story is a potential source. It may be made contemporary; children's sense of history is of limited development.
7. *Questions are not rhetorical.* If you pose one, give time for at least a few responses.
8. Be enthusiastic and energetic.

9. Close with prayer, and if possible, have the children join hands. Encourage them to say "Amen," by repeating the phrase, "And let the children say, Amen."

BAPTISM OF JESUS

January 10, 1993

TEXT: **Matthew 3:13-17**

THEME: God is pleased when people—infants, children, adults—are baptized.

Note: If you have not read the section on children's sermons, page 417, please do so.

If the baptismal font is not near where children usually sit for the sermon, invite them to gather around the font. If it is a bowl, it should be put in the middle where all can see.

What is in this? *Encourage them to put hands in the water. Talk with them about the feel and the sound of the water.* Do you know what we use this for?

Have any of you been baptized? *Know as much as possible who has, encouraging those who don't respond.* Some of you were babies when you were baptized. We baptize people when they are all ages. *Get the children seated.*

There's a story about Jesus I want to tell you. *Summarize Matthew 3:13-17.*

Who do you think said, "This is my Son, the Beloved, with whom I am well pleased"? *Affirm answers: "heavenly parent," "father," "God."* God was pleased when God's child, Jesus, was baptized. And, everytime someone is baptized, God is pleased again, because that means someone wants to be like Jesus. I like to think about God's being happy.

Let's join hands and pray.

We are glad, heavenly parent, that you were pleased with your son. We want to please you, too. And let the children say, Amen.

FIRST SUNDAY IN LENT

February 28, 1993

TEXT: **Genesis 2:25–3:7**

THEME: The best way to deal with guilt is to ask for forgiveness from the one you hurt. God forgives readily.

Note: If you have not read the section on children's sermons, page 417, please do so.

Sometimes we do things we shouldn't. Sometimes we don't share with a brother or sister, or we throw a toy when we are mad. This week I . . . *relate a concrete experience of doing something wrong for which you made amends.*

I felt really bad inside. *Tell what you did to make amends.* When we ask forgiveness from the person we have hurt, we are doing what God wants us to do. The minute we say, "I'm sorry," that is when God forgives us—as quick as a snap of the fingers.

Let's join hands and pray.

Dear loving God, thank you for forgiving us. Help us not to repeat the same wrong things that hurt others. And let the children say, Amen.

THIRD SUNDAY IN LENT

March 14, 1993

TEXT: **Psalm 95**

THEME: God wants us to express our praise. Although we can do that alone, we are encouraged to praise God together.

Note: If you have not read the section on children's sermons, page 417, please do so.

Have a copy of the Good News Bible in hands.

There's a book in the Bible—almost in the middle *(open up to Psalms)*—called Psalms. It sounds like "song," and that is what is in Psalms: songs to God and about God.

Psalm 95 tells about worshiping God—a happy time. It invites us to sing, to make a joyful noise to God. Let me show you a picture in this Bible. *Turn to Psalm 150.* What are the people doing?

We can also praise God by ourselves. *Turn to Psalm* 9. What is this person doing? It's good for us at the beginning and end of the day to tell God how great God is.

Psalm 95 tells us to go into a place of worship—like our sanctuary—and sing. It also tells us we can show that we believe God is great by kneeling. So by what we say and what we do, we show we believe in God. We come to the altar rail to pray and to receive Communion. Let's all find a place at the altar rail and kneel to have our closing prayer.

Let's pray.

We praise you, great God, and are happy to be in your church today to worship you with our special church family. And let the children say, Amen.

SECOND SUNDAY OF EASTER

April 18, 1993

TEXT: **John 20:19-31**

THEME: Jesus' earthly ministry did not end on Easter morning. Appearances to disciples established credibility of the resurrection. Easter is a day and a season.

Note: If you have not read the section on children's sermons, page 417, please do so.

To help continue the festive spirit of Easter, have juice and Easter bread or Paskha, a cream cheese dessert, after the service.

If I said this is Easter, you might think I'm crazy, or at least mixed up. Last Sunday many of you were here, and it was an exciting day in our church. *Remind them of specifics in your parish's celebration; do not emphasize new clothes worn.*

We talked on Easter Sunday about Jesus' resurrection—

coming back to life after he was crucified. But there are more stories in the New Testament about Jesus' being with the people who loved him and believed in him, *after* the resurrection.

Once Jesus appeared to the disciples when one of the disciples, Thomas, wasn't there. Thomas told the others he would need to see Jesus for himself to believe Jesus was alive. Eight days later he came to them again, and this time Thomas *was* there. He had had his doubts, but after Jesus spoke to Thomas, he made a statement that showed he did believe: "My Lord and my God!"

So this *time* of Easter is the most important time in our church. It is a season to help us know and believe in God and to let God be in charge of our lives.

If Easter foods are to be served, announce that.

Let's join hands and pray.

Oh, God, who lives today, thank you for being alive and for the joyous season of Easter. And let the children say, Amen.

PENTECOST SUNDAY

May 30, 1993

TEXT: **Acts 2:1-21**

THEME: We celebrate the birthday of the church!

Note: If you have not read the section on children's sermons, page 417, please do so.

Enlist the help of upper elementary children to cut, then distribute red crepe paper "stoles" as the people arrive for church. A birthday cake after the service would be great. Balloon lifts are not environmentally sound.

Does anyone see anything different in our church? *(Red "stoles" on members, red paraments, and clergy stole(s).* Do you know whose birthday we're celebrating today? The church is nearly 2,000 years old! Two thousand candles on a cake would make a big, bright light. I am so glad we have the church and that today, Pentecost Sunday, we can celebrate that.

What do you like to do in church?

I think we could sing Happy Birthday to the church and invite everyone else to join us. *Sing* Happy birthday to you . . . dear church . . .

Let's join hands and say a prayer.

Dear God, we are so happy to be a part of your church. Here we can feel love and are wanted. We know that love comes from you. And let the children say, Amen.

THIRD/FOURTH SUNDAY AFTER PENTECOST

June 20 or 27, 1993

TEXT: **Genesis 25, 27, 33**

THEME: We are to forgive, as God forgives us.

Note: If you have not read the section on children's sermons, page 417, please do so.

Jacob and Esau were brothers. Jacob pulled a lot of tricks on Esau, so Esau was very, very mad. Esau was so mad, that Jacob decided he'd better leave home and return when Esau cooled off.

It was about twenty years before Jacob decided to go back home. Remember I said Jacob had tricked his brother, Esau? Jacob had stolen from Esau. Do you think Esau was still mad?

The great thing is that Esau came out to meet Jacob as he was coming, and Esau had gifts to give to Jacob! Jacob could hardly believe it. He said that seeing Esau was like seeing God. They hugged each other.

I think Esau did that because God wants us to forgive people—yes, people who hurt us. Esau was able to forgive, because he had learned to love God.

If you are mad at someone now or get mad at someone this week, remember Esau who forgave his brother. Saying, "I'm sorry," and hugging are both better than fighting.

Let's join hands and have a prayer.

Loving God, help us to forgive like Esau. Thank you for forgiving us when we do wrong. And let the children say, Amen.

SEVENTEENTH SUNDAY AFTER PENTECOST

September 26, 1993

TEXT: **Matthew 21:28-32**

THEME: God expects us to do what we can to build up the kingdom—the "family business"—not give it lip service.

Note: If you have not read the section on children's sermons, page 417, please do so.

This is a simple parable to enact, requiring only three people. Invite children down for "front row seats." Possible scenario: a mother says her son needs to help that day in the family business. He says he's too busy, not interested, etc., and won't. But he feels bad about it later and goes. The mother says to her daughter, same message. She says, "Sure, Mom, I want to help you and Dad out," but never shows up.

After enactment, discuss with the children the following questions. Keep the characters there, and go to them so children are clear about whom you are speaking.

1. What did the daughter say she would do? What did she do?
2. What did the son say he would do? What did he do?
3. Which one did what the parents wanted and needed?

Let's join hands and pray.

Living Parent, help us to do what you want us to do, and not try to fool people with how good we are by saying one thing, but doing something else. And let the children say, Amen.

NINETEENTH SUNDAY AFTER PENTECOST

October 10, 1993

TEXT: **Philippians 4:1-9**

THEME: Christians are happy people, filled with God's peace.

Note: If you have not read the section on children's sermons, page 417, please do so.

Being a Christian lets me be happy, because I know God cares about me and will be with me. Being a Christian doesn't mean I don't sometimes have a hard day. Let me tell you about one. *Relate a personal story, or one known to you, about a time of being anxious and how looking to God for help cleared your mind so you had peace.*

Let's join hands and say a prayer.

Dear God, thank you for happy times. Help me to remember to thank you for those times, and to call on you for help when the hard days come. And let the children say, Amen.

TWENTY-THIRD SUNDAY AFTER PENTECOST

November 7, 1993

TEXT: **Amos 5:24**

THEME: We can stand up for our beliefs only through God's strength. That is part of being a disciple.

Note: If you have not read the section on children's sermons, page 417, please do so.

Martyrdom is not a usual topic for children, so this must be handled with care, paying close attention to choice of words. It is, nonetheless, an important sermon. For more information or a book on the Civil Rights Memorial, call the Southern Poverty Law Center in Montgomery, 205-264-0286.

In Montgomery, Alabama, there is a memorial to people who were killed 20–40 years ago in our country. There were people killed who thought that the way blacks were being treated in the United States wasn't fair.

The memorial has two parts. One is like a giant table, made of beautiful, smooth, black rock. On that are carved the names of the people. Water is running over it, and you can run your fingers through the water and over the table.

Behind the giant table is a wall, with words from a prophet in the Old Testament, Amos. "But let justice roll down like waters, and righteousness like an everflowing stream" (Amos 5:24). The

Reverend Dr. Martin Luther King, Jr., liked to quote that verse. He also died for his beliefs.

Some terrible things happened then in our country. I pray we learned enough lessons not to repeat our mistakes. God doesn't want any of God's children to be hurt like that. But I hope you remember that standing up for what we believe in is something God does want us to do. That takes believing in God and the fairness of God; that will help us be brave. I can't be brave without praying to God for strength.

When you are at school, or with friends, or anywhere there is something happening that is wrong—like cheating, lying, someone being unfair, hitting another person, or talking bad to someone—then God wants you to stand up for your beliefs. Standing up may mean not doing what others are doing. Sometimes it means telling others when something is wrong. Then you have helped God bring fairness and peace into our world.

Let's join hands and pray.

Dear God who wants fairness, help me to be strong for you, even if I am scared. Help me do the right thing. I know you love all your children and want us to be fair, truthful, and kind to each other. And let the children say, Amen.

THIRD SUNDAY OF ADVENT

December 12, 1993

TEXT: **John 1:19-23**

THEME: To take part in celebrating Jesus' birthday, we have to prepare and be prepared.

Note: If you have not read the section on children's sermons, page 417, please do so.

Once upon a time, a girl named Sally Ann decided she wanted her friend Michael to have a birthday party. Now this is what she did to get ready. She had her parents buy her a new dress. She bought cake and ice cream, and then ate it. She bought a gift for Michael and played with it.

This is what Sally Ann didn't do. She didn't tell Michael about the party and she didn't invite friends. She didn't have a place to have the party!

Do you think she was ready for the party? What should she do or not do?

The birthday of Jesus will be celebrated in thirteen days. We call it Christmas. Just like Sally Ann's party, if we don't do the right things, we won't have the right kind of party for Jesus.

In our church . . . *tell ways you're helping people get ready for Christmas, e.g., preparing services, the building and sanctuary physically, and sponsoring outreach projects—stressing doing for others.*

What are ways you can get ready for Jesus' birthday?

Let's join hands and pray.

Kind God, we want to be ready to have a great party for Jesus. Help us see ways to share the joy of Jesus' birth. And let the children say, Amen.

Benedictions

□

Now to God who is able to strengthen you according to my gospel and the proclamation of Jesus Christ . . . to the only wise God, through Jesus Christ, to whom be the glory forever! Amen. (Rom. 16:25, 27)

. . . Beloved, be steadfast, immovable, always excelling in the work of the Lord, . . . [and may] the grace of the Lord Jesus be with you. (I Cor. 15:58*a*, 16:23)

The grace of the Lord Jesus Christ, the love of God, and the communion of the Holy Spirit be with all of you. (II Cor. 13:13)

May the grace of our Lord Jesus Christ be with your spirit, brothers and sisters. Amen. (Gal. 6:18)

Now may the Lord of peace himself give you peace at all times in all ways. The Lord be with all of you. (II Thess. 3:16)

"Beloved, we are God's children now; what we will be has not yet been revealed. What we do know is this: when he is revealed, we will be like him, for we will see him as he is." Go forth in peace believing. Amen. (I John 3:2)

Go forth in peace, knowing that "whenever our hearts condemn us . . . God is greater than our hearts." Amen. (I John 3:20)

Now to him who is able to keep you from falling . . . to the only God our Savior, through Jesus Christ our Lord, be glory, majesty, power, and authority, before all time and now and forever. Amen. (Jude 24-25)

The LORD bless you and keep you; the LORD make his face to shine upon you, and be gracious to you; the LORD lift up his countenance upon you, and give you peace. (Num. 6:24-26)

Peace I leave with you; my peace I give to you. I do not give to you as the world gives. Do not let your hearts be troubled, and do not let them be afraid. (John 14:27)

Go therefore and make disciples of all nations, baptizing them in the name of the Father and of the Son and of the Holy Spirit. . . . And remember, I am with you always, to the end of the age. (Matt. 28:19, 20*b*)

May the God of steadfastness and encouragement grant you to live in harmony with one another, in accordance with Christ Jesus, so that together you may with one voice glorify the God and Father of our Lord Jesus Christ. (Rom. 15:5-6)

Offertory Sentences

□

In all this I have given you an example that by such work we must support the weak, remembering the words of the Lord Jesus, for he himself said, "It is more blessed to give than to receive." (Acts 20:35)

Let your light shine before others, so that they may see your good works and give glory to your Father in heaven. (Matt. 5:16*b*)

Do not store up for yourselves treasures on earth, where moth and rust consume and where thieves break in and steal; but store up for yourselves treasures in heaven, where neither moth nor rust consumes and where thieves do not break in and steal. For where your treasure is, there your heart will be also. (Matt. 6:19-21)

In everything do to others as you would have them do to you; for this is the law and the prophets. (Matt. 7:12)

Let love be genuine; hate what is evil, hold fast to what is good; love one another with mutual affection; outdo one another in showing honor. Do not lag in zeal, be ardent in spirit, serve the Lord. Rejoice in hope, be patient in suffering, persevere in prayer. Contribute to the needs of the saints; extend hospitality to strangers. (Rom. 12:9-13)

You know the generous act of our Lord Jesus Christ, that though he was rich, yet for your sakes he became poor, so that by his poverty you might become rich. (II Cor. 8:9)

The one who sows sparingly will also reap sparingly, and the one who sows bountifully will also reap bountifully. Each of you must give as you have made up your mind, not reluctantly or under compulsion, for God loves a cheerful giver. (II Cor. 9:6-7)

There is great gain in godliness combined with contentment; for we brought nothing into the world, so that we can take nothing out of it. (I Tim. 6:6-7)

Do not neglect to do good and to share what you have, for such sacrifices are pleasing to God. (Heb. 13:16)

Every generous act of giving, with every perfect gift, is from above, coming down from the Father of lights. (James 1:17)

Do not love the world or the things in the world. The love of the Father is not in those who love the world . . . the world and its desires are passing away, but those who do the will of God live forever. (I John 2:15, 17)

Sermon Contributors

□

Barbara Bate
Director of Preaching Ministries
The General Board of Discipleship
United Methodist Church
1908 Grand Ave.
Nashville, TN 37202

The Rev. Dr. Ralph K. Bates
First United Methodist Church
518 N. 19th Street
Birmingham, AL 35203

The Rev. Dr. John K. Bergland
Sr. Minister Haymount United Methodist Church
1700 Fort Bragg Road
Fayetteville, NC 28303

The Rev. Robert Eric Bergland
Grace United Methodist Church
800 Smith Street
Clinton, NC 28328

The Rev. H. Michael Brewer
Crescent Springs Presbyterian Church
710 Western Reserve Road
Crescent, KY 41017

The Rev. Dr. Michael Brown
Sr. Pastor Boone United Methodist Church
341 E. King Street
Boone, NC 28607

The Rev. Robert G. Bruce, Jr.
Ortega United Methodist Church
4807 Roosevelt Blvd.
Jacksonville, FL 32210-5998

Bishop William R. Cannon
Bishop United Methodist Church
Plaza Towers 12F
2575 Peachtree Road, NE
Atlanta, GA 30305

The Rev. M. Claire Clyburn
Chaplain Methodist College
5452 Ramsey St.
Fayetteville, NC 28311

Professor John Wesley Coleman
Professor METHESCO
3081 Columbus Pike
Delaware, OH 43015

Bishop Emerson S. Colaw
United Theological Seminary
1810 Harvard Blvd.
Dayton, OH 45406

The Rev. Donald William Dotterer
Christy Park United Methodist Church
29th St. at Beal
McKeesport, PA 15132

The Rev. T. M. Faggart
Sr. Minister Benson Memorial United Methodist Church
4706 Creedmoor Road
Raleigh, NC 27612

The Rev. Dr. Wallace E. Fisher
Holy Trinity Lutheran Church Pastor Emeritus
85 Briarwood Circle
Pinehurt, NC 28374

The Rev. Martha H. Forrest
Cedar Grove United Methodist Church
3430 Bouldercrest Road
Conley, GA 30027

The Rev. Susan Gladin
Orange County Churches in Action
Hillsborough, NC

The Rev. James A. Harnish
St. Lukes United Methodist Church
4851 S. Apopka-Vineland Road
Orlando, FL 32819

The Rev. Dr. James F. Jackson II
Sr. Minister First United Methodist Church
1411 Broadway
Lubbock, TX 79401

The Rev. Louise Stowe Johns
Chaplain Tutwiler Prison
4037 Strathmore Drive
Montgomery, AL 36116

The Rev. Jerry Lowry
First United Methodist Church
Box 1707
Pembroke, NC 28372

The Rev. Dr. James R. McCormick
Parkway Heights United Methodist Church
2420 Hardy Street
Hattiesburg, MS 39401

The Rev. Alton H. McEachern
Lovejoy United Methodist Church
1951 Mt. Carmel Road
Hampton, GA 30223

Chaplain Milford Oxendine, Jr., LCDR, CHC, USN
Native American Chaplain, U.S. Navy
48 Puritan Drive
Middletown, RI 02840

The Rev. John B. Peters
Braddock Street United Methodist Church
115 Wolfe Street
Winchester, VA 22601

The Rev. Dr. William Kellon Quick
Metropolitan United Methodist Church
8000 Woodward Avenue
Detroit, MI 48202

David W. Richardson
615 Bain Street (Box 156)
Dexter, MO 63841

The Rev. Carla Scanlan
South Denver Counseling Services
2465 S. Downing, Suite 207
Denver, CO 80210

The Rev. Donna Schaper
First Congregational Church
103 First Street
Riverhead, NY 11901

The Rev. Marjorie J. Thompson
208 Charleston Drive
Goodlettsville, TN 37072

The Rev. Dr. Thomas H. Troeger
Iliff School of Theology
2201 South University Boulevard
Denver, CO 80210

The Rev. William R. White
Bethel Lutheran Church
312 Wisconsin Avenue
Madison, WI 53711

The Rev. Dr. Herman S. Winberry
1217 E. 8th Street
Lumberton, NC 28358

The Rev. Michael C. Wolfram
Shepherd of Peace Lutheran Church
Box 36
Sergeant Bluff, IA 51054

Scripture Index

□

OLD TESTAMENT

I Corinthians

II Corinthians

Galatians

Ephesians